Women in Politics and Media

Women in Politics and Media

Perspectives from Nations in Transition

Maria Raicheva-Stover and Elza Ibroscheva

BLOOMSBURY
NEW DELHI • LONDON • OXFORD • NEW YORK • SYDNEY

BLOOMSBURY INDIA
Bloomsbury Publishing India Pvt. Ltd
Second Floor, LSC Building No. 4, DDA Complex, Pocket C–6&7,
Vasant Kunj, New Delhi 110070

BLOOMSBURY, BLOOMSBURY ACADEMIC INDIA and the Diana logo are
trademarks of Bloomsbury Publishing Plc

First published in India 2023
First published 2014

This edition published with permission from Bloomsbury Publishing Plc,
50 Bedford Square, London, WC1B3DP, UK

ISBN: 978-93-93715-20-3

Typeset by Fakenham Prepress Solutions, Fakenham, Norfolk, NR21 8NN
Printed and bound by Manipal Technologies Limited, Manipal

To find out more about our authors and books
visit www.bloomsbury.com and sign up for our newsletters

Contents

Acknowledgments

This volume emerged with the support, help and encouragement of a large number of people. We owe special gratitude to Washburn University, and specifically to Dr. Kathy Menzie, chair of the Mass Media department, and the College of Arts and Sciences, for the financial support, release time, and invigorating opportunities to teach innovative courses, and Southern Illinois University Edwardsville for providing the research opportunities that made much of our scholarship possible.

We also would like to thank all the scholars and researchers from all parts of the world who responded so enthusiastically to the initial book call. Space limitations did not allow us to publish all the manuscripts, and specifically the section with testimonies from political women from Turkey, Belarus, Bulgaria, and India. Above all, we would like to express our appreciation to the 20 contributors to this volume who patiently worked with us over the last 15 months to bring this project to fruition. This project is over, but we are fortunate to be left with a global network of connections which, we hope, will set in motion future collaborations. Our sincere gratitude goes to Bloomsbury Publishing for making this book happen and to the anonymous contributors who offered astute advice. We thank all the women in our lives—mothers, friends, mentors, and role models—for leaving an indelible mark on us. Lastly, this project would not have been possible without the unending encouragement and unconditional love of our respective families—Mike and Addison Stover, who've always been my biggest champions, and Sami, Adam, and Marc Moussawi, who are the greatest inspiration one might hope for. We dedicate this book to them.

Maria Raicheva-Stover and Elza Ibroscheva
February 2014

Notes on Contributors

Ingrid Bachmann received her doctoral degree in Journalism from the University of Texas at Austin in 2011. Currently, she is an Assistant Professor in the School of Communications at Pontificia Universidad Católica de Chile. A former reporter and blogger, her research interests include news narratives, gender, political communication, and content creation, with emphasis in cross-national comparisons. A constant theme that runs through her research is how news media shape and reinforce several identities and meanings within the public sphere. Her recent research has been published in *Feminist Media Studies*, *Howard Journal of Communication*, *International Journal of Communication*, *Journalism Studies*, and *Journalism & Mass Communication Quarterly*, among others.

Maryam Ben Salem is a doctor in political science and a university teacher. She works as a researcher at the Center of Arab Women for Training and Research—CAWTAR—on the theme of political participation of women. Her research themes focus on political activism, religious commitment, cyber activism, and media visibility of women politicians. She is a member of several scientific associations: Observatoire Tunisien de la Transition Démocratique, the association Mediterranean College for Scientific Research, and the Tunisian Association for Political Studies.

Claudia Bucciferro is assistant professor in the Department of Communication Studies at Gonzaga University in Spokane, Washington. She has a Ph.D. in communication from the University of Colorado at Boulder and a Master's degree in linguistics from the University of Concepción, Chile, where she also completed her undergraduate studies in communication and journalism. Her research focuses on topics in international/intercultural communication, cultural studies, gender, and media studies. Her work has appeared in the *Handbook of Gender, Sex, and Media*, the *Journal of Mass Communication*, the *Journal of Global Mass Communication*, and the *Journal of American Culture*. She is the author of *FOR-GET: Identity, Media, and Democracy in Chile* (University Press of America), and editor of *The Twilight Saga: Exploring the Global Phenomenon*

(Scarecrow Press). She is currently working on another book that will focus on popular culture, gender, media, and transnational information flows.

Tania Cantrell Rosas-Moreno received her doctoral degree in Journalism from the University of Texas at Austin in 2009. Currently, she is an Assistant Professor in Loyola University Maryland's Department of Communication. A former public relations practitioner, her research interests include (international) news narratives, political communication and diversity, with emphasis in cross-national comparisons. A question that underlies her research is, "How do news stories affect citizens' daily lives?" She has published in *Journalism Studies*, *Howard Journal of Communication*, and *International Journal of Communication*, among others. Her book on Brazilian media, which compares social, political, and cultural themes found in news stories, and a concurrent telenovela, is forthcoming from Lexington Books.

Munira Cheema is a Ph.D. student (final year) at the School of Film, Media and Music at the University of Sussex, U.K., where she is also working as an Associate Tutor. For her doctoral thesis, she is looking at the production and reception of gender-based content in Pakistani television. Munira holds Master's Degrees in International Relations (University of Karachi) and in International Communications (University of Leeds). Previously, she has worked as a Research Assistant for the Project of Ford Foundation at the Department of International Relations at the University of Karachi. She has also worked as a feature writer for a weekly publication (*Star*) in Pakistan. Prior to starting the doctoral program, Munira worked as a visiting faculty for the course of Gender Studies at the Shaheed Zulfiqar Ali Bhutto Institute (SZABIST) in Karachi. Her research interests include politics/representation of gender in South Asia, gendered citizenship and religion, and evolution of mediated public sphere in Pakistan.

Sara Chinnasamy, University of Technology MARA, Malaysia. She has been a senior lecturer in broadcast journalism in the Faculty of Media and Communication Studies, University of Technology MARA, Malaysia, since 2006, after working as a broadcast journalist for the public broadcaster, Radio Television Malaysia, Kuala Lumpur from 1999–2005. There, her role focused on parliamentary reporting, political assignments, and related analyses. In 2014, she completed her Ph.D. in media and politics at the University of Adelaide, Australia.

Camelia Cmeciu is an associate professor in the Department of Communication Studies at the University of Bucharest and a postdoctoral researcher at the Romanian Academy (Iasi Branch). Her research interests cover semiotics, organizational and political communication, advertising discourse, and linguistics. She is the author of *Strategii persuasive în discursul politic* (*Persuasive Strategies in Political Discourse*, 2005, Universitas XXI, Iaşi, Romania) and *Semiotici textuale* (*Textual Semiotics*, 2011, Institutul European, Iaşi, Romania). Her work on political discourse, social semiotics and organizational discourse appears in academic journals like *Semiotica*, *Public Relations Review*, *International Journal of Humanities and Social Science*, *Styles of Communication*, and *Cultural Perspectives—Journal for Literary and British Cultural Studies in Romania*.

Sonila Danaj has an M.A. in Contemporary European Studies from the University of Sussex, U.K., and another in Political Science from the Central European University, Hungary. She has worked as a political science lecturer at the Faculty of Social Science, University of Tirana, and later at the European University of Tirana. She is currently working on her Ph.D. in Sociology at the Department of Social Sciences and Philosophy, University of Jyväskylä, Finland. Her area of expertise is democratization and social movements, with a special focus on under-represented groups such as women, migrants and political communication. She has collaborated with various national and international organizations as a research consultant for the preparation of reports, analysis and policy papers in the above-mentioned areas.

Jonila Godole is a lecturer in journalism and political communication at the Department of Journalism and Communication, University of Tirana. Godole studied first at the Faculty of History and Philology in Tirana, then read political sciences and sociology at Goethe University in Frankfurt am Main, Germany. She was one of the first journalists after 1990, especially well-known for her interviews of high level politicians and political articles. Godole is author of several articles on political journalism and media analysis. In another communication field, literature, she has won important awards in Albania and abroad, for her prose as well as her translations of German literature. Her Ph.D. dissertation was about journalism culture in postcommunist Albania. Other research interests include the professional ethos of journalism in Albania, comparative media systems, and political communication.

Mary Griffiths is Associate Professor, in the Discipline of Media at the University of Adelaide. Previous academic positions included leadership roles at Monash University and the University of Waikato, NZ and international journal editorial boards. Research interests: eparticipation, digital citizens, online and offline governance, digital humanities, and participatory media. Publications in 2012 include: "Empowering citizens: A constructivist assessment of the impact of contextual and design factors on the concept of shared governance"; "Real time political news: Designing information flows in an online scenario"; and guest editor for "China," in *Communications, Politics and Culture*, 45.2, 2012. Published in 2014: "Notions of guardianship" in *The way we are governed: Investigations in communication, media and democracy*. Philip Dearman and Cathy Greenfield (eds) Cambridge: Cambridge Scholarly Press.

Farida Jalalzai received her Ph.D. from the University of Buffalo. She is an Associate Professor and Chair of the Department of Political Science at the University of Missouri–St. Louis. Her research focuses on women national leaders (*Women and Politics 2004*; *Politics & Gender 2008*; *International Political Science Review 2010*; *Journal of Women, Politics, & Policy 2010*; *German Politics* 2011). Her first book *Shattered, Cracked and Firmly Intact: Women and the Executive Glass Ceiling Worldwide* (Oxford University Press 2013) offers a comprehensive analysis of women, gender, and national leadership positions. Currently, she is conducting and analyzing field work examining Laura Chinchilla (Costa Rica), Dilma Rousseff (Brazil), Cristina Fernández (Argentina), and Michelle Bachelet (Chile) for a book manuscript on female presidents of Latin America. She also has published on the topic of Muslim political behavior (*Politics & Religion* 2009; 2011).

Twange Kasoma has a Ph.D. in media and society with emphasis on international and development communication from the University of Oregon. She recently joined Radford University in Virginia as an assistant professor of journalism. She currently teaches courses in newswriting, reporting, and specialized journalism. Prior to joining Radford University, she taught courses in journalism, international communication, research methods, media and society, and study abroad at Emory & Henry College, Virginia, for five years. Her research interest areas are: journalistic professionalism, development communication, gender and the media, role of the media in African society, and media regulation.

Einat Lachover, Ph.D., is senior lecturer in the School of Communication, Sapir Academic College, Israel. She teaches primarily courses in mass communication theory and gender and communication. She is particularly interested in feminist media research. She has published in international journals such as *Communication Theory*; *Journalism*; *Feminist Media Studies*; *Median and Zeit*; *Global Media Journal*; *Communication, Culture and Critique*; *The Journal of Israeli History*; *NASHIM*; *Israel Affairs*. She received her B.A. and M.A. from The Hebrew University, Jerusalem, and Ph.D. from Tel Aviv University. Her thesis focused on the gendered structure in the written media in Israel. She is one of the founders of Sapir Feminist Forum, promoting academic and social activism in the south of Israel.

Atidel Mejbri is a Ph.D. student and university teacher. She carried out her postgraduate studies on the institutional communication and e-training. Since 1999, she has been manager of the Department of Information and Communication of the Center of Arab Women for Training and Research (CAWTAR) and Chief Editor of its periodical with ten years' experience in audio-visual media, and in charge of media and communication issues for a number of national and international organizations. She produced discussion programs on social issues broadcast by the Tunisian Satellite Channel. She won the creativity award as the best conference moderator in the Radio and Television Festival of Cairo (2002). She also won the Prize of the Association of Tunisian Journalists for the best women's production (gender-based violence). She set a number of strategies on media and communication for some institutions. Ms. Mejbri also coordinated the three-year program on "Gender and Arab Media" for CAWTAR and the United Nations Development Fund for Women (UNIFEM). She is a member of the Association of Tunisian Journalists.

Teke Ngomba has a B.A. in Journalism and Mass Communication with a Minor in Political Science and Public Administration from the University of Buea in Cameroon. Shortly after obtaining his B.A., he worked as an Administrative Assistant in the Public and Alumni Relations Office of the University of Buea before traveling to South Africa in 2005 to undergo an intensive Media Training, with a focus on critical analysis of Africa's development, at the South African Institute of International Affairs in Johannesburg. Upon returning from South Africa in 2006, he obtained the EU-funded Erasmus Mundus Master Scholarship to study for an M.A. in 'Journalism and Media within Globalization:

The European Perspective' at the University of Aarhus, the Danish School of Journalism, the University of Amsterdam, and the University of Hamburg—where he went on to specialize in Public Spheres and Comparative Media Systems Analysis.

Elizabeth Gackstetter Nichols is a Professor of Spanish and Chair of the Department of Languages at Drury University in Springfield, Missouri. Dr. Nichols earned her master's degree and doctorate from the University of Kansas. Dr. Nichols specializes in Latin American cultural studies with an emphasis on women's literature and popular culture, and has worked extensively in Venezuela. Dr. Nichols' has previously published a variety of books, articles and encyclopedia entries on Venezuela, including: *Venezuela: In Focus* (with Kimberly J. Morse), Santa Barbara, CA: ABC-Clio, 2010; "Taking Possession of Public Discourse: Women and the Practice of Political Poetry in Venezuela" in *Bottom Up or Top Down? Participation and Clientelism in Venezuela's Bolivarian Democracy*. David Smilde and Daniel Hellinger (eds.) Durham: Duke University Press, 2011.

Monica Pătruţ is a Senior Lecturer in Political Science at Vasile Alecsandri University of Bacău, Romania. Her domains of research are political communication and computer science applied in social and political sciences. She is a member of the editorial advisory board of *BRAND: Broad Research in Accounting, Negotiation, and Distribution*. She has published several academic books on applying computer science in educational, social and political topics, and papers in international journals like *Public Relations Review* and *Journal of Media Research*.

Pedro G. dos Santos received his Ph.D. in Political Science from the University of Kansas in 2012 and is now Assistant Professor of Political Science at Luther College. He was also a Junior Researcher at the Graduate Program in Comparative Studies on the Americas (CEPPAC) at the University of Brasília in 2010–11. His dissertation, titled "Gendering Representation: Parties, Institutions, and the Under-Representation of Women in Brazil's State Legislatures," uses a mixed-methods approach to address the issue of female under-representation in Brazilian state legislatures. His main research focus is on Brazilian political institutions, paying special attention to electoral institutions and campaign finance. Within that framework he has more recently focused on women's descriptive and substantive representation in Brazil at all levels of government. He has published articles in *Latin American Politics and Society* and the *Journal of Women, Politics and Policy*.

Liudmila Voronova is a Ph.D. student at the Centre for Baltic and East European Studies in the research area of Media and Communication Studies, Södertörn University (Sweden). In her doctoral project she analyzes meanings and roles of gender in political journalism cultures in Russia and Sweden. Her research interests lie within the intersection of gender media studies, political communication research, and comparative studies of journalism cultures.

Tatiana Zhurzhenko is Research Director of the Russia in Global Dialogue Program at the Institute for Human Sciences (IWM) in Vienna, Austria. She studied Political Economy and Philosophy at V.N. Karazin Kharkiv National University (Ukraine) and received her Candidate of Science (equivalent to Ph.D.) in Social Philosophy in 1993. From 1993–2010 Tatiana Zhurzhenko was Assistant, later Associate Professor at Kharkiv University; she was also a co-founder and co-director of the Kharkiv Center for Gender Studies. From 2007–11 she held an Elise Richter Fellowship doing research on the politics of memory in Eastern Europe at the Department of Political Science, University of Vienna. In 2012–13 Tatiana Zhurzhenko worked at the Aleksanteri Institute (Finnish Centre for Russian and Eastern European Studies), University of Helsinki. She was awarded research fellowships at Harvard, Toronto University and London Metropolitan University. Tatiana Zhurzhenko has published widely on gender politics and feminism in Ukraine, on borders and borderland identities and memory politics in Eastern Europe. Her last book *Borderlands into Bordered Lands: Geopolitics of Identity in Post-Soviet Ukraine* (Stuttgart: Ibidem 2010) was awarded with the Best Book Prize 2010 of the American Association for Ukrainian Studies and with the Bronze Award of the Association for Borderland Studies (2012).

1

Introduction

As the world population grows closer and closer to complete parity between the sexes with the very real possibility of women outnumbering men, public discussions about the role of women in politics are no longer a thing of the past. On the contrary, women's roles in local, national and international politics have become the staple of democratic discourses all over the world, with trends in both female representation and political empowerment often used as evidence that gender dynamics are undoubtedly shifting and that women are often the moving force behind this phenomenon. In this regard it is worth quoting the core vision of the Inter-Parliamentary Union Plan of Action adopted 20 years ago: "The concept of democracy will only assume true and dynamic significance when political policies and national legislation are decided upon jointly by men and women with equitable regard for the interests and aptitudes of both halves of the population" (Plan of Action n.d.).

Indeed, there have been some notable breakthroughs in female political participation that have caught the attention of media audiences, political commentators, and analysts the world over. It is perhaps safe to assume that no member of the international community who describes him/herself as politically involved will argue against former Secretary of State Hillary Clinton's status as a powerful political player, who has a serious bid for the U.S. presidency in 2016, or the centrality of German Chancellor Angela Merkel, ranked number five on Forbes' 2013 Most Powerful People list, and described as "the backbone" of the EU (Forbes 2013). Yet, the media have been fixated on these powerful politicians not only because of their "gravitational pull"—a recent article in the *New York Times Magazine* described Clinton's political relevance as "Planet Hillary"—but also because they are, after all, essentially women doing unwomanly things who often need to be reminded of their proper gender label as was the case of Germany's *Bild* magazine, which dubbed the Chancellor's role in leading the 2007 G8 Summit as "Miss World," or the provocative *Time* magazine cover featuring a giant high heel accompanied by the title "Can anyone stop Hillary?" (Blake 2014; Chozick 2014; Lünenborg n.d.).

Outside of the Northern hemisphere, the recent presidential elections in Chile set a powerful precedent in having two female presidential candidates—Michelle Bachelet and Evelyn Matthei—compete for the highest post of the land, proving to be yet another indicator of the changing status of women in politics on a global scale. Interestingly, this example comes from a nation from the Global South, an area of the world that in many ways has recently demonstrated a much higher propensity to allow female players into the political arena. Another important milestone comes from Eastern Africa, where in 2008, thanks to a gender quota,[1] Rwanda became the first country in the world to boast a majority-female parliament, with women holding 56 percent of the seats, including the speaker's chair.

Indeed, things have changed in the past fifty years. Historically speaking, in 1960 Sri Lanka became the first country with an elected female head of government; in 1974 Isabel Perón of Argentina made history as the first woman president and in 1999 Sweden became the first country where female ministers outnumbered their male colleagues (Guide to Women Leaders n.d.). As of January 2014, there are nine female presidents and 15 female prime ministers worldwide (Guide to Women Leaders n.d.), though this number still represents a minority in the global leaders' club, which remains a predominantly male preserve (Jalalzai 2013). The statistics on overall political participation are sobering as well. From 1995 to 2013, the percentage of women parliamentarians increased from 11.6 percent to 20.9 percent (UN Women n.d.). Currently, there are 37 states in which women account for less than 10 percent of parliamentarians in single or lower houses (UN Women n.d.).

These trends have been alarming to both advocates for women's increasing political participation and academics alike. As Norris and Inglehart (2008), two scholars who have been mapping the trajectory of global gender equality for decades, noted, progress is taking place at a "glacial pace" so much so that "without intervention it would take more than a century and a half for women parliamentarians to achieve parity with men" (6). And despite global efforts to improve the political agency of women, including a pledge by the UN Beijing Platform for Action for a 50:50 parity between male and female politicians worldwide, there's still "unfinished business," to quote Hillary Clinton,

(Walshe 2013). Clearly, the world of politics is far from achieving gender parity (Inglehart and Norris 2003; Jalalzai 2013; Norris and Inglehart 2008) and gender remains relevant when examining electoral politics in the twenty-first century (see Carroll and Fox 2006, for a detailed analysis of this point within the context of the United States; and Norris and Inglehart 2008, and Jalalzai 2013, for a global overview).

Naturally, the intersection of politics and gender has received a wide scholarly attention within the United States. Space limitations do not allow for a comprehensive overview of the rich literature on this topic, yet the latest research from the field of politics indicates that even if women, including incumbents, who run for office "do as well as men," they have to nevertheless make significant investments in quality above and beyond that of men so that they would not be penalized electorally (Fulton 2012). As Fulton concluded, "relative to men, women have to work harder at developing greater political quality to be equally competitive" (310). Empirical research on how gender influences the decision to run for office in the United States also indicates that women are less likely to seek political office than their similarly situated male counterparts, thus influencing the "supply side" of the equation (Lawless and Fox 2010, 174–5). And even though overt bias against women politicians in the United States has been declared "largely a thing of the past" (CQ Researcher 2008, 269), the institutional and structural barriers to women's advancement in positions of real political power across the globe remain largely intact and often calcified in social norms and cultural practices (Norris and Inglehart 2008).

The role of media

The question of whether media can be blamed, at least partially, for the low representation of women in politics has been debated for several decades among scholars and international organizations. As van Zoonen observes, discussions of gender and politics "have accompanied the emergence of female political leaders ever since the feminist movement of the 1900s, what distinguishes the current generation from their predecessors is their ascendance to power in profoundly mediated contexts" (van Zoonen 2006, 288). Undoubtedly, the rapidly evolving media landscape, characterized by new digital technologies, the tabloidization of news and introduction of a 24-hour news cycle, foregrounds the need to pay closer attention to the interaction between political players and media (Aalberg and Strömbäck 2011; Dahlgren and Alvares 2013; Lawrence and Rose 2010; Ross 2010b). Some scholars observe that politics has become "mediatized" (Strömbäck and Van Aelst 2013, 354) to the point where political actors need to take media logic[2] into consideration regardless of whether they try to successfully promulgate their campaign messages to voters or counteract the effects of bad (or good) publicity. What needs to be acknowledged is that, as vital channels of information, "media are never mere neutral conduits: they have their own varying contingencies and logics, which serve to refract communication and cultural patterns in specific ways" (Dahlgren and Alvares 2013, 52). Framing theory has been frequently evoked by media and feminist scholars as a useful framework for explaining, interpreting, and analyzing the process through which news media construct and present political actors (see for example Bystrom, Robertson and Banwart 2001; Norris 1997; Ross 2010b; Tuchman 1979). The process is multifaceted and contextual. Norris (1997) reminds us that "frames are located within a particular culture and are the product of a complex interaction between sources, media and audiences" (7).

The close connection between news media and politics, therefore, raises questions about the nature and impact of media coverage on women politicians. Given the minority status of women politicians in the political field, it should be expected that their coverage would be mired by gender stereotypes. Seminal work on the effects of media coverage on women politicians was provided by Kim Fridkin Kahn (1991, 1992, 1994, 1996) who discovered through several systematic studies that, regardless of the status of the candidate (an incumbent, a challenger, or a candidate for an open seat), or the competitiveness of the race, women who were running for political office in the 1980s received less attention from the press than men. Moreover, the coverage showed preoccupation with the "horse race" frame, with greater attention to negative horse race information for women candidates that stressed their lack of viability or lack of campaign resources (Kahn and Goldenberg 1991, 109). Kahn's conclusion was that unequal coverage has an effect on women's electability because voters are less likely to consider candidates they are unfamiliar with or perceive as less viable (Kahn 1994, 172).

Another notable work has been the volume on *Gender, Politics and Communication* (2000) edited by Annabelle Sreberny and Liesbet van Zoonen, which, among other contributions, foregrounded distinctions between the public and private spheres. Extending the scope of examination from news media to popular culture, the volume underscored media's role in framing politics and femininity as antithetical (13). In spite of what the editors perceive as fundamental fragmentations of the concepts of "publics" and "arenas," the volume reaches the overarching conclusion that "the underlying frame of reference [for understanding the distinction between public and private] is that women belong to the family and domestic life and men to the social world of politics and work; that femininity is about care, nurturance, and compassion, and that masculinity is about efficiency, rationality, and individuality" (17).

Since the 1990s, feminist scholars responded resoundingly to Sreberny-Mohammadi and Ross's (1996) call to examine the "manner in which the mediated presentation of politics is gendered" (103). Scholarship of how media portray women politicians from the United States, Canada and the United Kingdom has revealed that media coverage tends to be more negative than that of their male colleagues, focuses more on trivialization and personalization than on issues, and reinforces masculine and feminine stereotypes (Banwart 2010; Braden 1996; Byerly and Ross 2006; Gallagher 2001; Gidengil and Everitt 1999; Robinson and Saint-Jean 1991; Ross 2002; Ross and Sreberny 2000; Trimble, Wagner, Sampert, Raphael, and Gerrits 2013). More recently, Liesbet van Zoonen has been interrogating the link between gender, politics and popular culture, outlining the "perilous grounds female politicians tread when trying to comply with the requirements of celebrity politics, namely personalization and popularization" (van Zoonen 2006, 296).[3]

An overview of the most recent research on media coverage of women running for political office within the United States reveals that the gap in terms of volume of coverage might have closed yet women who sought higher, more executive office, are still receiving more gendered coverage than men (Meeks 2012). This observation is supported by empirical research "across eight newspapers, in differing regions of the United States, and over a ten-year time span," suggesting that "media continue to cast women as novelties and norm breakers" (Meeks 2012, 187–8). The latest findings from the U.S. resonate with the results of a large scale, longitudinal study from Canada which found that, while personalized press coverage of women politicians did not increase between 1975 and 2012, women did receive more attention to their physical characteristics and personal lives thus underscoring the gendered nature of personalization in political reporting (Trimble, Wagner, Sampert, Raphael, and Gerrits 2013). Moreover, experimental research by Bligh et al. (2012) reminds us that politics is still perceived as a gender-incongruent profession for women, i.e. one that violates feminine gender roles, which takes its toll on those who strive to break the glass ceiling. Even if women are judged as competent for the job, media have a particular influence on the public's judgment of politicians' likability, which has implications not only for the electoral success of women running for office, but also underscores the need for women candidates to pay close attention to their media(ted) image and the relationships they cultivate with journalists. A mini-symposium in the September 2013 issue of *Political Research Quarterly* brings attention to how the specific context in which women seek office in the United States affects the news agenda, namely how variations in type of electoral race, political party affiliation, and much needed examinations of race and ethnicity correlate with the amount and quality of coverage they receive.

It is important to note that beyond matters of reproducing masculine ideologies about the nature of the political process, media are also directly involved in the very mechanisms that make these processes possible. On their part, "journalists – consciously of not – [uphold] the gendering of political offices," as indicated by the latest research examining the connection between a journalist's gender and gendered campaign news coverage (Meeks 2013, 68). The study, sadly, observed that even in 2012, the newsrooms, just like American politics, remain a largely "masculinized" domain where women represent only 38 percent of journalists (Meeks 2013, 60).

If the process of producing meaning and sustaining the existing social norms surrounding the political discourse is carried out by the institutional channels of media, how have women politicians adapted to this logic? Within the backdrop of "mediatized" politics, women politicians are growingly cognizant of the importance of maintaining an image as well as who has the power to control the message. In fact, research on women politicians reveals that they are as equally adept at campaigning as men (Kahn and Gordon 1997), are reluctant to allow the public and media into their private lives (van Zoonen 2006) and consistently try to avoid gender stereotypes in their self-representation (Banwart 2006; Dolan 2005; Niven and Zilber 2001; van Zoonen 2005), although there are indications that gender stereotypes could work to the advantage of women, especially in situations where their outsider status or feminine traits are perceived as valuable by voters (CQ Researcher 2008; Dolan 1998; Kahn 1996). As technology changes and the political impact of social media like blogs, Facebook and Twitter is weighed, more attention should be given to when or how political women strategically use these new media to yield control over the message.

The above findings not only provide evidence as to the gendered nature of political reporting and politics, but remind us that women still meet greater obstacles when they try to break the political glass ceiling. And while at this point we have enough research to provide some evaluation of the interactions between women politicians and media from established democracies like the United States, Great Britain, and Canada, we are *de facto* missing wide-ranging research on the experiences of women politicians. The present volume emerged as a response to feminist media scholar Karen Ross who, in her book on *Women, Politics and Media* (2002) laments that "much of the work on women politicians and the media has a strongly American orientation since many of the communication scholars working in this broad area are American-based" (3). Admittedly, several volumes on gender and media, have managed to provide a broader international perspective (Carilli and Campbell 2005; Carter, Steiner and McLaughlin 2014; Ross 2012) yet the political dimension is largely missing from these otherwise notable works.

The impetus behind the present collection, therefore, can be found in persistent calls to expand the scope of research on women in politics. Thus, while acknowledging the achievements in the field, we would like to extend our attention to the interaction between women politicians and media in an expanded international context. At the core of this attempt is the assumption that a more nuanced understanding of the interconnection between political women and media could be achieved through a closer attention to countries with different historical trajectories as well as political and cultural configurations. Ultimately, we were hopeful that we could make two specific contributions to the study of women, politics and media by: (1) shifting the focus of attention to countries in transition, which have not been the usual suspects of scholarly investigation, and (2) featuring a diverse group of scholars who could provide valuable insights into the latest developments in each region. In addition, we also wanted to take a more encompassing theoretical approach to mapping the debate on the role of media and gender in politics by stressing the importance of studying the construction, cultural function, and symbolic interpretation of women politicians. In this sense, we followed the method Karen Ross outlines in *Gendered Media* (2010b), focusing on representation, identity, and agency, where she argued for understanding gendered identity as constructed both in and by the media, but also recognizing that these constructions can be challenged by individuals through alternative modes of self-expression.

In an attempt at consistency, the selection criteria for the countries in this volume followed the categorization Inglehard and Norris (2003) applied in their *Rising Tide* book, which examined the relationship between gender equality and cultural change in 70 nations. Relying on measures from the Human Development Index (HDI), Inglehard and Norris categorized postindustrial societies as those with an HDI score over 0.900, industrial as nations with an HDI that ranges from 0.740 to 0.899, and agrarian as nations that have scores lower than 0.739. All countries included in this volume fell in the industrial and agrarian society categorizations, with Israel being right on the verge with a score of 0.900[4] (Table 1.1). We chose to refer to this group of countries as "nations in transition,"[5] primarily to distinguish them from established, Western democracies or what Inglehard and Norris (2003) called "old democracies."[6] As a cluster, our selections feature countries that have undergone rapid and, in many instances, fundamental developments in recent decades.

A different way to approach the countries featured in this volume would be geographic distribution, which aligns closely with Freedom House regional categorizations (Table 1.1). Our goal was to achieve a more or less even distribution among different regions, which was met with the 17 countries under examination, yet we would like to underscore the continuing need to provide a more inclusive overview of gender and political communication from such under-theorized regions as Middle East and North Africa (MENA), Sub-Saharan Africa and Southeast Asia. We also would like to acknowledge this volume's heavy emphasis on women engaged in the formal political sphere, which still leaves a gap in cross-national research on the intersection of gender and new ways of doing "politics" as part of informal politics and/or new media environments. And while most of the chapters cover a single country, they address comparable questions of media or mediated self-(re)presentation thus contributing to our understanding of the relationship dynamics between gender, political power and the media.

In line with our second goal, this volume aimed at achieving a greater diversity of contributors in terms of origin and specialization, which is seen as a valuable heuristic strategy. Special attempts were made to reach out to researchers who reside and work outside of the United States and who come from diverse disciplinary backgrounds. The result is a compilation of original essays by scholars and researchers who have long-standing professional and personal experiences with the countries they write about. In most instances, they also happen to be natives with deep understanding of local history, politics, culture, and languages—all becoming tremendously advantageous when exploring how gendered manifestations are situated within the political and cultural milieu of a given country.

In searching for a meaningful way to present the research from the countries included in this volume, we decided to eschew geographical categorizations. Instead, a thematic categorization emerged that presents us with an opportunity to look at both sides of the coin—including media representations of women politicians and mediated self-representations or evaluations—although a great number of essays espouse multi-perspective approaches. A third section goes beyond the narrow focus on media into the intersection of history, culture and politics.

In the first section, *Framing the Message: Mediated Representations and Journalistic Practices*, authors inquire into the presence of gendered coverage or question journalistic practices of gendering across different types of media. Einat Lachover interrogates the presence of a feminist discourse in the way Israeli popular women's magazines cover Tzipi Livni, a prominent politician and current Minister of Justice, and Daphni Leef, an anti-establishment activist. Mary Griffiths and Sara Chinnasamy highlight the role of online news portals as sites for making visible the counter-discursive practices of Malaysian human rights lawyer Ambiga Sreenevasan and the *Bersih* rallies she became a spokesperson for. The editors make a contribution to this volume with a historical analysis of the newspaper portrayal of Bulgarian women politicians, spanning from the communist era to post-communist times. Twange Kasoma provides a close look at the press coverage of women members of parliament in Zambia, which is supplemented with interviews with the journalists who wrote the stories, to uncover the reasons behind women MP's limited coverage. Maryam Ben Salem and Atidel Mejbri undertake a multifaceted analysis of the obstacles to visibility in traditional and new media for women active in the political sphere in Tunisia after the revolution. Munira Cheema's chapter offers a glimpse of the gender dynamics of political talk shows in Pakistan through a triangulation approach that involves textual analysis and in-depth interviews with the hosts of this new genre. Liudmila Voronova's chapter sheds light on the attitudes of Russian journalists toward the process of media production and representation of women politicians and highlights the contradictions between the ideas, practices and ideals present in the "quality" press in Russia. In the last essay in this section, Tania Cantrell Rosas-Moreno and Ingrid Bachmann undertake a tri-continental comparative analysis of how the national press in Germany, Chile and Liberia covered the second successful election bid of their respective heads of state—Angela Merkel, Michele Bachelet, and Ellen Johnson-Sirleaf.

The essays in the next section, *Managing the Message: Self-representations*, turn attention to the experiences of women politicians with traditional and new media as part of their election campaigns or their position as elected officials. Teke Ngomba's chapter examines how the meticulous campaign style of Edith Kah Walla, who was one of the first two women to run for president in Cameroon, made her a media sensation in the context of this Sub-Saharan nation. Pedro dos Santos and Farida Jalalzai closely analyze the creation of the "Mother of Brazil" narrative as part of Dilma Rousseff's successful presidential campaign in 2010, highlighting the strategic use of campaign messages during Brazil's Free Electoral Advertisement Hour. Camelia Cmeciu and Monica Pătruț inquire into the presence of gender stereotypes in the visual self-representation of Romanian women politicians on their campaign blogs. Sonila Danaj and Jonila Godole's interviews with women parliamentarians from Albania shed light on how they view their relationship with traditional media, which the authors enhance with data from monitoring studies on the portrayal of women politicians after the introduction of a gender quota in 2009.

The last section, *Navigating the Public Space: Class and Beauty*, presents the reader with rich historical and cultural analyses of the different routes successful political women have taken in their ascent to power. Claudia Bucciferro offers a "moving portrait" of Chile's Michelle Bachelet, who won a second term as president in 2013, evaluating her legacy against the backdrop of contradictory political and social developments. Elizabeth Gackstetter Nichols makes a dual contribution to this volume with essays on Venezuela's "public women" and two of Argentina's most famous female politicians—Eva Duarte de Perón (Evita) and Cristina Fernández de Kirchner. Nichols convincingly argues that, in the context of Venezuela, media representations as well as the public perceptions of Irene Sáez, a successful politician and former Miss Universe, and Lina Ron, an activist and revolutionary, point to a fundamental set of androcentric social expectations for women seeking to enter public life. In the case of Argentina, a connection between the historical trajectories of Evita and Cristina de Kirchner allows for an insightful analysis of the intricate process of managing and controlling one's public image. The last essay in the collection is by Tatiana Zhurzhenko who uses the metaphor of Yulia Tymoshenko's body to first explain the seductive power of her political celebrity status in Ukraine, and then to show how, when imprisoned, her tortured body becomes a stage for the drama of repressed democracy, which is unfolding for Western eyes.

Table 1.1 HDI score and rank for countries in the volume

Geographic categorization*	HDI (rank) 2012 data
Middle East and North Africa	
Israel	0.900 (16)
Tunisia	0.712 (94)
Sub-Saharan Africa	
Cameroon	0.495 (150)
Zambia	0.448 (163)
Liberia	0.388 (174)
Europe	
Albania	0.749 (70)
Romania	0.786 (56)
Bulgaria	0.782 (57)
Germany	0.92 (5)
Eurasia	
Russia	0.788 (55)
Ukraine	0.740 (78)
Asia Pacific	
Malaysia	0.769 (64)
Pakistan	0.515 (146)
Americas	
Argentina	0.811(45)
Brazil	0.730 (85)
Chile	0.819 (40)
Venezuela	0.748 (71)

* Regional categorization from Freedom House

Note: The Human Development Index (HDI) is a measure of human development around the world created by the United Nations. The Freedom House provides comparative assessment of global political rights and civil liberties.

We see the present collection of 16 essays as an opportunity for enlarging the frame of reference for women in politics. It emerged out of our desire to contribute to the dialogue about the barriers to women's empowerment and full participation in the political process. Our hope is that it could serve as a useful resource in attempts by North American and global audiences to gain better understanding of developments in other parts of the world.

Notes

1 The quota debate has been the focus of a growing body of literature, with quota proponents and opponents discussing implementation and outcome variables.

2 Media logic implies consideration of the "institutional, technological and sociological characteristics of the news media, including their formats, production and dissemination routines, norms and needs and standards of newsworthiness" (Aalberg and Strömbäck 2011, 169–70).

3 Notably, van Zoonen (2006) characterizes Angela Merkel's experience with celebrity politics as a "risky confrontation" (297).

4 The inclusion of Israel in this volume could be seen as contentious by some, yet we believe it could be justified from a cultural standpoint. If we take into consideration a broader measure of democracy, which the *Economist* defines as one that includes "aspects of society and political culture" to account for the "quality of democracy," then we can see that none of the countries featured in this volume, except for Germany, fall in the "full democracy" category. In fact, eight of the featured countries (Chile, Israel, Brazil, Argentina, Bulgaria, Romania, Malaysia, and Zambia) fall in the "flawed democracy category," six can be categorized as "hybrid regimes" (Ukraine, Tunisia, Albania, Venezuela, Pakistan, and Liberia) and two classify as "authoritarian states" (Russia and Cameroon). In addition, because of the media-centric focus of the volume, the inclusion of Israel is supported by a large-scale, cross-national study examining journalism culture, which did not place Israel within the group of "western journalism culture" as exemplified by Austria, Australia, Germany, Spain, Switzerland and the United States, but positioned it instead in the group of "peripheral western" journalism cultures together with Brazil, Mexico, Bulgaria and Romania (see Hanitzsch et al. 2011).

5 We purposefully chose to avoid such deterministic terms as Third World, now retired by the World Bank.

6 Old democracies were defined as "states with at least twenty years' continuous experience of democracy and a Freedom House rating of 5.5 to 7" (the Gastil index used by the Freedom House was reversed to align high score with high level of democracy) (Inglehart and Norris 2003, 23–4).

Part One

Framing the Message: Mediated Representations and Journalistic Practices

2

The Portrayal of Women Politicians in Israeli Popular Women's Magazines

Einat Lachover

Over the years research analyses have argued that women politicians are represented in the media in a gendered and sex-stereotyped way (e.g. Norris 1997; Ross 2002; 2010; Sreberny and van Zoonen 2000). Recently, Charlotte Adcock (2010, 136) stressed the importance of studying various textual characteristics of political coverage within and between specific news formats and market sectors. The present paper conforms to Adcock's suggestion and focuses on a specific arena of news media—popular women's magazines.[1]

After years in which feminist critique chose to position feminism outside of popular culture, beginning in the 1980s feminist representations started appearing in the popular media (Hollows and Moseley 2006). Studies of popular women's magazines indeed show that contemporary magazines are well informed about feminist ideas (Gill 2007). Against the background of this emerging development in feminist representations, the present study considers the issue of how women politicians are covered in Israeli popular women's magazines. Are they covered in a stereotypically gendered manner, or does an alternative feminist report manage to filter through?

An analysis of how women politicians are represented in popular women's magazines is linked to the issue of the relationships among the popular media, politics and the public sphere in democratic societies. Popular women's magazines are not normally considered to constitute a journalistic format that exposes its readers to information of democratic importance (Ytre-Arne 2011, 258). Hence, a survey of women politicians as represented in women's magazines can offer us an interesting case study about the encounter between the popular media and civilian political content.

The present study focuses on two major female leaders in current Israeli politics, representing establishment parliamentary politics as well as non-establishment, non-parliamentary politics. In 2009, Tzipi Livni (1958–) became the first Israeli woman to run for the office of prime minister,[2] and between 2009 and 2012 she served as leader of the opposition. Daphni Leef (1986–) was one of the initiators of the 2011 housing protest in Israel, which evolved into a far-reaching social justice protest involving hundreds of thousands of protesters.

Tzipi Livni's candidacy in the 2009 parliamentary elections generated a discussion of the gender issue in Israeli politics, manifested in her campaign and in the media coverage respectively. A gender-related disparity also emerged in the voting, with more women than men voting for the Kadima party headed by Tzipi Livni despite similar policy preferences (Gedalya, Herzog and Shamir 2011). The portrayal of Daphni Leef in the women's magazines is of particular interest. Because the social protest she headed expressed a civil agenda and values, she was identified with what society and culture perceives as feminine. Indeed, the Israeli social protest was recognized as having explicit feminist dimensions due to the numerous women who led it and stood at its forefront, and also owing to what was termed "the mothers' protest."[3] The present article examines whether the representation of Livni and Leef was stereotypical and gendered or whether it constituted an alternative feminist representation?

News media representation of women politicians

Studies have indicated that the news media constitute one of the major factors working against women politicians. In the main, the media depict women as exhibiting qualities and behaviors that run counter to those expected of politicians, thereby increasing the disparity between the political figure and the normative woman (Fogiel-Bijaoui 2010). Despite the fact that research points to some improvement in the coverage of women politicians over time, recent studies (e.g. Garcia-Blanco and Wahl-Jorgensen 2012; Ibroscheva and Raicheva-Stover 2009; Ross and Comrie 2012) still show the unbalanced media coverage given to women, both in quantitative and in qualitative terms. In other words, less coverage is devoted to women than to their male counterparts, and women politicians are depicted in the same gendered, sexualized, sex-stereotyped manner as are women in general (e.g. Adcock 2010; Norris 1997; Ross 2002; 2010; Sreberny and van Zoonen 2000).

Israeli studies examining how female politicians were represented in the 1988 and 1996 election broadcasts showed that the meager exposure they were accorded focused on familiar women's issues, such as education, health, and welfare (Lemish and Tidhar 1991; 1999). A more recent study that focused on television news relating to women in Israel's 2008 local elections found that although coverage mirrored the patriarchal power structure—primarily the subordination of women to men—it also offered a forum for a genuine feminist discourse (Author 2012).

The complex gender discourse in popular women's magazines

For many years, classic feminist critique condemned the way in which women's magazines perpetuated and disseminated gender identity. Researchers and activists of the second wave of feminism fiercely criticized these periodicals, claiming that they served as an ideological mechanism for relegating women to the domestic world as part of a scheme of patriarchal repression and domination (Byerly and Ross 2006).

In the early 1980s this liberal feminist critique was gradually replaced by a neo-Marxist one which drew on the concept of hegemony as defined by the Marxist theoretician Antonio Gramsci (Gill 2007) in 1971. By adopting the concept of hegemony, scholars could now claim that women's magazines constituted an arena not only for the repressive ideological manipulation of women, but also for civil society's political negotiations between the interests of domination and submission (Gough-Yates 2003). Janice Winship (1987) adopted Gramsci's approach and maintained that women's magazines display survival skills pertaining to feminine dilemmas relevant to each period. The present study adopts this approach, emphasizing the diverse voices, versions, and contradictions inherent in the representation of women not only at different periods, but also at the same time and in the same publication.

The political dimension of popular women's magazines

The public sphere theory has recently emerged as a new line of theoretical thinking with regard to popular women's magazines (Saarenmaa 2011; Ytre-Arne 2011). It offers two different perspectives. The older of these two perspectives, the critical-normative approach put forward by Habermas (1962/1989), claims that the media's role is to provide citizens with information that will enable them to understand and participate in political processes. This approach differentiates between journalism that belongs to the public sphere and journalism that belongs to the private one (Ytre-Arne 2011) and allocates popular women's magazines to the private sphere. A supplementary viewpoint is the postmodern-cultural perspective, such as the feminist critique of women theoreticians like Nancy Fraser (1990) and Sheila Benhabib (1992). This perspective rejects existence of a priori boundaries between the private and public, arguing that boundaries are determined by a struggle pertaining to power relationships—a struggle that is structural, economic, political, and social in nature, albeit symbolic and cultural as well. Fraser (1990) also argues that defining something as "private" may be a rhetorical strategy that delegitimizes the interests, opinions and topics of others. Similarly, Behabib (1992) states that according to the Western political school of thought this differentiation serves to restrict women and delineate spaces that are characteristic of women in the realm identified as "private." According to this approach, the discourse of popular women's magazines is not necessarily classified as private space.

In the wake of the feminist critique with respect to the differentiation between public and private space, Ytre-Arne (2011) argues that broader definitions should be adopted when defining journalism relevant to the public. Rather than discussing the question of whether women's magazines provide information about public matters, we should underscore the covert roles played by women's magazines in constructing the public space.

Popular Israeli women's magazines

The study of popular women's magazines in Israel is in its early stages. *La'Isha*, the most popular Israeli women's magazine, came into being close to the establishment of the State of Israel in 1947, and *At,* its closest competitor, was founded in 1967. Despite some differences between the two magazines in the sixties (Author 2009), during the last decades both magazines are known for stressing topics such as leisure time and entertainment and avoiding explicit political content (Almog 2004). *Lady Globes*, a women's monthly founded in 1989 as an insert to the daily Israeli financial newspaper *Globes*, seeks to interest businesswomen or the wives of businessmen (Cheker Institute 2009). Lately, Author (2013) has demonstrated the amalgam of different varieties of feminism in *Lady Globes*.

More than a decade ago Herzog (2000) referred to the lack of a comprehensive study of Israeli women's magazines and called for examination of this fertile ground. She stated that Israeli women's magazines appear to present different images of women and aspire to create diverse models of femininity.

The research

The research corpus comprises the three major commercial women's magazines in Israel: *La'Isha*, *At* and *Lady Globes*. It includes all items that focus[4] on either of the two women leaders during the periods in which they played a part in the public discourse: 2001–12 in the case of Livni, and 2011–12 in the case of Leef. The analysis focuses on a variety of verbal and visual texts. The findings reveal 19 items: 15 for Livni and four for Leef. *Lady Globes*, which caters to the business community, contained the most articles (13): 11 about Livni and two about Leef. *La'Isha* was second with five articles: four about Livni and one about Leef. *At* contained only one item for the period under examination, and it was about Leef.[5] These 19 items were accompanied by 53 photographs that were analyzed as well.

The texts were analyzed using the critical discourse analysis method, an interpretive method that focuses on structures, series of arguments, and narratives, and on the cultural meanings reflected in them and constructed while using them. The patterns and topics in the texts were examined based on the notion that ideology is discursive, and therefore often pragmatic and contradictory.

Two levels were integrated into the analysis: the textual and the intertextual. On the textual level, the linguistic-rhetorical and visual elements of the text that reflect and generate hidden messages were analyzed. The intertextual level involved a comparative analysis whereby the text was compared to other common texts and widespread myths and ideologies. The study adopted a multicultural perspective with emphasis on identifying gender dimensions. In this context the study attempted to locate contradictory and unique voices that digress from or offer a challenge to the text's main voice.

The topical and the symbolic

Women politicians are not commonly covered in Israeli commercial women's magazines, though they are not entirely excluded. A methodical examination reveals that Livni and Leef were presented in two fundamental contexts in these magazines: in news items and symbolically. Four of 15 items pertaining to Livni appeared close to elections—three items prior to the 2009 parliamentary elections and one prior to the 2012 party primaries. Livni was elected to the Israeli parliament in 1999 and was appointed minister in the 2001 elections. Yet only in 2004, when she was appointed minister of justice, did the women's magazines begin to cover her. The scope of this coverage substantially increased in 2008 when she was a candidate for the office of prime minister, an issue that evoked a public discourse on gender (Halevi 2012; Gedalya, Herzog and Shamir 2011).[6] Similarly, three of the four items about Leef, leader of the social protest, appeared in the summer of 2011 when the social protest was at its peak and took top billing on the public agenda of Israeli media. After the protest was relegated from the first pages of the newspapers to the inside, only one other item about Leef appeared, even though her public activities continued.

Livni and Leef were also covered in the women's magazines in a symbolic context with dual significance relating both to gender and to the public space. A considerable part of this coverage appeared in the *Lady Globes*' "Fifty most influential women" project. Every year the magazine lists fifty noteworthy women in Israeli society, with special emphasis on women who have been influential in the economic sphere. The fact that Livni and Leef were on this list reflects and constructs the perception of their status in Israeli public life. Livni first appeared on the list in 2004, and in 2005 was named the most influential woman of the year. From 2006 through 2011[7] she was among the top-ranked women each year. Activist Leef was named as the most influential woman in 2011—the year of the protest—and was still on the list in 2012.

Similarly, in 2009 Livni starred in the Jewish New Year's holiday issue of *La'Isha* in the magazine's "Woman of the Week" column, and in September 2011 the magazine crowned Leef as "Our Woman of the Year." Livni, the most senior female parliamentary figure in Israel, symbolizes the public achievements of Israeli women and was therefore also featured on the cover of *La'Isha* published "in honor of International Women's Day" in 2012.

Femininity and politics

Unlike the traditional research argument claiming that representations of women politicians in the media are stereotypical and characterized by contradictory expectations of femininity and politics, Livni's coverage in Israeli popular women's magazines does not, on the whole, exhibit such tension. Rather it depicts her as a political and idealistic woman, and reveals no friction between her femininity and her public role. The articles about and interviews with Livni focus on the political aspects of her career, including her political standpoints in various contexts. Her deep and unqualified ideological dimension is reflected in descriptions of her right-wing family background, while at the same time Livni is shown as being ideologically flexible and willing to accept political compromise—a duality put forward as a relative advantage. In addition, Livni is shown as an honest and genuine person, a fighter for quality in public government and someone who rejects political wheeling and dealing. Yet she is not devoid of ambition and resolutely seeks to become Israel's prime minister. Thus, for example, the headlines say: "*Zipiot gevohot*" [great expectations],[8] (*La'Isha*, September 26, 2008, issue no. 3207: 48), or "I will be prime minister. Full stop." (*La'Isha*, February 2, 2009, issue no. 3225: 26). Alongside her ideology and politics she is also shown as a private person: a family member, a woman who has friends and enjoys her free time (sports, dancing), and in this context her long and strong relationship with her supportive husband is underscored.

These findings with regard to Livni are compatible with the findings of Gedalya et al. (2011: 244) who showed that most of the reports on Livni in Israel's two leading daily papers during the 2008–9 campaign avoided mentioning her family status, her age and her physical appearance and refrained from using grammatical construct states (a Hebrew grammatical form implying dependence). The vast majority of articles referred to her professional functioning, not to her gender.

On the other hand, the way in which Leef was depicted in the commercial women's magazines mainly reflects the tension between femininity and politics. Some of the headlines label Leef as a leader, among them the headline "Leader of the protest," (*La'Isha*, September 5, 2011, issue no. 3363: 39) or the subheading "A column on inspiring women," (*At*, August 5, 2011, issue no. 731: 30–1). Other headlines diminished or belittled her, mainly based upon her young age. One such heading, "The rebellion of a young girl," (*La'Isha*, September 5, 2011, issue 3363: 39), alludes to the fact that the social protest Leef was leading was nothing more than a youthful folly. *Lady Globes* depoliticized her. The main reference to the interview with Leef, chosen as Woman of the Year in 2011, appears on the magazine's front page and underscores her personal story: "On loss, loneliness, rape and fall," (*Lady Globes*, September 2011, issue no. 156:1).

The article positions Leef's motivation for leading the struggle in the context of her personal history, and mainly that of her emotional experience. Her ideology, values, and political perceptions are not mentioned, and the entire article avoids any structural analysis of the reasons for and significance of the protest.

Nevertheless, a year later *Lady Globes* published an entirely different interview with Leef, drawing attention to the ideological dimension of her character. The headline defines her as a leader: "Leader of the social protest" (*Lady Globes*, September 2012, issue no. 168: 70), and the subhead highlights her political endeavor: "Leader of the largest social protest ever in Israel, now in its second year. This year she founded a social organization (*Yisrael Machar* [Israel tomorrow]), led several demonstrations and was even arrested by the police" (ibid.). The entire interview focuses on her social endeavors and ideological leanings, dubbing her a political and principled woman. Thus, for example, in response to a question about the most important events of the past year, she spoke about the social organization she founded, saying: "Perhaps the work invested will push people to go into politics" (ibid.). When she was asked how she felt about the past year, she responded that it represented "the choice to continue fighting for a better society" (ibid.). As is the nature of popular journalism, the interview did not lack a personal dimension, though this too had a political nuance. Thus, for example, when asked about the greatest difficulty she had faced during the past year, she responded: "Not to let violent and aggressive behavior define my behavior" (ibid.). When asked which profession she would choose if she could go back in time, she replied: "Teacher" (ibid.).

Visual representation

Feminist critique of the media places emphasis on the stereotypical representation of women in photojournalism (Global Media Monitoring Project 2010, 8). This critique stresses that women politicians are photographed in a way that accentuates their feminine dimension and obscures their political orientation.

In contrast, analysis of the visual representations of Livni and Leef in commercial women's magazines reveals a complex picture of stereotypical alongside nonstereotypical depictions, though the visual representation appears more stereotypical than the verbal representation, which, as we saw, shows a prominent trend toward gender blindness. This is not surprising based on other studies examining the depiction of women in news media. News pictures very often serve to attract readers' attention by depicting emotion, drama, or sexuality, and women are quite suitable for this purpose (Gallagher 2005, 52–3). Again, this is more obvious in visual depictions of Leef.

In general terms, Livni's photographs in women's magazines show a professional and well-groomed woman. She wears pants suits in subdued colors or monochromatic knee-length dresses. In her photographs she is shown wearing light makeup and simple gold jewelry, with her light-colored hair at shoulder length. In most cases she is not photographed in positions that can be construed as particularly feminine or masculine. At times the articles include photographs from different periods in her life: family photos from her parents' home, childhood photos, and photos with a professional context, such as a lecture or meeting with Israeli and international political leaders. The photographs reflect an exemplary, active and professional woman. Among the scores of photographs that appeared in women's magazines not one was taken in her home, with her spouse or her children, or during her leisure time activities. Livni's political and public portrayal is notable in the *Lady Globes*' project on the most influential women of 2007. Each of the women on the list was requested to choose a site for her photograph to be taken. Livni, who had practiced law for ten years and served as Minister of Justice, chose to be photographed in the courtyard of the Foreign Ministry against the background of the Supreme Court.

In the context of Livni's predominant visual representation combining the feminine and the professional, a staged series of photographs that appeared in December 2009 was striking (*Lady Globes*, December 2009, issue: 135: 1, 49, 51–2, 54), as it depicted Livni in a stereotypically feminine manner. This series of photographs, titled "Everything is Political," was published in an issue that focused on politics. Livni's photograph on the front page can even be considered seductive. She is wearing tight black pants and a top. The sleeves of her blouse are gathered and puffy at the shoulders, according her a doll-like appearance. The photograph is fragmented and conceals the lower third of her body. She looks as if she is leaning backwards against the table. The fingertips of one hand are resting on the table and her other hand is raised behind her head, touching her hair. Her head is tilted to the side, though she is looking straight ahead with an expression that conveys amazement and surprise. Her mouth is partially open. In contrast to this visual representation, the headline of the article on the front page was extremely political: "A War Criminal? Me?—Zipi Livni is not afraid of being arrested abroad." In two additional photographs in this article Livni is sitting on a light-colored couch upholstered in a floral embroidered pattern.

She is wearing the traditional feminine little black dress. Her bare crossed legs are prominent in the center of the photograph, and she is wearing high heels. The position of her body is frozen and her smile reveals embarrassment. Other photographs in this article show Livni leaning rather than standing upright or erect, and her posture conveys discomfort.

The visual depictions of Leef reflect noticeable tension between the feminine and the professional. Some of the photographs do not suggest any tension of this kind but rather show a liberated young woman who is not at all pedantic about her appearance. Her hair is unkempt, and she is wearing a simple t-shirt bearing the protest logo (*At*, August 5, 2011, issue no. 731: 1; *La'Isha*, September 5, 2011, issue no. 3363: 38). Other photographs in the same issue of *At*, which published only one item included in the research corpus, portray Leef as a young vulnerable woman and obscure her leadership dimension. Thus, for example, three photographs reflect her diminished image (*At*, August 5, 2011, issue no. 731: 30–3). One photograph shows her sitting on a bench and speaking on the phone. As in the photograph on the first page, here too she is shown as a young woman dressed in a protest shirt and shorts, wearing Teva sandals, her face serious and preoccupied. In another photograph she is shown sitting on a straw mat on Rothschild Boulevard, looking down and not facing the camera, her arms hugging her bare legs, her body bent, and her body language expressing embarrassment and shyness. In the center photograph of the three, which are spread over two pages, Leef appears in the classical sleeping position. She is shown wearing a short dress, lying on her back on a leather couch on the boulevard. Her eyes are closed, and one arm is folded, pillowing her head. Her image in this photograph conveys a lack of awareness and vulnerability.

The way in which Leef is portrayed in *Lady Globes* is also complex. Some of the photographs depict a soft feminine figure devoid of any political affinity, while others show her as a political figure whose femininity is indistinct. Thus, for example, in two photographs Leef is shown together with female partners to the protest. One is a group photo of five women protest leaders, and the other shows Leef with the woman identified as her second in command. In both photographs Leef is wearing a light-colored dress made of soft fabric and high heels. In both photographs the women leaders are standing with their backs to each other without any eye contact, thus conveying the absence of sisterhood. Leef's facial expression is serious, while her posture is slack and unstable as she is balancing her weight on one foot. An unusual object appears in the photographs: each of the protest leaders is holding an open fan. While a fan may indeed be a useful item during the hot Israeli summer, it is rarely used among Israeli women. Moreover, in a Western context a fan is seen as symbolizing upper-class women, running counter to the socialist values Leef was preaching (*Lady Globes*, September 2011, issue no. 156: 50, 52). On the front cover of the issue Leef is seen turning toward the camera, looking straight ahead, with the fan she is holding hiding her upper body. The graffiti drawings characteristic of Tel-Aviv streets are visible, though they are not political in spirit (*Lady Globes*, September 2011, issue 156: 1). Thus Leef, who during the protest was depicted in the news media in an urban space, perspiring, sleeping in a tent with no air conditioning, speaking on platforms, calling out, carrying signs, and together with her friends leading mass street demonstrations, is in these *Lady Globes*' photographs portrayed as an individualist in a space devoid of context. Her feminine identity is marked as symbolizing softness and the upper classes. Her face is serious and devoid of expression, and she makes no political statement whatsoever.

In contrast, other photographs appearing in the 2012 *Lady Globes* article identifying Leef as "leader of the social protest" combine femininity and political identity in depicting her. In one, her long hair is well groomed and she is wearing light makeup, but the photograph zooms in on her face and hands. Leef is looking at the spectator with a serious and penetrating gaze. Her arms at the center of the photograph are crossed in a gesture of opposition according to the body language employed in the Tel-Aviv protest demonstrations. In another photograph her hair is carelessly tied back behind her head, she is holding a video camera (symbolizing her profession as a video film director and editor) and again she is looking straight at the spectator (*Lady Globes*, September 2012, issue no. 168: 70, 72). In yet another photograph she is wearing a blue buttoned tunic reminiscent of a blue work shirt. This "worker" look is complemented by her high and unadorned rubber boots. Leef is standing facing the camera with her legs apart, her posture erect, her hands on her hips, and wearing the hat that has become her visual symbol. She is the epitome of confidence and resolve (*Lady Globes*, September 2011, issue no. 156: 44, 46).

Feminist representation

A feminist discourse does exist regarding the way in which Livni and Leef are portrayed in popular Israeli women's magazines, though this discourse is not prominent. The image of Livni is not shown directly in the context of the feminist discourse, and certainly Leef's image does not appear in this context either. The headlines and even the subheadings do not make any direct references to issues related to the status of women or to women's rights. Such issues are rather hidden away in small print and relegated to less prominent spots inside the articles.

Nevertheless, over the years the portrayal of Livni's image has shown considerable development. Whereas in the early years of her career there was no sign of feminist discourse, beginning with her candidacy for prime minister in 2008 and following her campaign's intentional focus on the gender context (Gedalya, Herzog and Samir 2011; Halevi 2012), feminist representation trickled down to women's magazines as well.

A leading theme in the feminist representation of Livni in women's magazines relates to the home–work conflict. In several interviews Livni is portrayed as someone who has experienced "the sequence of stages that all women are familiar with, the entire gamut of pangs of conscience" (*La'Isha*, February 2, 2009, issue no. 3225: 30). A prominent item in this context appeared in *Lady Globes* in 2012 (*Lady Globes*, August 2012, issue no. 167: 20–1). In this op-ed piece, in which Livni expresses greater affinity than in the past to women's magazines in general and to *Lady Globes* in particular, she refers to an article titled "Why women still can't have it all," by Anne-Marie Slaughter, an American State Department official who left her job in order to devote herself to her two adolescent sons. Slaughter's article was published in the July 2012 issue of *The Atlantic* and aroused lively discourse throughout the world, including Israel. The timing of Livni's column was not accidental. When it was published she was debating about becoming the chairperson of a new party in the Knesset, and was most probably trying to prove her "femininity" to female and feminist audiences and demonstrate that she had learned to "speak like a woman." In the column, Livni compared herself to Slaughter and focused on the conflict she had experienced throughout her career. Nevertheless, Livni put forward a weak critical and political standpoint regarding the reality working mothers were facing in Israel and did not call for a change in the public agenda and definitely not for public action. The item was framed as an individual opinion based on Livni's personal experiences as a career mother.

Another theme in Livni's feminist image emerges in her portrayal as a woman who has undergone a sobering process with respect to the feminist idea and her own feminist identity. Livni is depicted as a woman who denied the dimension of gender in the past, but became empowered through meetings with women voters: "Time and again I hear the same things from women—you have given me strength. I began to understand my part as a woman in this campaign, and I feel it big time" (*La'Isha*, February 2, 2009, issue no. 3225: 30). Similarly, when Livni was asked about who she would choose as Woman of the Year for 2011, she mentioned a woman who had been recently promoted to major general in the Israel Defense Forces (*Lady Globes*, September 2011, issue no. 156: 74). These examples and others offer concrete evidence for the liberal affinity of Livni's feminist image. She strives to achieve equal opportunities for women without rejecting or challenging the existing social-political order.

On the other hand, Leef's image reflects a weaker affinity to feminism. The three items about Leef that appeared in 2011 did not include any explicit feminist representation. A slight change can be seen in a fourth item in 2012. Leef's choice for Woman of the Year was Keren Neubach, a journalist identified with social struggles in general and with feminist ideas in particular (*Lady Globes*, September 2012, issue no. 168: 72). Moreover, Leef states that the person she considers most promising is "someone I have not yet met. I have the feeling that we will see a great deal of feminine strength rising up, women who will undertake leadership and will become dominant in social change" (ibid.). Thus, Leef is not depicted as a woman brandishing the feminist flag, but rather as one with an affinity to feminism.[9]

Summary

The representations of both Livni and Leef in popular Israeli women's magazines are complex, reflecting both a prominent trend toward gender blindness and a gendered representation that is at the same time both stereotypical and alternative. Gedalya et al. (2011) and Halevi (2012), who analyzed Livni's 2008–9 campaign and its coverage in the media, also found a complex representation. Their analysis, however, stressed the dominance of a hegemonic gendered representation based on chauvinist thinking patterns expressing a stereotypical standpoint according to which politics is a man's world and belongs to men. They argued that this representation was undermined in the election campaign and that over time a new political discourse evolved about Livni, one that offered alternative values or a renewed definition of the political leader.

Nevertheless, this discourse was introduced into the campaign belatedly, and was not sufficiently focused.

The present article examined whether the representations of Livni and Leef were stereotypical and gendered or whether they constituted an alternative feminist representation? The findings of this study point to a less stereotypical representation of women politicians compared to traditional media representations in general. This is particularly true in the case of Livni. Thus, the findings support previous studies arguing that contemporary women's magazines are *au courant* with feminist ideas (Gill 2007). Moreover, similar to the findings of the present study, previous studies revealed shades of a liberal feminist discourse and avoidance of a radical discourse (McCracken 1993).

The findings of the present study also point to differences in the ways in which these two women politicians are portrayed. The portrayal of Livni, a consensual, veteran, and experienced politician, largely reflects gender blindness and to a lesser degree stereotypical and alternative representations. In contrast, for the most part Leef's representation is stereotypical due to her status as an outsider and her anti-hegemonic agenda. These differences may also reflect the role of the political players themselves. As an experienced politician with professional media resources at her disposal, Livni managed to channel the coverage along the lines of what she identified as her political needs. Leef, in contrast, was inexperienced and devoid of any professional resources and had less say about the manner in which she was portrayed. Nevertheless, as we have seen, Leef's portrayal developed considerably over time, from a stereotypical representation in 2011 to a gender-blind representation with a touch of feminist affinity in 2012.

Contrary to the image of popular women's magazines as being apolitical and perhaps even anti-political, political portrayals can be detected in these magazines, alongside some differences between the publications. *Lady Globes* is geared to the business community and reflects a more conservative portrayal, while *La'Isha* is directed at a less homogeneous and broader audience and reflects a less conservative representation. *At* put forward an extremely political agenda, devoting an entire special issue to the social protest, with Daphni Leef on its cover. Nevertheless, she was represented in a stereotypical manner. We can therefore conclude that these magazines are not perceived as an irrelevant arena for public discussion of civil and political topics. The political representation in these magazines focuses on the personal coverage of women politicians. Articles about and interviews with women politicians, as found in this study, appear in the context of current affairs—usually prior to elections—or in the symbolic gender and public context in order to celebrate the achievements of Israeli women and empower them. The prominent trend toward portraying Tzipi Livni as a political woman without creating the traditional tension between femininity and politics exemplifies the potential of popular women's magazines to offer a political discourse that challenges the traditional categories of private vs. the public, as discussed by feminist women theoreticians such as Nancy Fraser (1990) and Sheila Benhabib (1992).

The trend toward gender-blind representations or toward alternative-feminist (liberal) gender representations reflects the changes taking place in Israeli society in its perception of the status of women in the public-political arena. Until the 1970s motherhood was defined as a woman's main role. In the wake of the second wave of feminism worldwide and the far-reaching social movement in Israel in the 1970s, women's status in Israel has reached a turning point and a feminist discourse has developed (Herzog 2006). Since the early 1990s these changes have filtered down to the public-political arena and to public opinion (Ishai 1999).

The world of Israeli politics is still masculine and hegemonic, yet it is gradually and continuously changing. Part of this process can be seen in the creeping but constant increase in the number of women in the Israeli parliament (Fogiel-Bijaoui 2010). In addition, the development of a gendered election in Israel as early as the 2009 elections (Gedalya, Herzog and Shamir 2011) is worthy of mention. This process may deepen the role of popular Israeli women's magazines as a more significant public arena for political coverage in general, and for women politicians in particular.

Notes

1 I use the terms "popular women's magazines" and "commercial women's magazines" as synonymous collocations.

2 Golda Meir did not run but rather was appointed party leader after the death of Eshkol and thus became prime minister.

3 The terms "mothers' protest" or "March of the Baby Carriages" refer to a group of educated and working women who took part in the 2011 social protest in Israel. This group called for introducing free education from the age of three months and providing affordable housing.

4 The items collected focused primarily on Livni or Leef. Items that only mentioned them were not included.
5 In none of the magazines is there computed archive, therefore I had to look up the relevant articles in each issue. Surprisingly, there was no article about Livni in *At*. I have confirmed this finding through an interview with *At*'s editor-in-chief for the last 14 years.
6 Only four items about Livni were found between 2001 and 2007, while 11 items were found about her between 2008 and 2012.
7 In 2012 the magazine's list of influential women did not include politicians, most likely due to the proximity to the upcoming elections in January 2013 and based on an attempt to avoid political influence. A separate issue was devoted to women politicians.
8 A play on words: in Hebrew Livni's first name is similar to "expectation" (*tzipiya* in Hebrew).
9 The topics raised by the social protest in Israel are identified as "feminine" areas: education, welfare, housing, poverty and concerns for everyday life. Furthermore, the social protest made use of the contemporary feminist discourse in Israel, which is not primarily a liberal feminist discourse but rather a discourse that criticizes the existing social order (Herzog 2013). Yet the media does not identify radical feminist discourse as feminist and thus did not specifically frame Leef as a feminist.

3

Ambiga Sreenevasan and Malaysian Counter-Publics

Mary Griffiths and Sara Chinnasamy

Introduction

This chapter focuses on the role of new technologies as zones for increased democratic participation in Malaysia, through contextualized analysis of media representations of the activism of a prominent human rights lawyer, Ambiga Sreenevasan. The counter-discursive practices of women activists as opposed to those of women politicians have as yet received scant attention, especially when the women are located in non-Western parts of the world. The civil society activist described here does not see herself as a politician, though she has been thought of as one, by opponents as well as supporters.[1] Sreenevasan's productive civil society interventions into deliberations about democracy have, however, changed Malaysian politics. She anchored emerging reformist counter-publics, as the new Malaysian online news portals, enabled by a censorship-free Internet, became spaces where alternative voices on the need for electoral reform could finally be heard.

The chapter's aim is to illustrate how, despite the specific difficulties faced by a high-profile professional woman in the public sphere when she speaks "truth to power"—in this case, to powerful elements in a political culture dominated by one party since independence, the Barisan Nasional (BN)—the woman becomes a model for other citizens as she publicly exercises democratic rights and responsibilities. A significant issue facing women who take up non-traditional, public advocacy roles is the official and unofficial attempts to silence them, for example, by belittling the views expressed, name-calling, deliberate misrepresentations of what they are saying or doing and, in multi-ethnic societies, by deploying of conservative cultural and religious attitudes about the proper public conduct expected of women. Some repressive strategies go further. In a state where race-based policy and the national Constitution itself favors the ethnic group rights of the majority Malays, Sreenevasan is not just represented as a "difficult Indian woman" and an unworthy political dissident, she has also been bullied by disrespectful opponents, implicitly threatened with revocation of citizenship by BN's elder statesman, Mahathir, and compelled to defend herself against government charges that she breached the Peaceful Assembly Act (2012). Significantly, however, she was simultaneously voted *Malaysiakini.com*'s "newsmaker of the year" (*Malaysiakini.com* 2012a), she remains a popular heroine locally, and internationally is recognized for her human rights work as twenty-fourth President of the Malaysian Bar Council (2007–9). The United States Department nominated her as one of eight "International Women of Courage" in 2009. Accepting her award from Hillary Clinton and Michelle Obama, she acknowledged the national and international aspects of activism in the service of democracy, calling for individual courage, and a keen commitment to the rule of law and pursuit of tolerance (*Thestar.com* 2009). Chosen to represent others accepting the award, she spoke at the ceremony of the democratic struggle against "the forces of the old" as "cultivating the souls of our nations," focusing attention on effecting democratic reform through implementation of procedural changes in the apparatuses of democracy, that is, in the material processes themselves. This civic and rational approach, within legal boundaries, describes her principled activism.

Sreenevasan's major stake in political culture began with co-leadership of, and highly visible participation in, Gabungan Pilihanraya *Bersih* dan Adil (Coalition for Clean and Fair Elections). *Bersih*, "Clean," a popular reform coalition of non-governmental organizations (NGOs) and political parties, was launched in 2006. *Bersih* announced its mission by challenging the "legitimacy of a state" with "flawed electoral processes" (Bersih 2006). *Bersih*'s overall aims thus contain the possibility of political upheaval. Specifically, they are to: apply continued pressure on the Election Commission Malaysia (EC) to ensure free and fair elections; demand that the EC begin by cleaning the electoral roll; reform postal voting; ensure the use of indelible ink; introduce a minimum 21-day campaign period; allow all parties free access to the media; and put an end to electoral fraud (Bersih 2006).

A brief overview of the rapid development of *Bersih* is given here as part of our argument that Ambiga is seen as synonymous with the movement by mainstream, alternative, and international media (Gooch 2011). The initial *Bersih* rally (1.0) was organized on 10 November 2007, in preparation for

General Election 2008. Critics had argued that the electoral roll favors the BN, and that this explained its apparent reluctance to investigate voting discrepancies. *Bersih* attracted diverse media coverage, not simply because the issues could not easily be conceived of as ethnically-based, but because supporters were reported as being between 10,000 and 40,000 strong (Bernama.com 2007). *Bersih* 1.0 was immediately seen as a significant movement with a clear focus and effective leadership under its co-chair. Plans for a further rally of up to 100,000 people stalled, as protesters gathered at different locations, and as efforts to raise people's participation by circulating pamphlets and carrying banners were barred by police. The *Bersih* 2.0 rally, known by the less provocative name, "Walk for Democracy," in July 2011 continued the momentum, reportedly attracting 20,000 participants (Boo 2011). After these popular successes, *Bersih* gained support from the opposition party, Pakatan Rakyat (PR), where it started to exert real political influence and attract more BN resistance. By *Bersih* 3.0, the ruling regime was negotiating *Bersih* demands for cleaner election processes, but also trying to frame the movement and its leader as oppositional and unruly.

Since 2007, Sreenevasan's public statements, which previously identified her interests as human rights and religious tolerance, have primarily focused on the practical achievement of electoral reform through *Bersih*. The pressure exerted has resulted in the BN government's implementation of a Public Select Committee (PSC) to investigate roll discrepancies (*Thestar.com* 2012). The movement has thus gained traction quickly. "Ambiga," as Sreenevasan is familiarly called in public, emerged as its pivotal figure; in and through this organization, she commands broad support beyond minority ethnic and religious groups. Governmental attention has focused on her whenever *Bersih* activities are reported because coverage of *Bersih* driving philosophies and activities inevitably gives voice to information about regime failures. Thus, in Malaysia's dominant development journalism news model, reportage of Ambiga and *Bersih* contrasts discursively along a political fault line, depending on whether it originates from mainstream print media, or "independent" Internet news sources. On both sides of the fault line, Ambiga is seen as the voice of the reformist movement. She lends her legal knowledge and performative authority to the solidification of requests for change. Her rational approach to political debate redefines, for others, a citizen's democratic responsibility despite a media landscape where, in mainstream media at least, legitimate disagreement can be represented as working against an imagined national unity.

The chapter proceeds as follows: it provides an explanation for the use of counter-publics to analyze news coverage over the weeks between *Bersih* 2.0 and 3.0. It contextualizes the comparative state of gender equality in Malaysia, its political practices with special regard to women, and Ambiga's emerging public role in *Bersih*. In addition, an explanatory section is included on the bifurcation in Malaysian media caused by ownership, regulation, and political affiliations. Next, the methodology is described briefly. Summaries follow of the contrasting coverage of Ambiga in her role as *Bersih* leader from a representative mainstream news source and reportage from two independent online news portals. The chapter concludes with an assessment of the counter-discursive civic rationalities assembled in the citizen activist, Ambiga Sreenevasan.

Theoretical approach: "Counter-publics" in the Malaysian context

Scholarly work on decision-making in democracy has produced useful approaches to the analysis of available public speaking positions. Habermas (1991) describes political deliberation beyond the realm of representative government in democracies as operating in the "public sphere" and his later work emphasizes the importance of citizens' participation in that realm; Benedict Anderson's work on "print nationalism" describes the way that daily reading of newspapers helps form national belonging in place and time, and identification with the state (1991), and this insight explains in part the ruling regime's support of the development journalism approach of mainstream media as a governmental technique for unification of a multi-race nation, following decolonization in Malaysia. Asen (2000) links the concept of "counter-publics" to networked interleaving of separate groups in the public sphere; and Warner (2002, 49) notes not only their deliberate visibility, for example, as a crowd which shares space and witnesses its own actions, but also how they are constituted in the readership of texts. Since this scholarship, Internet news and social media have disrupted a sense of the universal shared public sphere, as online readerships fragment and reassemble and niche civil society publics form for activism, deliberation, and public debate (Griffiths 2014).

We use these insights to argue that counter-publics around Ambiga and *Bersih* formed when two factors converged: first, when hegemonic power excluded minority voices from political deliberations in civil society, thus giving rise to the need on the part of those excluded to find alternative platforms for the expression of divergent views; and second, when contingent factors like Ambiga's individual agency, and independent media platforms such as *Malaysiakini.com* and *Themalaysianinsider.com* helped constitute deliberative publics by representing and mobilizing the expressive powers and street visibility of reformist forces.

BN's grip on hegemonic power is vigorously exerted through invasive government regulation of mainstream print and broadcast media, in the name of governing a potentially volatile and ethnically divided society. Rajaratnam, following previous scholarly analysis (Anuar 2000; 2005) notes the strong links between political and media elites, responsible for repressing open-minded journalists (Rajaratnam 2009, 35). The Internet news portals, on the other hand, are not so restricted, as they became beneficiaries of an unforeseen loophole in regulation when the Internet was left free of censorship in the interests of the country's business development. Counter-publics around the "independent" news portals are a direct result. Their existence may explain some mainstream media ambivalence about Ambiga, because the mere presence of independent online media increases the likelihood of a challenging new factor in political culture: a range of diverse opinions, and more supportive narrativizations of reformist ideas and activities. The news portals reframe the dominant representations of street protests by posting photographs of police violence; disputing the mainstream accounts of the number of rally supporters with eye-witness accounts; and deploying citizen-journalists on the ground to send in live mobile footage of events as they occur. This reportage legitimates a movement, makes visible a leader's counter-discursive power and, conversely, it also opens up exploitable controversies around that leader's representative qualities for the majority of Malaysians who are Muslim.

The bifurcation in the mediascape means that news outlets fall into broadly politicized categories: government "partners" (mainstream media) or government "critics" (independent news portals). *Malaysiakini.com*, Malaysia's first commercial independent Internet media, was set up in 1999, and although reformist publics constitute themselves around it, it is read widely throughout the country including by its rivals, the government "partners." It is an independent publication and it offers news in English, Bahasa Malaysia, Chinese, and Tamil, with nearly 800,000 visitors daily. It helps disclose irregularities in mainstream media reporting, fulfilling a "watchdog" role on government and government media. The co-founder of *Malaysiakini.com* has stated: "Malaysia is a democracy.

We have freedom of speech, but no freedom after speech. There is freedom of movement, but no freedom of assembly. We have a plethora of publications but we don't have a free press" (cited in Rajaratnam 2009, and Tang 2005). Since the 2008 General Election, *Malaysiakini.com* has given voice to the voiceless, such as the Hindu Rights Action Force (*Hindraf*) and the *Bersih* movement. It offered free access to its subscription-based website during *Bersih* protests, thus helping legitimize and broaden the movement's support base. These democratic interventions are possible because, unlike the print and broadcast mainstream media, *Malaysiakini.com* does not require annual licensing, and thus the consequent lack of guaranteed independence, from the Home Minister. After it began providing alternative news, "many Malaysians for the first time felt they had been misled and began to lose faith in the official media" (Samad 2001, 1). *Themalaysianinsider.com* was set up by a group of liberal-minded businessmen after the 2008 general election, as a business opportunity, following the proven success of *Malaysiakini.com*'s news model.

Utusan Malaysia is a pro-government Malay-language daily, owned by the Utusan Group. According to the AC Nielsen media consumption report in 2009, *Utusan Malaysia* started in Singapore in 1939 and is the highest circulation newspaper with a daily readership of 1,497,000. Yet, Audit Bureau of Circulation figures in 2011 show that, as with print news circulation across the world, *Utusan*'s daily sales shrank 20 percent between June 2006 and June 2010. The combination of factors just described present the ideal conditions for counter-publics to form. The next section deals with the unique Malaysian context of gender politics, which bears upon public participation by women.

Background to gender politics in Malaysia

Malaysia is a multi-ethnic and multi-religious society, with a large Malay Muslim majority, consequently opportunities for women, relations between men and women under the law, and speaking positions in public life are affected in complex ways. This section first deals with the constraints caused by gender expectations which demonstrate the impact of Ambiga's agency in taking a *Bersih* leadership role, and also help explain the discursive tactics used by mainstream media to diminish it.

Malaysia scores low on the gender gap in the East Asia and the Pacific region at 56 points, which is 13 points below the region's average of 69, and well below those of its neighbors (Social Watch 2012).[2] Another measure, the *Gender Inequality Index Malaysia*, places the country at 43 out of 146 countries (United Nations Development Programme 2011). According to these indices, women in Malaysia are still disadvantaged, although their legal status is gradually improving. *Article 8 (2)* of the *Federal Constitution*, for example, prohibits discrimination on the basis of gender. Malaysia also ratified the *Convention on the Elimination of All Forms of Discrimination against Women* in 1995, but with reservations particularly in relation to rights in the family and in marriage. The country has thus progressed in the education of women, their increased participation in higher-paying occupations, their greater involvement in business activities, and their improved health status (United Nations Development Programme 2007). Despite the advances cited by the United Nations, the World Economic Forum in 2010 reported that the country's women still remain unequal to men. The existence of the dual legal system of civil law and multiple versions of *Shariah Law* (Islamic law) contribute to gender discrimination, particularly in marriage and family relations.

Ambiga has taken a lead as a public advocate of the principle of equality before the law, and made a difference. She fought for the administration of justice in the "March of Justice" organized to call for judicial reforms and these public actions, after six months, led a Royal Commission to find a corrective action (Malaysian Bar 2011). Ambiga's activism for religious freedom and women's rights brought other controversies. She intervened, for example, in former Muslim Lina Joy's religious apostasy case. Ambiga argued, as President of the Law Council, that Article 121 (1A) of Malaysia's Federal Constitution does not deprive Muslims from freedom of religion (Ismail 2011); and that a citizen's conversion to another religion should be recognized on official documents (Sreenevasan 2011). The case was emblematic of the greater struggle in Malaysia for religious tolerance as it pertains to gender.

Ambiga's high profile and controversial activities were reported by *Malaysiakini.com*, and *Themalaysianinsider.com* which also condemned the ban on the ethnic Indian activist group, Hindraf, and the detention of its leaders under the Internal Security Act (ISA). So, although Ambiga has eschewed the label of "politician" (Loone 2012), representations of her indicate that she is seen—correctly—as a potential threat to the political status quo. The heterogeneous nature of *Bersih* support has arguably focused more attention on a female leader who steps outside traditional expectations of women, even professional women, in Malaysia.

In political life, although women in Malaysia have an equal right to vote in general elections, to be elected and participate in public life, equal political representation has not followed. The World Economic Forum in 2010 reported that women make up only 10 percent of Malaysia's parliamentarians and 7 percent of ministerial positions. The United Nations Committee on the Elimination of Discrimination against Women (CEDAW) in 2006 reported that the structures of most political parties are not conducive to women's involvement, as women's participation and movement within the party is generally restricted to the women's wings. Women's participation in Malaysia's electoral politics is thus still at the lowest level. Women nevertheless choose to participate in the *Bersih* rallies, led by a high profile spokesperson like Ambiga.

Ambiga's visibility as a leader makes her a target for diverse, powerful opponents. When Ambiga led *Bersih* calling for fair elections, the government used the violent turn of events as a platform from which to increase its attacks on *Bersih*'s leader. An article discussing the fate of women leaders in Malaysia observes that "Ambiga's name could scarcely be mentioned among government insiders without some measure of vitriol attached to it". The piece then provides a quote by Prime Minister Najib who reportedly told a crowd in the run-up to the *Bersih* 2.0 rally "Who doesn't know Ambiga. She's the one who threatened Islam." Ambiga was described as "*Awas! Ambiga wanita Hindu yang berbahaya*" ("Warning! Ambiga is a dangerous Hindu woman") on the leaflets distributed by Malay rights group, Perkasa (Martin 2012). Yet, in an instance illustrating the complexity of Malaysian politics, the racial and religious edge to hostility towards her drew sharp critiques on an influential progressive Muslim website, where it was named as "offensive" (Islamic Renaissance Front 2012). In other examples of intimidation practices, she has received death threats; local traders held a religiously abusive protest outside Ambiga's house; and a group of army veterans arrived to shake their buttocks in her direction as part of an impromptu "exercise" (*Malaysiakini.com* 2012b). Further, groups have held protests outside her home, one even presenting a memorandum detailing the need for Ambiga to leave the country if she did not apologize (they were non-specific about to whom an apology was owed). Though Ambiga called the veterans' protest "crude" and an "invasion of privacy," she was personally civil, even gracious, to protestors, according to the news story, with attached video. Nevertheless, the representations of Ambiga's treatment make the gap between gender policy and repressive sexist practices, nuanced by racial hatred and religious intolerance, even clearer. In recounting such events at a university Law school public talk overseas, Ambiga pointed out the need for "an elevation of national discourse," and suggested that the forceful tactics deployed against *Bersih* demonstrated that BN "did not get" people's desire for change (Sreenevasan 2011).

Method

To understand how reformist counter-publics work in practice, we analyzed content from *Utusan Malaysia*, *Malaysiakini.com* and *Themalaysianinsider.com* between *Bersih* 2.0 which took place on July 9, 2011 and *Bersih* 3.0 which took place on April 28, 2012. The period under consideration encompasses coverage surrounding the two rallies. *Utusan Malaysia* was chosen as representative of the mainstream press, for its close connections with the ruling political elite, and because of its Malay and English circulation figures. *Malaysiakini.com* and *Themalaysianinsider.com* were chosen as representatives of emerging online news. Keyword searches were conducted using "Ambiga" and "*Bersih*" as separate terms. These returned 45 news reports from *Utusan Malaysia*, 88 news reports from *Themalaysianinsider.com*, and 128 from *Malaysiakini.com*. Notably, the independent media sources returned more news coverage of events involving Ambiga and *Bersih* than *Utusan Malaysia*. The relative frequency of online news items both demonstrates the perceived newsworthiness of the protests and reflects the potency of the digital news platforms, that is, the immediacy of web reporting as opposed to time-based print news schedules. When media visibility is accorded, a reformist movement is capable of tapping popular support and can establish its aims.

Analysis, as key themes were identified, showed that *Utusan* news items proved antagonistic to, and online media fairer and more supportive of, Ambiga and *Bersih*. *Utusan* stayed true to the country's dominant development journalism model, representing national politics through a lens of government authority, national harmony and national interests, and characterizing *Bersih* as "unruly" and disloyal. The two online portals gave more space to explaining reformist aims and strategies. They reported police violence against protestors, quoting extensively Ambiga's refutations of mainstream press suggestions that the protests would turn violent, and boosting the *Bersih* co-chair's status as a strong and rational leader, a local heroine.

Utusan Malaysia: Constructing "us" and "them"

The 45 *Utusan Malaysia* articles reveal an implicitly antagonistic tone against *Bersih* and Ambiga. The Malaysian government is represented as working in the "strict father of the family" conservative mode of national politics, to paraphrase Lakoff (1995).[3] Overall, *Utusan* coverage treats *Bersih* as a movement whose main aim is illegitimate. Representation of street demonstration "unruliness," for example, deflects the issue of a citizen's entitlement to democratic disagreement and protest, and to the democratic expression of citizen criticism of perceived failures in electoral processes. In addition, as Ambiga's name is linked so closely to *Bersih*, and news items routinely portray *Bersih* negatively, comments about Ambiga's relation to government's "firm father" are embedded and made by association, rather than expressed as a direct personal attack. Foregrounding Ambiga's statements on the rationales for protest would have meant mainstream journalists being required to negotiate the reformist issues raised, and that would mean treating her not—by association—as an "unruly" daughter of the state but as a serious civil society leader. The rhetorical technique triggers stereotypically conservative notions that women are out of place simply if they are in public expressing views, and leading or helping mobilize rallies.

At the same time that the reformist cause was gaining popular support in face-to-face meetings, visible attendance was increasing at rallies, and discussion of *Bersih* was reverberating in the blogosphere inside and outside the country, mainstream media was attempting to starve it of oxygen: for example, by framing the street protests as a public order and policing issue, and connecting its multi-ethnic and multi-stakeholder support to Malaysians' alarm about the potential return of violent inter-ethnic divisions. Other stories include calls to reject the upcoming *Bersih* rally, reminding readers of earlier economic losses, and framing the legal right to protest as a disruption of the real business of life—trade (*Utusan Malaysia* 2011a). This consolidates the "us" versus "them" discourse, highlighting the dichotomy between protestors and peaceful citizens, presenting *Bersih* not as a popular movement, but one in the hands of anti-government forces and non-elected participants. In a skillful play on words—"*Bersih Atau Kotor*? (Clean or Dirty?)" a headline from April 4, 2012 turns the *Bersih* name around, to direct attention to a discourse of economic disruption and intentional damage (Hassan 2012). A June 27, 2011 news report entitled "Related NGO Donors' Clean Christian Movement?" triggers such a combination of Muslim Malay anxieties by mentioning foreign, Christian, and

NGO financial support for *Bersih*, and linking the organization to opposition parties (*Utusan Malaysia* 2011b). *Bersih* is again represented as promoting changes unsettling to domestic security. The phrase "detected active aid through the Net" implies *Bersih* deceit and illegality, and reawakens Malaysian fears about what influences and dangerous ideas the unregulated Internet might be bringing into Malaysia. The news story implies that strong government surveillance and vigilance are necessary.

In related rhetorical maneuvers, *Utusan*'s representations of rally protestors abroad in two May 2012 reports indicate they are destructive and heretical: the April 28 *Bersih* 3.0 was held simultaneously in Mecca and Medina as a sign of Malaysians protesting around the world in solidarity with rally protestors at home. Supporters attended rallies, using the original *Bersih* banners and T-shirts. This was treated as a *Bersih* provocation, because the protest took place without, apparently, proper respect for Islamic religious places (Amran 2012).

As tension mounted before rallies, stories of the successful police break-up of protests used the words "pre-emptive measures," "bridling" and "thwarting," with connotations of military strikes, runaway horses, and the forceful curbing of another's purpose; and reported the arrest of leaders, including Ambiga and others, who were portrayed as criminals and a national threat (*Utusan Malaysia* 2011c). Ambiga, in response, spoke about a government disconnected from the people. In an interview with Patrick Teoh for Media Rakyat, she said that government was no longer appealing to "the hearts and minds of people" (see July 9, 2012 report entitled "Police managed to bridle *Bersih*") (*Patrick Teoh* 2012).

Utusan also published ex-Prime Minister Mahathir's advice to the government calling for an amendment to the Constitution to strip "errant" lawyers of their citizenship for the act of protesting against the government. "The government needs to amend the constitution if it wants to strip citizenship of lawyers such as *Bersih* co-chairperson S. Ambiga, who go against the government. To strip a person's citizenship, you need to amend the constitution. And to amend the constitution you need two-thirds majority in Parliament," said former Prime Minister Dr. Mahathir Mohamad. "So, I ask that you give two-thirds majority to the BN government," he added, in response to a question after giving a talk on national security and the constitution in Cheras, Kuala Lumpur. He was asked how the government would go about stripping away the citizenship of "errant" lawyers like Bar Council leaders, and Ambiga. However, Mahathir did not go into the specifics of what he meant and what part of the constitution needed to be amended (Hazlan 2013). The ultimate act of a "strict father" is to threaten to expel an errant daughter, even if it is an idle threat. *Utusan* also quoted a statement released by the Islamic association that it was not "appropriate" (*haram*) to support Ambiga because, according to Islamic principles, the chairperson is not supposed to have attitudes that contradict Islamic principles. This news story referred to the earlier statement released by Ambiga about her equality-based attitudes to sexual preferences. The opportunity presented itself to inflame inter-ethic religious sentiments by adding interpretive commentary, but *Utusan* refrained this time, and Ambiga also showed restraint.

Overall, though, in the 45 articles, *Bersih* is depicted as illegal, divisive, and unruly; and its leader deserving of threats of forfeiture of citizenship, as a dangerous woman whose organization does not respect Islam, economic prosperity, or public order. All these accusations Ambiga disputes at *Bersih* meetings, interviews, and public discussions, and she has been provided a new platform by independent Internet media.

Malaysiakini.com and *Themalaysianinsider.com*: Counter-publics

Every year, for over a decade, *Malaysiakini.com* has named a top newsmaker, defined as "someone whose actions make news headlines, who affects the course of public discourse and creates an impact in Malaysian politics, for better or worse." Ambiga was the newsmaker of the year in 2011 (*Malaysiakini.com* 2012a). Later the same year, *Bersih* 3.0 was picked as the top news story. Of the 128 *Malaysiakini.com* articles, a third involve direct coverage of Ambiga's press statements; a third canvass opposing arguments from government leaders, and the final third report favorably on Ambiga's leadership role and *Bersih*'s probity. Of the 88 news items from *Themalaysianinsider.com*, half focus on Ambiga's press statements, a third focus on *Bersih* 3.0 activities, and 13 condemn *Utusan*'s reportage of *Bersih*, openly criticizing mainstream media coverage. Examples targeted by *Themalaysianinsider.com* include statements made to the Malaysian Human Rights Commission, reported in a story headlined "Utusan tried hard to portray *Bersih* as 'evil'" (Kamal 2012), that mainstream negative portrayals actually strengthened violence against protestors in the view of media watchdog representative, Ding Jo-Ann, from the Centre for Independent Journalism. In the independent media's coverage of the *Bersih* rallies, Ambiga is shown articulating popular discontent, or "unhappiness." References to

Ambiga appear as calls-to-action and conceptual rallying points, particularly in reportage by *Malaysiakini.com*. For example, on August 23, 2012—"Ambiga: Continue to fight the good fight"; May 19, 2012—"Ambiga: Do not underestimate Malaysians" and, April 28, 2012—"300,000 at *Bersih* 3.0, Ambiga claims success." The above are examples of *Bersih* news focus on the prominent civic and representative role played by Ambiga in *Bersih*.

In an article published by *Malaysiakini.com* on October 22, 2011, the headline refers to Ambiga's routine claims not to be seeking the political limelight: "Ambiga: A people's hero but no politician." Ambiga resolutely dismisses accusations that she is anti-government in front of a "largely Indian crowd," stating, "We are not fighting for BN (Barisan Nasional) or Pakatan Rakyat. We are fighting for you. We want your vote to mean something. We want to make sure they do not steal the value of your vote. Whoever comes into power, we should be able to remove them in five years if they are not good." She refers here to the polity's capacity to change governments through regular fairly conducted elections, the distinguishing characteristic of democracies.

The independents' news coverage overall demonstrates that Ambiga and *Bersih* are being labeled and treated as a threat to the BN government by opponents. In *Malaysiakini.com*'s report from July 9, 2011 entitled "Top leaders arrested; Anwar injured" it was reported that when five marches began, "the police responded with tear gas and water cannon fire. The crowd was estimated to be 10,000 strong. Several unsuccessful attempts to disperse the crowd resulted in a standoff. Meanwhile, *Bersih* 2.0 chief Ambiga Sreenevasan, PAS[4] president Abdul Hadi Awang and Batu MP Tian Chua have been arrested." The numbers reported here show how large numbers of supporters resolutely stayed on the streets even in the deteriorating circumstances.

On its part, *Themalaysianinsider* gave balanced coverage in the tense days before *Bersih* 3.0, portraying Ambiga as principled and firm. On April 24, reporting that "*Bersih* says it will call off rally if PM guarantees polls reforms," reporter Shannon Teoh dedicated most of her columns to quoting Ambiga verbatim, and documenting police rejection of *Bersih*'s request for help at the planned demonstration on 28 April. Ambiga, always photographed with the *Bersih* yellow scarf to show that she was speaking as *Bersih* co-chair, had previously been reported as confirming that *Bersih* would try to convince police to allow the street rally into the main square in Kuala Lumpur, Dataran Merdeka. The news on April 27 had reprised the eight *Bersih* demands. Early on the 28th, Ambiga's call to action to her fellow citizens was published in full online. The

Bersih co-chair writes with pride of the day that "Malaysians join hands across time and distance" in order to "reclaim for the *rakyat* [common people] their right to assemble peacefully in public places" (Sreenevasan 2012).

Conclusion

Ambiga Sreenevasan represents the possibility of democratic change, and the arrival and spread of a reform activism supported by counter publics, anchored by independent Internet media. The *Bersih* period has profited from uncensored online news platforms as places for the dissemination of alternative views in the demos. A woman in the *Bersih* leadership who argued that democratic change was possible, used her knowledge of the law to support her arguments, insisted on staying within the law, and showed that citizens could use logic to disagree, also meant that many women supported *Bersih*. People dared to speak about an alternative government, and imagine changing the government. It took courage to do so.

The conduct of the April 28 clash between *Bersih 3.0* and the Kuala Lumpur city government, which attempted illegal bans on assembly, was scrutinized later in 2012 at the Human Rights Commission hearings. Repressive pre-determined government actions against *Bersih* had apparently been planned. Witness evidence was reported by *Malaysiakini*'s Koh Jun Lin, under the headline "Early warning suggests crackdown pre-planned," and noted that allegations were made on December 6, 2012 that Seputeh MP, Teresa Kok, believed the police crackdown during the *Bersih* 3.0 rally was pre-planned, claiming she received an ominous warning from a Kuala Lumpur City Hall (DBKL) enforcement officer just five minutes earlier. "*Kalau nak balik, cepatlah. Mereka nak bertindak*," Kok said she was told. (If you want to go home, do it quickly. They are about to take action.) This report was re-posted on Kok's blog the next day ("Sassy MP" 2012), and illustrates the networked nature of the reformist counter-publics made possible by the Internet, and responsible for breaking government control over political expression.

Ambiga's role as a human rights lawyer also gave her the opportunity to hone her strategic skills in representative cases. She has been *Bersih*'s articulate, passionate spokesperson, from its first mass rally before the 2008 General Election, to the July 9, gathering in 2011 and the April 28, 2012 sit-in protest. Despite *Bersih*, the government's poll reforms still seem perfunctory. "There is nothing genuine about their intention to reform. Nothing," she lamented in an interview with *Themalaysianinsider.com* (Chooi 2013). Yet, *Bersih* became the catalyst for the civil society movement, and for engaged citizens.

Once the skills of democratic participation are learnt, they are difficult to repress. For example, *Bersih* 2.0's "citizen observers" are ordinary people who cast their own ballots on the polling day, but they are armed with special training from local election experts on how to spot possible fraud and what to do with that information. With the "citizen observers" initiative, a campaign called "*Jom Pantau*" (Let's Monitor) re-launched along with "*Jom 100*," which is a part of the group's attempt to ensure that the thirteenth General Election was conducted fairly.

Ambiga Sreenevasan's rise to national prominence, as a spokesperson for reformist citizen groups, has depended on counter-publics facilitated by the independent news portals. The portals gave her a speaking position denied by mainstream reportage. As participants in street rallies, Malaysians read about their struggles through press reports on *Bersih* activities. These reports made it possible to recognize themselves as citizens sharing a position with other Malaysians, and yet not see themselves necessarily as party loyalists; nor "illegal" insurgents about to launch regime change or destroy national unity, but citizens exerting rights and accepting responsibilities. In this chapter we have aimed to demonstrate the importance of a convergence of the new media as political platforms with a strong and determined leader expressing people's frustration both in argument and peaceful protest. Ambiga's own courageous agency and grace; the legal expertise which helped her to focus the movement's attention on addressing change to the apparatuses of power; and her civic insistence on abstaining from calling up ethnic or religious divisiveness have modeled how to be a citizen.

Notes

1 In a *New York Times* interview, for example, she firmly dismissed suggestions of a future political career: "I don't have the stomach for it" (Gooch 2011).

2 *Social Watch* measures the gap between women and men in education, the economy, and political empowerment across the world.

3 Rajaratnam (2009) makes a similar use of Lakoff in a study of agenda setting theory in the *Star*'s and *Malaysiakini.com*'s treatment of BN in the 2008 election coverage.

4 Parti Islam Se-Malaysia (PAS).

4

The Girls of Parliament: A Historical Analysis of the Press Coverage of Female Politicians in Bulgaria

Elza Ibroscheva and Maria Raicheva-Stover

Research demonstrates that women occupy far less prominent space than men in both political power and representation (Herzog 1998; Kahn 1994, 1996; Ross 2002). In Eastern Europe, this phenomenon has intensified with the collapse of the Berlin Wall, which brought about what has been called the "masculinization" of the democratic transition. The political trend has been accompanied by a widespread use of stereotypical images and representations of women in the popular press. As Sarnavka et al. (2002) point out, even when women achieve a measure of political success by joining the parliament, they are still not safe from insults and humiliation based upon their gender.

Stereotypical depictions in the media perpetuate gender norms that deny the complexity of both women's issues and women's interests. While women's interests and issues are extremely varied and complex, the media generally fail to capture this diversity and is often aided in this process by the female politicians themselves. As Mead (1997) contends, this is not an unusual phenomenon. Rather, she argues, women are forced into clichés well past their use-by date and the media often ignore the discrimination women face today. The media are more likely to comment on women's personal appearance, discussing their hairstyles, weight, clothes, or shoes than on their stance on important issues.

One way to explain such prevalence of gendered coverage is through the theory of gendered mediation. The gendered mediation thesis rests on the assumption that:

> ... the way in which politics is reported is significantly determined by a male-oriented agenda that privileges the practice of politics as an essentially male pursuit. The image and language of mediated politics, therefore, supports the status quo (male as norm) and regards women politicians as novelties. (Ross and Sreberny 2000, 93)

The gendered nature of news can be traced to the "gendered structure of news production" (van Zoonen 1994, 43). Indeed, media coverage of elections often uses metaphors that compare politics to a battle, a boxing match, or a horserace, which add "an additional point of reference to domains until recently denied women" (Jamieson 1995, 175; Kahn 1994). As such, the news does not simply reflect the fact that politics is still very much a man's world. It plays an active role in perpetuating a stereotypically masculine conception of politics and reinforcing notions of the "proper" role of women (Jamieson 1995; Rakow and Kranich 1991).

The purpose of this study is to look at what part gendered mediation plays in the representation of women politicians in the Bulgarian press. We analyze press coverage of female politicians dating back to the first elections in which women ran for office, through communism to the present day. Our goal is to engage in an analysis of the intricate relationship between gender, sexualities, political power, and the media in Bulgaria in the hope of exposing the mechanisms—both socially sustained and politically motivated—that create an atmosphere in which the discourse of gender equality becomes nothing more than a token of ironic symbolism that serves the interests of those in power, regardless of their political and ideological orientation.

Method

This study employed textual analysis to identify the patterns of press coverage of women politicians in Bulgaria. A less "objective" methodology (in comparison to quantitative content analysis) was chosen with the intent of discerning the implicit meanings, themes, and patterns used to describe women politicians. It is a technique that eschews quantification in favor of an inductive search that locates the texts within their deep social and historical contexts.

To develop a full understanding of how female politicians were portrayed, we collected and reviewed selected issues of the top Bulgarian newspapers from before and after the fall of communism. For the communist period sample, we chose *Rabotnichesko Delo* ("Workers' Deed") because it was the organ of the Bulgarian Communist Party's Central Committee and Bulgaria's highest-circulation newspaper. After the fall of communism, the readership interest has been mainly focused on two national dailies, *Dneven Trud* ("Daily Labor") and *24 Chassa* ("24 Hours"), which garner a combined readership of between 50 and 70 percent of all adults aged 18 and older. Because *Dneven Trud* (*Trud* hereinafter) and *24 Chassa* are owned by the German press group Westdeutsche Allgemeine Zeitung, and tend to have similar layouts, editorial staff and tone as well as advertising choices (Popova 2004), we chose to analyze only *Trud* for the postcommunist sample. *Trud* represents an "interesting 'glocal' event, combining the characteristics of a serious broadsheet with features of a sensational paper; very serious features and newsroom work appear alongside a barely dressed beauty on its 32nd page" (Danova 2006, 121).

The sample is comprised of articles about women politicians that appeared in *Rabotnichesko Delo* and *Trud* in the six-week period before and after each

Table 4.1 Distribution of newspaper articles by period and newspaper

Parliament	Number of articles
Communist period	*Rabotnichesko Delo*
1945–6	0
1946–9	0
1950–3	0
1954–7	3
1958–61	11
1962–5	9
1966–71	7
1971–6	22
1976–81	19
1981–6	17
1986–90	12
Total	**100**
Postcommunist period	*Trud*
1990–1	8
1991–4	4
1995–7	9
1997–2001	18
2001–5	49
2005–9	73
2009–current	90
Total	**251**

election, starting with that in 1945.[1] Both authors read and analyzed the full content of the 100 articles in *Rabotnichesko Delo* and 251 articles in *Trud* (see Table 4.1). Included in the analysis were articles, interviews, and commentaries plus accompanying headlines and pictures. Content referring to gendered nouns or adjectives, metaphors and descriptions of the candidates' psychological or physical characteristics, and their competency was underlined and, using an inductive approach, was gradually arranged into several emergent themes.

Media portrayals of female politicians during communism

In 1945, Bulgarian women entered the national parliament for the first time in the country's history (Table 4.2). Since then, and until 1989, female legislative representation was determined by the Communist Party, which set a quota of between 20 and 30 percent. During communism, the one-party rule guaranteed the continued and virtually uncontested electoral success of the Communist Party. Because of their potential to serve as propaganda opportunities, elections received wide press coverage, which is why around election time *Rabotnichesko Delo*, which normally contained four pages of news, devoted at minimum two of these to election coverage.

The textual analysis of the portrayals of political candidates during the communist period, however, revealed that the press did not devote much space to introducing the candidates to the readers, regardless of whether they were male or female. In fact, the scarce coverage of the candidates for Representative at the Communist Party Congress (which served as the equivalent of a democratically elected parliament) consisted mostly of feature profiles. The approach was to cover a broad range of candidates from all walks of life and include a comparable number of men and women. Nevertheless, women's profiles were construed following some clear themes, both culturally and ideologically informed by the existing gender norms of the socialist way of life.

The ordinary peasant woman

One of the more common frames emerging in the profiles of female representatives from the communist period is that of the "ordinary peasant woman." Prior to communism, most of the Bulgarian population lived in villages and were therefore mostly engaged in agriculture, so one of the major goals of the party was to "modernize" and "convert" the retrograde peasants, which historically have been somewhat resistant to the communist ideology. A popular approach of inculcation was to include more party members from among the rural population.

Women were seen as particularly well fitted for this role as they could wield influence in both the public and private spheres. In several profiles of women nominated as party delegates, the peasant theme was strongly pronounced, to a large degree defining the essence of the candidate as well as her political aspirations. In a April 19, 1971, profile of Yana Ivanova, nominated for a delegate post, we read, "I was just an ordinary peasant woman. In 1946, I joined the Party and then became a delegate representing my village. Now, my life is full of meaning—without the Party and my comrades, I would be lost" (Profile: Yana Ivanova 1971, 2). In a similar vein, another delegate candidate, Nenka Ivanova, is quoted as saying "I am often asked—what is the Party in my life? The answer is simple—everything! When I was little, I lived a poor life, with no light and no heat, but now, we walk boldly along the path determined by the Party on a road to progress!" (Profile: Nenka Ivanova 1971, 2).

While the ideological undertones of these "confessions" are hard to ignore, what is quite curious is that these women are almost completely devoid of any feminine or even individual features. It is hard to figure out how old they are or what their feelings are, for, as Marody and Giza-Poleszczuk (2000) point out, the socialist woman, "is above all a social being: one element of several different social structures (family, company, planned economy, and socialist society) that demand 'rational' behavior from her" (158). In her political role, the socialist woman, identified only as "an ordinary peasant woman" is exactly that—ordinary, yet critically important to the propaganda effort of the Communist Party.

A father's daughter

The crucial role of family background and origin in describing the qualifications of the female communist activist emerged as another common theme. Communist lineage was frequently mentioned in the pre-election stories, particularly stressing the women's familial ties on their father's side. In a society where patriarchal gender conventions were never rejected by the communist leadership, emphasis on the role of the father figure in the character formation of a young female political activist is not a coincidence. Thus, in a April 15, 1971, story about a prospective congress delegate, Margarita Eftimova, we read about her concerns as to whether she will be able to handle the honor and high level of responsibility bestowed on her in representing the people. However, the focus of her profile appears to be her father's communist past: she is frequently referred to as "her father's daughter." In fact, two out of the four paragraphs in the story are completely devoted to Eftimova's father, whose contributions to the party are seen as the greatest asset she can offer, by virtue of her family ties. In the final paragraph, we read her mother's words: "Hurry up, your father needs a rest," which encourage Eftimova to not only quickly take over the party duties but also act as a responsible daughter and alleviate the burden of work on her father's shoulders (Profile: Margarita Eftimova 1971, 2). It must be noted that most of the female candidates profiled in the press appear to have been fairly young and, therefore, in need of fatherly guidance and encouragement—another patriarchal notion that, as Lukic (2000) argued, only reinforces the prevailing patriarchal stereotype that women are so weak and childlike that they need constant guidance by a male father figure or mentor.

The well-decorated worker

One of the most prominent spheres in which the Communist Party propagated gender equality was the labor market, where women and men were expected to contribute equally to the progress of building socialism across the country and the world. On the pages of *Rabotnichesko Delo*, the majority of women profiled as political candidates occupied menial, low-paid jobs; in the few exceptions, women in positions of leadership, such as school principals and doctors, were profiled. Most of the featured occupations fell within "feminized" low-paid jobs, as in the textile, leather, shoe, and clothing industries, where women represented more than 75 percent of the workforce (Daskalova 2000). Women were also largely over-represented in the fields of healthcare and education, which, although prestigious by Western standards, were seen as typically "female" professions, saturated with sexual bias at the workplace and pay discrimination (Daslakova 2000).

During election time, the typical profile of the female political candidate contained mostly descriptions of the woman's profession and work responsibilities instead of a discussion of her political preparedness to represent her constituencies. The woman was defined through her work and not her intellectual capacity, even if she had demonstrated potential for making significant contributions to both political and social life. This trend was also reflected in the visual representations of the candidates, whose photos showed stern-looking women of determination, rarely wearing make-up or fashion accessories, dressed in modest and conservative, yet highly functional attire. More importantly, in instances when women were featured in positions of leadership, their legitimacy was often satirized, as in the profile of Ivanka Vasilieva, chief brigadier of a television assembly line. Her male co-workers trivialize her leadership authority when they are quoted as saying, "We can't believe we lived to see a woman ordering us around! Let's see, it might actually work out!" (Profile: Ivanka Vasilieva 1976, 2).

The mother figure

Socialist gender ideologies have actively exploited the figure of the woman not only as a representation of the values of the socialist revolution but also as its most valuable reproductive tool. As Kotzeva (1999) pointed out, "women's reproduction was underlined as the 'natural' function, rather than an activity of women, as their duty rather than as their right" (86). Even though the idea of equal political participation and gender parity at the workplace signaled a change in the stereotypical patriarchal conception of gender, the portrayals of femininity remained bound within women's traditional obligation to reproduce and thus preserve the nation. A frequently appearing theme in the coverage of women candidates is their role as mothers, not only to their own children but also to all children under their influence, to the labor collectives where they work, and, ultimately, to the entire nation. Thus, when we read the political profile of a female doctor we see her worth and character portrayed primarily through her devotion to her young patients, to whom she is "more than a medical professional, she is mother to all children" (Profile: Dr. Anka Angelova 1976, 2).

A particularly interesting narrative appears in the profile of young Muesin Durgurova, who had been elected to attend the Party Institute to train, and eventually represent, her fellow workers at the National Assembly. Muesin, whose name we learn in the seventh paragraph of the story, is anxious about leaving her newborn baby behind, immediately seeking her husband's approval. "What will my husband say?" she asks herself in the story, describing her fear of abandoning her family obligations (Profile: Muesin Durgurova

1971, 4). Her husband's approval follows shortly, reinforced by her in-laws' reassurance that they will not abandon her children: "Go ahead, set a bright example," they encourage her (4). Interestingly, only in the last paragraph do we find out that Muesin has actually been working as a high school teacher and a political activist for a long time, including being an active member of the Bulgarian Women's Committee—credentials that should be considered as an impressive testimony to her ability to be involved in the political sphere. Yet the predominant frame through which her achievements are presented is of the mother figure, whose political potential comes second to her responsibility as a caregiver and provider for the family: "Women are the best representatives of collective life and the collective values of socialism—they are named 'national heroines' as mothers, toilers, and social activists," (Kotzeva 1999, 86) but rarely as independent human beings, whose decisions to pursue a political career are matters of personal choice, and not a duty to the family, the party, or the nation.

Media portrayals of female politicians after the fall of communism

The first democratic, multi-party elections, in 1990, registered a drastic drop in women's parliamentary representation (see Table 4.2). Kostadinova (2003) explains the trend as a result of changes in the electoral system that favored popular candidates[2] and the highly competitive nature of politics in the first years. Other scholars see the withdrawal of women from political life as a natural consequence of the communist past where forced "emancipation" policies made women politically apathetic or eager to return to their domestic duties, which was seen as a new wave of emancipation (Spirova 2007). In the case of Bulgaria, the proportion of women MPs fluctuated within narrow boundaries until 2001, when it jumped to 26 percent. Since then it has remained at a steady 21–2 percent.

Although the number of women in positions of power did increase from 2001 to 2009, several important factors need to be considered. First, ever since Bulgaria put forward its EU candidacy and became an EU member in 2007, there has been a push to satisfy a number of quotas, one of which is higher female political representation. Second, starting with the 2001 parliamentary elections, a number of parties have effectively managed to court women's political formations. One recent example comes from the time of Bulgaria's

Table 4.2 Women members of the Bulgarian parliament

Parliament	Total MPs	Women MPs	Percentage women MPS
1945–6	279	16	5.7
1946–9	465	38	8.2
1950–3	239	36	15.1
1954–7	249	39	15.7
1958–61	254	41	16.1
1962–5	321	65	20.2
1966–71	416	70	16.8
1971–6	400	75	18.8
1976–81	400	78	19.5
1981–6	400	87	21.8
1986–90	400	84	21.0
1990–1	400	34	8.5
1991–4	240	34	14.2
1995–7	240	31	12.9
1997–2001	240	27	11.3
2001–5	240	62	25.8
2005–9	240	51	21.3
2009–current	240	52	22.7

Source: http://www.parliament.bg

former prime minister, Boiko Borisov, whose party allowed a woman to become the first president of parliament and also helped seven female MPs (out of a total of 17 candidates) to be elected to the European Parliament. Borisov's strategy to involve a legion of qualified women in politics was hailed internationally as "heralding what some are calling a sexual revolution in the politics of this abidingly macho Balkan country" (Bilefsky 2010, n.p.). On the other hand, critics argue that Borisov's female entourage is little more than "a window-dressing in a society that still devalues women" (Bilefsky 2010, n.p.).

Compared to the communist period, the postcommunist press coverage of women politicians included not only a higher number but also a more diverse array of articles, but the diversity of coverage could be attributed to the radical changes to the Bulgarian press system after 1989. The postcommunist period also registers a disproportion in the amount of coverage awarded to women in comparison to men. A clear pattern emerged (see Table 4.1), where the coverage of women politicians was scarce during the period of decreased women's political participation (1989–97), as if symbolically reflecting the absence of women's voices in the public sphere at that time. Even after the 2001 elections, when the number of female MPs increased substantially, women politicians rarely occupied prominent space in *Trud*. For example, out of the 110 published photographs of women politicians in the 2005 parliamentary elections, only four made it to the front page, and the ones that did only confirmed stereotypical portrayals of women.

Girls of parliament

Physicality emerged as the dominant theme in *Trud*'s coverage of women politicians for the entire postcommunist period, where discussions of women's beauty and style were inextricably linked to their public personae. One early mention of physical beauty as a sufficient reason for political success appeared in a 1991 interview with Emilia Maslarova, then Minister of Social Policy, where she was asked: "You are pretty, Mrs. Maslarova. Does this prove to be helpful to a minister?" to which she modestly replied "It's mostly charm, which indeed proves to be helpful in my work" (Radeva 1991, 1–2). The same theme is reinforced by another article from 1995, in which we read: "The female part of the political spectrum might be multicolored, but it is pleasing to the eye. Because, if the old saying is correct, beauty (in this case women) will save the world" (Nikolova 1995, 10). Women who entered the public sphere around this period were consistently portrayed as women first and as viable political candidates second. A 1997 interview with then Deputy Prime Minister Alexander Bozhkov focused on his love and appreciation of women and his denunciation of platonic love. Suggestively featured as part of the interview is a picture of Bozhkov and another male politician, both "flirting simultaneously with the charming Nadezhda Mihaylova," as we read in the caption. Mihaylova, who was dubbed the "pretty Nade" by the press, was Bulgaria's foreign minister for the period 1997–2001 (Veleva 1997, 9).

Ironically, with the larger number of women politicians on the election lists in 2001 came an increased incidence of gendered language to introduce them to the public. This is how one *Trud* article introduced a female candidate in the 2001 parliamentary elections: "The television anchor, Juliana Doncheva, can drive crazy every man, and every voter for sure, with her low, raspy voice."

As if to reinforce the sexual innuendo, the article placed the above words next to two images of equal size—one of topless Italian porn-star-turned-politician Cicciolina on a beach, and one of Doncheva in a reclined position covered by a blanket yet revealing enough to suggest that she is naked underneath. The same article had this to say about Doncheva's reasons to be involved in politics: "Juliana is a woman who has everything—son, husband, men who adore her. Even more—nice house, and a SUV[…] The only thing she did not have was a place in politics. Now she has it." The same article introduced the female incumbents in the following way: "These three women were beauties 10 years ago, now they need to be very careful not to embarrass themselves in front of the young female group" and moved on to discuss some of their fashion faux pas (Petkova and Bratovanova 2001, 10–12). As a sidebar to this long piece appeared the following commentary, which served to aptly summarize the perceived shift in women's role in politics:

> The new parliament will be twice as gentle and elegant. In the previous the ladies were only 28 out of 240, but starting July 5 they will be 58, all beautiful … Most female MPs will have to get in and out of a limo followed by the watchful paparazzi. In these moments they are often caught in awkward situations. (*Trud*, July, 1 2001, 11)

Another article, published after the 2005 elections, spoke of Bulgarian MPs as "the girls of parliament," downplaying the level of maturity, expertise, and political clout women politicians bring to the table. "There is going to be grace, charm and vanity, because gals from a wide range of occupations—from politicians to fashion models—are riding atop of many election tickets," (Apostolova, Krusteva, and Avramova 2005, 17), the authors wrote, not only trivializing the immense effort put forth by female candidates to enter the electoral race but also implying that women politicians win because of their attractiveness and not because of their qualifications and preparation to guide domestic and international policy decisions.

The same issue featured a commentary entitled "Vanity Fair" that focused exclusively on the physical appearance and style of the new MPs. The piece described in detail the reaction of the male members at the sight of their female counterparts—the men were described as "resting their eyes," "washing their faces in the sight of beauty," "pleasantly distracting themselves," "stumbling over signs of beauty." In line with the gendered mediation thesis, women MPs were described as, "strutting on the red carpet," "super elegant," and having "delicate faces" or as nothing more than objects of male gaze. The article concludes with the following observation about the composition of the new parliament: "If beauty is said to save the world, then this year's parliament is certainly in safe hands" (Apostolova et al. 2005, 16–17). As prominent female politician and diplomat, Elena Poptodorova, admitted in another *Trud* article: "When a man stands on the podium they listen to him first and then they look at him—with women it's the opposite" (Tokeian 2001, 11).

The latest manifestation of gendered coverage appeared in July of 2008 when Boiko Borisov introduced the female wing of his political party. The event was significant in that it gave his party a solid female base, yet the tone of *Trud*'s coverage was captured masterfully by the accompanying photograph, which showed a line of crossed female legs with the caption: "The ladies in the female club showed true style and perfect pedicures" (Borisov with a club of 700 women, 2008). And, although Borisov gave a long list of reasons why he prefers to work with women—which featured prominently (and ironically we might add), women's loyalty and work ethic—the tone and language used by *Trud* downplayed the significance of his words by suggesting that it was "almost a love admission" and that Borisov "flirted for a minute or two with the audience" (Borisov with a club of 700 women, 2008: 5).

As part of the theme of objectification emerged a secondary theme of demonizing women politicians who violated expectations of "proper" gender roles by exhibiting such qualities as strength and power, which are typically associated with male politicians (Jamieson 1995). Powerful women are suspected of "'being men' beyond metaphorical representations, or androgynous, such as the former Turkish premier, Tansu Ciller; former British Prime Minister, Margaret Thatcher; or former U.S. Secretary of State, Madeleine Albright" (Popescu, cited in Roman 2001, 6). In the case of Bulgaria, if a woman politician failed to exhibit what are deemed to be highly desirable physical characteristics of femininity, *Trud* took immediate notice. An interesting case at hand is Ekaterina Mihailova, who suffered a severe media backlash in her first term as one of the leaders of the Union for Democratic Forces (UDF). Mihailova, who often stood shoulder to shoulder with Nadezhda Mihaylova (the head of the right-wing UDF and former foreign minister), was a powerful political player yet was often ridiculed for her lack of grace, beauty, and style. In fact, the media coined a rather condescending nickname for Ekaterina Mihailova, "*Klasnata*," a derogatory term used to describe a rigid communist teacher and ideologue whose behavior and lackluster appearance would plague her leadership skills and political abilities. Yet, in the 2005 elections Ekaterina Mihailova underwent a dramatic makeover of her image and demeanor, appearing more feminine and less threatening, which immediately attracted the attention of the media, placing her among the frontrunners for nomination in her political party. *Trud*, closely following her new image, noted that Mihailova was finally looking "more human, more down to earth," and "visibly beautified," thus implying that exhibiting masculine traits is a risky move which could potentially damage one's political career (Apostolova et al. 2005, 16). Thus, Mihailova's political qualifications were legitimized by nothing short of a fashion makeover, topped with the appropriate media blitz.

A sidebar story in the same section of this issue of *Trud* focused on the oldest female MP and leader of the People's Union, Anastasia Moser. In describing her personality, hairstyle, and preference for conservative clothing, the article barely mentioned the fact that, in spite of being the only female member of this parliamentary group, Moser was its leader. The piece spent a disproportionate amount of space proposing that her presence in the Union imbued it with its only signs of elegance and class. Moser's political wisdom and extensive experience, therefore, gave way to a lengthy discussion of her conservative hairstyle and dress, implying that a clear connection must exist between a woman politician's appearance, her personal ideology and political agenda.

Good wives and mothers

While most of the female politicians in the postcommunist period have more than satisfactory qualifications as lawyers, doctors, accountants, or engineers, their qualifications often seem to appear in the context of their family ties. In a very traditional fashion, and probably as yet another manifestation of Bulgaria's patriarchal society, women politicians were often defined and represented by their association with a powerful male, usually a husband.

For example, when a 2001 article discussed the political qualifications of Vessela Lecheva, a popular Bulgarian athlete who had won numerous international awards in shooting, the reporters mentioned that her husband is her "most secret weapon […] it's certain that her decision to become a MP was stimulated by him" (Petkova and Bratovanova 2001, 11). A profile of another female MP from the same period, Hristina Petrova, presented her as a "lady who is in touch with everything feminine. She likes to dress nice and travel" and later informed readers that her husband "George claims that he is not jealous of his young wife because he trusts her" (Profile: Hristina Petrova 2001, 7).

In 2005, in two consecutive articles about Maria Kapon, voted as Miss Parliament (by a jury of four male journalists and one female political party speaker), the reporter mentioned Kapon's extensive line of professional credentials—an economist, a production manager, and physics engineer, who has worked in a variety of important positions. In a familiar pattern, most of the piece focused on her affiliation by marriage with a famous family and her qualities as a great wife and a mother. Kapon is further described as a "blonde but not in 'the blonde' joking sense of the words," "the blonde fury," who has an "aristocratic taste" (Todorova 2005, 12). Similarly, an article discussing the political qualifications of the newly-elected forerunner of the UDF, Eleonora Nikolova, described her as "window display case" of over 28 years of successful marriage (Veleva 2005, 15), implying that her ability to juggle both her professional responsibilities and the responsibilities of family life are significant indicators of her ability to perform in the political scene.

The "good wives and mothers" theme was further reinforced in *Trud*'s coverage of the 2009 parliamentary elections. An in-depth profile of Tsetska Tsacheva, the first female chair of the parliament in its 130-year history, is entitled "A real blonde in charge of parliament" (Nikolova 2009). In another *Trud* interview from the same period, Tsacheva is asked: "Beside being the first female chair of the parliament, how would you like to be known in history," to which she answers "As a wife and a mother" (Apostolova 2009). Gender expectations in Bulgaria might necessitate the need for women politicians to win sympathy by placing their traditional role as mothers and wives above everything else. In fact, it is rarely imagined that women might be able to successfully juggle professional and family responsibilities. Any exception is duly noted, as in the 2009 profile of Yordanka Fandakova, the first woman major of the capital city, Sofia, where the author mentions that Fandakova "is a rare example of a woman with a successful career who has also managed to preserve her family." The article visually frames the Sofia major in terms of her domesticity by including a picture of her holding her baby grandson (Mihaylova 2009).

Loyal worker bees

When women politicians' performance and success are discussed, the media emphasize the hard work and diligence it took to reach such a position but also find a way to link these qualities to their loyalty to the male leader and subsequently present the women as weak followers. Women politicians do not become successful because they are smart or skilled; they move up the ranks because they are diligent and loyal. Probably the best summary of how women politicians have been perceived since 1989 can be found in the following sidebar, which appeared in *Trud*:

> The parties have always donned themselves with the presence of women, but their political breakthrough was mostly done [by] … women establishing themselves as officers who have passed faithful service in the party apparatus … They are faithful to their [male] leader, some are even happy that they live at the same time *he* works and creates. They are loved by the electorate who chronicles the ascent of 'their girl' … And if women were getting recognition as worker bees, now they land on the party lists as multicolored birds. They are pretty, without any political baggage, popular and tantalizingly aggressive. (Petkova and Bratovanova 2001, 12)

The frame of the worker bee recurs when successful women politicians are introduced in *Trud*. For example, readers are introduced to Miglena Tacheva as potential minister of justice with the headline "Working girl again in power" (Hristova 2007, 8) or we learn that the "4 ladies [are] at full speed in the Europarliament" (Dimitrova 2007, 13).

Most recently, the "loyal worker bee" theme was used by *Trud* to explain the noticeable ascent of women politicians after the 2009 elections. Boiko Borisov's party was elected on the basis that it would clean up the mess in what was perceived as Europe's most corrupt country. Women in Bulgaria were seen as less prone to corruption and hence ideally situated to fill some prominent political appointments like the justice ministry, speaker of parliament and mayor of the capital city. When Borisov, commonly referred to by the media as "The General," brought women to positions of power first as a major and then as prime minister, a number of articles appeared in *Trud* underpinning the idea that those women were promoted namely because they were his hardworking and loyal followers, or, as the media dubbed them, "Borisov's good girls" (Bilefsky 2010). The theme is encapsulated by the title of a *Trud* article published right after the 2009 elections that refers to the recently elected mayor, Fandakova, as "The General's worker bee" (Mihaylova 2009).

Discussion and conclusion

The textual analysis of the coverage of women politicians in the Bulgarian press has revealed that, regardless of political ideology and time period, media portrayals continue to rely heavily on stereotypes and predictable gender conventions that, we argue, obfuscate a well-rounded and thoughtful representation of the role of women in the political discourse. Whether on the pages of the communist *Rabotnichesko Delo* or the postcommunist *Trud*, women politicians received gendered, and in some cases strongly stereotypical, coverage, that reinforced their traditional roles as good mothers, wives, daughters; loyal worker bees; or simply objects of the male gaze. In particular, during communism the dominant themes were propagandistically engineered to represent women's roles as defined by the communist understanding of their social and political significance and served the purpose of preserving the status quo. We see a celebration of women, achieving a notable measure of success, appearing not only as active members of the workforce, but also as visible political actors. This sense of empowerment, however, rested on shaky grounds, as it was framed within a patronizing and often trivializing conceptualization of the socialist woman as following political directives issued by an overwhelming(ly) masculine political institution. The identified themes of the ordinary peasant woman, the father's daughter, the well-decorated worker, and the mother figure follow deeply ingrained gender conventions that reinforce the dominant masculine ideology of communism while masquerading as socialist emancipation and women's political empowerment.

In spite of all the promising changes in the political and media institutions that occurred after 1989, the postcommunist period did not mark any dramatic improvements in the coverage of women politicians. Overall, the identified themes were just as gendered as the communist themes, but with an added emphasis on physicality and objectification. Just like the coverage of their communist predecessors, the coverage of women politicians in the postcommunist period followed the standards of deeply engrained, patriarchal conventions, additionally mixed with the tantalizing sexist language and images that were sure to sell.

Despite the recent rise of women politicians to power, stereotypical conceptions and representations of their roles still linger, some of which were clearly reflected in the discursive narrative of the "worker bee." For example, even as Fandakova was elected as mayor of Sofia, the deputy mayor suggested that promoting women to powerful positions could pose a liability at a time of crisis, using as an explanation his belief "that women are moodier than men and rule based on intuition rather than facts. During a crisis a woman can transform very quickly from being a politician to being a human being, and this can be bad" (as quoted in Bilefsky 2010, n.p.).

Thus far, the transition has not been overly kind to women. State paternalism and masculine democracies form the cultural-political framework within which identities are gendered in differently formed public and private spheres. Without fundamental restructuring of gender relations in both private and public discourses, particularly in political participation, women will continue to bear the burden of the pseudo-emancipated communist past and the postcommunist transitional illusion of political power. Democratization of gender relations in the political sphere is a sorely needed, but sadly neglected, aspect of social transformation that contributes to the shaping of gendered identities and is additionally directly translated into media content.

Indeed, a fundamental shift in both gender norms and media conventions is needed to bring about the beginning of a new era of democracy—one in which equality of the sexes is more than an utopian idea or a remnant of a pseudo-emancipated communist past. While society's gender lens has been significantly blurred by an intoxication with masculine power, it is important to note that, in the case of Bulgaria, women are equally responsible and silently contributing to the creation of the barriers of sexism and gender inequality. More importantly, the media, a significant proportion of which is made up of female reporters and editors, support sexism by portraying women politicians in a manner that discredits their political importance and influence. Thus, we often read interviews and see pictures in which women politicians speak about their favorite recipes, give fashion and shopping tips, and share their wardrobe secrets and undergarment preferences (Sarnavka, Mihalec and Sudar 2002). In order for a palpable change to ensue, women should cease to participate in the marginalization of their own representatives, first and foremost by challenging and transforming media conventions and newsroom rituals in favor of a more balanced and impartial approach to covering both women politicians and women's issues. While this study offers only a preliminary exploration of the complex relationships between media, politics, and gender, it is nonetheless an important contribution to the literature on gendered mediation that also serves as a timely and long-awaited glimpse into the dynamic nature of building and redefining relationships between the press, politicians, and informed publics in the postcommunist transition.

Notes

1 Website addresses have not been provided for all *Trud* articles as the archive from which these articles were retrieved is a subscription service.

2 Under the reformed electoral system, a party needs to pass the 4 percent threshold to get representation in the parliament. Yet women were on the lists of a significant number of parties that failed to meet this threshold in the 1990 elections (Kostova 1998).

5

Zambian Women MPs: An Examination of Coverage by the *Post* and *Zambia Daily Mail*

Twange Kasoma

Introduction

With only 18 women (out of 150 elected) Members of Parliament, Zambia is one of five African countries with the lowest number of female parliamentarians. This dismal statistic is in stark contrast to Zambia's ratification of the Beijing Declaration and Platform for Action, which advocates for at least 30 percent minimum representation of women in decision-making positions. Additionally, that statistic also contradicts the promise that the Patriotic Front (PF) party made when campaigning to form the next government. The PF, which won the elections on September 23, 2011, publicly declared that the gender policy under its predecessor—the Movement for Multiparty Democracy (MMD)—had been a complete failure. The PF noted that, like the United National Independence Party (UNIP) before it that ratified the Convention on the Elimination of All Forms of Discrimination Against Women in 1985, the MMD made no significant progress in improving the representation of women. Both UNIP and MMD failed to formulate a national policy that would mirror the policies of the regional and international conventions on women.

The PF government asserted that it would prioritize the domestication of international protocols on women and gender. Furthermore, in redressing the marginalization of women in mainstream decision-making organs—within the PF's first year in power—President Michael Sata appointed the first woman inspector general of police in the history of the country. He also appointed women to the helm of the Anti Corruption Commission and the Drug Enforcement Commission. Other milestone appointments Sata made were in the judiciary where he appointed Lombe Chibesakunda and Florence Mumba as chief justice and deputy chief justice respectively. However, their appointments have remained contentious as they are both past retirement age and, as stipulated in the Constitution, no one above the age of 65 can occupy such offices. Sata's enthusiasm for appointing women to decision-making positions has not extended to parliament. Despite the fact that the Constitution empowers the President to nominate eight MPs, none of his nominations were women. Additionally, his record on appointing women as cabinet ministers is far from impeccable. In Sata's inaugural cabinet, women only accounted for 10.5 percent of cabinet ministers (Table 5.1).

Moreover, the two women cabinet ministers occupied portfolios that are generally considered "soft." These were: minister of local government, housing, early education, and environment protection, and minister of chiefs and traditional affairs. Although it may be too soon to provide a holistic evaluation of the PF's performance on women and gender, a pattern is emerging where women politicians are consistently underrepresented and marginalized in the political sphere. The full list of explanations for this pattern is, undoubtedly, long, as well as beyond the scope of this chapter. The goal of this study is to provide an overview of how the Zambian press reported on the 18 women MPs during the PF's first year in power. The significance of this study lies, first, in its rare approach of studying the media coverage of female MPs in unison with journalists' insights into the coverage; and second, in helping to fill the void that exists in feminist scholarship on studies on women, politics, and the media from sub-Saharan Africa.

Overview of the representation of women in Parliament

To contextualize the representation of women in the Zambian Parliament, it is imperative to elucidate its composition. As noted earlier, the Zambian

Table 5.1 Gender representation in PF's inaugural cabinet

Portfolio	Number of women	Percentage of women	Number of men	Percentage of men	Total number
Cabinet ministers	2	10.5	17	89.5	19
Deputy cabinet ministers	4	21.1	15	78.9	19
Provincial ministers	1	11.1	8	88.9	9

Note: By July 2012, the Cabinet was expanded and a third female minister was appointed to preside over the Ministry of Tourism and Arts.

Parliament comprises 150 elected members and the President nominates eight. The President and the Speaker of the National Assembly are also considered MPs, which brings the total composition to 160. However, dating back to the independence era, the representation of elected women MPs compared to their male counterparts has remained minuscule, and has never grown beyond 14.6 percent (Table 5.2). Ironically, this highest percentage was attained under the MMD between 2006 and 2011.

Literature review and theoretical framework

Countries such as Rwanda, where women hold 56 percent of seats in the lower house of parliament, and is Africa's champion in this regard, show that parity can be achieved. It is also worth noting that Rwanda, unlike Zambia, is one of the African countries that have introduced a quota system, which reserves 30 percent of parliamentary seats for women, while the remaining 70 percent are open to both sexes. Lack of a quota system is not the only deterrent to the adequate representation of women in parliament. Zambian tradition instructs women to follow men in public and not to lead (Sampa 2010). Moreover, as Sampa notes, politics is viewed as a dirty game in which a woman is always targeted and destroyed while

Table 5.2 Representation of elected MPs in Zambia by gender since 1964

Time period	Number of women MPs	Percentage of women MPs	Number of men MPs	Percentage of men MPs	Total elective seats
1964–8	5	6.7	70	93.3	75
1968–72	2	1.9	103	98.1	105
1973–8	7	5.6	118	94.4	125
1978–83	6	4.8	119	95.2	125
1983–8	5	3.4	120	96	125
1988–91	6	4.8	119	95.2	125
1991–6	6	4.8	119	95.2	125
1996–2001	16	10.6	134	89.4	150
2001–6	19	12.6	131	88.3	150
2006–11	22	14.6	128	85.3	150
2011–16	18	12	132	88	150

Sources: Sampa (2010); Zambian Parliament (http://www.parliament.gov.zm/); and Electoral Commission of Zambia (http://www.elections.org.zm/past_election_results.php)

a man is protected by the system. Sampa's observations correlate with how the Zambian media have generally treated women. Morna and Mtintso (2005) wrote that in a self-reflection exercise, journalists participating in a gender-training workshop noticed the invisibility of women as sources and active participants:

> At ZNBC [Zambia National Broadcasting Corporation] participants picked up on how TV election coverage of a rally focused on the speakers (all of whom were men). The few interviews with people who attended the rally were all men. Women were seen dancing, serving the food, and wearing cloths with the faces of the male political figures. They said nothing at all. Participants conjectured that if they had spoken, their main concerns would be for a peaceful election and end to corruption. (67)

In analyzing the representation of South African women politicians in the *Sunday Times* during the 2004 presidential and general elections, Katembo (2005) found a similar disturbing trend. Women politician news sources only accounted for 7.67 percent of the 588 stories analyzed. The picture in Malawi—prior to the first woman president Joyce Banda who automatically succeeded Bingu Wa Mutharika, having been his deputy at the time of his untimely demise—was even gloomier. A workshop by Gender Links in 2009 revealed that women politicians only accounted for 2 percent of news sources across Malawian print and electronic media (Gender Links 2003). At a broader level, the Gender and Media Baseline Study conducted in 2003 in the 12 Southern African countries showed that women on average constituted only 17 percent of news sources (Gender Links 2003). In West Africa Yeboah (2011), who took a cursory look at the literature on news sources and gender in Ghana, found a tendency by female reporters to use more female sources than their male counterparts. She is, however, skeptical about whether female journalists' tendency of using more female sources is indicative of any special interest in opening up the news to female sources.

Notwithstanding the fact that studies on women, politics, and the media have been abundant in the West, Africa has had a short trajectory. The few and scattered studies available have mainly focused on women as news sources. Epistemologically therefore this study can benefit from looking at what has been done in the West. A popular term that has been used to explain the invisibility of women in the media is the symbolic annihilation concept popularized by Tuchman (1978). It posits that the media largely ignore women and relegate them to stereotypical roles. Symbolic annihilation also addresses trivialization and condemnation of women in the media. Yet the West also provides examples of how some women politicians have used trivialization to cause a media frenzy and win elections—a case in point, "the naked politician" in New Zealand (Fountaine and McGregor 2002).

One popular conceptual tool that has been used in examining the coverage of women politicians is framing. Its premise is that the media select some aspects of perceived reality and make them more salient in a communication text (Goffman 1974). The power of framing lies in its ability to define the terms of a debate without the audience realizing it is taking place (Tankard 1997). Devitt's (2002) study, which examined gender framing of gubernatorial candidates by the press in 1998 helps explain this point. Although the study found that newspaper reporters treated female and male gubernatorial candidates equitably in terms of the quantity of coverage, readers were more likely to read about a female candidate's personal traits such as her appearance or personality. By contrast, they were more likely to read about a male candidate's stand or record on public policy issues. According to Kahn (1994) these gender differences in news coverage may not only reflect stereotypes newspeople hold, but may also be problematic for women candidates. This is because the news media, through the news selectivity process, have the ability to shape rather than mirror the political landscape. Works in the media's agenda-setting function have also emphasized this point. Therefore, the role that journalists play in the construction of meaning cannot be overlooked.

In building on the existing scholarship, this study has a two-pronged goal: (1) to examine the quantity and scope of press coverage of women MPs; and (2) to inquire into the ways journalists explained their coverage of women MPs. The specific research questions addressed are:

RQ1: How much coverage did each of the 18 women MPs get in the *Post* and *Zambia Daily Mail*?

RQ2: What topics were present in the press coverage of the 18 women MPs in Zambia?

RQ3: How did journalists evaluate their coverage of the 18 women MPs?

Method

The two newspapers studied were selected because of their circulation and ownership patterns. With a daily circulation of 45,000 copies, the *Post* is the most widely circulated privately-owned newspaper, and its government counterpart, *Zambia Daily Mail*, has a daily circulation of 20,000. Traditionally, Zambians had grown accustomed to expecting hard-hitting investigative journalism from the *Post*, in line with its motto, "The paper that digs deeper." Today, however, the thinking has changed and critics have noted that the newspaper's allegiance to the PF government has compromised its watchdog role and turned it into a lapdog. It is overly critical of opposition leaders and mellow on the ruling PF—a government it aggressively campaigned for. As far as *Zambia Daily Mail* goes, the expectation of it being a government mouthpiece by nature of its ownership has been consistent.

This study utilized two primary methods—content analysis and face-to-face interviews. The selected timeframe covered the PF government's first year in power (September 23, 2011 to September 23, 2012). The method used in generating the stories studied was an electronic name search for each individual MP. In the case of the *Post*, the stories were obtained directly from the editor and categorized by name of MP. Only news stories and news features were examined. The unit of analysis was the individual story. The main topics were not treated as mutually exclusive, so each story could include multiple topics. The results provided a springboard for qualitative interviews with the journalists behind the stories. By-lines showed that there were 48 journalists—31 from the *Post* and 17 from *Zambia Daily Mail*—who wrote the 126 stories analyzed. Although all the journalists were approached with a request to participate in the interviews, only half of them were forthcoming. For example, some reporters from the *Post* who had since been appointed to positions in government and in diplomatic service following the PF's victory, preferred not to participate. The journalists were queried on why they covered the women MPs the way they did, and why they made the omissions they made.

Findings and analysis

Overall, the two newspapers published a total of 126 stories on the 18 women MPs for the selected one-year period. The *Post* accounted for 69 percent of the coverage (87 articles), while *Zambia Daily Mail* accounted for 31 percent (39 articles). Overall, the coverage in both newspapers focused on one MP and the topic of "corruption."

The findings also showed that over a third of the 18 women MPs received no coverage in the *Post*, save for a news feature providing demographic characteristics such as age, marital status, education, etc., for the new entrants to parliament. In the *Zambia Daily Mail*, the number of annihilated MPs was much higher—10 out of 18 never received any coverage (55.6 percent).

In response to RQ1, an aggregation of the stories by the two newspapers showed that three MPs—Dora Siliya, Professor Nkandu Luo, Minister of Chiefs and Traditional Affairs, and Sylvia Masebo, Minister of Tourism and Arts—accounted for 68 percent of the coverage (Table 5.3). Siliya, however, garnered most of the coverage. The controversies that surrounded her, which are elaborated subsequently, the fact that she was a former newscaster at ZNBC, and being a spokesperson for MMD made her a media magnet.

As for Luo and Masebo, there are a number of reasons why they attracted the decent media coverage they did. First, both have been vocal on "soft" or "female" issues, which Kahn (1994) defines as those where women are seen as superior and include health, education policy, etc. In this study some of the "soft" issues, which Luo and Masebo were vocal about, such as the banning of

Table 5.3 Frequency of MP coverage by newspaper (September 23, 2011 – September 23, 2012)

MP's name	**The *Post* (n = 87)**		***Zambia Daily Mail* (n = 39)**	
	Frequency	*Percentage*	*Frequency*	*Percentage*
Dora Siliya	31	35.6	13	33.3
Sylvia Masebo	16	18.3	7	17.9
Nkandu Luo	11	12.6	8	20.5
Josephine Limata	9	10.3	1	2.5
Jean Kapata	4	4.5	3	7.6
Emerine Kabanshi	4	4.5	2	5.1
Inonge Wina	4	4.5	2	5.1
Catherine Namugala	2	2.2	3	7.6
Victoria Kalima	3	3.4	0	0
Sarah Sayifwanda	2	2.2	0	0
Alfreda Kansembe	1	1.1	0	0
Lubezhi Moono	0*	0	0	0
Christine Mazoka	0*	0	0	0
Esther Banda	0	0	0	0
Annie Chungu	0*	0	0	0
Berina Kawandami	0*	0	0	0
Getrude Mwendaweli	0*	0	0	0
Dorothy Kazunga	0*	0	0	0

* Denotes MPs who were only covered by way of being incorporated in a compilation outlining the educational backgrounds, marital status, and professions of the new entrants to the Zambian Parliament.

street vending to maintain sanitation and cleanliness in the cities, were deemed controversial. The sheer numbers of women (in comparison to men) that depended on street vending as a source of livelihood made banning it controversial. Second, by virtue of having shifted camps from MMD to PF, Luo and Masebo were labeled "political prostitutes"—a label used to designate someone who switches allegiance from one political party to another. Political prostitutes tend to be perceived as lacking in principles. Although this label is commonplace in Zambian politics, its connotation where women MPs are involved is unfavorable. Another reason, where Luo is concerned, is that of prominence. She made history by being the country's first female professor in the field of medicine, and when she joined politics in 1996 under MMD she was subsequently appointed minister of health.

RQ2 asked about the predominant topics that emerged in the coverage, which are presented in Table 5.4. "Corruption," which covered stories that focused on abusing one's power in order to gain political mileage and self-fulfillment, was the most frequently discussed topic. The fact that the majority of stories focused on this topic should not be surprising as fighting corruption is the legacy that the PF government declared it wanted to leave in continuity of the work started by the late President Levy Mwanawasa.

Two main sub-categories emerged under this topic, namely electoral malpractices and financial irregularities. To elaborate on electoral malpractices, the *Post* (April 14, 2012) reported that Siliya, who belongs to the opposition

Table 5.4 Topics in the *Post* and *Zambia Daily Mail*

Topics	**The *Post* (*87 stories*)**	***Zambia Daily Mail* (*39 stories*)**	**Total**
Corruption	23 (26%)	14 (35.9%)	37
Women's issues	18 (20.7%)	4 (10.3%)	22
Development	14 (16.1%)	2 (5.1%)	16
Ceremonial appearances	6 (6.9%)	8 (20.5%)	14
Social issues	7 (8%)	5 (12.8%)	12
Tourism and UNWTO	6 (6.9%)	4 (10.3%)	10
Parliamentary affairs/debates	4 (4.6%)	3 (7.7%)	7
Private appearances	5 (5.7%)	1 (2.6%)	6
Portraits	6 (6.9%)	0 (0%)	6
Party protocol	5 (5.7%)	0 (0%)	5
Total number of topics	94	41	135

Note: Totals do not add up to 100% because some stories had more than one topic.

party, illegally used government vehicles while campaigning for re-election. She was also reported to have abused her power as communications minister by broadcasting derogatory radio remarks against the PF without paying for the services. According to the *Zambia Daily Mail* (April 14, 2012), these derogatory remarks included disseminating false information that if voted into power the PF would introduce gay rights (a culturally touchy subject) and stop providing farming inputs to the people. Although Siliya won re-election, her opponent challenged the victory in court alleging corruption. The High Court upheld her victory, but she lost in the Supreme Court. Her seat was nullified and she was barred from re-contesting. There were also other women opposition MPs who endured electoral malpractice petitions.

From electoral malpractices to financial irregularities, both newspapers extensively covered Siliya's charge and subsequent arrest in connection with the irregular sale of the state-owned Zambia Telecommunications Company (ZAMTEL) to a Libyan company while she served as communications minister. Interestingly, it was during this charge and arrest process that the reference to "physical appearance" surfaced.

> Clad in an expensive-looking smart red suit that matched her red lips and shoes, Ms. Siliya was clearly sweating and looked uneasy when she was asked by the commission to defend herself regarding the numerous allegations leveled against her surrounding the questionable sale of ZAMTEL to Lap Green. (The *Post*, October 30, 2011, 1)

Unlike the West and elsewhere, however, the inference in the excerpt is that Siliya had enriched herself via corruption. Another reference to the "physical appearance" frame surfaced in relation to a re-election campaign speech Siliya gave in Petauke. Siliya urged men "not to engage in homosexuality," which she had accused the PF of advancing, but instead "to admire her beautiful and soft buttocks and not their fellow men's." (The *Post*, October 7, 2011, 1)

The buttocks narrative even made its way to Parliament during elections for a new speaker of the house:

> Siliya, who was dressed in a cream white body fitting suit and a matching Queen's hat, stood up and after leaving her seat, turned around facing her neighbor Kunda and posed for the ruling PF legislators, much to the amusement of the members. Her action attracted more laughter as information minister Given Lubinda shouted: "bokosi!" (buttocks!). (The *Post*, October, 17 2011, 1)

The study found that Siliya was the only MP whose coverage was punctuated by "physical appearance" references and that, in some instances, she invoked objectifying language as part of her openly anti-gay rhetoric.

Another significant topic, particularly in the *Post*, was attention to "women's issues," (Table 5.4), which focused on stories whose emphasis was women's empowerment, gender based violence, health, and sanitation. The poster child for women's health was Kapata, a nurse by profession and one of the new entrants to Parliament. She used the media to publicize her breast and cervical cancer screening as a way of encouraging more women to take charge of their health. Wina, on the other hand, carried the banner for empowerment, and in commemorating the International Day for Elimination of Violence against Women, she urged Zambians to take advantage of the constitution drafting process and make submissions that would ensure that the national constitution entrenched the empowerment of women. Conceding the low number of female representation in Parliament, Wina was reported by the *Post* (26 November 2011) as saying that the PF had made great strides in increasing the number of women in key decision-making positions in other spheres. An example was the justices Chibesakunda and Mumba appointments. But as mentioned earlier, being past retirement age, their appointments were viewed unfavorably. Some sectors of society attributed the appointments to tribalism, to which Masebo responded thus:

> … the issue of Judge Lombe Chibesakunda and Florence Mumba should not be perceived as tribal but that the two were qualified to hold office. We need to get as many women as possible into decision making positions. (The *Post*, 24 June 2012)

Another central topic, which like the "women's issues" featured more prominently in the *Post* than the *Zambia Daily Mail* was "development." This category encompassed stories whose focus directly related to what needed to be done, both at the micro and macro levels, to develop the country and better people's lives. Partly personifying this type of coverage was Limata, the minister for North Western Province. Her province was turning into Zambia's development belt following the discovery of precious stones and the mushrooming of mines, particularly in a town called Solwezi. Limata was reported urging civil servants to change their sloppy attitude towards work. The *Zambia Daily Mail* (September 20, 2012) covered her castigating the Zambia News and Information Services staff for incompetence: "You are not here to drink beer every day, you are here to work." Ironically, Limata was also wary of the fact that civil servants were undermining her because she was a woman. She warned that she would not let that continue (the *Post*, September 2, 2012). Limata's experience of feeling undermined can be explained against the backdrop of the public–private divide outlined by Sreberny-Mohammadi and van Zoonen (2000). More specifically, in the rural area where Limata's ministerial purview lay, the gender divide is so overt that the expectations of a woman's role in society are confined to the private sphere. Two other MPs associated with the "development" topic were Luo and Masebo. The former's emphasis was on integrating traditional leaders into the development agenda, arguing that they were such a critical, yet overlooked, mass. The latter articulated her stance on development from the perspective of admonishing Zambians for having an inferiority complex, which was the source of the lack of development in the country.

The topics of "social issues" and "tourism and UNWTO" were synonymous with Luo and Masebo respectively and tended to be specific to their ministerial portfolios. During the period under examination, Zambia had been selected to co-host the United Nations World Tourism Organization (UNWTO) General Assembly with Zimbabwe. As a tourism minister, Masebo was covered touring and meeting with various stakeholders in Livingstone, the town where the gathering would take place. Cleanliness and getting street vendors off the streets in readiness for the international event became Masebo's personal mission. Luo, as a Minister of Chiefs and Traditional Affairs, also weighed in on the street vending. Luo was also preoccupied with social policy, which dominated her coverage. Her ban on the infamous potent spirits known as tujilijili, which were being abused by youths because of easy accessibility and affordability, was widely covered, including the controversies that followed.

Although by virtue of being MPs the expectation would be that "parliamentary affairs/debates," which comprised stories on voting and contributions made during debates in Parliament, would be one of the prominent topics in the coverage of the 18 women MPs, the results showed otherwise. The only MP whose contributions were covered during the timeframe studied was Namugala. Of the two stories the *Post* carried on this former tourism minister in the MMD government, one was on her questioning the government's decision to donate fuel to Malawi during that country's presidential bereavement. She challenged the PF government to explain to the Zambian people, who faced a massive fuel shortage shortly after the donation, why it donated 5 million liters of fuel valued at $7 million without securing national reserves. Another issue Namugala was reported questioning in Parliament was the implementation of the newly introduced minimum wage for domestic, shop, and general workers. Labor minister, Fackson Shamenda, on July 4, 2012, signed Statutory Instrument No. 45 of 2012, which increased the minimum wage for the above-mentioned workers from the K250,000-K400,000 (US$50-US$80) range to K700,000 (US$140) per month. Namugala's concern was how low-income workers such as teachers would afford to pay their maids following the revised minimum wage, and that this would inevitably lead to high levels of unemployment (*Zambia Daily Mail*, July 14, 2012). Away from questioning government policy, Namugala was also reported praising the PF in Parliament for increasing the number of provinces from nine to ten. Namugala noted that splitting Northern Province where her constituency was into two was commendable as this would help give it a fair budgetary shake. Prior to the split, Northern Province, which had 13 districts, received the same budgetary allocation as provinces with less than seven districts (*Zambia Daily Mail*, October 22, 2011).

Finally, as indicated in Table 5.4, there were also a few stories that discussed sundry topics such as ceremonial appearances where women MPs were invited to grace traditional ceremonies (eight in *Zambia Daily Mail* compared to six in the *Post*), and private appearances at weddings (five in the *Post* compared to one in *Zambia Daily Mail*). The *Post* also covered two additional topics, i.e. party protocol and portraits, that *Zambia Daily Mail* did not. In a nutshell, when coverage by the two newspapers is compared, it is evident that *Zambia Daily Mail* placed a lot of emphasis on the topic of corruption in line with the PF government's manifesto. Conversely, beyond corruption, the *Post* also emphasized women's issues and development.

Journalists' insights into their coverage

Out of the 48 journalists who authored the stories studied, a total of 14 agreed to be interviewed. The aggregated gender breakdown of journalists who participated in the interviews was about 70 to 30 percent in favor of men. In response to RQ3, the journalists justified the strong evidence of symbolic annihilation (refer to Table 5.3), by explaining that these MPs had no controversies or scandals to contribute to the news narrative. This insight coincided with the fact that the most covered MP—Siliya—was also the most scandalous, controversial and outspoken. Examined from the perspective of today's news media becoming more and more sensationalistic, this insight from the journalists was not surprising. An excellent example is when Siliya exploited stereotypes and went rogue on matters of sexuality beckoning men to admire her "soft bums" while campaigning for re-election. A male journalist from the *Post* said that the media find sexually explicit content "very juicy."

The journalists further noted that the seven MPs who did not receive any press coverage lacked assertiveness. One journalist bluntly put it: "As much as it is our job to speak to these people, they also need to come out in the open to state their positions on certain issues. Concentration is mostly on sources who are ready and not afraid to speak." Another explanation the journalists gave for not covering these MPs was that they rarely debated in Parliament, adding that the newspapers had little funds to follow them in their constituencies. What was interesting though was that the MPs that enjoyed the most coverage were not necessarily the ones who contributed to parliamentary debates. Other, more unflattering explanations, included: "Lack of both expertise and knowledge" and that these "MPs [were] hostile towards state media," thus hinting at lack of rapport between some women politicians and the press. Not all of the surveyed journalists absolved themselves of all blame for not covering these MPs. There were some who conceded that ignoring these MPs was "a weakness" on the journalists' part to "get them on [record on] various issues concerning the nation."

Finally, the journalists were given an opportunity to self-evaluate their coverage of the women MPs on a scale of 1 to 10, where 1 was poor and 10 excellent. The highest score the journalists gave themselves was 8 and the lowest was 1. The two who rated their coverage as 8 were male reporters from *Zambia Daily Mail*. One commented that *Zambia Daily Mail* was "the only newspaper in Zambia with a GENDER desk, with reporters and an editor." Yet the results of the content analysis revealed that the *Zambia Daily Mail* was outperformed by the *Post* in terms of amount of coverage and range of issues. Overall, the average rating of the journalists at *Zambia Daily Mail* was 5.5, which was higher than the 4.5 average rating of their counterparts at the *Post*. On aggregate, female journalists fared worse than their male counterparts. The female journalists had an average rating of 4 compared to 5.3 for the males. The reasons for the low rating for female journalists could be various and could range from perceived structural constraints on the job to the realization that so much still needs to be done culturally to achieve gender parity in coverage. Journalists from both publications attributed their poor scores to lack of gender training. In fact, the two *Zambia Daily Mail* journalists who gave themselves an 8, attributed their high rating to the fact that they had received gender training.

Discussion and conclusion

The coverage of the 18 women MPs in Zambia mirrored the country's culture and status quo. The unprecedented levels of corruption in society, which go against the African humanistic philosophy of ubuntuism, justified the emphasis on the "corruption" frame. Ubuntuism stresses the centrality of education and collectiveness in the uplifting of African people. According to Worthington (2011), grounding news frames in ubuntuism, which privileges educating the public, facilitating dialogue, and eradicating social hierarchy, can challenge cultural discourses that resist a progressive reform. Although emphasis on the topic of "corruption" was not surprising, how the corruption fight was being conducted and reported was. It gave the impression, particularly where electoral malpractices were concerned, that the ruling PF was bent on amassing majority seats in parliament. Therefore, opposition MPs perceived as obstacles were slapped with corruption charges that were hence covered profusely. For women in the opposition, where there was any slight suspicion of corruption, the stakes were even higher. This is because, as aptly put by a female journalist from *Zambia Daily Mail*:

> Women are regarded with the highest esteem by society. Therefore, when these women are engaged in any controversies it is of interest by the public to know why and how they found themselves in such situations and what they do to get out of them.

This journalist's insight helps explain why Siliya was the most covered of the 18 women MPs. The corruption charges and controversies that surrounded her made her fair game. So did the actions of Luo and Masebo, numbers two and three on the salience list, who were labeled "political prostitutes" for switching parties. Indeed, media newsworthiness standards dictate that news stories that are controversial or contain conflict would be heavily reported, regardless of gender. Yet the gendered implications come into play when women politicians are subjected to higher standards and scrutiny (Sreberny-Mohammadi and Ross 1996).

What is important to note, however, is that the media should not hide behind the guise of culture when it comes to annihilating or framing women politicians in unfavorable light. The overall results of this study reveal that most of the women MPs were either invisible on the pages of the Zambian press (except for three newsworthy MPs) or covered in 55 percent of the time in connection to three topics—corruption, women's issues, and development. Although there was limited evidence with regard to media references to appearance, this study found what Carroll and Schreiber (1997) called a "problem of *omission* rather than one of *commission*" (145). The presented picture of women MPs might have been correct, but was incomplete in the sense that it lacked detailed coverage of the activities of women politicians in Parliament or was missing stories where women politicians were shown as active decision makers on a broad range of issues. The few women MPs who were covered by the two newspapers were linked with either a potentially career damaging and controversial topic (corruption) or women's and development issues which, as pointed out earlier, were also closely linked to the "soft" ministerial positions assigned to women parliamentarians. This is not to suggest that women's issues and development are unimportant or irrelevant in the context of Zambia, yet such coverage could create the perception that women MPs are active mostly around topics that concern women. Thus the analysis of the press coverage of women MPs over a one-year period indicated that not only were few women politicians visible, but when they were, they were the ones who were most controversial and outspoken and linked to a narrow range of issues. Furthermore, interviews with journalists behind the stories revealed that they evaluate their job of covering women politicians as average. The present study is just a first step in understanding the amount and content of press coverage of women politicians in Zambia. Future research should explore in depth newsroom culture as well as the tone of media coverage of women politicians or how coverage of women MPs compares to that of their male colleagues.

As a first step, investing in gender training with the goal of achieving gender mainstreaming is a feasible starting point that both newspapers should consider in order to enhance their coverage. In fact, training should also extend to the MPs themselves, particularly the ones who were ignored by the press, to learn how to effectively deal with the media. Finally, ensuring the availability of and strict adherence to style manuals that are designed to eliminate gender stereotyping would not only serve journalists at the two newspapers well, but would also ensure consistency in coverage of Zambian women MPs.

6

Media Visibility of Tunisian Women Politicians in Traditional and New Media: Obstacles to Visibility and Media Coverage Strategies

Maryam Ben Salem and Atidel Mejbri

On December 17, 2010, Mohamed al-Bouazizi, a street fruit vendor, set himself on fire in protest at the confiscation of his wares by the authorities. This act sparked a revolution in his country of Tunisia and influenced similar pro-democracy movements in North Africa and the Middle East.

The revolution drew attention to Tunisian women who became omnipresent in the international media. Newspaper front pages and news channels were constantly relaying images of women—activists and ordinary citizens—at the heart of demonstrations and on all fronts. The images of committed and politically active Tunisian women, which those reports conveyed, contrasted sharply with the stereotypical image of passive Arab women confined to the private sphere. Yet contrary to Western media's enthusiasm for Tunisian women's active engagement in the sweeping changes, local media kept women marginalized from the media sphere. In essence, there was a sharp contrast between the international and local media representations of women as agents of change.

This chapter undertakes an analysis of women politicians' media visibility after the revolution in Tunisia. It explores the challenges that women politicians face when it comes to media visibility, whether in traditional or new media, and women's level of consciousness of its impact on their political career. It also tackles the question of sexist abuse, highlighting barriers to women politicians' presence in new media platforms. By uncovering the subjective (inherent to women politicians) and objective (related to stereotypes and gender based discrimination) barriers, this study questions the media coverage of women in politics through the paradigm of recognition.

Representation of Tunisian women in the political sphere

Although it is difficult at present to provide a thorough analysis of women's entry into politics since the revolution, the data below suggest that women are still under-represented in the political sphere in spite of all the changes that have been introduced to allow easier access for women to decision-making positions.

With the law on parity in electoral lists for the October 2011 elections for the National Constituent Assembly (NCA), 30 percent of women were able to enter the NCA (65 women out of a total of 217 elected). Although it marks a slight improvement compared to the presence of women in parliament under the regime of Ben Ali (28 percent), this rate remains below expectations. Only two women were appointed ministers in the Government of Hamadi Jebali,[1] one in the environment department and the other holding the portfolio of women and the family. The new government, headed by Ali Laariadh and formed in March of 2013 after the resignation of Jebali, includes only one woman who is the Minister of Women, Family and Children Affairs.

Moreover, women are far from being well represented in the decision-making positions in political parties or trade unions. In the last elections of the executive board of the General Labor Union there were four female candidates yet none was elected. Our data also indicate a low presence of women in the political bureaus or executive boards of political parties (Table 6.1).[2]

Theoretical background

The relationship between social reality—namely the effective participation of women in public life—and media representations is at the heart of this study, which seeks to analyze the media coverage of women politicians in Tunisia by taking stock of the presence of women in traditional media (print, audio-visual) and new media. The issue of media coverage of women politicians is strongly linked to the notion of recognition. Axel Honneth (2005) stresses in this context that "recognition depends on the media that express the fact that the other person is supposed to have a social value" (45). As such, media visibility would be a key issue for women politicians insofar as media coverage is a form of a symbolic recognition, towards recognizing a right to participation which enshrines the status of a political actor.

Table 6.1 Representation of women in the executive levels of political parties in Tunisia after the 2011 revolution

Party	Number of women members	Overall number of political bureau members	Percentage of women
Republican Party	1	17	6
Ennahdha	1	14	7
Call for Tunisia (Nidaa Tounes)	11	57	19
Ettakatol (Democratic Forum for Labor and Liberties)	11	41	27
Tunisian Workers' Party (PCOT)	4	21	19
Congress for the Republic	1	9	11

Source: Maryam Ben Salem, Traditional and new forms of young women's political engagement in a transitional context. Tunisia as example, CAWTAR 2013 (data collected in March 2013 and updated in October 2013)

Note: Percentages rounded to the nearest whole number.

Also, as noted in Derville (1997), media coverage exerts a selection effect on politicians by strengthening the pre eminence of those who are considered political heavyweights (109). Thus, media influence recognition at two levels: the recognition by the public and the recognition by the political organization and its members. If we consider visibility as a form of recognition, it is necessary to examine women's political awareness of such issues and the impact of media visibility on their political careers. This study questions the existence of claims of visibility for political women in both traditional and new media.

Finally, Honneth (2005) emphasizes the close link between recognition and the representation we make of the social value of an individual (50–6). The positive or negative value that is attributed to a person determines the act of recognition. Thus we cannot address media visibility or invisibility without giving consideration to clichés, stereotypes and sexist insults in the media. Emphasis will be placed here on the image of women politicians in new media, namely Facebook, because such messages deliver, without the filter of political correctness or linguistic correction imposed in traditional media, the perception users (and potential voters) have of women politicians. This analysis allows us to raise the issue of the impact of sexist insult on the visibility strategies adopted by women in politics.

Method

This chapter is based on the results of three projects conducted by the Center of Arab Women for Training and Research (CAWTAR). Each project deals with a different aspect of media visibility, i.e. as expressed in local media, as understood by TV producers, and as approached by women politicians themselves. We believe that a triangulation approach allows for a broader understanding of the phenomenon of visibility in the context of postrevolution Tunisia. Below is a list of the projects:

1. A quantitative analysis of traditional media outlets in the Arab region in the framework of the Fourth Global Media Monitoring Project conducted on November 10, 2009 to which CAWTAR contributed with data from Tunisia;[3]
2. Qualitative interviews with TV producers regarding the absence of women politicians in post-revolution current affairs talk shows;[4]
3. The results of a comprehensive qualitative research on young women's participation in politics in Tunisia[5] which is based on:
   a) A corpus of 41 semi-structured in-depth interviews conducted with young men and women active in politics (conventional and unconventional) and formulated to trace the trajectories of social actors.
   b) Two focus groups: the first, involving cyber-activists and women active in the traditional political sphere, was aiming to define this practice with respect to participation in political parties or associations. The second, bringing together men and women internet activists, was seeking to follow the way this practice has changed one year after the revolution and examine discrimination based on gender in this sphere.[6]
   c) The observation of the internet activity on Facebook of 12 cyber activists[7] chosen for their reputation (not just in the media) and the diversity of their profiles. This is an in situ observation of debates, comments of internet users on the publications and status of internet activists as well as the relationships between actors. This observation, which is part of the above mentioned research, was conducted from May 2011 to May 2013.
   d) A monitoring and analysis of conversations and publications on Facebook[8] relating to women politicians (a woman minister, deputies in the National Constituent Assembly and the president of the Tunisian Journalist Union)

combined with monitoring of their Facebook accounts or pages. This monitoring lasted for one month and was conducted in March 2013.

Results

The visibility of women in traditional media outlets

In Tunisia, the relationship between social reality and media representation corresponds to the hegemonic ideal type as defined by Macé (2006). The latter, which is characterized by "lack of problematization of gender relations […] is spontaneously sexist" (114). It should first be noted that this problem is not specific to Tunisia and is not specific to a particular political context either.

The invisibility of women in politics in the Arab world in general and in Tunisia in particular is evidenced by many surveys as well as monitoring projects of the media. The Middle East media monitoring conducted in 2009 could be used as a benchmark of what kind of visibility women had in print and broadcast media before the Tunisian revolution (El Bour and Mejbri 2010). The report shows that in the Arab region, the percentage of women who are interviewed by the media and/or who become the focus of news stories is very low. Also noteworthy is the fact that political news casts, which are the most widespread genre, give voice to only 10 percent of women. The report also reveals that women appear only up to 19 percent of the time as experts and only 12 percent of the time as spokespersons. As a source of information, they represent only 16 percent of the sample.

Keeping in mind that the media field has been traditionally reserved for men, the monitoring revealed a positive trend, i.e. a feminization of the information sector since 57 percent of news presenters are women and so are 33 percent of the reporters. Finally, this study also revealed that news from the region generally reinforces stereotypes based on gender. An overwhelming percentage of news (81 percent) conveys stereotypes against women, while only 4 percent is opposing them.

A report entitled *Media coverage of women's political participation in Algeria, Morocco and Tunisia* focused on the media treatment of women active in politics before the revolution (El Bour 2009). This study showed that the Tunisian media (print, audiovisual, and electronic) do not reflect the diversity of women's political participation.

The revolution did not bring significant improvement to the media visibility of women politicians in Tunisia, despite the transition context that encourages the participation of women in public life. During the transition period, the situation does not appear to have improved since monitoring of the media shows that women political actors continue to receive extremely limited coverage with 10.4 percent for radio, 10.21 percent for television and only 2.85 percent for newspapers (Women and gender 2011).

Barriers to the visibility of women politicians in current affairs talk shows

The observed media quasi-invisibility significantly reduces the symbolic power of women active in politics, insofar as their exclusion from the media scene is a form of implicit denial of their skills and legitimacy to act in the political arena. These observations lead us to look for the causes of the exclusion of women from the media, particularly in current affairs talk shows, which have become a popular genre in Tunisia. Does the exclusion relate to gender stereotypes, a fortiori the idea that the quality of a debater, understood as "specific political competence necessary in dealing with political professionals" (Bourdieu 1981, 6), is just for men?

The answer to this question is provided by qualitative interviews conducted in early July 2011—five months after the Tunisian Revolution. The sample included producers and presenters of current affairs talk shows (11 men and five women) in the framework of the Arab Network of Monitoring the Image of Women in the Media. The 16 interviews conducted with participants from three Tunisian state-run and one private TV channel allow for a better understanding of the reasons behind the absence of women in the broadcast space.

A content analysis of interviewees' responses revealed entrenched biases toward women. The results show that TV producers are deeply convinced that male participants are more numerous, more motivated, and more willing to discuss public affairs. Furthermore, the interviewees noted that when it came to involving female participants, unavailability (due to family responsibilities) and the need to refer to the husband or family members to participate in the talk shows, in addition to their fears of not performing properly, are among the main reasons presented as barriers to women politicians' participation in the shows.

In addition to production conditions that require instant answers to urgent requests for participation, other reasons were mentioned, including, among others, the desire on the part of women politicians to be presentable or "look good." Also cited among the reasons for the marginalization of women politicians was the fact that they lack understanding of how to interact with media. Women politicians were perceived as insensitive to the role of the media: as demanding and selective with respect to the nature of other participants and as lacking self-confidence or media experience. As Jamel Arfaoui, former member of the editorial board of the private Nessma TV, observed: "When women participate, I noticed that the majority of them are uncomfortable when they face the camera."

Paradoxically, what also emerged from this analysis was that the TV producers and presenters believe that the few women who get to participate in their shows, although they are marginalized, are good debaters. Women politicians go straight to the point, initiate constructive, sharp, and rational debates, prepare well for their interventions, respond immediately to questions, and in general are considered bold. Similarly, most of the time, they lead the other participants to meet some debate ethics like respect for others, observing speaking time, or adherence to subjects discussed. According to the interviewees, women's rhetorical style differs from men's by a rigorous, pragmatic and precise argument away from all abstract, theoretical extrapolations. Women politicians also exhibit higher propensity than men to create new themes and place politics in a social context.

Overall, the interview results point to a more complex set of obstructions to the media visibility of women other than stereotypes: lack of time or flexibility due to family and work constraints, lack of self-assurance, and their inexperience when dealing with media. Without denying the existence of gender stereotypes, this leads us to turn our attention to women politicians themselves to better understand the origins of invisibility. Do they perceive access to visibility as a form of political recognition? Is media visibility for women politicians a driving force for their political career? Do they adopt media strategies or are they fighting for visibility?

The challenge of media visibility for women politicians

This section presents some of the results of a larger research project on the political participation of young women in Tunisia, based on 41 in-depth interviews with politically active men and women, two focus groups, the observation of cyber activists as well as the monitoring and online observation of Facebook accounts of women politicians.

It appears from the in-depth interviews that women active in politics, whether party members, community activists, or trade unionists, do not all have the same understanding of visibility and do not grant it the same importance. Indeed, when asked about their visibility, women in politics do not always link this term to media visibility. Spontaneously, respondents speak about the visibility of their political actions through direct contact with the electorate. They associate visibility with face-to-face interactions that are spatially and temporally limited, which corresponds to Voirol's approach to immediate visibility as opposed to media visibility (Voirol 2005, 95–7).

When asked about their access to visibility through the media, the majority of interviewees consider this aspect as secondary to their activities. But it needs to be pointed out that this is specific to a particular profile of women politicians who consider their work as "acting behind the scenes." It is something they do by choice, not because they are forced to. Staying behind the scenes does not mean that these women have a minor role, but refers to what might be termed as "disinterested fieldwork." The binary vision that some of the respondents have of the political action: interested, that is to say, serving their own interests, on the one hand, and disinterested, i.e. promoting the general interest, on the other hand, is the origin of this negative position vis-à-vis media visibility. Media visibility is seen as a strategy of personal visibility designed to satisfy the political ego, thus it is avoided or considered as secondary.

One participant, Lamia, provides a good example of this attitude toward media. She is actively engaged in a political party and was a candidate for the National Constituent Assembly in 2011. Lamia places greater importance on the impact of her political actions on her close circle, than on media. She even cites the confidence parents give her as a sign of her political popularity. According to her, her reputation and authenticity, the values she carries, and her honest actions give her more legitimacy than television appearances, which, she said, do not reflect the political weight of women:

> In the days of the revolution, the image of a woman in the middle of many men attracted attention; it does not end there, it is also the ability of women to have weight. Indeed, many parents want me to teach their children because I do not offer private tuition and I am authentic. Once, I had problems with a director, an RCDist,[9] because of my political position, but I had always sent reports to the

> Minister because of his behavior. Legitimacy is acquired only with a real fight for citizens' rights. (Lamia, woman politician, interviewed April 2011)

The above quote underscores the distinction some of the interviewed women were making between media visibility and political fieldwork, the first being less important than the latter.

Other interviewees, however, suffer from a lack of visibility in the media, which they perceive as misrecognition of the work they do within the party organization. They remain, nonetheless, less numerous than the first group. In this case, obstacles to visibility pertain, essentially to malfunctions at the party or union level that favor men and relegate women to a secondary role, that of shadow workers.

In addition, when there is a real awareness of the media invisibility of women politicians among respondents, it is not clearly problematized, or seen as an object of struggle.

> In general, they are large gaps. We saw … even if women were very visible in the photos of the events, they have contributed a lot, they have coordinated, they have played a very important role in the dissemination of information among bloggers … etc. … the media, shows, debates … very little, it is very, very little, that is to say, there are very few women [present in media]. [The attitude is] we do not call them, we call them only to talk about women's issues, I think … Well, this is a fact everyone knows and there is probably a job to be done. (Raoudha, trade unionist, interviewed September 2011)

Thus, we noted in the interviews the scarcity of the media visibility strategies at the individual level. As for the collective level, they are totally non-existent. There is not, strictly speaking, struggle among women politicians and activists for visibility and recognition in the media. At this point, any actions in that regard are limited to training initiatives implemented by NGOs and international organizations or associations. The latter is limited to a few groups acting for women's rights.[10]

New media and strategies for visibility

Some user-generated content platforms, especially Facebook, have gained a great importance since the revolution. The major role played by cyber activists during the revolution—in mobilizing and relaying information collected from the media and the public—has brought legitimacy to their cause. It has turned them into true political actors, whereas before the revolution they were considered part of the marginal protest culture. This is how social media tools are becoming indispensable instruments of political communication. Considering that these platforms give instant visibility to individuals and do not require intermediaries as is the case with traditional media where women's participation is dependent on their invitation by media professionals, we examined the existence of strategies for visibility through women politicians' use of these platforms.

Web 2.0 applications have brought about a paradigm shift by allowing consumers to move from the status of receiver to that of participant (Jenkins 2006). By extension, we can say that the digital environment has provided women politicians with the opportunity to expand the scope of their activities and their ability to manage their image formation. Indeed, through its interactive nature, the Web offers a medium through which politicians can play a dual role—that of creators of information and that of receivers. The first role accords women politicians the opportunity to provide visibility to their actions. Furthermore, the interactive aspect of new media could help politicians gain a better understanding of their political popularity ratings and how the public receives their speeches and actions. Although these tools are somewhat of a barometer of the popularity or unpopularity of politicians regardless of gender, women politicians do not seem to be aware of this opportunity. Our research indicated that the interviewed women politicians do not use new media in a systematic way and even less as a tool for visibility. Rather, for them it is a means to access information. They often simply follow the news, share publications on Facebook or comment on them.

An examination of the Facebook accounts of the NCA women who were elected in 2011 shows that only 38 out of 65 women members are on Facebook, and only 21 of them have public pages while the rest have private Facebook accounts. Public pages indicate the willingness of women politicians to put their actions and their persons in the public domain, while personal accounts confine them to the private sphere. This choice reveals a gap at the level of presentation and self-representation among those who define themselves and present themselves as politicians and those who use social media like ordinary citizens. The overall conclusion is that for a great number of women politicians in Tunisia, Facebook is either irrelevant or primarily a means to communicate with their friends and entourage and not a tool for political communication.

The case of sexist abuse as a barrier to women politicians' presence in new media

Though they do not commit heavily to new media platforms, women politicians are nevertheless present in these forums. In fact, their speeches and public appearances are almost always relayed on Facebook and heavily commented on. Women politicians' presence in new media deserves particular attention because the reactions they create tell much about the gender stereotyping in a public arena that overlooks political correctness. Facebook thus provides yet another facet of gender stereotyping against women politicians that differs from the instances conveyed in mainstream media. As our research indicates, in mainstream media, women politicians are mostly excluded from public debate, and when they are represented, they are perceived first as women, i.e. with reference to their gender, confined to issues related to women's rights, and often relegated to their traditional roles as mothers. It is important, therefore, to explore what types of stereotypes are conveyed in new media and how they are different from those we encounter in mainstream media?

We observed that Facebook has become the preferred place for public debate, but also a popular platform for criticism and vilification of politicians be they from the government or the opposition (depending on the partisan preferences of the user). The insults, taunts, sarcasm, and verbal abuse are certainly not limited to women, but we have seen that when it comes to women politicians, the register is explicitly sexist. We define "taunt [as] a serious and intentional insult designed to prejudice the honor or reputation of a person but that does not contain the elements of defamation or slander because it does not refer to a specific fact" (Hoebeke 2008, 89). Our purpose here is to undertake a discursive analysis of internet users' comments on Facebook in order to identify the purely sexist content of insults hurled and examine the differentiated responses of women politicians to them. The analysis of sexist insults aimed at women politicians has the advantage of better understanding the stereotypes about women in the political realm.

Insults are considered sexist when they attack women's moral integrity and concern them specifically and personally. Oger (2006) showed in the case of French women politicians that sexist insults increase after women politicians speak in public or when they become more publicly visible. We noted that this is also the case with Tunisia, since publications, videos shared by users, and the debates, often occur after an action or statement by a woman politician.

The reference to the sexual identity of women politicians contained in the sexist insults, in addition to being hurtful, symbolically excludes political actors from the political arena and affirms the persistence of the idea of masculine domination in this field. Insults are often accompanied by a questioning of parity laws that would have allowed the "incompetent" to enter the political arena even though they do not have the required skills and talent.

The first type of insult confers a negative and demeaning status to women. The term most commonly used in the Facebook lexicon to designate the incompetence of women politicians is that of "*Harza Hammam*," which means employee responsible for body care at a public bath[11] who is usually from the lowest classes of people. In the Tunisian collective imagination, bath workers are closely associated with gossiping, typically a female attribute, and a trade strongly devalued.

The most common insults involve the morality of women: thus women politicians are often referred to as "immoral," "divorcees," "prostitutes," "sluts," "lesbians," or "witches." For women politicians, these insults represent a denial of their social value, which is inherent to their honor. Insults about physical appearance are also common, referring to women in terms of "ugliness," or as "mannish," or "frumpy." It should be pointed out that the words rarely involve the content of a speech or action taken by the women politicians. They rather pertain to their status as women.

The second type of insult relates to the discriminatory perception of the roles of men and women, with the explicit assumption that the public arena is reserved for men. The inference is that women should naturally remain in private. Indeed, there are many insults that define the role allotted to women, including domestic tasks and pointing openly to the illegitimacy of the political position of women.

A good example is a video posted on Facebook of a member of the National Constituent Assembly that received 148 comments of approval. This video, which was overwhelmingly insulting, proclaims that women's access to the political arena can be only lead to bad results: "The house where the hen does the job of a rooster is doomed to ruin."

Conversely, the "praise" addressed to women politicians involves either their moral integrity (wife of morality) or their perceived possession of manly qualities. The use of the term "*Rajil*" (man) or "*rjouliyya*" (virility in the literal sense but not understood in the sense of male dominance, but male social attributes) is not always pejorative for those who use it, although it is in itself highly gendered. This so-called "compliment" implies that women politicians demonstrating political competence, expertise, and know-how cannot be women because women lack these qualities. Possession of these skills implicitly involves the annihilation of their femininity and highlights their ability to internalize the "masculine" rules of power in order for them to find a place in the public sphere (Sourd 2005). The most telling example is that of a woman politician whose photos of attending the funeral of Martyr Chokri Belaid (funerals are reserved by custom to men) were posted on Facebook with comments linking them to a politician who was not present there. In a clear misuse of the rules of conjugation in Arabic, the verb in this comment is conjugated as male to assert the "virility" of the woman politician, while the second verb is conjugated as female so that it would underline the inferiority of her male colleague: "M (the woman politician) has come and X (Tunisian male politician) did not come."[12]

The third type of observed insults involves age. The emphasis on celibacy, using the term "old maid" indicates the belief that women's political engagement was made possible by their deviation from the norm, i.e. to be married and become a mother. For example, to the outbursts of insults on Facebook which appear under the video statement of a female NCA member, one of the internet users responds in a condescending tone: "No, stop saying this, she is a sour-tempered woman, because she is older and it is common in a seraglio for the concubine who is aging to become a sour-tempered woman dealing with the affairs of the harem in the Caliph's palace." This type of insult embodies the idea than an old woman has no value in society as long as she has no reproductive role. The sexist insult thus deflects the subject of criticism by questioning altogether the presence of women in political life. The gender characteristics of women politicians become, again, sole focus of those insults. Their femininity and the traditional role assigned to them are the only aspects likely to be noticed and used to justify their incompetence. Even professional incompetence that is supposed to be criticized, regardless of gender, becomes through the sexist insult, an aspect inherent to women politicians, since it is exclusively related to their femininity.

Finally, the discrimination revealed by insults is not just sexual. The analysis of the insults on Facebook also reveals the presence of racial slurs or even calls to violence. For example, on the Facebook account of a woman minister, a comment on a video she posted said a dozen times: "rape her then prosecute her!" In addition, openly racist insults involving the N word addressed to the President of the Tunisian Journalists' Union, are seeking to minimize her contributions by referring to the color of her skin. Such insults are meant to suggest her racial inferiority and thus her subservient position, which justifies the insult. The racial slur reduces the insulted to "the only aspect of this person perceived by the racist: pigments of his [or her] skin" (Guard Dogs 2000).

Faced with these insults, the reactions of women politicians encompass a variety of nuances, ranging from indifference to self-affirmation through justification. Some women politicians fully assume their positions and actions, ignoring critics and sexist insults. Others, however, are obliged to have a critical look at this social tool, which they perceive as a "space of gossip." This is the case of Kaouther which explains why she refrains from using Facebook in this way:

> Honestly, I use it to participate in discussions more than for anything else and this is why I told you that Facebook had a role in the revolution, but now you feel that it has become something totally different. It has turned into a space for gossip where people trade insults, [it's] not like before. Even if Facebook users put an event, the comment is never objective. They share information accompanied necessarily by a comment, which is often subjective and an insult to a political party, do you understand? And personally, I am against this. I always want to discuss with people what they think provided we discuss with mutual respect. Either I will convince you or you convince me. (Kaouther, woman politician, interviewed May 2011)

The overall effect of this registry of insults is that, by reducing women politicians to their skin color, physical appearance, or morality, they subtract women's qualities as political players and thus question their legitimacy to intervene in the political sphere.

Conclusion

The results of three studies conducted by CAWTAR between 2011 and 2013, converge towards the same conclusion: Tunisian women politicians suffer from a lack of visibility in traditional media as well as social media and their image is affected by gender stereotypes which create an impact on the recognition of their status as political actors. Facebook emerged as a privileged spot to propagate gender stereotypes against women politicians. A sexist insult is one aspect of symbolic violence against women politicians, whose quality as a politician or public woman is continually questioned due to the simple fact of being a woman.

Invisibility is generally interpreted as a form of discrimination due to the exclusion of women politicians from the media spotlight by media professionals. Yet, both the survey conducted by one of the authors, and the survey on the political participation of young women in Tunisia (CAWTAR/IDRC), demonstrated that the causes of invisibility are much more complex and are due in part to women politicians themselves. It is clear from these surveys that, among women politicians, there is not, strictly speaking, a true awareness of the importance of media visibility or of the need to adopt media strategies. Television producers immediately admit that they rarely invite women to their current affairs talk shows, but they also insist that women politicians or female experts are generally reluctant to participate. Moreover, the majority of interviewed female politicians tend to avoid media appearances as they are deemed as contrary to their perception of political action and their perceived need to be selfless.

This observation thus originates questions that deserve, in our opinion, to be dwelt on in depth, namely: Why do women politicians not grant importance to media visibility? Why do they not perceive it as an issue of political legitimacy? What are the differences in the profiles of women politicians which explain their differentiated relationships with the issue of media visibility? Moreover, taking into account both the state of the visibility of women politicians in the media and their relationships with their media image, this study questions the notion of recognition. This chapter shows that media invisibility isn't always seen as unfair and doesn't induce collective action against this injustice.

From this point of view, the priority to increase media visibility of women politicians is to make them aware of the impact of media exposure on the success of their political careers. In addition, the various obstacles faced by women, such as their exclusion and marginalization in traditional and new media, the prevalence of sexist insults, etc., require the establishment of training sessions on strategies of visibility as well as greater emphasis on mastery of communication techniques.

Notes

1 The government of Troika is composed of the Ennahdha party, FDTL and CPR. It was formed in the wake of the National Constituent Assembly (NCA) elections in October 2011.

2 The list of political parties is based on their representation in NCA while also taking into account created coalitions. Some parties represented at the NCA are not mentioned due to lack of data.
3 The fourth project on global media monitoring was completed on November 10, 2009. The Arab region, as well as other parts of the world, took an active part in this project, which represents the largest and longest existing international research project on the theme of gender in the media. Arab participation was ensured by five countries: Tunisia, Egypt, Jordan, the United Arab Emirates and Lebanon.
4 Survey conducted by Atidel Mejbri in July 2011 with 16 TV producers.
5 Research titled "Traditional and new forms of young women's political engagement in a transitional context. Tunisia as example" realized by Maryam Ben Salem and initiated by CAWTAR in February 2011 with the financial support of the International Development Research Centre (IDRC).
6 Two other focus groups were conducted in the framework of the above-mentioned study on young women's political participation in Tunisia. One focus group dealt with gender relations within party organizations and the fourth, which addressed senior–junior relations, focused on the issue of intergenerational transfer of political know-how and knowledge.
7 They are six women (Bent Trad, Henda Hendoud, Fatma Arabicca, Jolanare Jo, Massir Destin, Amira Yahyaoui) and six men (Z, Aziz Amami, Hamadi Kaloutcha, BigTrap Boy, Kerim Bouzouita and Chut Libre).
8 We opted for Facebook from the range of available tools because of the greater popularity it has enjoyed in Tunisia compared to others (Twitter, blogs, etc.). We observed in this regard that even the most prominent cyber activists tend to favor this tool.
9 Belonging to the ruling party under Ben Ali, Constitutional Democratic Rally-RCD
10 They are training initiatives on communication for women politicians implemented by NGOs and international organizations or associations.
11 As in a Turkish bath.
12 “ما جاتش (سياسيرجل) ف -جاءو (سيسية مرأة) -م-”

7

Understanding the Gender Dynamics of Current Affairs Talk Shows in the Pakistani Television Industry

Munira Cheema

The media landscape in Pakistan transformed in 2002 with the policy of liberalization under which several private broadcasting channels were launched. With diminished control from the government, the content in media started resonating with the realities on the ground. Along came another phenomenon based on inviting political representatives as discussion panelists in current affairs talk shows. This, in turn, led to a reduction in the huge gap between voters/public and politicians. While reforms in relation to media were being introduced, the percentage of women parliamentarians also increased to 22.5 percent in the Lower House and 16.3 percent in the Upper House (IPU). This increase in number gradually became reflected in the panels of talk shows as well. It thus marked a shift from almost no visibility of female politicians to their vivid presence on television and in the government, respectively.

There is clearly a gap in the academic literature with regard to examining the presence of Pakistani women politicians in broadcast media. In acknowledging this void, the goal of this study is to analyze the gender dynamics of current affairs talk shows in Pakistan. Therefore, this research attempts to understand how female politicians' participation in talk shows is affected by the gender dynamics of Pakistani society. It observes how traditional gender biases of male politicians become visible on talk shows and provides insights into the rhetorical style of Pakistani women politicians. In addition, this chapter also examines how male and female hosts understand and conceptualize the participation of female politicians in their talk shows. Lastly, it attempts to understand why gender-based issues are not high on the agenda of the current affairs talk shows.

The political and journalistic culture of Pakistan

Traditionally, the political parties in Pakistani politics have been divided between the secular/liberal and religiously inclined elements. However, in the last decade, the political culture in Pakistan has witnessed another dividing line that separates the political parties on the basis of their stance regarding the Taliban (anti-Taliban and pro-Taliban). In 2002, the political dynamics were such that Pakistan came forward as an ally in the War on Terror that the U.S. launched in response to the attacks of 9/11. In doing so, the government had to curb rising extremist elements and introduce a liberal approach toward religion and politics. In this context, a policy of liberalization of media was introduced that paralleled increased representation of women in parliament.

Syed Ali (2013) noted that since this move women in the parliament have been able to move certain bills but the reality on the ground for women has not changed. According to the Global Gender Gap Report (Insight Report 2012), Pakistan is second to last of 135 countries on the Gender Gap Index, whereas in terms of political participation it ranks 54. The rate of gender-based violence against women in Pakistan is also increasing by the day. "As many as 451 women had been killed in Pakistan in honor killings by the end of July 2013 compared to 918 killed in 2012" (Yusuf 2013). This situation has recently worsened with rising radical Islamist elements who oppose women's participation in the public sphere. As a result, ordinary female citizens as well as political activists find themselves under a constant threat (Female Pakistani minister 2007).

The existing literature on women politicians in South Asia emphasizes the region's rich history in terms of having women as national leaders (Anderson 1993; Lenneberg 1994; Richter 1990–1), yet highlights that most of them have only furthered the legacy of their families. Therefore, family ties have played a major role in the politics of this region (Lenneberg 1994). The literature on women politicians in Pakistan tends to focus exclusively on Benazir Bhutto. For instance, Anderson's work (1993) engages with the dynastic politics attached to the Bhutto family and how Benazir Bhutto rose through family as well as party politics to assume the office of prime minister. However, Anderson also notes how Benazir Bhutto had to experience the gender binds in the field of politics. Under the last tenure of Pakistan's People's Party (PPP), which is Bhutto's party, the country had its first ever woman Speaker of the National Assembly, who also formed the Women's Caucus that actively engaged in taking up women's issues at the policy level. Hina Rabbani Khar is another example of a young and educated woman, she served as the Foreign Minister to Pakistan from 2011 to 2013, but as Imtiaz (2011) argues, "as part of the political elite, Khar's elevation to Foreign Minister has very little to do with women's rights, and more perhaps, to do with the lack of candidates in PPP to serve this office."

Moreover, the political elite is known to have feudal background and the patriarchal culture of Pakistani politics is deeply rooted in the feudal system where "constituencies are often controlled by the local landowner who can draw on the support of thousands of workers come election day" (Crilly 2013). Anwar (2013) notes that "feudalism has become a strong part of the political system, so both the government and feudal dictatorships are inter-related." Therefore, if women parliamentarians have worked actively in favor of women's empowerment as noted by Palmieri (2011), the enactment of such laws becomes yet another struggle.

The issues of shame and morality are also regulated under the patriarchal culture or under Shariah, or Islamic law. In Pakistani society, shame is a dense concept. As Alvi (2013) explains, the "meaning of the term *sharam*, so often invoked in relation to the veil, is far richer than its usual English translation 'shame,' which is often associated with modesty, morality, piety, and female sexuality and its control." As part of an expanded definition, Alvi proposes to explore:

> additional meanings of *sharam* as aspects of concealment as a value, like nakedness of humans and sacred items, virginity, beauty in concealment, honor in responsibility and as embodied self-control, affinity, self-respect, dignity, pride, reverence for the other, self-sufficiency, vulnerability, security and protection, embarrassment, an obligation to be humble, humiliation, shyness, reservedness, restraint, as well as women of the house, in particular, daughter and sister. (178)

In the context of Pakistan, most of these attributes constitute the appropriate form of behavior for women.

The journalistic culture in Pakistan is also unique in terms of approaching socio-political issues. As insiders to society, journalists cannot be abstracted from the dominant practices. According to a recent study conducted by Pintak and Nazir (2013) that surveyed 395 Pakistani journalists: "almost 60% said the government should not pass laws that contradict *Sharia* law" (647). It was also observed that "more than 96% of respondents said the mission of Pakistani journalism is to 'analyze complex issues,' and no issue is more complex than the multifarious relationship between elements within the Pakistani political establishment, military and intelligence agencies, and the U.S. on one hand and the forces of Islamist militancy on the other" (648). Pintak and Nazir conclude that the overall approach of Pakistani journalists "is a synthesis of Western practices and the development journalism of Southeast Asia: objective but respectful, independent but cooperative … this approach is, in part, expressed within the idiom of Islam" (662).

Political communication across cultures

The existing literature in this field is significantly defined by Western scholars who have aimed to look at the representation of female politicians in media (Dolan 2005; Kahn 1994; Lovenduski 1996; Sreberny-Mohammadi and Ross 1996). Sreberny-Mohammadi and Ross (1996) have pioneered work on how women politicians view their complicated relationship with media. The work in this direction is taken further by Ross (2002) who builds upon the relationship between women politicians and the political sphere by elaborately describing their struggles to rise within their parties, as representative of women voters, and also their complex interactions with media. In the East, Lee (2004) contributed to a somewhat different portrayal of female officials in Hong Kong. Lee attempted to examine how positive coverage can obscure the entrenched hierarchies of gender and "alert us to how the 'game' of gender in the political arena is structured" (222).

Several studies (Dow and Tonn 1993; Hayden 1999; Jamieson 1995; Robson 2000) have also contributed towards feminine rhetorical style and how women as public speakers have tried to employ different strategies to make their style effective. In a study on the rhetorical style of Ann Richards, former governor of Texas, Dow and Tonn (1993) noted that the "synthesis of formal qualities of feminine style evident in Richards' rhetoric … with an alternative political philosophy reflecting feminine ideals of care, nurturance, and family relationships functions as a critique of traditional political reasoning that offers alternative grounds for political judgment" (289). While analyzing the ways in which Jeanette Rankin, the first U.S. female elected official, used her feminine style in the early twentieth century, Hayden (1999) argued that Rankin negotiated the gender dynamics in such a way that her rhetoric style played a part in "obscuring the threat to men's power that woman suffrage posed" (100). As a rhetorical strategy, the feminine style often reflects the rhetor's efforts to negotiate the power relations that gender entails.

Jamieson (1995), on the other hand, attempted to understand rhetoric in the sense of double binds. She argues that a double bind is a "rhetorical construct that posits two and only two alternatives, one or both penalizing the person being offered them" (13–14). Her work provides justification for how a long history of sexual stereotyping has connected male traits to intellect and rational faculties and female traits to the heart and emotional capacities and have even established a connection between lower (male) pitch and authority so much so that "female candidates are coached to increase their credibility by lowering their pitch" (121). Yet Jamieson argues that those bipolar opposites "can and usually do characterize the same person" (125). In essence, the "double bind is durable, but not indestructible. Examined as rhetorical frames, double binds can be understood, manipulated, dismantled." (20)

Another study in this regard was undertaken by Robson (2000) who explored how Senator Barbara Mikulski transcended the femininity/competence bind through her negotiation with three stereotypes: orientation toward family, availability, and aggression. Robson analyzed how in the case of Mikulski, "the power of the femininity/competence double bind has diminished as the gendered stereotypes/expectations of women are brought into the public sector and assigned value by female politicians" (219).

The literature on political communication in Asia has not received wide circulation in the West due to the fact that many of the studies have not been translated or have only appeared in regional publications (Willnat and Aw 2008). Further confounding the problem is the unequal volume of scholarship on the region, with nations like China, Hong Kong, Taiwan, Korea, Japan, Singapore, and Indonesia receiving the focus of attention. Willnat and Aw also point out that the "realization that there are important political, social and cultural differences between the West and East should … encourage us to test established media theories in different contexts" as a way to establish their validity (481, 487). In particular, concepts relating to individualism/collectivism, "saving face" (Willnat and Aw 2008) or *sharam* in Pakistani context could open new venues for understanding the dynamics of political communication and gender.

Method

This study uses a multi-method approach. As a first step, I employ textual analysis to understand the gender dynamics of media texts produced under the genre of current affairs television talk shows. The structure of these shows is such that three to four panelists from different political parties are invited to discuss a current political issue. The selected six shows (see Table 7.1) run three to five times a week in different time slots (including prime time) and are faring well in terms of ratings. Women politicians are not as frequently invited as male politicians; therefore, to get an overall understanding of the gender dynamics, a purposive sample of fifty shows featuring the participation of female politicians was collected over a period of one year (May 2012–April 2013). All of the shows were originally aired on commercial television networks, but were accessed through YouTube or Awaz.TV.

Hartley (2003) noted in his account on textual analysis, that "this method for reading literary as well as television text enables one to talk about universal themes in the social imaginary, both public (politics, war, news) and private (sexuality, identity, drama). But at the same time it focuses on very specific features that could be isolated and discussed" (31). Therefore, the researcher's informed act of extracting particular themes out of a media text and reading in

Table 7.1 Sampled current affairs talk shows

Title	Anchor	Channel	Frequency (air time)	Sampled
Off the record with Kashif Abbasi	Kashif Abbasi (m)	ARY News TV	4 (20:05–21:00)	10
Kal Tak (Until Tomorrow)	Javed Chaudry (m)	Express News TV	4 (22:00–23:00)	10
Eleventh Hour with Waseem Badami	Waseem Badami (m)	ARY News TV	4 (23:00–00:00)	10
Ab Tak (Until Today)	Sadaf Abdul Jabbar (f)	ARY News TV	5 (17:00–18:00)	10
Hai Koi Jawab (Do you have any response?)	Nadia Mirza (f)	CNBC	2 (19:05–20:05)	5
Baat Se Baat (Conversation to Conversation)	Maria Zulfiqar (f)	Express News TV	3 (19:05–20:00)	5

Note: The sex of the anchor is listed in parentheses

relation to his/her social disposition is crucial to understanding several attitudes that run in society. Likewise, I have also extracted themes that were useful in reading gender dynamics of talk shows and later used them as the basis for my questions to the talk show hosts. In this way, the use of textual analysis complemented the interview method by providing appropriate interview questions.

The second method incorporates ten in-depth interviews with popular hosts of current affairs talk shows to understand how they view participation of women politicians in their own and other shows, and how these responses resonate with the results of the textual analysis.[1] In understanding the responses of interviewees, Walford (2007) noted:

> [They] will always have subjective perceptions that will be related to their own past experiences and current conditions. At best, interviewees will only give what they are prepared to reveal about their subjective perceptions of events and opinions. These perceptions and opinions will change over time, and according to circumstance. They may be at some considerable distance from "reality" as others might see it. (147)

With this in mind, I approached the anchors with a view that respondents involved in practices of cornering female politicians would not readily acknowledge doing so in their interviews.[2] I also interviewed three popular female anchors to achieve a better understanding of the gender dynamics of this genre. The questions were framed in a way that allowed respondents to distance themselves from the practice while still commenting on such a culture in the industry.

Findings of textual analysis

The textual analysis reveals four noteworthy patterns with regard to understanding the gender dynamics of current affairs talk shows.

The first identified pattern is that female politicians are often *not taken seriously*. This is to suggest that, while female politicians argue for their stance on issues, their competency is questioned in a way that portrays them as unsuitable for politics. Consider, for example, how Shehla Raza (PPP)[3] was cornered by Inamullah Niazi (PTI) on not being able to defend her position concerning her party's stance on restoring the Local Government Act of 1979. He referred to her as an "embarrassment to her party and should therefore be banned from appearing on television." In addition, he not only questioned her suitability for the office of deputy speaker in the province of Sindh, but also picked on her voice saying that it was too masculine. Raza, on the other hand, did not take these remarks personally and continued defending her party's position.

In another show, an argument between Sharmila Farooqi (PPP) and Rtd. General Rashid Qureshi (APML) escalated to a level where Qureshi referred to his opponent as a "pleasant looking lady yet foolish." Farooqi reacted by saying that "the General does not know how to talk to women." A similar situation was faced by Fauzia Wahab in *Kal Tak* when she refused to comment on issues she considered irrelevant to the discussion. As a result, Javed Chaudry, the male host of the show said: "since you don't know anything … you do the easiest bit, tell us how to perfectly boil an egg." Wahab replied to this (smilingly): "I don't know that as well, I am good for nothing, you have made a wrong choice by inviting me." In this context, it is noteworthy that when female politicians refuse to comment on certain issues they are often portrayed as unsuitable for their positions or not having enough knowledge.

Stereotypical attitudes are not new to Pakistani women in politics. In the past, Benazir Bhutto's suitability for the office of prime minister was also challenged on the basis of Muslim law. A *fatwa* (religious pronouncement) was issued stating that "as the prime minister is not the *amir*, who is the head of state (i.e. the president) and who must be a man, but is rather the head of a political party, a woman can hold the office" (Anderson 1993, 55). Anderson also observes that "Experiencing the bind of many women in authority, [Bhutto] was repeatedly subjected to the gender-based charges that she was either too weak or too arrogant" (67). What Benazir faced then still resonates with the realities of women politicians and despite their presence in a mediated public sphere, women politicians still seem to struggle in seeking acceptance as equals.

In an attempt to make their rhetoric effective, women politicians also try to incorporate "masculine" discursive strategies (asserting, getting aggressive, loudness). Women politicians often raise their pitch when they are interrupted again and again. However, in stressing their point, they are reminded of the need to observe *appropriate behavior for their gender*. This is the second pattern identified in the textual analysis and is the most common tactic used by male politicians against female politicians.

In one of the shows the debate on new political alliances took a sharp turn when participants started talking over each other. Abid Sher Ali (PMLN) said to

Sharmila Farooqi (PPP) that: "you should have some decency; you are a woman … She should have some self-respect she is a woman (looking at the host) … you are a stain on women, you should not call yourself a woman." Refusing to get intimidated by the male panelists in this situation, Farooqi instead reminded Sher Ali of the etiquette of talking to women in Pakistani culture. Farooqi's style of rhetoric offers an interesting angle in this regard—she comes across as argumentative and assertive yet retains gender as her shield. Playing on the gender dynamic, some male panelists even challenge the rules of decorum with the suggestion that women politicians do not belong to the same talk shows as male politicians. For example, when Farooqi reminded Mustafa Kamal (MQM) to refer to her with the respect she is entitled to as a woman, he replied to this argument in the following way: "If you are so concerned [about how people should talk to you] then you should only go to talk shows for women only …" to which, in turn, Farooqi replied: "I treat you as my elder brother so talk to me with respect; if I will open my mouth then you will not be able to appear on this channel." In this verbal exchange, Farooqi backfired with similar verbal threats usually reserved for use by her male counterparts, but that made her look out of her character. What is noteworthy here is how gender is used by male politicians as a reminder of the expected norms of behavior by female politicians; women politicians, on the other hand, use it as a shield for respect.

The third pattern identified as part of the textual analysis is that of *intimidating new entrants*. The intimidation approach operates at two levels; the first tactic used against women politicians is to refer to them as *inexperienced/immature*, while the second tactic calls their *sexual honor* into question. Zaeem Qadri (PMLN) responded to Naz Baloch's (PTI) lengthy argument in such a manner: "I have been in politics for thirty years, you were born yesterday … you don't have any manners, ill-mannered woman … go away … send someone else who is more experienced," to which Baloch replied: "Yes you are experienced in corruption; your seniority is in corruption." In another talk show, Sharmila Farooqi was also criticized for her lack of experience in politics by Shahid Masood, an independent political analyst and ex-host of a popular talk show *Meray Mutabiq*, like this: "I know politics since when you were not even born … either you talk sense or just don't talk." Interestingly, both Baloch and Farooqi continue to struggle against this particular bias by getting their viewpoints across in a much louder pitch, thus turning the interaction into a dominance bout.

The second tactic used to intimidate those who are relatively new to the field of politics is that of *questioning their morality/sexual honor*. Such acts are registered by either directly attacking their personal character or through verbal innuendos suggesting that female representatives have used sex to succeed in the field of politics. Those who have experienced such attacks have remained silent on the air or walked out. In a society where honor and morality have great significance, such accusations can undoubtedly tarnish women politicians' credibility and reputation.

The first case in point in this regard is that of Farooqi who was questioned on her morality/honor by Sher Afghan Khan Niazi (APML). Entirely out of context, Niazi said: "Sharmila should feel ashamed. She has become shameless. You [Sharmila] have lost your sexual honor." While Farooqi preferred not to respond to this direct allegation, the host intervened and said that Niazi was getting personal, which was not in line with the rules of debate. However, it has been noticed that hosts have played a limited role in intervening to stop such character assassination of women politicians. Another case that demonstrates the role of the host in such situations is that of Javed Chaudry who did not intervene at the right time to stop the character assassination of Kashmala Tariq in his show. Firdous Ashiq Awan (PPP) took an argument to a level where she implied that Tariq (reserved seat holder) has used unpopular routes to advance in politics. She said, "Firdous Ashiq Awan [referring to herself] did not play bedroom politics to secure a seat in the assembly … [I] did not beg and plead for a seat in the assembly … I am very proud of the fact that I did not enter the realm of politics through *Heera Mandi* (the red-light area)." Firdous Ashiq Awan's rhetorical style was clearly confrontational and offensive. While Tariq initially struggled in responding to such an accusation, she replied: "I am sorry to say that absolutely risqué language is being used in your talk show."

Furthermore, it appears that there is not much difference in how male and female hosts handle such situations. For example, a female host did not take any notice of how Mushahidullah (PMLN) used verbal innuendos to counter Naz Baloch's defensive argument on her party's leadership. Referring to Baloch's party's leader Imran Khan, he said: "I am younger than Imran Khan. You will find me far more [sexually] capable." Baloch preferred to stay silent on this remark. Not reacting to such attacks is deeply rooted in the Pakistani culture of shame that dictates that women should stay silent on such issues. Even defending one's own sexual honor on a public medium can account for being shameless.

The fourth pattern notes that current affairs talk shows do not take up issues of women's rights as a priority topic. Despite the seriousness of such issues in relation to the gender-based violence in Pakistani society, they are not considered an urgent political problem or given attention in the current affairs talk shows. Out of the fifty sampled shows, only one addressed the issue of the importance of a quota for women in the National Assembly and how reserved seats for women can impact gender-based policies. Typically, women politicians are invited to discuss "male" issues such as intra-state politics and policy on war on terror. Yet, given the serious violations of women's rights in Pakistani society, the absence of a discussion on gender-related topics becomes a de facto censorship. The close link between journalism and religion discovered by Pintak and Nazir (2013) can serve to explain why gender-related issues are not high on the agenda of talk shows—such issues are strictly regulated under Shariah and religion therefore taking them up can also suggest taking issue with Islam.

Findings of the interviews

The study was carried further with four major questions extracted from the findings of the textual analysis to seek responses from the hosts of some of the most popular current affairs talk shows. The aim was to explore their understanding of the participation of women politicians in this public space and the role gender plays in it.

Motivations for inviting women politicians

The factors that seem to have influenced the criteria for inviting female politicians include those of being loud, combative, and flippant. All anchors acknowledged that such stereotypes compromise on the quality of debate but at the same time they lure audiences and contribute to higher ratings. Traditionally, all of the above stereotypes have been attached to women, except for aggression, as it is read as a male attribute. One talk show host, Muneeb Farooq, describes his rationale like this: "[those in media] invite women who are a bit flippant with her tongue, or someone who would also corner male counterpart or not let the anchor bully her or she can even give tough time to male anchor or be over loud on the show." Another host, Talat Hussain, notes: "I think they appear tireless … their attitude is such that you listen to me or else I will throw you out … they are combative and uncontrollable."

In this light, women politicians can be viewed as negotiating the traditional gender binds, on one hand, but at the same time reinforcing others by appearing to be flippant and loud or high-pitched. Jamieson (1995) acknowledges this trouble with expectations from women when she argued:

> When women try to establish their competence, they are scrutinized for evidence that they lack masculine (instrumental) characteristics as well as for signs that they no longer possess female (expressive) ones. They are taken to fail, in other words, both as a male and as a female. When women excel at female (expressive) behavior, the significance of their skills is undercut by the fact that these are devalued behaviors. (125)

Although male politicians continue to use aggression against female politicians as an expression of power, when women resort to this tactic they are seen as failing to match the decorum of their gender.

The attitude of anchors towards female politicians

This research traced patterns where talk show hosts were observed as taking women politicians lightly, especially in instances where the heated exchange of arguments has a propensity to go below the belt, allowing the "spectacle" to happen. As Gurevitch and Kavoori (1992, 415) note, "a street spectacle draws a crowd of passers-by. A television spectacle does more, it generates a national audience." There can be two ways of looking at this practice. First, it can be identified as an attempt to create spectacle out of the argument or the participants, and second, it can also reflect the authority hosts have in channeling a discourse. Therefore, this question was directly pursued with the male as well as the female hosts in order to encourage them to identify the pattern of taking female politicians lightly. Even though it is difficult for male anchors to admit such an attitude, this trend was acknowledged by one of them:

> As far as I remember, it was once that I grilled female politician a lot and she almost had tears in her eyes but that was just about exposing her … but it was not intentional that she is a woman … in fact it is usually the male politicians that I get a bit intimidating towards. (Khanzada Shahzaib, Host of *To the Point*)

Evoking professional norms, hosts argue that gender is not relevant when it comes to politics and surely in such platforms it is difficult to draw a line between following the etiquette of talking to a woman in the context of Pakistani society and holding a politician accountable regardless of his/her gender. Male anchors as well as politicians are often seen interrogating women politicians as their fierce rivals in the field while pushing the traditional boundaries of treating women with respect. One of the female hosts, Asma Shirazi, who refused to provide specific names, agreed to the discrimination against female politicians when she said:

> I do feel that male anchors do take female politicians lightly, it can be my personal feeling but that is how I feel. In my show, if there are female panelists, I introduce them in a way so they feel important that they are doing some good work, but I have observed that my male colleagues do not take them seriously.

Similarly, Mazhar Abbas, a senior journalist and host related such occurrences to the overall culture of Pakistan:

> The issue involved here is that of culture … even in abusive language in Urdu, we have references to the female sex rather male; it is a kind of an attitude that is prevalent, downgrading or treating women as inferior … Male domination reflects through all such practices, and it is not just restricted to Pakistan. In media, with female politicians, I wouldn't say that they are invited so they could be easily dominated by the male anchors, and even if there is a deliberate attempt, female members of parties are dominant enough to not let it happen.

Abbas is referring to the trend that some female politicians (usually more experienced in the field) do not seem to get affected by the pressure and stand their ground. However, when young female politicians backfire more aggressively and loudly, their rhetorical style is taken as an opportunity by male hosts and politicians to apply a gender bind and make them look emotional or unprofessional. Discussing the case where politicians are allowed to question the sexual honor of another female politician, the interviewed hosts argued that it is because of the way patriarchal culture operates in Pakistani society. One of the female anchors also pointed out that her male colleagues do not intervene in time to stop such verbal accusations. Referring to the incident described in the previous section where a female politician questioned the sexual honor of her counterpart, a female host, Sana Buchha, responded with the question: "Did you notice how [the male host] was letting it happen and not interfere to stop it?" Though the interviewed female hosts could easily identify such practices, some of them also allowed them on their shows. Clearly, the male hosts were the ones who acknowledged that Pakistani culture is such that it allows discriminatory practices, but refused to accept that there was an intentional bias towards women politicians on the talk shows.

Female politicians' engagement with gender-based issues on talk shows

The presence of women politicians in talk shows is promising in many ways for the process of democratization, but the textual analysis also revealed that gender-based issues are not taken up for discussion in political shows and female politicians are reluctant to comment on these issues. The hosts of the talk shows linked this to the fact that political parties are structurally male-dominated and women fail to transcend their party loyalties in favor of gender-based causes in their TV appearances. Furthermore, the gender-related cases are controversial in the sense that they focus upon the honor of a family and also fall under tribal customs and Shariah. Many of the elected women politicians also belong to families where the patriarchal structure is dominant. Most of the cases of gender abuse are reported by the constituencies of their male colleagues, which makes it even more difficult for women politicians to pursue the issue (and the rights of other women) on talk shows. For instance, Talat Hussain underscores how difficult it is for women politicians to speak on gender-based violence, " … if you ask me why it is not high on agenda on talk shows, frankly, there are not many women who can articulate such issues." Shahzaib Khanzada also points towards the constraints in this direction: "We, the talk show hosts, cannot go there on our own, we need a panel to discuss issues and certainly need a panel of politicians to go with such issues. So if the panel is not complete, it becomes a one-sided show."

This particular line of inquiry opens up many questions in relation to the participation of women in the mediated public sphere. For instance, it speaks to the fact that unlike many examples of the engagement of women politicians with "soft" areas of politics (health, education, childcare), the political culture of Pakistan allows them to speak on mainstream political talk shows about the economy and foreign policy, but it does not allow them to speak openly on issues that can alter the patriarchal structure of society. For instance, Mazhar Abbas, deputy director of ARY News TV, argues that while women politicians are actively participating in mainstream politics they are still unable to touch the real issues related to female voters in their own constituencies: "I think on talk shows these women have to protect their party's interest than further women issues."

It can be argued that women may be representing their party positions on issues raised in talk shows but not representing women's issues, to which they seem otherwise committed in the Women's Caucus. In his interview, Abbas also raised the point that Pakistani society is living under a state of heightened fear where issues such as women's rights are considered controversial and can risk one being branded as Western or liberal. Therefore, anchors and politicians refrain from speaking openly about them. Besides, women are also not so powerful within the parties at the decision-making level to make such issues a priority, therefore mainstream media (and hence talk shows) happen to cover what is popular and high on the agenda within the parties. The interviewees in this study acknowledged that there are women parliamentarians who transcend the party differences among their folk and stand united to promote policies in favor of women's empowerment within the parliament, but face challenges while moving legislation in a male-dominated House.

Conclusion

This chapter attempted to offer an insight into how women politicians in Pakistan negotiate the gender binds in the mediated public sphere and how this negotiation is understood by the hosts of the talk shows. The findings of the textual analysis have identified four p patterns in participation. First, women politicians are not taken seriously and their knowledge and competence is questioned; second, if they try to assert their position, they are reminded of the appropriate behavior for their gender, yet they use gender as a shield as well; third, young female politicians are intimidated at two levels—calling them inexperienced or questioning their sexual morality; fourth, talk shows do not cover gender-based issues. The findings of the in-depth interviews reveal that the male hosts do not take women politicians seriously either and often allow the "spectacle to happen." Although the hosts in my sample did not openly admit to any practices of gender bias against the female politicians on their own shows, they linked such practices to the cultural values and social injustices in Pakistan. In terms of issues, it seems all current affairs talk shows follow closely the top issues on the government agenda while gender-based issues are non-existent. This trend was directly linked by the hosts to the status of women politicians as unequal participants in the political arena.

This study demonstrates that women politicians use multiple strategies to get their message across. They can adopt an aggressive, loud or expressive style, which in turn, is used against them to make them appear inexperienced, emotional, and foolish. They also prefer not to respond to questions raised about sexual morality as this is deeply rooted in the tradition of shame. It is also noticed that although women politicians have moved legislative bills in the House, they are unable to represent a voice in defense of gender-based issues on talk shows. As Lovenduski (1993) points out, "In democratic societies, the representation of a group's interests has two dimensions: the presence of its members in decision-making arenas and the consideration of its interests in the decision-making process" (2). In the scenario of Pakistani politics, policy-making on gender-based issues may not have alienated the women representatives' contribution to it, but the male predominance has led to "distorted policy implementation" (to use Lovenduski's phrase).

Although this study has only aimed to identify the rhetorical styles of women politicians rather than critically analyze them in detail, it is important to note how women abstain from using specific feminine qualities such as nurture and care, and how they selectively use masculine strategies such as being assertive and aggressive to prove their toughness. Given the rigid gender expectations within Pakistani society, women politicians find ways to broaden the range of "acceptable" behaviors. It also suggests that trends are changing and there are more opportunities for women in terms of their participation in the political and mediated spheres. In this sense, Pakistan offers a unique case where women politicians are invited to discuss matters of mainstream politics (mainly intra-state politics and policies on war on terror). Yet the general belief is that women politicians are high-pitched and emotional, and often are unable to articulate issues at the same level as their male counterparts. The hope is that this preliminary research in the area of gender and political communication in South Asia and Pakistan in particular is contributing to an expanded understanding of the power asymmetries of gender.

Notes

1 In total, 17 interviews were conducted, 12 with hosts and five with women politicians. Due to space limitations, I am unable to use the politician interviews here but they have significantly informed this study.

2 The length of each interview varied from 40 minutes to more than an hour at times, where several dynamics of the talk shows were discussed with particular emphases on a set of questions crucial for this study. The selection of the hosts was determined through the popularity of their shows and also their availability for the interview.

3 Party abbreviations are as follows: Pakistan People's Party (PPP), Pakistan Tehreek-e-Insaf (PTI), All Pakistan Muslim League (APML), Pakistan Muslim League Nawaz (PMLN), Muttahida Qaumi Movement (MQM).

8

Between Two Democratic Ideals: Gendering in the Russian Culture of Political Journalism

Liudmila Voronova

> *In Russia this [women in politics] is, well, not exotic, but something uncommon. The society, well, probably is not yet ready to perceive women politicians seriously and view them as professionals. In Russia when women politicians are talked about, two images occur: either somewhat marginal persons, or people who came to politics either just out of interest, or to reach their somewhat selfish goals, but not seriously dealing with it, not doing it professionally [...] So media confess to the same position, and do not yet take women politicians seriously.*
>
> International reporter, *Kommersant*

Introduction

After a 20-year period of transition, Russian media and political culture have achieved stability and established new political practices (Vartanova 2013). However, the complex process of transformation of the media system was not linear (Vartanova 2009), and today's Russian "government-commercialized" media model is characterized by the traditionally strong interconnection between the Russian media and the authorities, where "the media still has the role of an 'obedient child'" (Vartanova 2013, 109, *translation by author*).

In the process of transition, gender power hierarchies were shifting as well, raising the question of whether the changes can be considered fully democratic[1] (Azhgikhina 2006, 2008). Today, according to the Global Gender Gap Report, Russia ranks in 94th place (out of 135 countries) when it comes to the political empowerment of women (Hausmann, Tyson, Bekhouche, and Zahidi 2013), with 13.6 percent of women parliamentarians in the lower chamber, and 8 percent in the upper (Inter-Parliamentary Union 2013). The representation of women in high-ranking political posts is remarkably low: one female deputy prime minister (out of 8) and one federal minister (out of 21) (Russian Federal Government 2013), and only three women governors (out of 83) (Russian Federal Subjects 2013).

According to Russian political scholars, political power remains as one of the most impermeable "ceilings" for women (Zdravomyslova 2003). First, this phenomenon is explained by the fact that power, and financial and administrative resources are concentrated mainly in the hands of men (Gorshkov and Tikhonova 2002). Second, political appointments and recruitments are made from spheres, exclusively or predominantly occupied by men (Kochkina 2004). Third, according to politicians from both sexes, the partnership between women and men in politics is almost impossible due to the "naturally" built gender borders that exist along the same line as holding political power (Zdravomyslova 2003).

Media scholars relate the political participation of women, and voter recognition of female candidates, not only to political factors, but also to the quantity and quality of media representations women politicians receive (Falk 2008; Ross 2002), which is furthermore connected to the fact that media reflect and reshape our perceptions of selves and others, and function as a social technology of gender (Gamble and Gamble 2002; van Zoonen 1994). Scholars from all over the world have demonstrated that women politicians are poorly represented in media discourses, and when they do appear in the media content, they are rarely treated in the same way as their male counterparts: their gender is spotlighted, their private lives and appearance become the main focus of the stories, they are shown as unnatural and incompetent actors of the political process, which constitutes a problem for democratic developments in any country (Braden 1996; Falk 2008; Global Media Monitoring Project 2010; Kahn 1996; Norris 1997; Ross 2002; Ross and Byerly 2004; Sreberny-Mohammadi and van Zoonen 2000).

Together these patterns have been studied as "gendered mediation" or gendered framing (Gidengil and Everitt 1999). In this chapter gendered mediation will be referred to as "*gendering*," with an emphasis on the process of production of a complex set of media constructions. It should be noted, that while usually gendering is defined by scholars more narrowly as an emphasis on a person's gender when it is not of a specific relevance to the context (Devere and Davies 2006; Kroon Lundell and Ekström 2008), in this chapter I use the term as a broader concept, including both spotlighting of gender and gender stereotyping.

Research on gender in Russia has shown that women are seldom covered as active participants in political life (and when they are, they are discussed as voters rather than as politicians). Moreover, the problem of gender inequality in the political sphere is rarely raised in journalistic articles (Vartanova, Smirnova, and Frolova 2012). Hate speech, proverbs of sexist character, and gendered asymmetry of lexical and grammatical forms accompany women politicians' media portrayals (Smirnova 2010). Even the quality press (re)produces common myths about women in politics (Voronova 2011).

Western researchers have offered different theoretical explanations as to why women politicians' media representations are such. Among potential reasons, those related to the media industry dominate: its logic (viewing the journalism mission in reflecting and not shaping the societal trends, profit orientation), its structure and organization (domination of men at the top levels of the media companies and in the elite journalism units, lack of regulatory norms concerning gender balance in media content), and characteristics and background of content producers (gender socialization of journalists, their unawareness of their own cultural assumptions leading to unconscious use of gender stereotypes, lack of gender education and training) (Braden 1996; Byerly and Ross 2006; Falk 2008; Norris 1997; Ross 2002; Sreberny-Mohammadi and van Zoonen 2000). Whatever the reasons, the lasting observation is that "there is a necessary interdependence, since journalists need copy and politicians need exposure" (Ross 2010, 273).

Within the Russian context, Azhgikhina (2006) states that the reason for the imbalanced representation of female and male politicians in the Russian media is due to the "post-socialist patriarchate renaissance," and the unpreparedness of journalists to adequately address the significance of women's enhanced representation in the political sphere.

Despite the fact that political journalists are identified by scholars as the key "party at fault" as far as gendering of women politicians in the media discourse is concerned, they have remained silent subjects in the field of political communication. In particular, research examining the views of political journalists regarding the coverage of women politicians in the context of postsocialist Russian society is nonexistent. This chapter aims to close this gap by shedding light on the attitudes of Russian journalists toward the process of media production and representation of women politicians. It seeks to answer the following questions: How does the culture of political journalism influence gendering of women politicians? And what makes the Russian culture of political journalism unique when it comes to the coverage women politicians get?

Method

In December 2011, semi-structured face-to-face interviews were conducted with 21 political and international reporters and editors working for the newspapers *Kommersant*, *Novye izvestiya*, and *Moskovskie novosti*, and magazines *Kommersant. Vlast'*, the *New Times/Novoe Vremya*,[2] and *Forbes* (Russian edition) (see Table 8.1). The sampling method used a snowball technique, where once a journalist was contacted at a publication he/she was asked to identify other colleagues who might be interested in participating. All the interviewees were working journalists who, at the time, were actively involved in the process of news production.

The sampled media organizations are referred to as "quality" press and considered to be among the most influential actors of political communication. According to Resnyanskaya (2007), a medium's belonging to the "quality" or the "mass" category depends on the standards of informational behavior: reliability of facts, competence of experts, pluralism of opinions, argumentation of viewpoints, and deliberateness of critical evaluations, as well as non-engagement and non-bias. It makes quality media "the best space for the public dialogue" (Resnyanskaya 2007, 83). These high circulation publications are reaching a great number of politically active potential voters in Russia (Table 8.1), thus, becoming influential intermediaries in the process of what voters learn about politicians (Ross 2010).

The study applies an ethnographic approach that focuses on how journalists perceive the coverage of women politicians in the quality press and how they explain their production practices. The interviewees were viewed as "inhabitants" of journalism culture in Russia (Hanitzsch 2007; Nygren 2012). The empirical data was the starting point in the analysis. The data was sorted into categories, and labeled theoretically. Journalists' interpretations of women politicians' media coverage were placed in a structural framework of analysis, comprised of the components of journalism culture: ideas (political journalists' vision of the world and politics), practices (daily routines including interaction with politicians), and ideals (journalists' beliefs about their societal role in relation to external power and audiences, and professional ethics) (Hanitzsch 2007).

The interviewees in this chapter are anonymous, which was one of the conditions for granting an interview, yet the journalists' job title and affiliation are provided. The mentioned titles were valid for the time of the interview. The interviewees' gender is mentioned only where it is relevant to the analysis (as long as the subjective perceptions of the political actors are concerned). All the interviews were conducted in Russian and excerpts from them were translated by the author.

The chapter first addresses media producers' interpretations of the low number of women politicians in media content. It then turns to journalists' reasoning behind the different types of gendering that occurs. The chapter further highlights the contradictions between the ideas, practices, and ideals present in the journalism culture of the "quality" press in Russia. The concluding part discusses how media producers envision the future of media representation of women politicians and how this relates to the problem of gender inequality in the political realm.

Table 8.1 Number of interviewees from each publication, with information on circulation and years of publication

Title of publication	Number of interviewees			Type of publication	Circulation (number of copies)	Launched (year)
	Total	**Female**	**Male**			
Kommersant and *Kommersant. Vlast'*	9	1	8	United newsroom for the daily newspaper *Kommersant* and weekly magazine *Kommersant. Vlast'*	120,000 60,000	1992 1997
Novye izvestiya	5	3	2	Daily newspaper	108,200	1997
Moskovskie novosti	1	1	0	Newspaper. 3 times a week, plus a weekly supplement	30,000 (weekly supplement 100,000)	1930/2011
The *New Times*	4	1	3	Weekly magazine	50,000	1943/2007
Forbes	2	1	1	Monthly magazine	105,000	2004

Source: The circulation is provided by the Media Atlas (2013) http://www.media-atlas.ru/editions/?a=srch&reset=1

"Just as many as in real life": Absent women in the "fair media mirror"

According to the interviewees, the main explanation for the little attention political journalism pays to women politicians is their low representation in Russian politics and the fact that they "hold such positions, where their deals are rarely covered":

> Everything depends on the number. Earlier when Khakamada[3] was active, she was covered constantly, [media] sometimes even picked up her suggestions, initiatives! Here [in Russia], yes, everything is connected to the fact that we really have very few deedful women … So it doesn't depend on the media, media would write about them with pleasure if there were more of them. (Political reporter, *Novye izvestiya*)

Journalists constantly frame their role in producing women politicians' media representations through the restrictions imposed on them by the profession and voice their understanding of media's role simply as a reflection of society. This view emerges as one of the main justifications for the absence of women politicians in the media, and corresponds to theoretical discussions on the reflection ideal (see e.g. Graber 2005), extensively criticized in the gender and media research (e.g. Gill 2007; Ross 2002).

> I cannot imagine that at the level of the chief editor someone would say: "And now we write about women! 40 percent about these, 60 percent about those." You see, we [media] are a reflection of society. Not that we are tied to the chariot, but to a certain extent we pick up the societal trend. Probably we are the first ones to do it, but [the trend] is first born in the society, and then goes to the media. (Political reporter, *Forbes*)

Yet some journalists do not see the absence of women politicians as something "the society suffers from," or as an acute problem in the Russian context, given the existence of more pressing economic or political issues. However, other journalists express regret about the lack of active and charismatic women politicians. This regret is often connected to their overall evaluation of the democratic development of Russian society. Recalling the Russian feminist motto of the 1990s that "Democracy without Women is No Democracy," they think that the absence of women from today's politics can characterize Russia's political culture as an "exclusive club," to which women have very few chances to access, even if they have the potential and aspiration to be politicians. However, journalists emphasize that the problem is not only gender-related; the established rules do not allow access to the political sphere for "outsiders" in general:

> How can women get into politics? The political sphere is blocked from the start. There is a filter, all this "United Russia," where they share everything among themselves, so it is not a healthy democratic environment where everyone can compete on equal terms, but something like this, a strange quasi-scheme ... It is very difficult to get there from the street, if you want to uphold interests, if you try to make a political career. Who will take Chirikova to the Duma? No one! Though she is a good candidate. (Political reporter, *Novye izvestiya*)

The reference to Chirikova, who is an oppositional politician, suggests that journalists do not believe that the political sphere in Russia is open to all political actors, given the dominance of the United Russia party that holds the majority of seats in Russian parliament—the State Duma. "Outsiders" are excluded from official politics, which also restricts the access of many women who represent views that are oppositional to the dominant political discourse. Other journalists, however, claim that politicians' gender doesn't matter at all. Instead, they adopt an antagonistic approach to all politicians that expresses their disenchantment with the overall political process. Their lack of hope for meaningful changes within the entrenched political culture of Russia is evident in the following statement:

> [Women politicians] are the same corrupted, mainly unpleasant people. [... Politicians] are small screws in the wheels of the state, in the corrupt machinery, who are genderless in that sense. (Co-editor of international department, *Kommersant*)

In general, journalists acknowledge the absence of women in politics and use it as an explanation for their absence in media content. While some suggest that women in politics would make a difference if there were more of them, others claim that politics has no gender dimension in the context of Russia's political culture. But what happens when the few women politicians *are* covered by the media?

Gendering to contextualize, personalize and pep up: When women politicians' gender becomes important

According to the interviewees, it is the standards of quality journalism that play a key role in defining what women politicians' media coverage should be like. They emphasize that it is not the norms, but rather the culture of quality political journalism, with its roots in the 1990s, when a new type of journalism was launched, that defines the main values that journalists uphold—verification, neutrality, objectivity, and accuracy. These standards and values require that it is politicians' actions, programs, and strategies that should be the major focus of political journalism, and not their gender. These standards also set apart "quality" journalism from tabloid journalism. In the words of one interviewee:

> Quality journalism is a genderless journalism … For some reason, evaluative stuff—things concerning gender, emotional characteristics—are not popular. Well, they are all there—but in the tabloids. (Political reporter, *Forbes*)

Despite the claim that gender neutrality is "an indicator of quality, maturity and respect towards the audience" (international observer, *Kommersant*), journalists acknowledge that "gendering" exists even within the "quality" press. Still grounded in the standards of quality political journalism, some journalists do not see gendering in a negative light but rather as a newsworthy practice, especially when linked to exceptional and extraordinary achievements. For example, journalists state that the gender of politicians may be spotlighted when it is defined and justified as a true breakthrough for women in the context of post-Soviet politics:

> When it comes to Roza Otunbaeva, I think, I mentioned that she is the first woman president [of Kyrgyzstan], as this is really important for the region, the country, the political culture, in which there is a total masculine domination, and emergence of a female chief executive is indeed an important case, which is worth at least mentioning. (Co-editor of international department, *Kommersant*)

Another challenge for "genderless" political journalism is the trend toward personalization, which did not skip the Russian "quality" press. As journalists acknowledge, political coverage is less and less about figures and facts, and more and more about the personalities of politicians. Gender is an important characteristic of a politician as a person, and many journalists agree that the spotlighting of gender among other personal characteristics (whether belonging to a female or a male politician) in an article can pep up political journalism as a genre:

> Quality journalism doesn't have to be boring ... It is important to pep up. For example, when we write about elections in a country, there are two candidates winning, so we try to find something to catch hold of. We cover not just their programs, like, "Danish right—Danish left," which is not so interesting to us. In this case, being a woman is something to catch hold of. Here it is a woman, but it could be a former Olympic champion, or a football-player who came into politics. Something that stands out and thus attracts somewhat bigger attention. (International observer, *Kommersant*)

Some journalists justify the tendency toward personalization of women politicians in the media in terms of their novelty or "uncommon" status: being so few in the political domain, women politicians "strike journalists' eyes," as one of the deputy editors at the *Kommersant* pointed out. Others link the trend of personalization of politics to its feminization,[4] and, thus, suggest paying closer attention to women politicians' personalities (and, accordingly, to their gender):

> As women are significantly fewer [than men] in politics, it is not unusual that they tend to do everything in their own way, and, thus, it is important for us to show their personal qualities. A woman who comes to politics, who rises to prominence in politics, is a priori a big person. It is twenty men per each such woman, even in contemporary politics. Accordingly, we put a stress on women's personal features. (Editor of international department, the *New Times*)

On the other hand, some journalists believe that the personalization of politicians is strongly linked to the tabloidization of quality journalism, and this becomes especially evident in women politicians' coverage:

> Probably there are more "yellow" materials about women: for example, about their clothes, jewelry. Women are probably more exposed in terms of the details and tastes than men. Well, a man has his suit and watches, and a woman always has a certain image. This raises interest, and is often discussed. [For example,] Matvienko's innumerable furs were discussed, all these crazy jewels, hairstyles. Also about Lyubov Sliska there is always information that she spends most of her working time at the hairdresser. Yeah, these things appear more often about women than men. (Political reporter, the *New Times*)

Thus, journalists acknowledge that, even in quality political journalism, politicians' portrayals may become gendered, and that it happens more often when women politicians are concerned. Often framed as exceptional, the gendering of women politicians that is aimed at contextualization, personalization, or "pepping-up," nevertheless, is perceived by journalists as something natural, as, according to journalists, women politicians "provide" more material for gendering.

Gendering as a critical tool and an instrument of promotion

From the interviews it also became obvious that most of the journalists are well aware of media's (i.e. their own) power in the political process. In this sense, media's gendering of women politicians is a double-edged sword in that it can be constructed either as a tool for degrading women politicians or for benefiting their platforms. That means that the process of gendering of women politicians pursues certain journalistic objectives, and is not done out of ignorance. Journalists are well aware of the power of gendered media portrayals of politicians that they hold in their hands and of the different means of gendering that can be applied to cast a female (or a male) politician in a negative light:

> Note that if you want a woman to get bad press, you show her as a fright, if you want a man to get bad press, you show him as an idiot. (Head of the foreign information group, *Kommersant*)

The application of this power, however, is restricted by the institutional and personal journalistic ethics. One of the journalists I interviewed told me a story about a situation that she observed and discussed with her colleague, who, in her opinion, applied a dishonest method of stereotyping in order to achieve his journalistic goal of criticizing a foreign politician "between the lines":

> I know that my colleague from another big media—when Clinton was presenting in Vilnius about the OSCE [Organization for Security and Co-operation in Europe] and she strictly said that our elections are unfair and unjust—wrote something like "Hillary Clinton with her thin pony-tail" ... By introducing her quotation in this way he clearly disavows everything she said. Because it already doesn't matter what she said, does it? Even if she would say the very truth, this "thin pony-tail," is an image, which trumps all the rest. (International reporter, *Kommersant*)

Journalists also acknowledged that spotlighting of gender as such—a discussion of women politicians in terms of their "womanhood"—is another common tool for implicit critique against women politicians who are not perceived as independent political actors, but rather as transmitters of dominant political views.

> When now actress Mariya Kozhevnikova was elected to the Duma, then it raised the question: what is she doing there? And, of course, immediately her pictures in *Playboy* were laid out. But that is not an attitude of "there should be no women" [in politics]. This is a reaction to very particular strange people [who enter the political process]. (Editor of political department, *Kommersant*)

Paradoxically, the essentialist vision of women as "different," "essentially other," in the Russian context can lead not only to bad press, but also bring alleged benefits. Some journalists view women politicians as different in a positive way, and they suggest that gendering can be a tool for promoting both particular women politicians as well as the idea of gender equality in general. Some of the journalists suggested that when it comes to women politicians, the working principle is to be more friendly, more subjective, "to have compassion and mercy," and that "when it comes to women politicians, the objective approach is often sacrificed, because they are a weaker sex, because there is a need to be more considerate" (editor of international department, the *New Times*). Given the specific political and cultural context of Russia, some journalists even believe that the gendering of women politicians has the benefit of drawing the attention of audiences to feminist issues and thus promoting "more progressive" values. The end result, according to some interviewees, is making women more visible as political actors:

> In Russia, the society is quite conservative and patriarchal; it is still far from the Western tradition. Feminism has not yet come to Russia, and hardly will in the nearest future. So here it is often possible to see even contemptuous assessments, because representation of women in the organs of power and so on is inferior to the figures in the West. Thus, the society doesn't yet react in the right way. We, in the magazine, try not to skip, but, on the contrary, draw attention—if in a certain country a woman first becomes the leader of the country, we write about it indispensably. (Editor of international department, the *New Times*).

Overall, Russian journalists are well aware that gendering not only exists, but also that it may be not at all neutral. They acknowledge the power of critical gendering, and illustrate how spotlighting of gender or stereotyping can be used as critical tools against politicians. In the context of Russian political journalism, gendering can be also used to promote women politicians and the idea of gender balance in the political sphere. This approach is paradoxically built on journalists' essentialist view that women are different and therefore they require "more sympathy" from them.

Does the reporter's gender matter?

Some scholars have observed that increased presence of women in the journalistic profession could provide the opportunity to approach the coverage of women politicians differently (Norris 1997; Ross 2002). Yet among the interviewed journalists there were twice as many men as women (see Table 8.1), which is a reflection of the overall gender representation of reporters in the political and international press departments in the national media in Russia. Even though the general level of representation of women in the journalistic profession across the country reaches 80 percent (Azhgikhina 2006), or 64.9 percent among reporters and editors, and 58.5 percent in the top levels of management (Global Report on the Status of Women in the News Media 2011), men still dominate in political and international news departments.

From the interviews it becomes apparent that the presence of female journalists does not help with the existing gender imbalance in the quality press (as it has been discussed in previous research—see e.g. Braden 1996; Ross 2002). There is no gender solidarity established between female journalists and female politicians. Both female and male journalists often find it more convenient to interact with male politicians, and describe women in politics as "reticent" and "incomprehensible."

Moreover, internalized gender expectations seem to define to a large extent the interaction between journalists and politicians. Male correspondents stated that it is easier for them to interact with male politicians as they speak "the same language," while communicating with a woman implies that "you have to do it gracefully, you need to do your best" (political reporter, male, *Kommersant*). Female correspondents suggested that their communication with male politicians is more efficient because they can "play on these absolutely psychological tricks, like, you smile, look blank, play silly girl, so that they explain better" (political reporter, female, the *New Times*), thus relying on entrenched gender stereotypes. Yet a certain barrier exists when female reporters try to communicate with women in power:

> Men find it easier to work with women, and vice versa. It's easier to establish contact. I will give an example. The president's press-secretary is a woman, Natalya Timakova. So she has a much better relationship with male journalists than with female journalists in most of cases. It is on her side, so to say, a preference, and we feel a certain barrier in communication. We understand that she will tell and show everything we need, but anyway in communication she will prefer [men] … I at least find it much easier to communicate with male news-makers. It's good that there are more of them! (Political reporter, female, *Novye izvestiya*)

Female journalists do not reflect much upon their negative perceptions of communicating with women politicians. However, they try to be extra cautious when it comes to expressing their positive attitudes, keeping their sympathetic feeling under control in order to avoid breaking the rules of the "game" or getting "carried away."

> I think, when I was writing such materials I always thought: I need to keep to a certain degree of objectivity because I am a woman! But it wasn't so easy to keep to it: I also have this bias "Women can! Women rule!" as I share this view. (Political reporter, female, *Novye izvestiya*)

It appears that journalists from both genders perceive male politicians as more favorable subjects to communicate with, while women politicians seem reticent and less open to dialogue with the media. It is rather this overall subjective perception of women politicians, than the number of female political journalists, that, to a big extent, defines the interaction between Russian journalists and politicians.

The contradictory culture of Russian political journalism

If we summarize journalists' views of how media represent women politicians in Russia, we can see that in many ways the reasons for the low visibility of women politicians in the press, for the gendering of their portrayals, manifested both in spotlighting of gender and in stereotyping, align with existing media theories. Many journalists insist that their mission is to reflect the world and not to shape it, and that they cannot avoid being dependent on the news peg, leading them to write about the existing "reality." In addition, they perceive gender problems as not yet relevant to Russia's political journalism and justify their lack of attention to the issue of gender imbalance in the political sphere through the news value of newsworthiness—other issues seem more pressing, and therefore worth covering in the current state of affairs in Russia. Furthermore, gendering is not directly restricted by media norms and journalistic ethics, and consequently, some journalists might not see the gendering of women politicians as problematic.

However, there is another, more unexpected side, to journalists' attitudes towards the highly gendered media representations of women politicians and the production of these representations. While academics often claim that journalists are too dependent on their own socialization and cultural background and that they are unprepared to adequately perceive new tendencies (Azhgikhina 2006; Braden 1996), it occurs that the vast majority of journalists think of themselves as the avant-garde of society and explicitly welcome women politicians, both in politics and in media discourses, even if they continue to prefer male politicians as communication partners.

Similarly, it appears that the majority of Russian political journalists working for the quality media are gender-aware and value objectivity and neutrality. Paradoxically, this doesn't mean that they never spotlight women politicians' gender, or never apply gender stereotypes in their coverage. What it demonstrates is that the media producers are aware of the power they have and usually make conscious choices between the different types of gendering they employ.

Media representations of politicians have a very particular influence both on voter recognition of female and male candidates, and political participation of women and men (Falk 2008; Ross 2002). If the "quality" press, being an influential sector of the Russian media, contributes to the gendering of women politicians, it is possible to conclude that we observe what Sreberny-Mohammadi and Ross (1996) label "double gendering at work," a situation where both the representational politics and the media coverage have gendered nature, contributing to the marginalization of women politicians as the "outsiders" to the system.

Future of women politicians' media coverage in Russia: Between two democratic ideals

What makes the Russian culture of political journalism unique is the contradiction between the idealized vision of "quality" political journalism as "gender-less," and the simultaneous impossibility to avoid gendering, fulfilling various functions—reflection, contextualization, "pepping-up," and critique among them. This contradiction, representing a crucial challenge for the balanced and gender-neutral representation of women politicians, can be explained with the gap between two democratic ideals.

The first of the democratic ideals concerns the openness of the political sphere. Despite some scholars' evaluation of the current political situation as stable (Vartanova 2013), journalists in Russia believe that the political system should change and become more open to different views and people. Even if gender is not the most important political factor, women could make a difference at least in connection with the features society ascribes to them. Journalists hope that Russian society will soon acknowledge women as crucial political actors and that the increasing number of women politicians will lead to more visibility and active involvement, including in their interaction with journalists.

Another democratic ideal that political journalists value even more is the freedom of expression. The choice of critical tools to question the political decisions and efficiency of particular political personalities, according to this study's respondents, should remain free and unrestricted. Gendering of politicians occurs among these critical tools and since it most often affects female, not male politicians, women become the main object of this gendered critique. However, journalists consistently oppose any new guidelines, standards, or requirements that would regulate this part of their job. This has been strongly criticized by scholars, who claim that the gendering of women politicians in the media is often related to the gaps in the normative and ethical framework (see Voronina 1998). The reason why journalists react negatively to such suggestions is that they view any intervention into their culture as a potential threat to the democratic freedom of speech. As one respondent argued, "because if [gendering] is regulated, then the reader will immediately understand that this all [regulation] is handed down" (political reporter, *Novye izvestiya*).

These two democratic ideals—one concerning the openness of the political sphere, and another one—the freedom of journalistic expression—clash when it comes to the coverage of women politicians. As long as journalists apply gendering as one of the tools of critiquing the political sphere, this sphere will not be promoted and shaped as a space open for women. The changes, as it was suggested by one of the interviewees, can be initiated only within the journalists' community itself, when gendering is acknowledged as a problem and when this pattern begins to change, supported by a "very mandatory agreement that we should all work in this direction, concluded by the heads of the media—and I emphasize, not the owners, but the heads—the editors-in-chief" (head of the foreign information group, *Kommersant*). In this case, there is hope that the two democratic ideals will overlap—and gender balance in the political realm and political journalism alike can be achieved.

Notes

1 The famous motto of the Russian feminist activists of the 1990s was "Democracy without Women is No Democracy" (see Cockburn 1991).

2 The *New Times* is a Russian magazine, which previously had a title in Russian—*Novoe vremya* (*The New Time*).

3 A list of women politicians, as they appear in the course of the text:

- Khakamada, Irina—a Russian Parliament (Duma) representative in 1993–2003 and one of the leaders of the Union of Rightist Forces. In 2004 she ran in the presidential election, where she received 3.9 percent of votes.
- Chirikova, Evgeniya—a Russian political activist, member of the oppositional Coordination Council. Became well-known for her participation in the protests of the eco-movements defending the Khimki forest in the Moscow region.
- Otunbaeva, Roza—the President of Kyrgyzstan in 2010–11.
- Matvienko, Valentina—the Chairwoman of the Russian Federation Council since 2011. In 2003–11 the Governor of Saint Petersburg.
- Sliska, Lyubov—the First Deputy Chairwoman of the Duma in 2000–7, and a Deputy Chairwoman in 2007–11.
- Clinton, Hillary—in 2009–13 the United States Secretary of State. In 2001–9 the U.S. Senator from New York. A leading candidate for the Democratic Presidential nomination in 2008.
- Kozhevnikova, Mariya—an actress, and a Duma representative since 2011.
- Timakova, Natalya—the Press Attaché to the Russian President Dmitry Medvedev in 2008–12. Since 2012 she has been the Press Attaché to the Prime Minister.

4 Van Zoonen (2003) suggests that today's politics is compared to "soap opera" in the media with its focus on the private sphere, emotions, and conversation. In turn, when political problems are framed as a "soap opera" by the media, politics receives an accusation of feminization.

9

Becoming Less Gendered: A Comparison of (Inter)National Press Coverage of First Female Government Heads Who Win Again at the Polls

Tania Cantrell Rosas-Moreno and Ingrid Bachmann

As of 2013, only 19 female world leaders were in power, with 17 having been voted into office during their latest elections (McCullough 2013). This is not surprising, since women struggle to break into politics, let alone climb up the political ladder, due to gender-based media resistance they can encounter when going beyond their usual political roles. Yet, in the last three years, German, Liberian, and Chilean voters have elected women as their government heads *again*. In fact, in Germany, Chancellor Angela Merkel, from former East Germany, won her third successive election in September 2013. She currently stands to eclipse Margaret Thatcher as Europe's longest serving elected female government head. These events offer a timely opportunity to study *re*-elected female leadership within the dynamic, traditionally male public sphere.

Considering how news media portray elected women is critical, since their representation affects how public women are viewed. Printed media remain decision-makers' medium of choice, so their portrayal of public women can influence how the elite think about and interact with female leaders (Heldman, Carroll, and Olson 2005). How the elite interact with female leaders relates with how others within society react to their leadership (Hoogensen and Solheim 2006).

This tri-continental comparative analysis replicates Cantrell and Bachmann's 2008 study, addressing (inter)national news framing of German, Liberian, and Chilean *re*-elected female firsts during the time periods of their second elections, which were 2009, 2011, and 2013, respectively. Comparing first and second election coverage, it deciphers manifest and latent news content differences about female leadership in a global traditionally patriarchal system, teasing out media messages surrounding government heads within culturally and developmentally diverse nations. Comparative research, according to

Blumler and Gurevitch (1995), serves as an antidote to unintended narrowness, enforcing awareness of other systems. It also helps to understand news story normalization and routinization.

Gendered mediation refers to politics being covered largely as a male domain. Because these nations already have elected a female to a nation's most important office, and each leader led a fairly successful presidency with high approval ratings, we assume that the gendered mediation would have decreased over time. This could lead to a more gender-neutral approach to (inter)nationalistic covering of politics. This is not to argue that gender bias would completely disappear. Rather, the likelihood of bias and stereotypes suggesting that women do not belong in politics would decrease when former female state heads run for a second term in office and win.

In sum, Eastern/Western, Northern/Southern, First-/Third-World (inter) national news coverage of Angela Merkel in Germany, Michele Bachelet in Chile and Ellen Johnson-Sirleaf in Liberia in each leader's (inter)national newspaper of record is quantitatively and qualitatively analyzed. While most leadership comparisons are male–female, this woman-to-woman, second-election comparison enriches the female leadership discussion, particularly among diverse political and electoral systems, media systems and cultures.

The intersection between gender and politics

Despite evidence of increasing gender equality in political affairs (e.g. Inglehart and Norris 2003), throughout history women have had a hard time engaging in the world of politics, policy, and authority (e.g. Ross 2002). Media portray gender as a hindrance for those females trying to climb up the political ladder—rather than as an asset or a neutral trait (Ross 2002; 2004)—and research suggests women encounter some media resistance when they run within the masculinized domain of politics (Byerly and Ross 2006; Devere and Davies 2006; Falk 2008; Gidengil and Everitt 2003; Loke, Harp, and Bachmann 2011; Ross 2009).

For instance, the news coverage women politicians and leaders receive tends to be highly stereotypical, and news reports usually trivialize female candidates and officials (Byerly and Ross 2006; Devitt 2002; Niven and Zilber 2001; Ross 2009). Women in politics receive less coverage, are more likely than men to be paraphrased instead of quoted, and their platforms are usually second- or third-tier material, whereas their family issues, sartorial style, and personality traits are given high prominence (Bachmann and Correa 2013; Cantrell and Bachmann 2008; Devitt 2002; Heldman, Carroll and Olson 2005; Loke, Harp and Bachmann 2011).

As the media consistently treat women in politics qualitatively and quantitatively different than men, evidence shows that female politicians are seen differently by the public, especially in Western societies, where political offices at all levels have a masculine cast (Carlin and Winfrey 2009; Hoogensen and Solheim 2006; Jamieson 1995; Meeks 2012). More so, the figure of a political leader, as promoted by media discourses and supported by public opinion, is linked to stereotypical male attributes and qualities—such as assertiveness and ambition—which are deemed inappropriate for a woman (Devere and Davies 2006; Harp, Loke and Bachmann 2010; Hoogensen and Solheim 2006).

To a great extent, news frames reinforce the gender stereotypes that keep women out of the centers of authority and decision-making. They also inform citizens' impressions of candidates and officials, as they rely on the mediated images and stories to form their assessments (Bucy and Grabe 2006; Falk 2008; Ross 2009). As agents of socialization, the media play a key role in shaping the content of public expectations of a politician's job, the appropriate demeanor of a public official, and the markers that define social categories as gender. For example, Falk's (2008) analysis of coverage on female presidential candidates in the U.S. found that the media consistently argue that emotionality would render women incompetent at leadership, and beliefs about men's emotional suitability for politics act as a predictor of voter stereotypes about the ability of politicians to handle issues (Sanbonmatsu 2003).

Sreberny-Mohammadi and Ross (1996) labeled the media logic covering the political realm as the "gendered mediation of politics" and thus news coverage "privileges the practice of politics as an essentially male pursuit" (112). According to this approach, females in politics—let alone trying to break the last glass ceiling—remain scarce and are thus subject to disproportionate media attention. The dilemma for these women is that to succeed in politics, they must show masculine traits, but when they do they are portrayed as violating the deeply held notions of acceptable female behavior (Loke, Harp and Bachmann 2011; Ross 2009). The situation does not necessarily improve once the female candidate becomes an official (Bachmann and Correa 2013; Cantrell and Bachmann 2008) although there is evidence that the press is not always hostile to women and that the inroads made by several female leaders have open doors to less biased coverage (Meeks 2012; Norris 1997).

The role of news media framing and cognitive dissonance

Within the last several years framing has become increasingly attractive in media research and been relied upon to help make sense of communication phenomena. Generally, framing refers to the way events and issues are organized and made sense of among media, media professionals, and their audiences. In particular, news has become a prominent discursive site to understand what framing is and how framing works (D'Angelo and Kuypers 2010), since framing can explain to what extent news media affect citizens' understanding of politics (Lecheler and de Vreese 2012). Ultimately, framing affects citizens in their behavior of voting, in selecting one candidate over another.

According to Reese (2003), "Frames are organizing principles that are socially shared and persistent over time, that work symbolically to meaningfully structure the social world" (11). Frames are not to be confused nor underestimated as simple lenses through which to view a world (Tuchman 1978), nor as mere topics. Rather, they are ways of approaching, understanding, even evaluating various topics (Connolly-Ahern and Broadway 2008). Perhaps stated another way, frames should be understood as active, negotiated elements that tap into group mental imagery (schemas) through sometimes emotional visual and/or verbal prompts and connections (Rosas-Moreno, Harp, and Bachmann 2013). They can be so culturally and ideologically embedded that they seem invisible, or so common that they are taken for granted (Rosas-Moreno 2010).

Frames go beyond transferring issue salience from the media to the public, a common second-level agenda-setting notion; media frames provide a way to understand a message and tie into relationships and environment, requiring a stronger emphasis on causal reasoning (Maher 2003). They can enable audience members to rely on or connect with their familiarity of issues and events to influence or empower certain levels of understanding, or not (Han, Chock, and Shoemaker 2009). Through a selective function, a frame can affect an individual by stressing certain aspects of reality and de-emphasizing others (Lecheler and de Vreese 2012). In this way, certain issue attributes, judgments, and decisions are proposed (Scheufele 2000).

Cognitive Dissonance Theory (Festinger 1957) suggests that news frame creation and processing can be mediated by individuals' decisions regarding what to do with information. Individuals can seek out (selective exposure), tune out or pay attention to (selective attention), interpret (selective perception), and/or remember (selective retention) information in conjunction with their attitudes or beliefs. What citizens *do* with news frames from political news stories affects nations at their polls.

Frames also evoke ethical considerations because of inherent power. Framing power includes (un)conscious decisions by frame sponsors and frame receivers to negotiate a message's denoted and connoted meanings (Carragee and Roefs 2004; Rosas-Moreno and Bachmann 2012). Considering message manifest (informational) and latent (interpretive) content—or specific message inclusions as well as (un)intended omissions—through a cultural sieve increases framing power (Clarke and Everest 2006; Gamson 1989).

Study context and direction

Scholars swing in their research and opinions regarding gender-stereotyped media. Some argue coverage has improved (Rausch, Rozell, and Wilson 1999). Others claim misrepresentations persist nationally and internationally, although more women are running for office (Ross 2002).

What happens, though, when a woman who has previously won the battle at the polls, runs again *and* wins? This study aims to investigate this question. It considers three candidates who have each previously served as her nation's first female head and, broadly, how each is framed in her nation's newspaper of record. More concisely: How do the *Frankfurter Allgemeine Zeitung*, the *Star*, and *El Mercurio* frame their respective female-and-former-state-head presidential candidates, namely Germany's Chancellor Angela Merkel, Liberia's President Ellen Johnson-Sirleaf, and Chile's President Michelle Bachelet, in a subsequent successful election bid? It should be noted that South Africa's *Star* was chosen over any Liberian paper for three reasons. Like Germany and Chile, Liberia ranks as having had a free press at election time but does not seem to have a consistent daily newspaper from which news stories can be easily accessed for Johnson-Sirleaf national news coverage evaluation. Johnson-Sirleaf's role has been not only as the first female state head in Liberia but also in all of Africa. Further, South Africa is Africa's leading economy, and its daily *Star* is reputed for its national and international news coverage.

How these (inter)national press frame female firsts seeking, then winning, additional terms in office makes leading ladies' roles, decisions and actions salient to decision-makers and the public sphere. It is critical that these frames, then, are discovered and analyzed. It is expected that because of assumed familiarity with the female presidential candidate because of her previous tenure as first female, or the general election advantage associated with name recognition, gendered mediation would have lessened in subsequent election news coverage. This study's purpose is not to see the level of treatment of, for example, female leader attributes, but to see how that level varies under certain circumstances, such as an additional successful presidential bid.

Background: Leading ladies and their lands

Germany's Angela Merkel, Liberia's Ellen Johnson-Sirleaf, and Chile's Michelle Bachelet are among the world's most powerful women. In 2009, both Merkel and Bachelet were nearing the end of their first terms in office, and Johnson-Sirleaf was peaking in her six-year term. In its rank of the world's hundred leading women that year, *Forbes* weighed women who run countries, companies or influential nonprofits and scored them according to visibility (measured by press citations) and organization/country size that they lead (Egan 2009). That year, Merkel topped *Forbes*' list of the world's most powerful women, Bachelet ranked twenty-second and Johnson-Sirleaf ranked sixty-seventh.

Each comes from a culturally and developmentally different nation. The German, Liberian, and Chilean political systems differ—a parliamentary republic compared with two presidential republics, respectively. Times are changing, but few women participate in each nation's parliament.

Economic and media systems also differ strongly. For example, in 2009, on the heels of a global recession and the common year of comparison across these three nations, poverty rates ranged. Germany was at 14.3 percent (Isenson 2009), Chile was 15.1 percent (World Bank 2014), and Liberia's poverty level was an astounding 80 percent (UNICEF 2014). Also, each country offers very different life experiences, including information access opportunities. This unique blend of similarities and differences substantiates why this cross-cultural comparison is so compelling and interesting.

Methods

While an international approach to studying successive leading lady election was attempted, news story totals proved not to be viable. For example, *China*

Daily was researched to consider these leading ladies' return to power, but not enough reportage surfaced for a viable study. Hence, this study analyzes three (inter)national press: Germany's *Frankfurter Allgemeine Zeitung* (*FAZ*), South Africa's the *Star* (*Star*), and Chile's *El Mercurio* (*EM*).

Germany's *FAZ* and Chile's *El Mercurio* are each nation's newspaper of record. Reputed to be the country's top quality daily newspaper, Germany's *FAZ* is a daily conservative national newspaper with a 382,000 circulation as of January 2013 that manages its own correspondent network. Chile's *El Mercurio* is a family-owned, 160,000 circulation, national conservative newspaper. As previously noted, South Africa's *Star* was chosen over any Liberian paper for various reasons. It is South Africa's leading daily, liberal leaning, owned by the Independent Newspaper Group and enjoys a circulation of 117,874 (Audit Bureau of Circulations of South Africa 2012).

For comparison, each newspaper was searched one month prior to and one month following each leading lady's *second* election. Germany's four-year tenure with no stipulation preventing successive terms has allowed Merkel at least to run for office thrice. Meanwhile, President Bachelet is constitutionally limited from serving consecutive terms, and President Johnson-Sirleaf, according to Liberian law, is elected to serve a term of six years in office. For Merkel, who was re-elected her second time on September 27, 2009, headlined articles were pulled from August 27, 2009 to October 28, 2009, including one day after the election results were announced. A total of 95 articles surfaced, so every fifth article was sampled. This resulted in 19 *FAZ* stories. President Johnson-Sirleaf was re-elected November 11, 2011 following the second round with 90.7 percent of the vote, even though voter turnout was lower than the first round. Searching *Star* from September 11, 2011 to November 12, 2011 resulted in 33 articles. Once articles headlined with either her name or a synonym like "Nobel Laureate" were pulled, the sample included 14 articles.

In the case of President Bachelet, the time span to pull articles was expanded to include her run-off election. So, *El Mercurio* was searched October 17, 2013 to January 15, 2014 to include the December 15, 2013 run-off election. Once every fifth article was pulled, 80 stories resulted. Another sample of every fifth article was then pulled, culminating in a total of 16 articles for analysis. Table 9.1 summarizes this information.

Once the articles were pulled, two rounds of analysis occurred. First, each story (unit of analysis) was content analyzed very similarly to Cantrell and Bachmann's (2008) study. An acceptable level of intercoder reliability was calculated to ensure researchers followed systematic practices during open-ended data coding (Neuendorf 2002). Researchers also conferred to discuss any uncertainties. Second, a framing analysis was also conducted to assess what news frames would emerge qualitatively. In the Rojecki (2005) and Esser and D'Angelo (2006) traditions, this required more than a topical assessment. The authors weighed social, cultural, and political circumstances associated with each female first's second successful election bid, making connections to larger ideologies to uncover frames embedded within or alluded to by the news stories. This is crucial in cross-cultural comparisons (Benson and Saguy 2005).

Findings

The research questions consider how the (inter)national press frame female firsts seeking then winning additional terms in office. To reiterate, a national comparison helps unearth larger communication issues, such as the normalization and routinization of press practices and globalized frames of gender and gender roles. A general descriptive overview of press coverage precedes a deeper, more qualitative analysis of national storytelling.

The numbers

Overall, the 49 stories analyzed were mostly written by newspaper staff (57 percent) and averaged 623 words long. Almost three-quarters (74 percent) of the analyzed articles were hard-news stories, and about 40 percent addressed an election, rather than a specific issue, personal coverage, or the candidate's leadership skills. A neutral tone regarding the candidate was the most common (57 percent) and a negative tone was found in 18 percent of the sample. These evaluations usually stemmed from claims by personal sources (35 percent) or the reporters themselves (27 percent).

A quarter of the stories explicitly mentioned the candidate's gender, and 14 percent pointed out personal traits of these women. Both experience (75 percent) and leadership (78 percent) were often mentioned in the stories about these women; the former was most commonly cast within a neutral tone (62 percent) and the latter, within a positive evaluation (49 percent). Other stereotypically male and female traits were less commonly mentioned. Thus, assertiveness and toughness—typically male characteristics—were mentioned in 31 percent and 14 percent of the stories, respectively, whereas dependence and care—feminine traits—were brought up in 12 percent and 14 percent of the articles analyzed, respectively.

A breakdown by candidate reveals several differences in the coverage of each of these women. Coverage of Johnson-Sirleaf focused on the election itself (71 percent), whereas stories regarding Bachelet tended to pay more attention to issues such as the economy (38 percent). While a neutral tone was the most commonly used in the stories, in the case of Merkel and Johnson-Sirleaf the positive tone was the second most common (37 percent and 21 percent of the stories, respectively). Conversely, in the case of Bachelet, 25 percent of the *El Mercurio* stories had a negative tone regarding the eventual president-elect of Chile. The basis for such evaluations also differs. For Merkel, several of the stories based their evaluation on foreign policy (16 percent) and partisan strength (21 percent), and for Johnson-Sirleaf, claims by personal sources took center stage (50 percent).

Additionally, candidate gender mentions were more frequent in *Star*'s coverage for Johnson-Sirleaf. Thus, almost 80 percent of the stories on the Liberian president explicitly mentioned her gender, but only one of Germany's *FAZ* or Chile's *EM* did so. That said, the one story (2 percent) found to mention a physical feature of any one of the three candidates was from the German newspaper—regarding Merkel's hairstyle. One other story from the sample, also from the German newspaper, incidentally, included a mention of the candidate's outfit, which was a pantsuit.

The experience of each candidate was relevant in most of the national presses, particularly for Liberia's Johnson-Sirleaf (93 percent) and Germany's Merkel (83 percent), usually framed in positive terms. For Chile's Bachelet, the mentions of her past experience as a public official were less prominent—only 50 percent of the stories mentioned it, often with a neutral tone.

When it comes to the stereotypical traits, Merkel was presented as a competent, tough leader, with integrity, and as somewhat resourceful, albeit also dependent on others. Mentions of assertiveness were common, but usually with a negative evaluation. This means she was critiqued by the press as needing more assertiveness in her campaign, and that her assertiveness should carry over to her governance. Johnson-Sirleaf was cast as a caring, competent leader, somewhat motherly, empathic, and both resourceful and dependent, but whose integrity was often questioned. Thus, on the one hand her Nobel Peace Prize—awarded days before the election—was in contrast to the Liberian Truth and

Table 9.1 News story summary

Leading lady	Newspaper	Total articles	Sampled articles
Chancellor Merkel	*FAZ*	95	19
President Johnson-Sirleaf	*Star*	33	14
President Bachelet	*EM*	403	16
Total			*49*

Reconciliation Commission's report recommending that she be banned from public office due to her ties to former warlord-turned-president Charles Taylor. Bachelet, in turn, was described as a competent, assertive leader, somewhat empathic and resourceful. These traits were often presented in a neutral tone.

The (inter)national frames

Beneath the numbers, more microscopic study reveals two frames per national medium illustrating connections between returning leading ladies and nationalistic ideologies. While some of the frames carried over from the first election, indicating strong normalization and routinization of press practices, *how* the frames were latently manifest differed. In all instances, gendered mediation faded.

FAZ and Chancellor Angela Merkel

In the earlier study of national press reports on Angela Merkel's first election as Germany's state head, two culturally and socially connected frames percolated: *women über all—nationalism expounded* and *motherless motherhood*. German national press reports from her second election indicate that while both frames continue, the first is less inclusive; one woman, namely Angela Merkel, is über all.

Consider the newer, more inclusive frame, *Merkel über all—nationalism expounded*. The crucial element of this frame is not necessarily what was said about Merkel, but rather what went unsaid. With rare exception, no article clarified who Angela Merkel is. Familiarity and understanding were assumed. And when clarification was offered, it was to punctuate her presence and popularity. For instance, noting she is East German taps into the difference between formerly East and West German women; prior to Germany's 1989 reunification, and in the face of certain social movements, West German women had largely been socialized into a more patriarchal society where women were traditional homemakers. This contrasted with East German women of Merkel's generation who were socialized into a more progressive, Soviet-based, women-are-an-essential-part-of-the-(educated)-workforce culture (Lewis 1995).

Still, Merkel and her popularity unite German women. As one headline endorsed, "The *Women*'s Union Sees Merkel as the Debate Winner" (*FAZ*, September 15, 2009, italics added). Another headline was more inclusive: "*All* Hail the Female Chancellor" (*FAZ*, September 29, 2009). News reports also quoted Merkel saying she wanted to be the chancellor of "*all* Germans" (*FAZ*, September 28, 2009, italics added), and her campaign slogan, "*We* have the power," asserts majority rule.

Merkel's reputation crossed national and international boundaries:

> Luxembourg Prime Minister Jean-Claude Juncker decreed: "This woman should not be underestimated," followed immediately by the outgoing SPD parliamentary leader Peter Struck ("We actually have all underestimated her") and the CSU chairman and Bavarian Prime Minister Horst Seehofer followed – "Anyone who underestimates Angela Merkel has already lost … " (*FAZ*, September 10, 2009, punctuation as it appears in the story)

Press reports also clearly indicated her competence and intelligence are unquestioned. Guido Westerwelle, who would serve as Merkel's foreign minister in her second cabinet and as Germany's Vice Chancellor from 2009–11, said, "she is smart" (*FAZ*, September 10, 2009). Perhaps most revealing of this frame, the prime minister of Germany's most populous state, the North Rhine-Westphalia, Jürgen Rüttgers, said, "Our answer is Angela Merkel." (*FAZ*, August 31, 2009)

The latter press report straddles the second frame, *motherless motherhood*. While critiqued for needing "more emotion" in her second campaign (*FAZ*, August 31, 2009), Merkel gained national and international acclaim for her ability to weather the global economic downturn beginning in 2008. In Germany, she was presented as a saving figure, one who deployed "courageous policy" including a controversial government bailout of the German automaker Opel.

As the elected Mother of the Land, Merkel was widely recognized and admired for her consensual political approach. Press reports also highlighted that she takes care of the weak (*FAZ*, September 3, 2009), even though they directly describe her personally as "East German, Protestant and *childless*"

(*FAZ*, September 10, 2009, italics added). It also points out some parenting turmoil, with German youth in her own political party "rebelling against the party leader Angela Merkel" (*FAZ*, October 16, 2009).

Star and President Ellen Johnson-Sirleaf

International news reports of not only Liberia's, but all of Africa's, first female head winning a second term trigger similar frames from Johnson-Sirleaf's first election bid as covered by her own national daily, the *Liberian Times*. The former frame *Women heal nations* gains a timing component on the international scale to become *Women heal nations in stages*. The key component of this frame is not how it differs from a male incumbent asking for second chance at office, but rather how news reports propose Johnson-Sirleaf's request for another opportunity to lead. Consider:

> Analysts agree that throwing herself into the long neglected reconciliation efforts, while targeting poverty and massive unemployment of up to 80 percent, will be the best way forward for Sirleaf.
>
> "Considering her track record I think *she will reach out to each and every Liberian* ... " said Joe Pemagbi of the Open Society Initiative West Africa. (*Star*, November 10, 2011, italics added)

Further, news reports of the healing Johnson-Sirleaf began in her first term appeared gendered:

> Sirleaf said while her first term focused on *establishing peace* and development, her second would tackle problems such as job creation with unemployment running at a staggering 80 percent. (*Star*, November 11, 2011, italics added)

The news frame *Women heal nations in stages* is not entirely positive. It can cast an ominous shadow on the incumbent's work and plea to voters. One quotes exemplifies:

> While Sirleaf initially promised to serve only one term, she has said she needs more time to continue rebuilding the "broken country." (*Star*, October 18, 2011)

Sealing this frame, news during Johnson-Sirleaf's second presidential bid broke that she was awarded a Nobel Peace Prize along with another Liberian woman " ... for the practical ways in which they have brought peace to their country" (*Star*, October 21, 2011). Reports cited various international leaders emphasizing this frame. Norwegian Prime Minister Jens Stoltenberg said it was a prize that "recognised [sic] the role women play in reconciliation" (*Star*, October 8, 2011). South African President Jacob Zuma was reported as saying, "President Sirleaf is a worthy recipient given her dedication and commitment not only to women's emancipation, but also to peace, stability and prosperity in Liberia" (*Star*, October 7, 2011). Even "The [Nobel] committee paid tribute to Sirleaf for her contribution to securing peace in Liberia, promoting economic and social development, and strengthening the position of women." (*Star*, October 7, 2011).

The two Liberians shared the prize with a third female, Yemeni Tawakul Karman. Weaving this credential into most of the news coverage, African news reports advanced the former second frame, *Women depend on others to achieve.* A point of discussion peppering Nobel news reports was that Johnson-Sirleaf, or any one of the three women, did not *singularly* receive the award.

Within her own nation, and at the polls, it was also evident that "[w]hile a darling of the international community," Johnson-Sirleaf could not expect to achieve success within her native nation without assistance. "With security institutions still weak, the country is heavily reliant on an 8000-strong UN peacekeeping mission and international organisations [*sic*]" (*Star*, October 12, 2011).

While not unusual for male counterparts to also rely on rivals' backing to gain their constituents' support once they desisted in their run for office, Johnson-Sirleaf faced unique validation from potential backers. Former rebel leader Prince Johnson said he would support Johnson-Sirleaf not only because he thought her policies good for the country, but because he preferred " … to go with the lesser evil … [who] is the incumbent" (*Star*, October 18, 2011).

EM and President Michelle Bachelet

The coverage of Bachelet's road to a second (non-consecutive) term greatly differs from the media treatment received during the first months of her first term. Thus, while a previous analysis found that the main frames of the national press where her gender is her fault (she's not really a bad president), and that women are soft leaders, the current analysis shows that gender and soft leadership were not considered at all in the stories published by *El Mercurio*. Even though the criticism toward Bachelet remains to some extent—not really surprising, considering she was a left-wing candidate and *El Mercurio*'s conservative editorial standing—the pervasive attention to her gender and her so-called "feminine" leadership found in 2006 coverage disappears in 2013. Arguably, after serving a whole (and rather successful) term, gender stops being central in the coverage received, and the media start paying attention to other dimensions of a political career, including her platform, suitability for the job, and strength as a candidate. The lack of focus on gender is even more surprising when considering that Bachelet's main contender was another female, making this the first Chilean presidential election where the main two coalitions had women on the ticket.

Rather than gender, the principle guiding the coverage of Bachelet is one that acknowledges her competence, leadership skills, and assertiveness. Thus, one of the frames in *El Mercurio* is that *Women can be assertive leaders as well.* This frame gives credit to Bachelet's ability to get things done and command others, while recognizing that, rather than being soft, she is authoritative and self-possessed. For instance, her response to several politicians publicly making suggestions and recommendations about how Bachelet ought to comprise her cabinet, was praised and repeatedly brought up following her triumph in the December 15, 2013 run-off election:

> "Who makes it to a future cabinet is the exclusive responsibility of the president-elect and I will wholly fulfill that responsibility. It will be me who decides who will be part of the future cabinet of my administration", said the president-elect. (*EM*, December 18, 2013)

According to *El Mercurio*, much of this self-assuredness stems from her most-likely winner status. Indeed, having left office with an almost 80 percent approval rating, Bachelet was consistently named the obvious left-wing candidate and successor to the 2010–14 Piñera Administration.

While assertive, the press also warned that this authoritative Bachelet had to deal with a coalition with many inner conflicts. Thus, another frame is *The strong leader with a shaky foundation.* The message here is that for all her approval ratings and self-assured demeanor, the second Bachelet Administration could be undermined by her own allies, especially if she eventually proved herself unable to rein them in. For example:

> This time, Bachelet will have to govern with parties that are even weaker than four years ago, empowered congressmen and fresh memories of the bad times she endured due to the wayward politicians [from her coalition] that made her lose the legislative majority very quickly. (*EM*, December 22, 2013)

Similarly, her own platform and campaign promises raise suspicions and disagreements over her coalition, which could forecast problems during her second term in office. Thus:

> Although all the party presidents from the coalition showed satisfaction with the document [stating her platform], the Christian Democrats raised concerns about the promise of universal free education as the Communist Party showed reservation regarding a state-run pension fund. (*EM*, October 28, 2013).

Discussion and conclusion

This study has quantitatively and qualitatively considered how German, African, and Chilean (inter)national presses frame their respective female firsts seeking then winning an additional term in office. News stories have been pulled from each female first's second election in the 2009, 2011, and 2013 timeframes, respectively. Discovering and analyzing news messages from nations representing the East/West, North/South, First/Third-World should help make leading ladies' roles, decisions, and actions salient to decision-makers, news consumers, and other members of the public sphere. It should also help to erase coincidence among findings. Hence, this study's purpose has not been to see the level of treatment of, for example, female leader attributes, but to see how that level varies under certain circumstances, such as additional successful presidential bids across various boundaries.

Because of assumed familiarity with the female presidential candidate seeking re-election, coupled with the general election advantage associated with name recognition, gendered mediation did lessen in the subsequent election news coverage, with random mentions persisting. In the case of the German press, as represented by its leading daily the *FAZ*, two frames emerged during analysis: *Merkel über all—nationalism expounded* and *Motherless motherhood.* With regard to the African press, South Africa's *Star* revealed two frames with regard to President Johnson-Sirleaf: *Women heal nations in stages* and *Women depend on others to achieve.* In Chile, *EM* showed two frames through its coverage of President-elect Michelle Bachelet: *Women can be assertive leaders as well,* and *The strong leader with a shaky foundation.*

While some of the frames that arose in the earlier study were still present, the focus has shifted. This could indicate that while news normalization and routinization has occurred, cognitive dissonance has mediated gender in news reports. In other words, while gender mediation claims politics is covered as a male endeavor, women being elected to the top government seat breaks a glass ceiling, and constituents get more used to seeing female leaders. The exception becomes the norm, or normalized. The press, then, cannot cover the news event as a solely male endeavor and is forced to focus on platform and other issues, dismissing gender as a consideration and promoting the position for voter consideration.

Put perhaps another way, once a woman breaks the top-leadership threshold and attains a successful election, the tension of gender and how to report (or not) on it dissipates. The candidate becomes a leader rather than a woman trying to be a leader of a nation. Once she becomes familiar, it is the office that is seen and/or reported on, rather than the individual. This could explain why scholars have argued for quotas at least in political nominations (e.g. Htun 2005).

Comparing these results across boundaries geographically and culturally, the results are consistent. It seems disappointing that women need to prove themselves in the political public sphere, rather than just be a woman, that they need to demonstrate that they are competent, capable, even presidential, despite their gender. However, based on this tri-continental study, women can do it. To quote Merkel, "We have the power." Part of that power is to work to increase opportunity for media representation of women in power to further help the (inter)national media become less gendered in the first place.

Part Two

Managing the Message: Self-representations

10

"Cameroon's Female Obama": Deconstructing the Kah Walla Phenomenon in the Context of the 2011 Presidential Elections in Cameroon

Teke Ngomba

Introduction

Although there has been a modest increase in research examining the interaction between news media and female politicians in several non-Western countries, there has been an alarming paucity of empirical research exploring the news media portrayals of female politicians and their election campaigns in sub-Saharan Africa. To expand research in this area, this chapter examines the campaign style of Edith Kah Walla, a prominent female politician from Cameroon who made a bid for the presidency in 2011, and how the local print media constructed her political activities and achievements in the context of her bid for the highest political office in this country. This is one of the few existing studies that examine the media coverage of a woman's presidential candidacy from the African continent.

Edith Kah Walla earned her MBA degree in Management from Howard University in the United States of America, and in 2011 she was listed by *Newsweek* and the *Daily Beast* as one of 150 women who "shake the world." Beyond her education, her connections to the United States stretch right into the Democratic Party thanks, in part, to her recognition in 2009, with the Leadership in Public Life Award from Vital Voices, an NGO established by Hillary Clinton and Madeleine Albright. About a year before the October 2011 presidential election in Cameroon, 45-year-old Edith Kah Walla announced her resignation from the main opposition party, the Social Democratic Front (SDF), while declaring simultaneously her candidacy for the presidency.

She eventually competed in the election as the candidate from a hitherto little known opposition party, the Cameroon People's Party (CPP). As per the official results, out of the 23 candidates who contested the elections, she was the sixth best candidate, obtaining 0.72 percent of the vote. Although these official results look insignificant, Kah Walla's candidacy and campaign emerged as one of the most talked-about issues during the presidential elections principally because of what one analyst termed her "audacity to dream change" in the context of Cameroonian politics (*Eyeball to Eyeball* of November 14, 2010).

News media coverage of female politicians

Although research has shown that a gendered pattern of media coverage of politicians cuts across all levels of public office (Atkeson and Krebs 2008), women running for top executive positions such as the presidency, vice-presidency or prime ministry have tended to experience a particular kind of news coverage harboring on two important angles: mediated reflections of dominant sociocultural expectations of gender and power and the novelty of their pursuits.

With regard to the first angle, as Heldman et al. (2005, 316) aptly noted in the case of the U.S., executive positions like the presidency are "highly masculinized" and for journalists as well as the public at large, ideas about what it means to be a "woman" do not correspond well with expectations about what it means to be "president." These "ideas," which circle around notions such as the "woman's place is in the kitchen" and not in a public office, are also very recurrent across Africa (see Arriola and Johnson 2013). One important outcome of these gendered expectations has been their reproduction in news reports, especially when it concerns women running for the first time for positions like president or vice-president (see Meeks 2013). As concerns the second angle, because top executive political positions tend to be "highly masculinized," each time women aim for these positions, there is a tendency for the media to approach their candidacies as something novel through what Heldman et al. (2005, 319) referred to as a "'first woman' frame", which could have negative ramifications.

Whether by examining print or audio-visual media or different types of election campaigns, the arguments summarized above have been reached in studies from both established democracies (Meeks 2013; Vos 2013) and emerging democracies (Dan and Iorgoveanu 2013; Thomas and Adams 2010).

The fairly consistent evidence of gender biases in the coverage of female politicians by the news media (Heldman, Carroll, and Olson 2005, 316) clearly suggests that these biases are "not isolated but systemic" (Aday and Devitt 2001, 53). To conceptually capture this systemic nature of the gender biases in news media coverage of politics, Gidengil and Everitt (1999) have suggested the useful notion of "gendered mediation." The gendered mediation concept encapsulates the "stereotypically masculine narrative used in political reporting" which reinforces "traditional conceptions of politics as a male preserve" (Gidengil and Everitt 1999, 48). Gendered mediation also states that the most insidious form of bias appears "when conventional political frames are applied to female politicians" (ibid., 49).

The special hurdles which female politicians face suggest that, strategically, they need to adopt campaign communication strategies, which can enable them to surmount the gendered socio-cultural expectations and mediated discourses. Prior research comparing the campaign communication strategies of male and female politicians has shown that overall there is a tendency for male and female politicians to adopt similar campaign strategies. Kahn and Gordon (1997), for instance, found that even though male and female candidates for the U.S. Senate "present alternative agendas to voters," they "deliver these distinct messages in a remarkably similar fashion" (74).

The similarities notwithstanding, subtle differences identified in previous research indicate that women politicians are "more likely than men to make issues a corner stone of their campaigns" (Kahn and Gordon 1997, 74). According to Johnston and White (1994, 327), this emphasis on issues is perhaps because of "the desire by female candidates to firmly establish their competency and credibility in the minds of the voters."

Another important difference has been the identification of a tendency for female politicians to strategically appropriate socio-cultural gendered stereotypes such as women being "more compassionate and honest" than men, for their benefit (Kahn and Gordon 1997, 63). As Larson (2001, 107) noted, female politicians can do these by calling voters' attention to their "uniqueness as candidates and their political outsider status." Such strategies have been used successfully for instance, by Michelle Bachelet in Chile and Ellen Johnson-Sirleaf in Liberia (see Thomas and Adams 2010; Valenzuela and Correa 2009).

Women and politics in Cameroon

Since 1990, Cameroon, like most countries in sub-Saharan Africa, has been going through a process of democratization, which has been described as being "stalled" (Mbaku 2002). Like other emerging democracies, the democratization process in

Cameroon has been characterized by an immense "masculinization" of the political sphere (to borrow from Ibroscheva 2012, 19). The country has a population of about 20 million people (close to 51 percent of whom are women) yet, although women are the majority population-wise, they have historically been under-represented in political institutions like municipal councils, parliament or the cabinet.

Although the elections on September 30, 2013 led to a notable increase in the number of female parliamentarians, as shown in Table 10.1, over the course of the past two decades, women have been significantly underrepresented (see Bauer 2012).

It is against this background of a "masculinized" political sphere in Cameroon that we need to situate the importance and mediated portrayals of Kah Walla's candidature. The 2011 presidential election in Cameroon was historical in at least three ways. First, there were 23 candidates—the highest number of presidential candidates since the reintroduction of multipartism in 1992. Second, it was the first time that Cameroonians residing abroad were allowed to take part in a national election. Third, women were among the presidential candidates for the first time. Although two women, Edith Kah Walla and Esther Dang, made history simultaneously, Kah Walla significantly eclipsed Esther Dang during the campaigns. As Kah Walla put it, although there were 23 candidates for the elections:

> ... only about five candidates campaigned. Esther Dang was not one of them. She did not do any media appearances; she did not go out on the field. I am not quite sure what was the reason that she ran but she was not trying to convince Cameroonians of anything. So that immediately put us into two different categories. (See also *Le Messager* of October 11, 2011 for a similar analysis)

Table 10.1 Representation of women in the National Assembly in Cameroon

Legislative period	Total number of seats	Seats occupied by women	Percentage of women's seats
1992–7	180	23	12.8%
1997–2002	180	10	5.6%
2002–7	180	20	11.1%
2007–12	180	25	13.9%
2013–18	180	56	31.1%

Source: National Statistics Institute, Cameroon; and *Cameroon Tribune*

Since Kah Walla campaigned effectively and emerged as the "revelation" of the 2011 presidential election (*Mutations* of October 17, 2011), the present study poses the following questions: What campaign communication strategies did Kah Walla use? What kinds of mediated discourses emerged about Kah Walla's candidacy and her campaign and to what extent were these discourses "gendered"?

Method

The data used to answer the questions indicated above come from two principal sources: an in-depth telephone interview with Kah Walla and 163 newspaper reports about Kah Walla's candidacy and campaign. To find out more about Kah Walla's campaign communication strategy and her assessment of the way the news media covered her campaign, I conducted an in-depth telephone interview with her on December 14, 2012. The interview lasted for about 75 minutes. Furthermore, her official campaign website (www.kahwalla.com) was examined to gain an in-depth understanding at how she chose to present herself and her political program.

In order to find out how the news media covered Kah Walla's candidacy and her campaign, relevant content from the six daily newspapers in Cameroon at the time of the election was analyzed. These newspapers include the state-owned *Cameroon Tribune* and the following five privately-owned newspapers: *Le Messager*; *Mutations*; *La Nouvelle Expression*; *Le Jour* and *L'Actu*. These six daily newspapers are among the most circulated newspapers in Cameroon (Africa Media Barometer 2011). Except for *Cameroon Tribune*, which is published in the two official languages of Cameroon–English and French, all the other daily newspapers in Cameroon are published only in the French language. Relevant sections from these newspapers used in this chapter have been translated by the author.

To get the relevant reports, the websites of these newspapers were searched for the key words "Kah Walla." All reports mentioning Kah Walla, which were published between October 23, 2010 and December 31, 2011 were selected for this study. This timeframe was selected because, although the official campaign period for this election was September 25, to October 8, 2011, once Kah Walla declared her candidature on October 23, 2010, unlike other candidates, she immediately started campaigning. Also, although the election results were proclaimed on October 21, 2011, the news media still focused on these elections right up to December in their usual "re-cap of the year's major stories" series.

Beyond searching for stories mentioning Kah Walla on the websites of the six daily newspapers, a secondary search was done within the same timeframe in other Cameroonian newspaper websites, especially those published in English such as the *Post Newspaper*; *Eden Newspaper* and the *Sun*. Likewise, a similar search was done on the following five major Cameroon-focused online news portals: *Journal du Cameroun*, *Camer.be*, *Cameroun Link*, *Cameroun Info.net*, and *Camnet*. These portals—very popular, especially among the Cameroonian diaspora—act like news aggregators, collecting and republishing stories about Cameroon originally published on newspapers' websites. Some like *Camer.be* and *Cameroun Info.net* also publish news reports or opinion pieces written by their own freelancers.

By searching through these portals, relevant reports from both the six dailies and other weekly or bi-weekly newspapers in Cameroon were found. Although the secondary reports mentioning Kah Walla from these different media were read, the analysis presented below focuses on the reports published by the selected six daily newspapers. Table 10.2 shows the type of stories mentioning Kah Walla that were found in the six daily newspapers between October 23, 2010 and December 31, 2011.

Since the focus of this study is not so much on the volume of news media coverage that Kah Walla received but rather on the "quality" of the coverage, this study applies textual analysis to look for explicit and implicit meanings. All the articles were coded paragraph by paragraph, paying particular attention to words used to describe or refer to Kah Walla as an individual, her candidacy, her campaign, her political program, her stands on topical issues during the campaign, her chances of winning the election, and the impact of

Table 10.2 Type of report mentioning Kah Walla from *Cameroon Tribune*, *Le Messager*, *Mutations*, *La Nouvelle Expression*, *Le Jour* and *L'Actu*

Type of report	Number	Percentage
News story	106	65%
Feature	14	8.6%
Editorial/Opinion piece	22	13.5%
Interview with Kah Walla herself	12	7.4%
Interviews with other politicians/political party officials	9	5.5%
Total	163	100%

her candidacy. After collecting and arranging all extracts from these reports under each of the aforementioned headings, general patterns were noted as well as exceptions and these are what constitute the findings presented for this study.

Kah Walla's campaign communication strategies

To understand the overall tone of the news media coverage of Kah Walla and her campaign, it is imperative to grasp first the ways in which she designed and managed her campaign and the communication choices that she made. As will be evident subsequently, these decisions and actions in and of themselves, constituted an overarching frame, which the news media easily perched on to talk about Kah Walla as an individual, her candidacy and campaign.

Once the CPP elected her as its candidate for the presidential election, Kah Walla and her team adopted a hybrid campaign communication strategy hinged on a relatively sophisticated blend of the use of the internet, other news media, and extensive door-to-door campaigning. These strategies, carried out by a youthful team, were anchored under the catchy slogan of the campaign: "The Time is Now!"

As indicated earlier, the 2011 presidential election was the first time that the Cameroonian diaspora was allowed to vote. As a result, getting a strong online presence in order to reach the Cameroonian diaspora became sort of imperative for the candidates, and, as we will see shortly, mediated discourses about the Kah Walla campaign showed that her online campaign set itself apart from the others. According to Kah Walla, this was possible thanks in large part to the technical support she got from the Cameroonian diaspora and the professional campaign advice from her networks in the U.S., especially from her contacts within the Democratic Party. Part of her campaign communication strategy involved the crafting of Kah Walla's public persona—something which she did through her website and during several interviews with the media.

On her website, Kah Walla presented herself as a "45-year-old African entrepreneur" who is "internationally recognized for her expertise in management, her understanding of development issues and her strong stance on Africa, its women and youths." She further described herself as a "social entrepreneur and advocate" whose favorite words are "grassroots, grassroots, grassroots … " Her campaign website emphasized her professional experience, networks, and recognitions, her political engagement with the SDF, the "structural reforms" she initiated in the party; her fight for accountability and transparency in municipal and electoral governance as well as her work with women and youths. She reinforced these frames of herself in several newspaper interviews (see for instance *Mutations* of February 4, 2011 and *Le Messager* of September 22, 2011).

Beyond her age and a list of some of the authors whose books she reads, there is hardly any other personal information about Kah Walla on her official website. Even when she refers to her upbringing, she emphasizes competency, not family. For example, in several media interviews, she talks about how her upbringing influenced her political views. In an interview in *La Nouvelle Expression* of September 5, 2011 for instance, she said that:

> The first time that I took part in a political protest, I was 11 years old. My mother, who was in the United States took us to the protest. She took us from Pittsburgh to Washington DC to take part in a protest march against apartheid. That was the first time that I became aware of the need for action at the political level …

Through such discourses, she presented herself as someone with a long history of political activism who comes from a family that instilled in her, at a relatively tender age, the importance to fight for equality and freedom.

So how did the media frame Kah Walla and how similar and or different were these media frames from the way Kah Walla framed herself? Overall, the analysis shows that Kah Walla and her campaign were indeed a media sensation, a veritable electoral phenomenon hitherto unseen in the context of Cameroonian politics. Kah Walla and her campaign were regularly singled out in these media reports as major positive exceptions from the other 22 candidates. On July 23, 2011, *Mutations* for instance pointed out in a report that echoed the dominant media discourse about Kah Walla's campaign that her campaign:

> … is without doubt one of the most organized, most thought-through at the moment. At least in terms of its strategic design, including its financing … The little lady has not stopped travelling between Cameroon, Europe and America.[1] The campaign team of the candidate, Kah Walla Campaign (KWC), is now present in all ten regions of the country … To date, more than a thousand people work in her campaign … To succeed in the challenge to raise funds of about 34 million FCFA, Kah Walla's strategy has been the classic American-style fundraising. The

> KWC campaign has set up a collection system to encourage contributions whether one is residing in Cameroon or abroad. Payment in cash, by cheque, bank transfers, money transfers etc. And on the field, the candidate does not skimp on any medium of communication, Facebook being widely used to convey messages …

Kah Walla's political program in the media

As the literature reveals, one of the regular discussions concerning news media coverage of female politicians is the finding that the news media tend to focus on "soft issues" when covering female politicians. However, Kah Walla's political program was indeed detailed and touched on all sectors of the Cameroonian society and was reflected as such in the media. In several media interviews with her as well as news reports, she offered detailed policy proposals on issues ranging from the economy to security; structure of the state; corruption and the national football team (for some of these reports, see for instance *Le Jour* of July 22, 2011; *Cameroon Tribune* of September 21, 2011 and *Le Messager* of September 26, 2011).

Beyond the news media, Kah Walla also ensured that she "stayed on message" in different forums thanks to advice she received from the Democratic Party in the U.S. She pointed out in the personal interview that she is:

> Also very connected to people within the Democratic Party in the US. I had the privilege of talking to some of the key people who had run that campaign [Obama's 2008 campaign] and we drew a lot of lessons from them and one of which was to stay present on the Internet through our website, through Facebook, through e-mail correspondents to our network and that we did do, we did constantly …

On her website as well as her social media pages and through regular press releases, Kah Walla published documents with headings such as: "Vision of the Candidate"; "Outline of the Political Program"; and "Key Projects/100 Priority Actions." By being one of the very few candidates with such detailed policy discussions, she could easily attract attention from the information-hungry news media. The comparative absence of such information from other candidates easily earned her a good reputation among journalists.

Centrally, this clear strategic focus on policy issues in a context where campaigns have historically tended to center obsessively on personalities, constituted an indication of Kah Walla's desire to portray herself as an "outsider" with new ways of doing politics in Cameroon. The strategy is also aligned with extant findings indicated earlier that female candidates tend to focus on issues in their campaigns in a bid to boost their viability perceptions. The eloquence with which she presented her candidacy and policies in very fluent English and French as well as her meticulous combination of mediated and non-mediated communication strategies sufficed to earn her the praises she received from the news media—a point further examined below. Overall therefore, in several respects, Kah Walla's campaign communication strategies represented a break from tradition as far as political campaigns in Cameroon are concerned.

News media coverage of Kah Walla

The textual analysis revealed three dimensions of how the media framed Kah Walla's candidacy: Kah Walla as a courageous individual; Kah Walla in relation to her political viability; and overt and subtle gendered discourses about Kah Walla.

Kah Walla as a courageous individual

The overall tone of the media discourses about Kah Walla, from the 163 reports analyzed for this study, was positive. The most recurrent frames about her included descriptions of her as being courageous, intelligent, determined, hardworking, and full of conviction. On September 13, 2011 for instance, *Le Jour* reported that "at age 46, the political weapons of Kah Walla are her courage and her activism, which have earned her several arrests by the forces of law and order." Similarly, a report in *Mutations* of September 13, 2010 referred to Kah Walla as "one of the most visible female politicians in Cameroon" adding that she has brought a "strategic and methodic approach to politics: new technologies, marketing strategies, communication professionals, systematic analysis of the stakes and political factors etc., … all, a mini revolution in short, in the methods and approaches of politics."

When she went to campaign in the predominantly Muslim northern region of Cameroon, *La Nouvelle Expression* reported on May 19, 2011 that many Muslim women had come out curiously to see the "courageous woman" who had presented her candidacy for the presidential elections in a "society dominated by men." In a sense therefore, these mediated discourses aligned with the way Kah Walla framed herself during the campaign.

Kah Walla and her political viability

Although the media were clearly fascinated by Kah Walla's candidacy and her campaign, the reports examined did not carry any substantial articulation of a real possibility that she could actually win the presidential election. She constantly received the "newcomer frame" and reports about the strengths of her campaign were often tempered with reminders that she was contesting an election in a context unfavorable to the opposition in general and female candidates in particular. *Mutations* for instance pointed out on May 17, 2011 that "Certainly, her candidature does not constitute a special threat to the ruling system which has taken care to lock off the electoral game but she represents a matter of conscience and therefore a pebble in the shoe of the regime."

With regard to this notion of mediated political viability of female candidates in the context of election campaigns, two issues stand. The first is a current pragmatic viability assessment and the second a futuristic viability assessment. The first implies dismissing hopes expressed by Kah Walla throughout the campaign that she could win the presidency and in its place, discussing the most likely scenario given the nature of the uneven political playing field in Cameroon between the ruling party and the opposition parties as a whole. As an example of this dimension, on October 7, 2011, two days before the elections, *Mutations* concluded that the incumbent will win the elections and added that:

> For the first time since 1992, John Fru Ndi [the leader of the SDF, Cameroon's main opposition party] is not sure to be second. In fact, *the real issue* in this election is this second place … In Kah Walla's case, a second or third place is possible. It will be at the same time a surprise and a confirmation. Surprise because she is the Benjamin in the political landscape.[2] Confirmation because she is without doubt the most structured candidate, most organized on the field and one of the most mediatized. (Emphasis added)

By pointing out that the "real issue" in the election was who will come second and not who will replace the incumbent, the newspaper pragmatically "boxed" Kah Walla into where she seemed most viable—finishing in a "second or third place." While this sort of assessment might not be interpreted as inherently gendered, it is unapologetically pragmatic in view of the realities of the electoral terrain in Cameroon.

Futuristic viability assessments, on the other hand, include acknowledgments that the candidate may not have the capacity to succeed in a current election, but has the potential to win future elections or change the nature of a country's political game in some way. Kah Walla was said to have succeeded to "impose her image" on the country thanks to her "continuous presence" on the political frontlines (*Cameroon Tribune* of March 6, 2011). Before the elections, *La Nouvelle Expression* on September 5, 2011, declared her the "most popular female politician in the country" and after the elections, *Cameroon Tribune* (October 17, 2011 and October 24, 2011) wrote that she had to be counted now as one of the principal leaders of the opposition in Cameroon.

In the telephone interview with her, Kah Walla acknowledged that even though she did not win the elections, she was pleased because:

> We really wanted to get Cameroonians excited again about politics ... [and] We got them excited. By every possible measure, we had the most popular candidacy. People were very excited, we drew the biggest crowds. People were fired up again about politics ...

The excitement about her candidacy was aptly captured in an *All Voices* report (November 27, 2010) titled "Kah Wallamania Syndrome Grips Cameroon" published about a year before the presidential election. The report stated that the Kah Walla campaign, with its slogan "The Time is Now," created:

> ... a lot of enthusiasm in the youth and the women folk who see in her that Obama kind of veracity. The most interesting thing about Kah Walla is that she is young and full of life; a sudden and brave pure breath of fresh air, hope and change for Cameroon; Obama-like persona, Anglophone and Francophone, perfectly bilingual ... Cameroon seemingly has got her own Obama but this time a female Obama ...

This allusion to Barack Obama or the "American style" of campaigning featured regularly in the reports about Kah Walla. Similar to the quote above, on the day Kah Walla declared her candidature, one of Cameroon's most seasoned political commentators, Francis Wache, reported that her campaign style and slogan had "unmistakable echoes of Barack Obama's enchanting of 'Yes we can.'" (*Eyeball to Eyeball* of November 14, 2010)

In a context where recent elections in Cameroon have been characterized by significant levels of voter apathy, candidates like Kah Walla arguably have the potential to "reignite" political interest and the engagement of a broad section of the electorate. This capacity as well as assessments that she may eventually win elections in the future, constitute a futuristic viability of the candidacy of Kah Walla.

Overt and subtle gendered discourses in news media coverage of Kah Walla

Although the 163 reports examined for this study were largely without any outright gender bias, there were nonetheless instances in all six daily newspapers as well as in the other media that displayed gendered undertones in the manner in which they talked about Kah Walla or her campaign.

First of all, she tended to be described as a "female politician" and not just a politician, even though she strategically avoided putting women and traditional women's issues at the forefront of her political program or campaign discourses. This notwithstanding, she was often asked about issues like her "thoughts concerning a female candidature" and what she will do for women, children and youths if elected (*Le Jour* of October 8, 2011). Second, reference to her being intelligent and eloquent was often made alongside direct or subtle reference to her physical appearance especially her height (1.62m), but also included her age and marital status. In a special report profiling all the presidential candidates on September 25, 2011, state-run *Cameroon Tribune*, for instance, presented Kah Walla as follows:

> For those who meet Kah Walla for the first time, the surprise is big. Difficult to imagine in effect that this little bubble of a woman who looks almost timid and nervous, is the one who is causing all the public curiosity. But once she gets into a debate, we understand this emulation around one of the two female candidates for the supreme magistracy. Eloquent and sure of herself, Edith Kah Walla, president of CPP, is full of ideas ... Among other proposals if she is elected, the female politician aged 46 years, promises to reduce the presidential term limit to 5 years renewable once ... Single without children, Kah Walla is cited among the 150 most influential women in the world by Newsweek ... (See also *Le Jour* of October 6, 2010)

In contrast, the marital status of male candidates rarely surfaced, nor was there any reference to their physical appearance for that matter. Beyond the six dailies examined, other newspapers also contained similar discourses. For instance the newspaper of the ruling party announced the official kick-off of Kah Walla's campaign by reporting that "the diminutive Kah Walla began her campaign in Douala where she has worked for close to 25 years" (*L'Action* of September 27, 2011). The Xinhua news agency called her a "small woman" who was making men tremble (Xinhua, September, 9 2011). On February 27, 2011, the *Sun* reported that during a press conference granted by Kah Walla:

> … she was also questioned on her marital status. She said it is because she is a woman that is why her marital status is always mentioned. In response, she said "if you poke into the marital lives of some of my political contestants you will get more interesting stories that you will no longer be interested in mine. Those who have brought Cameroon to its knees are married men" she said.

Through that response, Kah Walla also played into the strategic use of traditional gender stereotypes implying that since men had "brought Cameroon to its knees" the country needed a caring mother to lift it up. As indicated earlier, such strategies have been used successfully by other female politicians such as Michelle Bachelet in Chile and Ellen Johnson-Sirleaf in Liberia. So, the overall media fascination and positive reports about Kah Walla notwithstanding, gendered discourses about her candidacy and campaign still emerged.

In an article published in 1991 and strikingly titled "The media: obstacle or ally of feminists?" Kahn and Goldenberg noted that "under certain circumstances, media treatment can serve as an obstacle to women's achievement of their political goals. In other circumstances, the news media can act as an additional resource" (1991, 104). In the case of Kah Walla's 2011 presidential campaign, it seems the latter scenario held sway. She acknowledges that "gender bias is real in Cameroonian politics" but she does not think it negatively affected the way she was covered by the media. According to her:

> I would say that I got probably more than my fair share [of media coverage] due to a certain number of factors that were particular to me and I am not sure that every female politician will get that. One is that I was breaking the political mold in Cameroon. The fact that I was a woman standing up to these 70-year-old men was more outstanding, astonishing and amazing to people … We do little surveys from time to time and if you say my name and say "what is the first word that comes to your mind when you hear Kah Walla?" The most pronounced word is "courage." So the media, the population, everybody was just like amazed that I was coming up against these guys as a woman. The other factor that I had was that I took them on intellectually. There was no question about it. I was the best debater out there … The journalists have amusing stories of people who showed up [for media debates] and found out that I was the one that they were going to have in front of them, and turned around and went back home. It became a David and Goliath factor [and this] was stronger than the gender factor in this particular circumstance …

Foregrounding the David and Goliath narrative instead of gendered perspectives introduces a supplementary approach in understanding gendered orientations in the mediation of politics as a process that is perhaps not necessarily a given but one which, depending on circumstances, can be foreshadowed by other contextual factors like the profile of a particular candidate (see Vos 2013).

Conclusion

The central objectives of this chapter have been to examine: (1) the campaign style of Edith Kah Walla; and (2) how selected print media in Cameroon covered her presidential candidacy and campaign. Overall, the analyses show that with the novelty of her candidacy (one of the first two women to run for president in Cameroon), her manner of "doing politics" (participatory party and campaign governance and well-informed policy-oriented debates), her excellent bilingualism, and her eloquence, she became a "media darling" and by default, one of the most visible candidates and a "phenomenon" during the 2011 presidential election in Cameroon.

All these did not, however, secure Kah Walla the presidency. Arguably, this failure was not purely because she is a woman but simply because of several other contextual factors in particular, the fact that she, like all the other opposition candidates, was fighting against a dominant ruling party, which undemocratically appropriates the benefits of incumbency as it attempts to hold on to power. Although her official results were dismal and instances of gendered media discourses still surfaced, Kah Walla's candidacy and campaign have undoubtedly set a bar against which future campaigns in Cameroon will be evaluated. Politics in Cameroon is significantly "masculinized" and prior to 2011, no woman had contested presidential elections. Through her remarkable candidacy, Kah Walla may not have entirely shattered the "political glass ceiling" but she has indubitably shown that women can henceforth effectively compete with men for the presidency.

The chapter has also shown that in relation to the "standard" aspects of research in this field—news media coverage of female candidates' viability, issues, and traits—Kah Walla received significant coverage of her political program on a wide range of issues and not just "women's issues"; she also received significantly *positive* coverage on her personal traits (such as her intelligence and courage) and some coverage focusing on her physical appearance and marital status, which was in line with previous research on these issues.

These findings, however, raise important issues worth reflecting on with regard to research in this field. The first is the need for female politicians not to be easily blinded by what may appear as a positive tone in the coverage but which merely reinforces gendered demarcations of the political sphere. For instance, Kah Walla framed herself as courageous and she was evidently pleased that she was framed in the media as courageous. While such framings, especially from the news media may lead to leaps of satisfaction, they nonetheless underscore an entrenchment of gendered perceptions of the political field and need to be challenged rather than celebrated.

The media, for example, highlighted Kah Walla's courage arguably because she was being judged as literally having the guts to attempt something meant for men. In line with Gidengil and Everitt's (1999, 48) gendered mediation argument, such framings subtly reinforce "traditional conceptions of politics as a male preserve." Why were the other male politicians who were contesting the elections for the first time not also seen as "courageous"? In a sense, therefore, the gendered mediation thesis resonates with this aspect of the findings, which point to an important dimension of the varied forms of manifestation of the thesis: subtle gendered demarcations of the political terrain disguised in mediated discourses as positive trait articulations. As Garcia-Blanco and Wahl-Jorgensen (2012, 437) concluded in a similar argument supporting the gendered mediation thesis, this form of the thesis manifestation subtly encapsulates the "discourses that perpetuate the gendering of female politicians and their assessment within patriarchal models of femininity which [in turn] discursively estrange women from the realm of politics."

Second, the political, socio-economic and cultural situation in the West and the election era political discourses around these spheres are significantly different from that which operates in many non-Western countries, especially in a place like Cameroon. In the case of Cameroon, it is true that there are particular "women's issues" like female circumcision or traditional widowhood practices that can be classified as "electoral women's issues" but these, as well as issues such as defense policy or international relations, are rarely prominent in election campaigns. In a context of generalized poverty, what often take center stage during campaigns are socio-economic development issues: unemployment, agriculture policy and provision of basic services like electricity, pipe-borne water, and health centers.

Given the widespread poverty and urgency to redress these issues, which affect men and women alike, all candidates tend to focus on them to attract as many votes as possible. As a result, the traditional "gendered demarcation" in policy prioritization that has been shown in the case of the West fails to emerge in such contexts. What we have rather is what can be called *an overall contextualized de-genderification of campaign discourse*, which describes a situation where there is no major coalescing of candidates' policy preferences along strict gendered lines and although candidates' campaigns may be "gendered" (targeting women's associations for instance) their overall central policy proposals are *de-gendered.* I would argue that it is through such lenses that one can understand the way in which Kah Walla framed her political program as focusing on the "majority of Cameroonians who are marginalized" and literally refused outright to "play the gender card" by consistently singling out women in her campaign discourses.

Last, the point above about a *contextualized de-genderification* of campaign discourses signals the need for more cross-national research across emerging democracies. This further research will need to focus on aspects such as the local factors that mediate male and female candidates' strategic appropriation of politically-relevant gendered opportunity structures and the role played by media constructions of electorally salient issues in shaping these strategies. By addressing these and related questions, we would be answering the call of the moment to further extend the empirical scope of research about media, gender and politics.

Notes

1 This is a direct reference to Kah Walla's height, a point addressed later.

2 The reference to "Benjamin" in this context is a biblical allusion to Benjamin, the last of Jacob's 12 sons as discussed in the Old Testament. This was pointing to Kah Walla being the youngest candidate and the newest political sensation.

11

The Mother of Brazil: Gender Roles, Campaign Strategy, and the Election of Brazil's First Female President

Pedro G. dos Santos and Farida Jalalzai

In 2010 Dilma Rousseff, popularly referred to as "Dilma," joined a small yet growing group of women executive leaders when she was elected the first woman president of Brazil. Dilma's victory was no surprise since she had the support of the very popular outgoing president Luiz Inácio "Lula" da Silva.[1] Nevertheless, the fact that Dilma is a woman is noteworthy given that Brazil's political system is overwhelmingly male-dominated at all levels of government (Araújo 2010; Miguel 2008). Dilma's significance also stems from the fact that, unlike most women national leaders around the world, she occupies a relatively strong presidency, gained office through popular election and lacked family ties to power (Jalalzai 2013).

In this chapter we explore the rise of Dilma from a competent bureaucrat to becoming the president of one of the world's most influential countries. In it we focus on two key interrelated aspects of Dilma's 2010 presidential campaign: the creation of the "Mother of Brazil" persona and the way her political party used this persona to consolidate the electoral victory. In the case of Brazil it is essential to discuss the importance of the Free Electoral Advertisement Hour (HGPE), the free hour in which political parties and candidates can broadcast TV and radio ads daily throughout the campaign period.

This chapter is divided in five parts. First, we briefly discuss women's political representation in Latin American and Brazilian politics, situating Dilma's rise to power within broader understandings of women in politics in the country and in the region. Second, we provide Dilma's biography, paying special attention to her political ascension. Third, we discuss campaign strategy in Brazilian presidential races and the role of the HGPE on campaign strategy. Fourth, we explore the creation of the "Mother of Brazil" persona, focusing on media portrayals of Dilma throughout her political ascension and the role outgoing president

Luis Inácio "Lula" da Silva had on framing Dilma's campaign as a natural, and gendered, continuation of his presidency. We conclude by briefly discussing the results of the elections.

Women in executive office and the Brazilian political scene: Some thoughts on Dilma's significance

Totaling only 89 cases to date, women prime ministers and presidents are political rarities but vastly increased their numbers over the last two decades. They exercise somewhat limited powers and arise from a very narrow array of circumstances, contexts, and backgrounds (Jalalzai 2008; 2013). Women worldwide are more likely to be prime ministers than presidents. Whereas parties select prime ministers, their powers are somewhat weak, and governance requires cabinet collaboration. This coincides with stereotypes of women's skills in working with others rather than acting independently. Women are less likely to become presidents holding dominant power gaining office by popular vote. Prevailing gender stereotypes work against strong women presidents; both their personal traits and the issues they address are deemed more masculine. Women leaders wielding dominant presidential powers are almost exclusively relegated to daughters and wives of male executives or opposition leaders, thus compensating for the traditional vulnerabilities women face in entering executive politics.

Latin American women comprise 12 of the 89 historical cases of female executives, eight of those acting as the de facto executive power of the nation. Latin American countries nearly universally adopted unified presidential systems and invested a great deal of authority to presidents. Brazil proves no exception and is very much a presidency-centered domain. Powers such as decree, amendatory observations, and appointment of their cabinet provides an agenda-setting power that is considerably higher than most presidents, including their American counterpart (Aleman and Tsebelis 2005; Cox and Morgenstern 2001).

The 2010 election of Dilma makes her one of the few "strong" female chief executives in contemporary Latin America. Women presidents in Latin America tend to share one thing in common: their family ties with established political leaders. In 1974, Isabel Perón of Argentina became the first woman president in the world. She succeeded her husband, President Juan Domingo

Perón, who appointed her as vice-president one year prior to his death (Weir 1993). Michelle Bachelet of Chile, who took office in 2006, was the daughter of Air Force General and Pinochet opponent Alberto Bachelet Martinez who died of cardiac failure during political imprisonment. In 2007 Cristina Fernández became the second female president of Argentina. Fernández succeeded her husband, President Néstor Kirchner, now deceased, who declined another bid (Rohter 2007). The father of Laura Chinchilla, elected as president of Costa Rica in 2010, Rafael Ángel Chinchilla Fallas, was a former national comptroller and still a very popular figure noted for his honesty (Jalalzai 2012). Dilma's election in 2010 marks the first time a woman president had no direct family ties with political leaders in Latin America.

Dilma's rise seems especially puzzling since the presence of women in Brazilian politics continues to be one of the lowest in South America at all levels of government and varies only slightly between legislative and executive positions, as well as among levels of government (local, state, and national). According to the Inter-Parliamentary Union (IPU) (n.d.), Brazil's 8.6 percent of women in the Chamber of Deputies (national lower house) ranks 123rd in the World Classification Rankings, making the country's representation of women in the lower house well below the Americas' average of 23.8 percent and even below the 14.3 percent average in Arab states.

While Dilma did not benefit from blood ties to any political figure, her connections to the outgoing president Lula proved pivotal to her ascension. Taken together, Dilma's significance, therefore, stems from her seeming divergence patterns evidenced among women leaders more generally and Latin American female presidents particularly. As someone invested with significant executive powers, lacking family ties, and ascending in an environment seemingly unwelcoming to female politicians, she presents an important opportunity to examine the role of gender in the election of a female president.

The rise of Dilma

Involved in the clandestine guerillas during Brazil's dictatorship regime in the late 1960s and early 1970s,[2] Dilma's formal political career started in 1986 when she worked as a party advisor for the *Partido Democrático Trabalhista* (Worker's Democratic Party [PDT]) in the state of Rio Grande do Sul (RS). Throughout the 1980s and 1990s Dilma was appointed to a number of key positions, including the State Secretary of Mines and Energy in RS. In 2000 she switched from the PDT to the *Partido dos Trabalhadores* (Worker's Party [PT]), continuing her tenure as State Secretary of Mines, Energy, and Communication. It was as State Secretary that Dilma started receiving attention from the PT and president Luis Inácio "Lula" da Silva. In 2001, during a national energy crisis, the state of Rio Grande do Sul was one of the few Brazilian states to avoid energy rationing. Her handling of the notorious *apagão* (the big "lights off") led Lula to appoint Dilma in 2003 as the Minister for Mines and Energy during his first term (Fernandes 2012; Souza 2011).

Throughout Lula's first term as president (2003–7) it became clear that he felt a political connection with Dilma. In 2005, after the *mensalão* (big monthly payments)[3] scandal rocked the PT's political structure, Lula appointed Dilma as his Chief of Staff—the most important cabinet role in the country. From that moment on pundits started to see Dilma not only as a powerful cabinet member but also as a potential presidential candidate. Lula, constitutionally barred from being president for a third consecutive term, needed to find a suitable successor. Some scholars and pundits argue that Lula wanted to pick his successor himself, not allowing the PT to make the decision collectively (Souza 2011). Some further speculate that the choice of Dilma, a newcomer to the PT when compared to lifelong politically powerful members, was a strategic move that would allow Lula to take power again in 2014 (Romero 2012). Regardless of the reason why Dilma Rousseff was picked by Lula and the PT, the fact that she was able to become a respected political leader in a considerably short time span is noteworthy. That Dilma is a woman makes this feat even more remarkable, especially in a country such as Brazil in which women's presence in politics is low and *machismo* is still perceived as a cultural issue (Baldwin and DeSouza 2001). Dilma's nomination showed that she was able to overcome her lack of political pedigree, such as family connections common among female heads of state, thanks to her effectiveness as a bureaucrat and her recent association with President Lula. It is irrefutable that Dilma Rousseff's connection to Lula, a president who exited the post with a remarkable 80 percent approval rating, was a deciding factor for her election (Alves 2012; Downie 2010). Nevertheless, Dilma still needed to be accepted by party members as the correct choice and, more importantly, convince voters that she was capable of being the president of Brazil.

Media, campaign strategy, and the free electoral hour

Since the return to democracy, Brazilian elections, especially presidential campaigns, have become highly competitive and professional. The 1989 election of Fernando Collor de Melo, a relative unknown at the national level at the time, ushered the era of elections that focus on the use of television and political marketing (da Silva 2011). The power of political marketing became more clear when Dilma's predecessor Lula was able, after three failed attempts, to win the presidency in 2002 on a well-run campaign that in many ways reinvented the candidate and depended heavily on his image in the media (Miguel 2006). The election of Dilma was no different than the previous five in the sense that political marketing and television exposure were keys to the development of a winning bid.

Television is still the medium politicians and electoral marketing strategists seek the most in Brazilian elections. Polls revealed that in the 1980s and 1990s between 86 percent and 89 percent of the population used television as their main source of information about politics (Kinzo and Dunkerley 2003). More recently, Azevedo (2006) claims that at least two-thirds of the population use television and radio as their source for basic information, including information about politicians. Television is still king in Brazilian elections because it reaches a large sector of the population, and that is key for political parties trying to reach the Brazilian voter. More importantly, television ads are highly regulated, free, and on primetime, during the elections. Brazil's *Horário Gratuito de Propaganda Eleitoral* (HGPE) runs twice a day, during the lunch hour and at night (primetime) for one hour each time during the two months preceding an election (Schmitt 1999; da Silveira and de Mello 2011). Paid advertisement outside the allocated "free hour" is not allowed. Therefore, parties rely and depend on exposure during this two-hours-a-day period to reach a majority of the Brazilian population during the campaign.

Political parties pay special attention to the HGPE. The time allocated to each party for the "free hour" are based on two criteria: one-third of the time divided equally among parties/candidates, and two-thirds of the time proportional to the coalition's share of representatives in the National Congress (Schmitt 1999; da Silveira and de Mello 2011). Therefore, campaign coalitions are negotiated many times among political parties to maximize their time on TV (and radio) for their preferred candidate. The nature of coalition negotiation in Brazil shows that political parties consider the HGPE a crucial aspect of their campaign strategy (Martins 2013). In other words, the effort parties and candidates put in their HGPE spots may be the determining factor in a successful campaign.

While advertisement space is free, the production of such ads is not. The rise of political marketing in presidential elections in Brazil led to a level of professionalization in the creation and production of television and radio spots that is costly yet effective. The pressure to convey the right message during the HGPE is high, and parties (and candidates) are willing to pay the price for the right message to reach Brazilians through their television sets. Campaign expenditures have risen considerably. For example, campaign expenditures for all presidential candidates in 2002 was a little over R$93 million (U$41 million), a number that rose to R$334 million (U$147 million) in 2006 and $589 million (U$258 million) in 2010 (Backes and dos Santos 2012). In the 2010 campaign Dilma and the PT spent over R$210 million (U$93 million), doubling what all candidates spent only two election cycles before (Abramo 2013). The costs associated with political marketing (and the hiring of the right people to convey that message) have also risen considerably. In 2002, Lula reportedly spent R$5 million (U$2.2 million) to hire a renowned *marqueteiro*, an amount superior to his whole campaign budget in 1998 (Miguel 2006). In 2010, Dilma reportedly spent over R$29 million (U$13 million) on "radio and television production," which included the production of television advertisements using high-definition "cinema-style" digital cameras and the creation of "soundtracks" for each television spot (Flor and Victor 2010).

The rise of the Mother of Brazil

> *Dilma is kind of the mother of PAC. She is the one who coordinates PAC. She is the one who takes care of it, who follows it, who makes sure the plan is working.*
>
> President Luis Inácio "Lula" da Silva 2008 (cited in Amaral 2011)

Because Dilma was a relative unknown both to party members—she was not a lifelong PT member—and to the general public—she was a powerful minister but was not "popular"—the PT had to work hard to create an image that would directly connect Dilma to Lula and would translate into the continuity of his presidential term. The connection had to be clear, but it also had to highlight how Dilma's presidency would not just continue his legacy, but move the country and Lula's policies forward.

Adding to Dilma's "anonymity," her personality was also a problem for the campaign. As one weekly magazine puts it, when talking about Dilma's job as a minister in 2006, she is a complex figure, "tough, but feminine, without being feminist." The magazine also pointed out that Dilma has a strong temperament, being an intransigent and technical negotiator (in Biroli 2010, 287). Other publications, political bloggers, and political pundits were less politically correct about Dilma's personality. Because of her abrasiveness as a minister, critics were not afraid to question her femininity and focus on aspects beyond her capacity as a politician to question her credentials. Therefore, not unlike other women in presidential campaigns (Carlin and Winfrey 2009; Heldman, Carroll and Olson 2005), Dilma's choice of clothing became a major topic of discussion, especially after it became clear that she would be the presidential candidate in 2010. For example, Milene Chavez, a writer for *Veja* (Brazil's largest weekly magazine) provided the following analysis about Dilma's clothing style: "Less skin means more credibility. Showing the armpits? Never. Red is good because it is the party's color. However, a very small part of society will vote on ideological leaning. This color also conveys fear. The blazer shows seriousness, but the ones she uses are too short, they accentuate her hips" (quoted in Queiroz and Martins Jr. 2011, 137). Queiroz and Martins Jr. (2011) state that after Dilma's wardrobe became a major topic of conversation, Lula himself asked for fashion stylists to help her select what to wear.

Dilma is complex because even though she is a woman and consequentially has feminine traits, she also possesses a leadership style that is distinctively "masculine." While such a personality trait may be okay for a bureaucrat working in the background, such characteristics in a woman can be problematic during an election campaign. In other words, the PT (and Lula) were worried about what Kathleen Hall Jamieson calls the double-bind effect, where women who are considered "feminine" will be judged incompetent while women who are competent will be judged as unfeminine and analyzed under a different lens from that applied to successful men (Carlin and Winfrey 2009; Jamieson 1995). Therefore, the *marqueteiros* would have to portray Dilma as competent candidate, but also as a "feminine" woman.

Dilma's profile in Brazilian politics rose at an abnormally fast pace. Therefore, media outlets and the population were playing catch-up to learn who Dilma was between 2003, when she was first appointed Minister of Mines and Energy, and

2010 when Dilma became Brazil's first woman president. As her profile rose, so did the scrutiny. As the Minister of Mines and Energy, most news outlets focused mainly on the policies her cabinet enacted and on the difficulties Dilma as the head of the cabinet would face during her tenure, while some journalists started questioning her past as a clandestine guerilla ("Brasil mantendrá su política económica," 2003). In 2005, when Dilma was appointed Lula's Chief of Staff, she was the first woman to ever fill that position. Therefore, there was some discussion in the media about that novelty and more discussion about her past as a member of the armed guerrillas, but most of the debate at the time was directly focused on the *mensalão* scandal and her appointment was seen as "natural" because of her competency as Minister of Mines and Energy (Carvalho 2005; Scolese and Flor 2005; Villaméa 2005).

At the moment Dilma became Chief of Staff for the Lula administration, rumors started to point to her as a possible presidential candidate, but nothing at that time indicated that either Lula or the PT were seriously looking at her as a potential candidate. At that time another woman was seen as the natural choice. Marina Silva was Lula's Minister of the Environment and provided another great "coming from nothing" story for the PT. However, disagreements over environmental policies (and arguably over Lula's decision to favor Dilma as the presidential candidate) led Marina Silva to leave the PT in August 2009, choosing to join the *Partido Verde* (Green Party—PV) and eventually running for president in 2010 for that party (Bonin 2009). Marina was also an important player in the 2010 elections as she was able to garner almost 20 percent of votes and come in third place in the first-round election, an impressive number given that presidential elections in Brazil had, since 2002, been a two-candidate (and two-parties—PT and PSDB) affair.

While Marina Silva may have seemed like the natural choice, "Lula in skirts" as some would call her (Alencar 2009), by February of 2009 Lula started to hint that his choice for his successor was Dilma. It was clear that the party leadership would approve whomever Lula decided would be the 2010 PT presidential candidate, and at that moment the unofficial campaign for Dilma started. From that point on Lula started to actively campaign for Dilma, using various official occasions to bolster her popularity, even though the presidential campaign could not officially start until June of 2010.

Because Dilma was a relative unknown in national politics, Lula had to work hard in "selling" her as the natural choice for his successor (Pires 2011, 140). Lula was aware that Dilma was not as charismatic as he was and went as far as calling

Dilma out and asking her to "change from this 'office' expression you always have" (quoted in Gomes 2011, 21). Moreover, as Lula became more assertive about his decision to choose Dilma as his successor, scrutiny over her possible candidacy and femininity increased considerably. It was in this moment, the beginning of 2009, that news coverage about Dilma took a distinctive gendered direction. It is here that the double bind—scrutiny under different lenses for women politicians—over Dilma's news coverage started to focus on aspects related to charisma, femininity, and fashion. For example, a 2009 article of *Veja* magazine was titled and subtitled "Body and Soul 2010. With diet, plastic surgery, and a radical change in her haircut, Dilma Rousseff shows the (good) results of her own PAC, a Plan for Cosmetic Improvement. It is the first step in her way to become Lula successor" (quoted in Gomes 2011, 23).

In April of 2009 Dilma was diagnosed with lymphoma, an issue that raised some questions about her ability to run as a presidential candidate in 2010 (Ribeiro 2009). After it became clear that Dilma was going to beat the cancer and continue her duties as Chief of Staff and, eventually, her presidential candidacy, once again the focus of attention was on something other than politics; fashion and personal appearance became central in media discussions about Dilma.[4] News outlets focused almost entirely on the fact that she was wearing a wig after her chemotherapy and radiotherapy treatment, and they also focused on her hairstyle after she stopped using a wig (Lago 2009).

Questions about Dilma's fashion choices, something more rare among male presidential candidates, also brings up the point that Lula, Dilma, and the PT were aware of the importance of showing Dilma as more "feminine." It is undeniable that there was a conscious effort to change Dilma's clothing style and to make her look younger. During the campaign Dilma dyed her hair a lighter tone and started using colorful clothes, something that was rare during her tenure as Minister and Chief of Staff. As Gomes (2011, 25) argues, the campaign "constructs a more feminine and sexually more interesting body, creating a stereotype of a 'light' and docile woman/politic." In other words, the presidential campaign choice for hair and style was a deliberate attempt to feminize Dilma and to differentiate her based on gendered expectations, arguably connecting her "visual persona" with the persona that was going to be *created* for the campaign.

In February of 2010 the PT made its official announcement of Dilma's candidacy. At this point in the process the party had to start thinking about a campaign strategy that would help voters understand that she was Lula's successor, but also that she would be a competent president. Among the political establishment and to a lesser extent the media, the focus was on her lack of charisma and abrasive (perhaps even manly) leadership style. As Lula and the PT devised a political campaign they would have to find a way to portray her as a competent leader but they also had to "humanize" her, or in other words, make her more feminine.

Dilma's campaign focused early on the term "Mother of Brazil," or "Mãe do Povo" (Mother of the People), as an identifier. Lula first used a variation of the term, calling Dilma "the mother of PAC" in a speech in the *Alemão favela* in Rio de Janeiro, during the unveiling of a development in the community that was part of the government's *Programa de Aceleração de Crescimento* (PAC, or Growth Acceleration Program). PAC is the largest development program ever launched in Brazil, aimed at building infrastructure and industrial capability throughout the country (Bertazzo 2012). Lula did not perceive Dilma as his picked candidate at that time, but he was seriously considering Dilma as his successor (Amaral 2011; Pires 2011). Nevertheless, the term "mother of PAC" allowed for the development of a campaign in which gender played a key role. By the time the official campaign kicked off in June of 2010 the moniker "Mother of Brazil" and "Mother of the People" became synonymous with Dilma. The use of symbols of motherhood and femininity were especially important given the fact that Dilma was notorious for her harshness and abrasiveness, characteristics normally associated with masculinity. For example, when asked about Dilma's toughness, Lula argued, "Dilma's toughness […] is the toughness of a mother. When we try to eat a bigger piece of meat […] It is the toughness that you know of a person who wants equality" (Preite Sobrinho 2010).

The strategy of focusing on Dilma's gender and exploiting the "Mother of Brazil" moniker was clear on June 13, 2010 when the official campaign was launched. During the whole event the color lilac was ever-present, sometimes overpowering the traditional red that is characteristic of PT events. Prior to the nomination speech (and Lula's speech), the convention honored women in Brazilian political history, highlighting their struggles under the slogan "*elas mudaram o país*" (they changed the country). In her nomination speech it also became clear that the campaign would focus on gendered differences to highlight certain characteristics that Dilma as woman could bring to the presidency, a strategy used by other successful women presidential candidates such as Michele Bachelet of Chile and Ellen Johnson Sirleaf of Liberia (Thomas and Adams 2010). For example, Dilma wanted to assure voters that this would not be a women-only government, arguing that "we, women, are 52 percent [of the population]. The other 48 percent are our sons, so it all stays 'at home' because women do not discriminate against anyone" (quoted in Gonzalez 2010).

Because Dilma was a relative unknown even to some of Lula's supporters the first weeks of official campaign and the spots on HGPE focused both on her biographical profile and her connection to Lula. In these television spots the fact that Dilma is a woman was discussed either directly or indirectly in virtually every program. At the end of almost all programs a video clip shows women from various ethnicities and age groups with a song on the background that included this section in its lyric:

> Women are divine fortresses/they are beautiful ballerinas/ they are black on with, warrior of faith/woman/women are *pulso firme* (strong, rigid)/but with the voice and love of a mother/ they are predestined to win/ this is a woman/ against insecurity/ for Brazil/ for order/ for progress/ we want woman. (Quoted in Pires 2011, 157)

On the first HGPE show in July of 2010, the theme of motherhood was distinctively part of the message the party was trying to convey to voters. During the program Dilma says, "I want to do, with the caring of a mother, everything that still needs to be done. This is my dream" (quoted in Pires 2011, 157). During that first program another jingle is introduced symbolizing Lula's exit from the government, and these lyrics are added to the catchy tune: "Now the hands of a woman will lead us/ I will continue missing all of this, but happy and smiling/ Because, my people has just gained a mother/ who has a heart that goes from the *Oiapoque ao Chuí* (north to south)" (quoted in Pires 2011, 157). In the program both the "Mother of Brazil" persona and the message that Dilma is Lula's successor are clear, and this is the message the party wants to convey early on in the campaign, especially to those voters who were not yet associating Dilma's candidacy with Lula's presidency. The connection between Lula and Dilma was essential for the campaign to be successful, and the HGPE program on May 13 (a PT sponsored program before the official presidential campaign), the national convention on 13 June, and the beginning of the HGPE on August 17 (with the songs and speeches described above) helped consolidate this connection and Dilma's position as the front runner (Alves 2012).

As the campaign gained ground, the use of the term "Mother of Brazil" and any association to Dilma as a mother figure became one of the most used rhetorical strategies of the PT. For example, the August 26 HGPE program profiles a seamstress named Marilane Dantas, and this is what she says about Lula and Dilma:

> The community calls Lula "father." Because he was a man who prepared himself for this. To lead our country, but thinking about equality, thinking about the lower classes. He entered the government with this "light" for the poor. That's understood. The father of the people. I hope Dilma Rousseff can be the mother of the people. (Quoted in Pires 2011, 157)

Dilma herself used such connections in a number of her speeches and interviews during the campaign. In her nomination acceptance speech, Dilma said, "It is time for a woman to govern this country. We women are born with a sense of caring, supporting, and protecting. We are unbeatable in our defense of our family and our sons" (Bencke 2010). Later, in a speech in Natal (Rio Grande do Norte state) Rousseff said, "The president left a legacy, that of taking care of the Brazilian people. I will be the mother of the Brazilian People" (Alvares 2010). The motherly figure and gendered assumptions about the role of women and mothers in society are clear aspects of the campaign when Dilma claims, in an interview with the Argentinean newspaper *El Pais*, that she will "continue Lula's model, but with the heart and soul of a woman. It is not repetition, it is progress. In my opinion, women have a great capacity for taking care while also nurturing. Of course men can do that too, but the women's view is different" (Pires 2011).

Throughout the official campaign period, from June until Dilma's victory in November, the persona of "Mother of Brazil" was skillfully used in the candidate's advertisements during HGPE and speeches conferred both by Lula and Dilma. The term was used to distinguish Dilma from her main opponent José Serra in gendered terms, but also to place Dilma as the candidate who would continue and improve on Lula's popular presidency. Nevertheless, it is important to point out that the focus of the campaign was not this gender difference but the continuation of Lula's presidency. Of the 40 programs shown during HGPE, 24 of them either referenced Lula directly or had him present in the program. The focus of these Lula-related segments was to reinforce the qualities of Dilma, connect her to the success of Lula's government, and mobilize Lula supporters to help elect Dilma (Panke 2011, 43). In other words, the fact that Dilma was a woman and the creation of the "Mother of Brazil" persona are important aspects of PT's campaign strategy in 2010, but this gendered aspect of the campaign is used in connection to one main theme: the continuation of widely popular outgoing president Lula. Therefore, while the "Mother of Brazil" strategy may not have been the deciding factor in the election of Dilma in 2010, it was an essential aspect of the campaign discourse adopted by the PT.

The 2010 elections and conclusions

Dilma's main opponent was José Serra, former Health Minister and Governor of São Paulo who hailed from the Social Democratic Party (PSDB). Serra had faced off against Lula in the 2002 presidential elections and was already a known politician. When Dilma failed to win a majority of the vote in the first round, this was not due to Serra, whose candidacy was largely lackluster, but to the traction Green Party candidate Marina Silva gained among more affluent and evangelical voters. Dilma also did not appear to be particularly gifted at campaigning. In response, in the second round Lula began devoting nearly all of his time campaigning for Dilma, going on the attack against Serra and the media. Dilma could largely keep a positive tone, but this could make her vulnerable to arguments that she was a woman needing Lula's protection (Goertzel 2011, 182).

Dilma's election with a 12-point margin in the November 2010 runoff showed that the "Mother of Brazil" strategy, as a complement to the strategy focusing on Lula's strength, worked, or at least it did not undermine her candidacy. Although Dilma did not receive a majority of the female vote in 2010, polls showed that vote intentions among women in Brazil changed in favor of Dilma after the image of "Mother of Brazil" became a key campaign strategy (Oms 2010). This allowed her to position José Serra as a gender opposite in the people's psyche (after all, men do not fight against their mother); establish the continuity of Lula's government and his description as the "Father of the People"; and provide her with much-needed charisma, pushing voters to see her as the first female president and not as the boring and rude bureaucrat.

Gender played a key part in Dilma's presidential campaign, and her role as a woman and a mother was artfully used by the PT to make her the ideal successor to Lula's political legacy. The birth of her grandchild during the campaign season allowed her to nurture the idea of a motherly figure even more (Guedes 2010). Therefore, even though gender was probably not the deciding factor in the election of Dilma it is arguable that Lula, Dilma, and the PT skillfully appealed to the candidate's feminine traits to consolidate her position as Lula's natural, female, motherly successor.

Notes

1 Murray (2010) aptly points to possibly negative repercussions of the media referring to female presidential candidates disproportionately called by their first names. We, however, reference Dilma Rousseff mainly as Dilma rather than Rousseff because this is how she is most commonly referred to by politicians, scholars, the press, the public, and, most importantly, her own presidential website.

2 Rousseff was involved in a number of leftist clandestine organizations such as the *Politico Operario* (Pollop—Political Worker), *Comando de Libreação Nacional* (Colina—National Liberation Command), and *Vanguarda Armada Revolucionaria Palmares* (VAR-Palmares—Armed Revolutionary Vanguard-Palmares) (Fernandes 2012). It is arguable that Rousseff's political career started during this period since a number of individuals involved in these clandestine organizations were directly involved in politics before the coup and many became politicians, establishing and re-establishing parties such as the Communist parties (PCB and PC do B) and the Worker's Party (PT).

3 This political scandal involved a number of politicians from the upper echelon of the PT and revolved around the payment of monthly fees to Congress members of different parties to guarantee they would vote in favor of Lula's policies. The scandal led to the resignation of Lula's previous Chief of Staff José Dirceu (Hunter and Power 2007; dos Santos 2007).

4 Dilma's cancer treatment was also a great opportunity to make the changes in appearance deemed necessary by the party and by campaign officials. Dilma allegedly underwent cosmetic surgery that went beyond the treatment of the cancer, and her choice in wardrobe definitely changed especially during and after the cancer treatment. It is clear that Dilma has changed her appearance to run for president, and that the main intention of this change in appearance was to make her more "friendly" and arguably more feminine. Therefore, there is a gendered component in how Dilma's looks changed in 2009, and it was clearly a strategic move by the candidate and the party in making her more appealing to voters.

12

The Visual Framing of Romanian Women Politicians in Personal Campaign Blogs during the 2012 Romanian Parliamentary Elections

Camelia Cmeciu and Monica Pătruț

Social media have emerged as a powerful tool to disseminate information and to mobilize and engage citizens during election campaigns. Politicians from the former Soviet bloc have been gaining awareness of the high degree of visibility that social media allow and they have been increasingly using blogs or Facebook pages as online strategies to represent themselves. Most of the existing research from Western scholars has focused predominantly on the verbal content of online self-representations yet attention should also be given to visual content as a powerful campaign instrument (Goodnow 2013). Since women are more often associated with a visual appearance (Dan and Iorgoveanu 2013), an emphasis should be placed on how women politicians have been using visuals during their election campaigns. This is the principal goal of our study. To our knowledge this is the first attempt to examine the visual self-representation choices of Romanian women politicians on their campaign blogs. Of particular interest will be the question of whether female candidates for parliament challenge or conform to gender stereotypes in their online identity construction.

Prejudices, discrimination, family responsibilities, stereotypes regarding women's lack of qualification, and limited access to election campaign funds are among the main reasons (Miroiu 2004; Paul Vass 2012) why female politicians are under-represented in the Romanian Parliament even after the fall of communism. In the present structure of the Parliament of Romania (Marcu and Nedelcu 2013, 19–21), only 11 percent of the seats belong to women politicians (68 out of 588 seats).

Within the political context of a significant under-representation of women in the Romanian Parliament, we will conduct a visual framing analysis of the blog posts of three women candidates (Alina Gorghiu, Rodica Nassar, Elena

Udrea) belonging respectively to the three main Romanian parties (National Liberal Party [PNL], Social Democratic Party [PSD], Democratic Liberal Party [PD-L]).[1] Our choice of photographic images as empirical data has two main justifications. First, voters respond more to their perceptions of visual images than to objective realities (Hacker 1995, xii) related to the candidate. Second, blogs have become self-promotional sites where candidates and the campaign staff may control what should be revealed or not. Besides being the most active female candidate bloggers in the four weeks leading to the Parliamentary Election Day (December 9, 2012), the three candidates had the highest number of votes in the colleges they represented. As the final results posted by Biroul Electoral Central (the Central Electoral Bureau) show, Alina Gorghiu (PNL) had 12,418 votes, Rodica Nassar (PSD) had 20,765 votes, and Elena Udrea (PD-L) had 11,978 votes.

Literature review—self-representations of women candidates

Besides the considerable research on media representations of female candidates, the studies on women running for political office in Western democratic societies also focus on their self-representation in advertisements, TV spots, and on Web 1.0 and Web 2.0 (Banwart 2010; Bystrom 2004; Bystrom, Banwart, Kaid, and Robertson 2004; Dolan 2005; Markstedt 2007; Niven and Zilber 2001).

Research on women politicians' self-representations in the offline or online environment examines how they negotiate deeply entrenched assumptions that competency, a typically male trait, is deemed as more valuable for a "good" politican than expressiveness, a typically female trait. The double bind (Jamieson 1995) that female candidates face during election campaigns, presents a challenge for how they approach their image development. Kathleen Dolan (2005) considers that "decisions about how to present themselves to voters can be tricky" (31) because the public's perception of women candidates is complex. Thus crafting "an electable image" (Banwart 2010, 269) turns into a real challenge. Research on how voters evaluate female candidates' communication highlights that women should develop "both an image of possessing the required male attributes for the job in concert with the expected—yet less valued—female attributes" (Banwart 2010, 269). Niven and Zilber's study (2001) on congressional websites indicates that, in their pursuit to overcome the gender-stereotypical label, women and men politicians communicate very similar messages. Some women politicians in the West have started to challenge media and voter stereotypes by changing their issue priorities on their campaign websites. Female candidates for the U.S. Congress seem to have shifted (Dolan 2005, 35) their issue priorities from a set of gender-stereotypical issues (education, health care, social security/medicare, environment, family issues, women's issues, abortion, and ethics/government reform), which reflect compassion traits, to a set of topics similar to those of their male counterparts, which reflect competence (business, economy, foreign affairs, defense/military issues, agriculture). Some research on campaign websites (Dolan 2005, 42) highlights that the dominance of certain issues in the self-presentation of female candidates should be mainly associated with party-based stereotypes rather than with gender-based stereotypes.

In our study we want to examine whether women politicians adopt or challenge issue and trait stereotypes in their self-representation in the context of an emerging democracy such as Romania. Research on women politicians in Romania is scarce (Dan and Iorgoveanu 2013; Marcu and Nedelcu 2013; Miroiu 2004; Țăruș 2008). Țăruș's study (2008) indicates that women politicians have changed their communication style in the 24 years since the fall of communism: from a lack of aggression and a high degree of decency and discretion in the 1990s to overt media confrontations with male politicians. Țăruș (2008, 72) highlights that this change should be associated with their increasing desire to become visible by making certain statements. The findings of Țăruș's qualitative study, which included interviews with seven women politicians, reveal that two important strands may be identified in the self-representation of women politicians in Romania. On the one hand, some female candidates try to omit personal matters from their speeches in order not to be accused of placing a greater emphasis on family than on political responsibilities. On the other hand, some female candidates, who put an emphasis on their appearance, consider that traits of femininity should be accompanied by masculine traits. Dan and Iorgoveanu's study (2013) on media coverage of Romanian female and male candidates for the 2009 European Parliament elections shows that women were more often associated with male-oriented issue frames than their male counterparts. Despite the salience of issue frames related to women politicians, Dan and Iorgoveanu (2013) point out that an equal treatment of Romanian female and male politicians cannot be proclaimed since "women were considered unable to deal with the issues they were linked to" (208).

Blogs—self-presentation tools in political communication campaigns

Blogs are considered to have a low media richness and a high degree of self-presentation (Kaplan and Haenlein 2010). The emphasis on self-presentation and the function of k(nowledge)-logs specific to blogs coincide with the personal and social construct of identity. Using blogs as social diaries (Blood 2005, 130; Lawson-Borders and Kirk 2005, 549), the candidate controls the information posted on this medium and provides favorable frames for his/her identity.

In Romania, political candidates have gradually become aware of the visibility benefits that new media and social media campaigns may bring to their self-presentation, given the rapid increase of internet usage from 35.5 percent in 2010 to 44.1 percent in 2011, as internetworldstats.com (2013) shows. In addition, a shift from forums to blogs (Cismaru 2012, 43) has been noticed, where the number of blogs jumped from 30,000 in 2008 to 70,000 in 2011. For Romanian politicians, blogs have a double function: to mobilize and communicate directly with devoted voters, and to influence the media agenda. The choice to promote themselves visually on blogs during the 2012 parliamentary elections seems to have been a good campaign tactic on part of the female candidates since political issues have the greatest impact (45 percent) in the Romanian blogosphere, as the Report on the Romanian Blogosphere (2011) shows.

Theoretical background: Visual framing theory

There is a constantly negotiated flow between what should be made visible and what should be hidden in blog posts, a flow which is specific to the concept of a frame. As "schemata of interpretation" (Goffman 1974, 21), frames are used to make sense of information or an occurrence, providing "principles for the organization of social reality" (Hertog and McLeod 2001, 140). Selecting those aspects of a perceived reality and making them more salient in a blog post, bloggers try to convey their opinions on certain events, issues and actors, but at the same time to promote their interests and values. In political communication, blogs are used as framing devices since the locus of control remains with the politician blogger. They provide in-depth visual and verbal information justifying the candidate's positive image (Bichard 2006, 331).

Our choice of a framing analysis for the present study has two reasons. First, visual framing is closely related to the position of the point-of-view. The photographer, by making certain compositional choices (camera angle, focus, and distance), highlights what is important (Burgin 1982, 146). Second, visual images tell a story about the social roles that political candidates assume in the process of their online identity construction. The research on blog posts shows that because candidates "need to emphasize current issues and appeal to voters with current imagery" (Bichard 2006, 340) during election campaigns, their blog posts include many photos and/or graphics (framing mechanism).

Starting from the literature on framing (Goffman 1974) and specially on (political) visual framing (Goodnow 2013; Jewitt and Oyama 2001; Messaris and Abraham 2001), we use Paul Verschueren's model (2012) of visual framing analysis, which blends a quantitative and a qualitative methodology. This model focuses on the use of social semiotics in visual framing analysis. Social semiotics (Vannini 2007, 40) places human beings as participants within context-bound and conflict-laden interpersonal interactions, attributes meaning to power, and investigates how semiotic resources are used in "specific historical, cultural, and institutional contexts" (van Leeuwen 2005, 3). Starting with the social semiotic toolbox (represented participants, interactive participants, composition, and modality), we provide a multilevel frame analysis (Verschueren 2012, 35) of the photographic images posted by the three Romanian women politicians. The ultimate goal of such analysis is to reveal the meaning potentials of the semiotic resources used by the three female candidates in their online self-representations.

The first level implies an observation of the *scene* which consists of a process (action, event, state of being), participants, and a circumstance (setting, means, accompaniments). The analysis focuses on the representational and interactive meaning potential. The participants belonging to different socio-demographic categories may be depicted within certain narrative structures (for example, a politician offering his/her help to an elderly person or shaking hands with a citizen). The interaction between politicians, other represented participants, and viewers is visually rendered through two factors: distance and point of view. Distance is associated with the "size of frame" of shots (Jewitt and Oyama 2001, 146), ranging from extreme close-up to extreme long. The types of shots highlight the relationships with possible voters/viewers that politicians promote through photographic images. For example, a close-up of the politician (head and shoulders) will suggest an intimate/personal relationship whereas a long shot (politician's full figure) may suggest an impersonal relationship. The types of angles within photographic images reveal the participants' point of view. For example, a low angle is associated with power over the viewer whereas a high angle renders the power of the viewer.

The second level implies a generalization of the scene into a *theme*, which designates some prototypical representations assumed by the visual participants in their self-representation. A woman politician engrossed in helping children is to be assigned the prototypical role of "a mother" or "a teacher" whereas a woman politician depicted within an office is to be assigned the prototypical role of "a business woman."

The last level focuses on a generalization of a theme into a *master frame* or *ideological orientation* with which the represented participants are to be associated. The semiotic resources that form the depicted scene and the represented role assigned to the participants form a paradigmatic set that specifies "a unity of culturally resonant and politically relevant contents and themes" (Verschueren 2012, 35).

Method

We employ a visual framing analysis of the images posted on the politicians' blogs during the four weeks (November 9, to December 8, 2012) leading up to election day (December 9, 2012). As primary units of our analysis, photographic images have the meaning potential of authenticity, integration, evidence (Bourdieu 1990, 19), by framing politicians as social actors performing certain actions. Our sample included 139 blog posts, of which 75 included visuals. Since a blog post may include several images, our final sample included 580 photographs. We did not include advertisements, posters, banners, or leaflets in our sample because they do not have the same referential nature as photographic images.

The study employs both a deductive and an inductive method. We used a deductive method by seeking to find how two interaction factors (distance and point of view) were represented. We coded all 580 photographic images taking into account the shots and angles as analytical variables for distance and point of view. In the existing literature (Kress and van Leeuwen 2006,

130), shots are coded as extreme close-up, close-up, medium close-up, medium, medium long, long, or extreme long, and angles are coded as low angle, eye-level, or high angle. The type of shots and angles was measured through their presence or absence in each photographic image. Both authors coded the images and we cross-checked our coding strategies to ensure that an agreement on the categories is reached. In order to determine intercoder reliability (Kappa), we coded 10 percent of the photographic images. The coefficient of agreement was computed to be 0.93, considered to be acceptable by researchers.

The inductive method was used for an in-depth analysis of the photographs in order to find the types of represented participants, the prototypical roles and the master frames visually assigned to the Romanian female candidates. The assumption is that every social action depicted in a photographic image is performed by represented participants. In social semiotics, participants are either the people, places, concrete, or abstract things. We coded the participants visually represented in the 2012 parliamentary election campaign blog posts in three categories:

a) political party staff (female candidate, party members, party high officials, political opponents, indexical objects depicting a candidate's profession);
b) local authorities (town/city officials);
c) socio-demographic categories (elderly citizens, middle-aged persons, families, children, students, members of the clergy, doctors, disabled people, factory workers, ethnic groups, young bloggers). The inclusion of these different categories may be explained in terms of Romania's social, economic and political context. The findings of The National Institute of Citizens and Public Opinion Survey (INSCOP) survey show that Romanians continue to trust the Church (over 65 percent) more than politicians (INSCOP 2013). Doctors' low salaries and medical staff cuts have always been on the political agenda, especially during election campaigns. The visual presence of disabled people and of ethnic groups may be explained in terms of political doctrines. Policies for disadvantaged people, diversity, and multiculturalism are three important aspects often included in the programs of Romanian parties. The increasing usage of the internet in Romania has prompted politicians to take into account a new category of voters, namely bloggers who may become their online promoters.

The presence or absence of a certain participant in the photographic image contributes to establishing a certain prototypical role and master frame meant to be attributed to the female candidate. We analyzed the prototypical roles and master frames taking into account the types of traits identified in the literature on gender stereotyping (Dolan 2005; Banwart 2010; Jamieson 1995): compassion traits (understanding, caring, gentle, warm) which correlate with "feminine" issues (education, health care, social security/medicare, environment, family issues, women's issues, abortion, and ethics/government reform) versus competence traits (knowledgeable, skillful, rational) which correlate with "male issues" (business, economy, foreign affairs, defense/ military issues, agriculture).

Our visual framing analysis focused on the blog posts of the three most prominent female candidate bloggers (Table 12.1) from three opponent political parties.

Elena Udrea served as Tourism Minister from 2008–9 and as Regional Development and Tourism Minister from 2009–12. Her name is associated with some scandals, which were on the media agenda: wearing expensive outfits, posing for the cover of a Romanian fashion magazine, having a privileged relationship with the president Traian Băsescu, being accused of embezzlement, and abuse of office. Alina Gorghiu serves as a vice president of the

Table 12.1 Female candidate bloggers during the 2012 Romanian parliamentary elections

	Alina Gorghiu	**Rodica Nassar**	**Elena Udrea**
Party affiliation	National Liberal Party (PNL)	Social Democratic Party (PSD, center-left)	Democratic Liberal Party (PD-L, center-right)
Member of the Romanian Chamber of Deputies	2008–present	2000–present	2008–present
Profession	Lawyer	Accountant	Lawyer
Election results	71.33%	51.23%	44%
Slogans	*Rămân avocatul tău în parlament* (I will remain your lawyer in the parliament)	*Pentru o Românie puternică* (For a strong Romania)	*Forța de a rezolva lucrurile pentru tine* (The force of achieving things for you)

committee for investigating abuses and corruption and for petitions in the Romanian Chamber of Deputies. Her name is associated with the Committee of Enquiry, which accused a former PD-L Minister of embezzlement in 2009. During the 2012 parliamentary elections, she garnered the highest percentage of the three female candidates and during the election campaign she personally updated her blog.[2] Unlike the other two female candidates, Rodica Nassar is an accountant and her name is associated with ethnic groups. Married to a Lebanese citizen, Rodica Nassar was the president of the Romanian–Lebanese Friendship Parliamentary Group.

Our visual framing analysis of the three Romanian women candidates' blogs during the 2012 parliamentary elections examines whether the photos used for their self-representation challenge or contribute to gender stereotypes. To that end, the present study addresses the following research questions:

RQ1: What types of participants were depicted in the photographic images posted by the candidates?
RQ2: What were the most salient types of shots and angles used in the self-representation of the candidates?
RQ3: What social prototypes did the candidates use in their photographic images?
RQ4: What master frames were present in the photographic images on their blogs?

Findings

During the 2012 parliamentary election campaign in Romania, Alina Gorghiu was the most active blogger (n = 84 blog posts), followed by Elena Udrea (n = 34) and Rodica Nassar (n = 21) (Table 12.2). Whereas Udrea used the structural feature of visuals in the majority of her blog posts (80 percent), Gorghiu used visuals in only 32 percent of her blog posts. Nassar had images in each post (100 percent), but she had the lowest number of blog posts overall (n = 21).

The three categories of represented participants depicted in the female candidates' photographic images (RQ1) may have the meaning potential either of authority (political party staff and local authorities) or of desired legitimacy (socio-demographic categories). Table 12.3 shows that elderly people, middle-aged people, children and families prevail in the visual framing of the Romanian

Table 12.2 Distribution of blog posts, blog posts with visuals and number of visuals per candidate

	Total blog posts	Blog posts with visuals (percent)	Visuals
Alina Gorghiu	84	27 (32%)	102
Rodica Nassar	21	21 (100%)	199
Elena Udrea	34	27 (80%)	279

Note: Percentages rounded to the nearest whole number.

women candidates. These dominant socio-demographic categories demonstrate that the crowd bath, where the candidate is portrayed as "one of us folks" (Semetko and Boomgaarden 2007, 163) is the best strategy to reveal a visual legitimacy.

What differentiates the Romanian female candidates in depicting their power through visual communication is the setting where these crowd baths as mass appeals take place. Whereas Udrea and Nassar are presented among elderly and middle-aged people, and children, in photographic images taken in markets, schools, or in the streets of Roman and Bucharest, Gorghiu chose the parliament building as the setting for being depicted among the people from Bucharest. The Open Doors Day at the Romanian Parliament, the workplace of the three Romanian women candidates, could have been the best strategy to show that women politicians should be considered in terms of their status as elected representatives. Alina Gorghiu was the only candidate who visually highlighted the competence trait. Besides the visual framing of her workplace setting (the Romanian Parliament), she also posted photographic images depicting objects (files, court benches, a gavel) as an indexical resource of her profession (a lawyer), which may be assigned the meaning potential of viability. Three other differences in the visual framing of represented participants can be noticed. First, Udrea and Nassar used photographic images depicting themselves and three important socio-demographic categories (doctors, priests, and disabled persons) whereas Gorghiu used photos that showed her in the company of bloggers as a means to appeal to young urban voters. Second, Nassar was depicted together with members of ethnic groups to reinforce her position as the former president of the Romanian–Lebanese Friendship Parliamentary Group. Third, Udrea was the only candidate who posted images (0.7 percent, $n = 2$) where she was the

Table 12.3 The salience of represented participants in Romanian women candidates' blog posts

Represented participants		**Alina Gorghiu**		**Rodica Nassar**		**Elena Udrea**	
		Frequency	*Percentage*	*Frequency*	*Percentage*	*Frequency*	*Percentage*
Political party staff	Woman candidate (alone)	0	0%	0	0%	2	0.70%
	Indexical objects—profession	3	3%	0	0%	0	0%
	Party members	8	8%	9	4%	12	4%
	Party high officials	3	3%	3	2%	5	2%
	Political opponents	3	3%	0	0%	1	0.30%
Local authorities	Town/city officials	1	1%	13	7%	18	7%
Socio-demographic categories	Elderly people	15	15%	49	25%	64	23%
	Middle-aged people	5	5%	56	28%	121	43%
	Families	26	25%	4	2%	0	0%
	Children	25	24%	9	4%	21	7%
	Students	5	5%	13	7%	16	6%
	Clergy	0	0%	6	3%	13	5%
	Doctors	0	0%	9	4%	0	0%
	Disabled people	0	0%	12	6%	6	2%
	Factory workers	0	0%	6	3%	0	0%
	Ethnic groups	0	0%	10	5%	0	0%
	Bloggers	8	8%	0	0%	0	0%
Total		102	100%	199	100%	279	100%

Note: Percentages rounded to the nearest whole number.

only participant depicted (see the use of medium close-up shots in Table 12.4). She used two images portraying herself alone, the emphasis being placed on her good looks (a blonde-haired beautiful politician with a flawless make-up). Elena Udrea and Elena Băsescu, the Romanian president's daughter, have been considered the two beauties in the Democratic Liberal Party.

Types of shots and angles—the meaning potential of interaction and power

Photographic images create "particular relations between viewers and the world inside the picture frame" (Jewitt and Oyama 2001, 145). Distance and point of view with their corresponding resources (RQ2) are two factors that play an important role in achieving the interactive meaning between viewers and represented participants. Table 12.4 shows the types of shots used in the images posted by the three Romanian women candidates. Alina Gorghiu and Rodica Nassar preferred long, medium long, and medium shots. Elena Udrea used medium shots as the most salient ones, followed by long and medium long shots. This difference of the types of shots in blog posts may be explained in terms of the degree in which the human figure (the candidate) was visually framed. On the one hand, the medium long and long shots, as means of the "one of us folks" strategy, present the full figure, the focus being laid on the surroundings and on the candidate accompanied by a group of possible voters. All three female candidates used the meaning potential of impersonal relationships, the long and medium long shots being "an index and instrument of integration" (Bourdieu 1990, 19). On the other hand, medium close-up shots imply cutting off the human figure from the waist up, the focus being laid on the political candidate and on one or two more represented participants. Elena Udrea was the female candidate who used the highest percentage of medium close-ups (9 percent, n = 24). Besides the meaning potential of a social relationship and even of a personal relationship with her blog viewers, the choice places an emphasis on her attractive appearance.

Table 12.5 shows the salience of angles in the framing choices of the three Romanian women candidates. The frontal-angle framings are the most frequently used since their meaning potential is the identification and involvement with other represented participants (possible voters). In political communication, photographic images may allow the candidate to symbolically relate as an

Table 12.4 The salience of shots in Romanian women candidates' blog posts

Types of photographic shots	Alina Gorghiu		Rodica Nassar		Elena Udrea	
	Frequency	*Percentage*	*Frequency*	*Percentage*	*Frequency*	*Percentage*
Extreme close-up	0	0%	0	0%	0	0%
Close-up	0	0%	0	0%	0	0%
Medium close-up	4	4%	7	3%	24	9%
Medium shot	22	22%	49	25%	103	37%
Medium long	33	32%	68	34%	66	23%
Long	41	40%	63	32%	76	27%
Extreme long	2	2%	12	6%	10	4%
Total	102	100%	199	100%	279	100%

Note: Percentages rounded to the nearest whole number.

equal to the people (Jewitt and Oyama 2001, 135). For example, in the photos depicting Alina Gorghiu, children, and their parents, the eye-level angle (71 percent) was used to increase involvement with represented participants who visited the Parliament of Romania during the Open Doors Day event. This use of "point of view" through a frontal angle may be noticed in the photos of Udrea and Nassar while they get involved in conversations with Romanian citizens.

Social prototypes and master frames in the visual framing of Romanian women candidates

We will next interpret the visual semiotic resources (represented participants, types of shots, and angles) of the parliamentary election scenes created by the

Table 12.5 The salience of angles in Romanian women candidates' blog posts

Types of angles	Alina Gorghiu		Rodica Nassar		Elena Udrea	
	Frequency	*Percentage*	*Frequency*	*Percentage*	*Frequency*	*Percentage*
Low angle	27	26%	85	43%	89	32%
Eye-level angle	72	71%	108	54%	176	64%
High angle	3	3%	6	3%	12	4%
Total	102	100%	199	100%	279	100%

Note: Percentages rounded to the nearest whole number.

three Romanian women candidates in their blog posts in terms of a thematic meaning (RQ3) and ideological orientations (RQ4).

Compassion is the prevailing master frame in the visual framing of Elena Udrea and Rodica Nassar. The photographic images depicting the crowd baths, posted by Elena Udrea and Rodica Nassar, seem to represent them as prototypical women sensitive to the needs of the people. The women candidates' age and dress code make a difference between the two instances of this social prototype. Rodica Nassar (55 years old) embodies the prototype of a protective mother, the low-angle shots rendering this thematic meaning as well. Elena Udrea (39 years old) may be associated with the prototype of a gentle and feminine companion. Considered as one of the most voluptuous and attractive politicians (Ţăruş 2008, 70) and often being associated with the misogynistic syntagm referring to blonde women's lack of intelligence, Elena Udrea rejects the idea of a masculinization process of women in politics. Her resistance to defeminization is visually framed through two semiotic resources: dress code and medium close-up shots. Being accused of wearing expensive outfits and high-heeled shoes in inappropriate contexts (for example, during floods in Romanian villages), Elena Udrea seemed to have adapted her dress code to the spatial context of her electoral college. Because of the unfavorable polls, she changed her college and moved from Bucharest to a college in South-East Romania (the Piatra Neamt county). Many of the photos depict her talking with elderly people from the countryside. Despite the choice of low-heeled shoes and trousers instead of tight dresses or skirts, the medium close-ups reveal her flawless make-up and emphasize her desire to display her femininity. Udrea is also the politician who is the most "visual" in her communication style. She has the highest number of visuals (n = 279) on her campaign blog, which is significantly higher than that of Gorghiu (n = 102) and Nassar (n = 199).

The salience of the socio-demographic categories towards which Elena Udrea and Rodica Nassar show their compassion highlights a discrepancy in the dominance of the social prototype. Whereas Udrea, the prototype of a feminine companion, visually frames compassion issues such as social welfare, education, and religion, which is in line with her party, Nassar visually depicts two other social domains: health and ethnic minority issues. The various forms of compassion promoted by Rodica Nassar during the 2012 parliamentary election campaign can be explained in terms of her political affiliation with the Social Democratic Party (PSD). The social-democratic ideology focuses on people as the most important resource of a society. PSD has been the governing party since 2012 and this advantage was visually exploited through the presence of the Ministry of Education and of the Prime Minister in the photographic images posted by Nassar. The emphasis on ethnic issues coincides with one important ideological aspect of the Social Democratic Party, namely multiculturalism, which highlights minority rights and espouses an open migration policy.

Nassar and Udrea's choice of clergy as depicted participants may be explained in terms of the collectivist society that prevails in Romania. Since Romanians trust the Church more than politicians (see Nineo'clock.ro), the two female candidates used members of the clergy as participants in their photos in order to highlight their closeness to traditional values in Romanian society and to attract the elderly religious voters.

Furthermore, the presence of doctors and disabled persons may be explained in terms of the party doctrines, thus highlighting Dolan's (2005) observation that the salience of certain issues is associated with party-related ideologies. As their party programs highlight, PSD (Social Democratic Party, PSD.ro 2013) and PD-L (Democratic Liberal Party, PDL.ro 2013) promote policies regarding the social protection of disadvantaged people. If physical disability may be automatically included in this social category, doctors as a group of disadvantaged citizens may constitute a society-related issue. Yet, in the context of Romania, where doctors receive low salaries and often choose to migrate abroad, candidates for office often address the dismal state of medical care during their election campaigns. In comparison, the reason why doctors were not included in Elena Udrea's photos might be explained by the fact that in 2010 the Democratic Liberal Party, as an incumbent party, decided to cut the medical staff and to close many hospitals. This budgetary decision proved to be quite unpopular among the people.

On the other hand, competence was identified as the master frame that prevails in Alina Gorghiu's blog posts. The visual framing of competence was associated with the prototype of an assertive, active, and rational lawyer. As mentioned, the first level of visual framing analysis was focused on resources revealing Alina Gorghiu's competence as a lawyer and as a deputy. Even her campaign slogan (*Rămân avocatul tău în parlament!*—I will remain your lawyer in the parliament!) renders the competence trait. Interestingly, she is also the politician who put the least emphasis on visuals (32 percent). At the same time, Alina Gorghiu was the only candidate whose photographic images depicted her meetings with young bloggers and with the people from Bucharest at her workplace (the Romanian parliament building). Dialogue, pluralism, diversity, and equality of chances are issues included in the PNL doctrine and Alina Gorghiu chose to promote an online dialogue, thus targeting the young voters.

Conclusion

Photographic images as a structural feature of blog posts during election campaigns should not be under-estimated during election campaigns since they have the meaning potential of authenticity, integration, and evidence. This study showed that female candidates, in total control of the visual content of their blogs, have the opportunity to either contribute to gender stereotypes or challenge the existing dichotomies.

Having photographic images as primary unit of our analysis, we adapted Verschueren's model of visual framing analysis to the photos posted by the three most active female candidate bloggers during the 2012 parliamentary elections in Romania. The comparative analysis of the images posted by the representatives of the three main parties highlights two important aspects.

First, the candidates avoided images that present them as part of the private sphere. None of the three female candidates used photos depicting them with family members or while being occupied with household matters. Second, the dominance of compassion as a master frame should be related to the candidate's background and to the party affiliation and not only to gender-stereotyped issues. The latter aspect highlights the findings of Dolan's (2005) study and Dan and Iorgoveanu's (2013) study: the party-stereotyped issues, the candidate, and the context may determine the dominance of certain female and male elements.

Also, the framing analysis of the represented participants showed that the prevalence of a certain socio-demographic category should be related to the Romanian social and political context. For example, members of the clergy are depicted as participants since the Church is the most trusted institution in Romania.

Medium and long shots were used by all three candidates in order to achieve the categorization of the populist "one of us" appeal. The analysis of the semiotic resources that compose the scene revealed that the meaning potential of the photographic shots highly depends on the setting in which the participants are portrayed. Streets or markets constitute the setting, which may be related to the compassion master frame (Elena Udrea and Rodica Nassar) whereas the work-related environment (the Chamber of Deputies) can be related to competence (Alina Gorghiu).

In addition, the candidate's background plays an important role in assigning a certain meaning potential to a photographic image. Elena Udrea represented herself as a feminine companion, highlighting her good looks through medium close-up photos (double those of her opponents). This type of framing is consistent with the voters' perception and mainstream media representations of Elena Udrea as the blonde-haired beauty in Romanian politics. To capitalize on her appearance may seem to be a strategic decision since "an emphasis on female qualities could be quite convenient" (Dan and Iorgoveanu 2013, 225) especially when voters place value on them (Dolan 2005). Rodica Nassar represented herself as a protective mother, emphasizing her political involvement in issues concerning ethnic groups. Unlike her opponents, Alina Gorghiu placed emphasis on competence by representing herself through her twofold profession: a lawyer and a member of the Chamber of Deputies. Even if the compassion frame seems to prevail in the visual images of two female candidates thus highlighting that they conform to the gender-based stereotypes, the picture is more complex and contextual. As discussed, the choice of some represented participants in the visuals was made on the basis of party affiliation and of the social and economic context. For example, doctors were possibly strategically not present in Elena Udrea's photos since the Democratic Liberal Party was accused of having brought the Romanian medical system to decay.

A visual framing analysis of photographic images during election campaigns is valuable in the overall analysis of female candidates since it provides an insight into the representation of the scene (participants and setting) and into the meaning potentials, which should be always related to the individual/candidate and the social, economic, and political context.

This study on the visual framing of Romanian female candidates indicates that women politicians should take into account two important aspects in the process of online identity construction: the increasing number of internet users in a former communist country and the meaning potential of photographs in producing an image of a candidate. Blogs, through the high degree of visibility and the total control upon the visual and verbal content posted, are a strategic tool to craft an identity, which may help female candidates with the issue of under-representation in the Parliament of Romania.

Notes

1 During the 2012 parliamentary elections, Elena Udrea ran for the electoral alliance, The Right Romania Alliance (ARD). The Democratic Liberal Party was the main party of this alliance. ARD was founded in September 2012 and it was dissolved on December 10, 2012. Even if Elena Udrea represented ARD, we will present her as a member of the Democratic Liberal Party in this study.

2 We assume that Elena Udrea and Rodica Nassar were closely involved with their blogs because they did not have a huge campaign staff. Even if they did not personally make the updates, they had a say in what got posted on their personal campaign blogs.

13

Gender, Politics, and the Albanian Media: A Women Parliamentarians' Account

Sonila Danaj and Jonila Godole

Introduction

Albanian politics have been male-dominated since the end of communism. National and international organizations have lobbied continuously to change this pattern. Eventually, a proportional system with a 30 percent gender threshold was introduced in 2008, which brought more women into the Albanian parliament. Entering politics put these women in the spotlight, given that politics has become a mediated process (Mazzoleni and Schulz 1999). Although there are many studies on how women are viewed by the media through content analyses of media products, the question of how women politicians view their media coverage has received limited attention (see Aalberg and Strömbäck 2011; Ross 2010; Ross and Sreberny 2000), especially in postcommunist countries. In this chapter, we contribute to the current literature on the perceptions of female politicians about their relationship with the media focusing on the context of a postcommunist emerging democracy: Albania.

The specific questions raised here are as follows: What are the dynamics of the relationship between women politicians and the media? How do women members of parliament (MPs) perceive their relationship with the media? What factors influence their presence in the media? These questions are relevant because media are the main intermediary between politicians and their constituents and the main source of information the latter have. Furthermore, media coverage has become crucial to the way policies and politicians are perceived by the general public (Iyengar and Kinder 1987), and competing for media's attention has become a fundamental part of the political race and control (Wolfsfeld 1997). We first present data from existing studies on media coverage of Albanian women politicians and compare the results with women

MPs perceptions about the political communication dynamics in Albania. Giving voice to the politicians themselves is important because their beliefs and attitudes influence their relationship with the media and this might also have an impact on their media coverage (Ross 2010).

Theoretical framework

Early studies on women politicians and the media were concentrated on their (in) visibility, and "symbolic annihilation," i.e. media's condemnation, trivialization and omission of women (Tuchman 1978). Results of the studies on visibility, however, have been inconclusive as some indicated women to be less visible than men, while others suggested that their unusualness makes women more newsworthy (Trimble 2007). Media and communication scholars have identified three determinants of parliamentarians' presence in the media: media pay more attention to the most active members (McQuail 1992; Tresch 2009), as well as to those in the high ranks (Tresch 2009), and show ideological, commercial or gender biases (Hallin and Mancini 2004; Kahn and Goldenberg 1991; Patterson and Donsbach 1996; Staab 1990). Although competing, these approaches are "not necessarily incompatible" (Tresch 2009, 69). Media, in particular in Western democracies, have become more independent in their agenda setting and the two first determinants clearly show that they are interested in the politicians that hold power and that produce more events (Tresch 2009). On their part, politicians continue to be dependent on the media to reach the public, as more of them perceive access and visibility in the media as "a prerequisite for political success" (Aalberg and Strömbäck 2011, 170). However, media selections of what is newsworthy are strongly shaped by their own or their media owners' political and economic agenda, often combined with a strong gender bias (Gidengil and Everitt 1999; Kahn 1994; Tresch 2009). Aalberg and Strömbäck (2011) argue that women politicians' relationship with the media is shaped by skepticism and Ross and Sreberny (2000, 96) explain that some women perceive that "the anti-women stance is simply a reflection of the norms and values of the wider society" and that sexist attitudes are so deeply embedded in the consciousness of journalists that they do not even notice their own gender bias.

The gendered mediation thesis explains that stereotyping has become more subtle within the frame of politics as a men's domain, therefore pushing media to concentrate disproportionately on behavior that does not match gender stereotypes. The "game" frame of politics as a male preserve explains why women who adopt "masculine" styles are portrayed as more aggressive, and therefore cast in a more negative light than their male colleagues (Gidengil and Everitt 1999). Confrontation is newsworthy and, as such, women politicians might be receiving more coverage because of their unusualness as women in politics and their confrontational behavior (Trimble 2007). Nevertheless, women politicians remain seriously misrepresented and penalized for their adopted masculine behavior (Gidengil and Everitt 1999; Lundell and Ekström 2008).

While there are a considerable number of studies on how media portray women politicians, there have been only a few that examine the relationship of women politicians with the media (Aalberg and Strömbäck 2011) and how women politicians view their relationship with the media (Ross 2010; Ross and Sreberny 2000). Aalberg and Strömbäck (2011) argue that there is a gender gap in the relationships of the MPs with the media, even in the most gender-equal countries in the world, such as Norway and Sweden. Their results show that male politicians have a closer and more adjusted relationship with the media, while women are more critical of it. However, Ross (2010) finds that it is personality and political power that mostly affect the relationship between politicians and media and that the gender of the politician (or the journalist) is not a significant determinant of difference in New Zealand, another country with a strong female presence in parliament.

Women and politics in transition

The transition from authoritarian regimes to democratic ones has been accompanied by a dramatic decrease in the number of women in assemblies. Communist regimes provided for state feminism, which promoted gender equality. The postcommunist period is characterized by a strong patriarchal political culture, weak state apparatuses that lacked social equality mechanisms, weak women's or feminist movements, unfavorable electoral systems, and male-dominated political elites, which served as party gatekeepers and eventually gatekeepers for the political realm.

In the period 1995–9, the recommendations of the Beijing Platform for Action started to be slowly accepted in former communist countries, including Albania. A "sandwich strategy" was undertaken, in which international organizations, such as the Organization for Security and Co-operation in Europe (OSCE), Council of Europe, United Nations Development Program,

United Nations Development Fund for Women, Kvinna till Kvinna, National Democratic Institute, Swedish International Development Cooperation Agency, and many other western foundations, in concert with the national and local civil society organizations put pressure on governments to pass gender equality laws and to design social equality strategies and action plans, thus combining top down (or external) pressure with bottom up efforts (Antić and Lokar 2006).

Female political representation in Albania

The participation of women in politics in Albania was granted by the communist regime when it came to power soon after the end of World War Two. During communism, female representation in the national assembly was the highest in history (see Table 13.1). There were six women (7.3 percent) in the first postwar parliament in 1946–50, and the figures peaked to 88 (35.2 percent) in 1974, remaining above 30 percent until the communist regime ended in 1991. In the first democratic elections, women's presence dropped to a minimal 4 percent, which has increased slightly during the transitional period but only once reached above 10 percent, until the proportional system was introduced in 2008 (OSCE/ODIHR 2009). Only rarely have parties promoted female candidates, and mostly women who already had a public profile and media exposure (Ekonomi, Sokoli, Danaj, and Picari 2006).

The new Electoral Code and the Law on Gender Equality in Society, adopted in 2008, require the participation of 30 percent or more of each sex in the list of candidates presented by political parties for parliamentary elections. No party in the country observed the legal provisions in 2009, and the two largest parties, the Democratic Party (DP) and the Socialist Party (SP), reached 29.3 percent and 28 percent respectively. Only 5.7 percent (DP) and 6.4 percent (SP) of these women candidates were at the top of the lists, while the rest were at the bottom. Smaller parties did not position their female candidates in winning rankings. As a result, in the 2009–13 parliament, women MPs were members of the two major parties only (ACER and ASET 2009). The new electoral code seems to have given a boost to female representation resulting in 16.4 percent or 23 women in the first round of elections in 2009, and slightly higher (17.9 percent or 25 women), in 2013. There were 16 newly-elected MPs out of 23 women in 2009, and another 12 newly-elected MPs out of 25 in 2013. Only nine of the newly-elected in 2009 were confirmed for a second mandate in 2013.

Table 13.1 Women in parliament in Albania

Year	Number of Members of Parliament	Number of Women in Parliament	Percentage
1921	78	0	0%
1925	75	0	0%
1929–39	57	0	0%
1946–50	82	6	7.3%
1950–4	121	17	13.9%
1954–8	134	16	11.9%
1958–62	186	17	9.1%
1962–6	214	25	11.7%
1966–70	240	39	16.3%
1970–4	264	71	26.7%
1974–8	250	88	35.2%
1978–82	250	81	32.4%
1982–6	250	78	31.2%
1987–91	250	75	30%
1991–2	250	10	4 %
1992–6	140	8	5.7 %
1996–7	140	21	15 %
1997–2001	155	11	7.1 %
2001–5	140	8	5.7 %
2005–9	140	10	7.1%
2009–13	140	23	16.4 %
2013–17	140	25	17.9 %

Source: The table is a complemented version of the publication of the Albanian Assembly's "Women in Parliament" (2003) with data from the Central Elections Commission accessible at www.cec.org.al

Media and politics in Albania

Albanian media experience a lot of interference from politicians, economic lobbies and media owners with either economic or political interests, or both. International monitoring of electoral campaigns and national studies all indicate that broadcasters show biases towards political parties in the elections, which is reflected not only in the amount of coverage, but also in its content (Dragoti, Tahsini, Dhëmbo, and Ajdini 2011; OSCE/ODIHR 2009). In her study about the professional culture of journalism in Albania, Godole (2013, 72) argues that "the media operate as secondary businesses used by their owners to strengthen their primary businesses, with the direct and indirect support of politics." Furthermore, due to a lack of journalistic tradition as neutral observers, Albanian journalists display strong political parallelism of the type

Hallin and Mancini (2004) called the "polarized pluralist model" (Godole 2013). As a result: "Journalists and media, due to their political alignment, minimize to the point of self-censorship various aspects of the news or highlight what is in harmony with their political or business allegiances" (OSCE/ODIHR 2011, 16). In other words, lack of financial independence and the division along political lines shape the relationship between Albanian politicians and media. Media outlets offer more coverage and a positive image to the politicians of their favorite party, while ignoring or describing negatively their opponents.

There are few studies conducted by Albanian think tanks and scholars that analyze media's coverage of women's issues in general (e.g. Gender Alliance for Development 2009) or in electoral campaigns (e.g. ACER and ASET 2009). Their results indicate that although there has been some progress in covering women in politics, there is still ample evidence that female candidates are covered in the media less frequently than their male colleagues in spite of a surge in their political representation. For example, during the 2009 campaign TV channels covered male politicians 94 percent and women only 6 percent of the time, whereas the major newspapers published articles about male politicians at the rate of 93 percent and women only at 7 percent (ACER 2010; ACER and ASET 2009). Some think tanks monitored the level of coverage by counting how many times each politician was mentioned or cited during the electoral campaign period in 2009. Their results show that only one woman, the Speaker of Parliament, appeared among the top ten most cited politicians. Furthermore, she is cited approximately four times fewer than the Leader of the Opposition and eight times fewer than the Prime Minister. The next woman is 13th on that list (ACER 2010; IDRA and FML 2009).

The same period registers some notable trends. The Open Society Foundation in Albania conducted a content analysis of the political discourses of the main political leaders in the country and how those were reflected in the five daily newspapers with the highest circulation rates for a six-month period during the 2009 and 2011 electoral campaigns (OSFA 2012). The results show that both the Prime Minister and the Leader of the Opposition discussed women's issues more than any other type of issue concerning socially disadvantaged groups, such as ethnic or religious minorities. Although their attention was directed predominantly to female political representation, mainstream media have not followed suit, covering ethnic minorities twice as much as women. Female political representation was the least covered topic, yet violence against women received most of the media's attention, which might be explained by the increased number of cases of reported violence against women in the country and the ongoing awareness campaign against it (UNDP 2013). Furthermore, with the exception of one newspaper, the rest covered women's political representation less in 2011 than they did in 2009, when the gender quota was introduced for the first time (OSFA 2012).

In another study, print media were monitored for three months prior to introducing the quota system. The results show that issues of women's representation were only sporadically present in print media, with 18 to 32 articles in each of the four newspapers in a three-month period. An in-depth analysis of the content demonstrated that most of them reported on the introduction of the quota system but rarely focused on individual women politicians. In three months the newspapers mentioned only 18 women politicians, 12 of whom were high status party members (Gender Alliance for Development 2009), which is in line with the second determinant of media coverage of politicians. The results indicate that politicians are not always the agenda-setters and that media in Albania function according to their own standards of what is newsworthy or not.

Apart from disproportionate coverage, media continue to perpetuate gender stereotypes. The image of women candidates described in the media during the 2009 elections was one of undeserving candidates who were on the lists because of the quota regime, not their merit. Media often used the "game" frame for the political campaign, describing it as a brutal and fierce political arena dominated by men (Ekonomi, Sokoli, Danaj, and Picari 2006), and thus "a male preserve." Consequently, they scrutinized women's behavior and criticized them either for being weak and not aggressive enough, or when some of them adopted masculine styles, described them as more aggressive than their male counterparts. Additionally, women were not given the opportunity to demonstrate their capacities and individuality, but were mainly presented under the party umbrella, which made them remain relatively anonymous in the eyes of the electorate (Equality in Decision-Making Women's Network 2010). In many instances their media profile mainly focused on their look and family matters rather than their political ideas (ACER 2010). The general trend was to select statements that give the impression that men speak about important things and women about unimportant ones, thus further trivializing and misrepresenting women politicians (Gender Alliance for Development 2009). Overall, most studies see the role of the media "in the best case as insufficient, and in the worst case as negative" (Dragoti, Tahsini, Dhëmbo, and Ajdini 2011, 26). Thus, it becomes important to look at how women politicians think of their coverage in the media in order to better understand the dynamics of this relationship and examine the perceived factors that influence it.

Method

In January and February 2013, we interviewed eight out of the 23 women parliamentarians in office for the period 2009–13. Five of them were representatives of the Democratic Party, which led the governmental coalition, and three were representatives of the Socialist Party, which was the main opposition party at the time (for a list of the participants see note 1).[1]

Most of the interviewees have had an academic career prior to becoming members of the parliament. They have also been high-level professionals and civil society activists. One of them is an actress, and there is only one case of a political career started in the party youth group, continued in the women's forum, municipal council, and finally the parliament. As MPs, they have all been engaged in various parliamentary commissions, such as education, media and communication, foreign policy, and the economy. The speaker of the parliament for the period 2009–13 was a woman as well and she was part of the sample.

The MPs were asked questions about their professional career, how they entered politics, their relationship with the media before and after entering politics, and their perception and understanding of their relationship with the media. A qualitative thematic analysis of the data was conducted, which highlighted themes such as political recruitment, media coverage, perception of media attitudes in general, and gendered mediation in particular. To avoid any tensions their responses might cause to their individual relationships with the media, we decided to code the respondents after each citation as WMP (women members of parliament) followed by the numbers one to eight randomly assigned to each of them.

Women parliamentarians and Albanian media

The analysis of the in-depth interviews shows that women MPs are perceived to be less covered than men, which confirms the media monitoring studies (ACER 2010; ACER and ASET 2009). Media's heightened interest in the new women candidates from civil society and academia at the early stages of their political careers was short-lived. Once their involvement was no longer new(s), new politicians say they experienced decreased media coverage, which is similar to that of more senior MPs. Furthermore, our respondents perceive a strong gender bias in the way they are covered by the media. In the following sections we examine their relationship with the media and the gendered mediation they notice.

The relationship between women politicians and the media

Most women politicians did not have a direct relationship with the media prior to their involvement in parliamentary politics. The only exceptions are the two civil society activists and one MP who acted as a party spokesperson. The interview data suggest that it has been easier for women to enter the elite (i.e. elected) level of politics if they already had a substantial visibility thanks to a successful professional career: "I think people selected to be members of parliament have something peculiar anyhow: a political career, a very good intellectual resumé … " (WMP4).

Some women think their involvement is a result of a strategy to help improve the national and international reputation of the party. As one of them said:

> I understand that the recruitment of people from civil society can be done for strategic reasons: for the undecided, new electorate … I think bringing new people has had a positive effect, a new perspective, a new image for the party in the eyes of Albanians but also the [international bodies] … (WMP6)

All MPs indicated that they were all recruited by the party leaders, which helps us understand why their candidacies were successful, but also explains why women were mostly portrayed under the party shadow during the campaign and received little personal coverage. The new party members brought in by the quota system also hinted at a sort of tension with the existing members, men and women, who perceived them as outsiders that took undeserved positions. The fact that they were also women did not help. These attitudes were shared by some media that described "quota women" as undeserving of their candidacies, as the results of media monitoring showed (Equality in Decision-Making Women's Network 2010).

Once in politics, all interviewees indicated that they received some media exposure. The most frequent interactions are with print media because of the commentaries they have written, citations from their speeches or press releases, and interviews. They are also present on TV, through media debates and talk shows, televised press conferences, as well as reports about their activity in office. Their presence in the various media supports the interpretation that media cover more political elites, albeit women, than rank-and-file members of the political party (Tresch 2009). However, even among members of parliament, holding a high-level parliamentarian office draws more media attention than being an MP, such as the case of the head of an investigative commission or Speaker of Parliament. Despite their elite status as members of parliament, for most of the female MPs the relationship with the media remains occasional (only one of them stated that she has frequent contacts with the media), and mainly issue- or policy-driven, i.e. they intensify when there is an important discussion in the law commission, or in the electoral districts they represent. As one of them said: "The frequency depends on events and developments ... The liability suit against me and other colleagues who denounced [lack of transparency about the acquisition of public property by a person related to a member of the majority] received a lot of media attention." (WMP7)

All respondents say that the media have shown to be positive and supportive during important campaigns about social issues such as that of violence against women. As one of them indicated: "When I have asked for their help, they have supported me" (WMP4). Such response confirms that media tend to cover more the active members of the parliament, as well as what they consider the most newsworthy events (McQuail 1992; Trimble 2007). Thus, the Albanian case seems to confirm Tresch's results (2009) that elite status combined with high level of activity produce newsworthy content and greater media coverage.

However, the media are not the only ones that search for news. From some of the interviews we infer that contact with the media is initiated by the MPs as well, mainly to serve the needs of the party and sometimes their individual needs. The proactive approach to achieve media coverage confirms the theoretical interpretation of media as the main channel of information about policies and the necessity politicians feel to draw their attention (Aalberg and Strömbäck 2011; Iyengar and Kinder 1987; Wolfsfeld 1997). In the words of one of our interviewees: "In general it has been the media who has been contacting me, but in some cases, we have also gone to the media to promote our projects. So, there has been a mutual relationship" (WMP2).

The relationship between members of parliament who have been civil society activists and the media is more complex than the other MPs. When their candidacies were made public they became something unexpected and newsworthy (Bell 1991). Therefore, they have received a lot of media attention mainly asking and discussing the reasons for their involvement in party politics. As one of them explained:

> For the media ... my involvement in politics was a surprise. For a few months, at the beginning of my involvement in politics, there has been an increased interest on the side of the media to learn how I made such an important decision, how I was perceiving my involvement and feeling about politics. (WMP7)

Yet, once the novelty wore off, their media coverage was similar to that of other women politicians. Some of our interviewees have actually noticed a decrease in media coverage. As civil society representatives and human rights activists, they had frequently been featured in all the media and invited to talk shows, but since their involvement in party politics, certain media stopped covering them as they used to: "I have noticed that some TV stations have not invited me to their programs since I entered politics" (WMP6). Or "With my involvement in politics, I miss some screens and print media. I am not their 'favorite' anymore, officially" (WMP7).

All our interviewees expressed concerns about what they perceived as the agenda of the media. In some cases they have noticed that while the list of questions focuses on the political life of the interviewee, in the published version some answers are either partial or completely excluded. In some cases, politicians have noticed a tendency to publish trivia they might have briefly mentioned but not their political and policy statements: "some of the media do not cover my political activity and do not cite me, and even when they do, quotes are short and not about the important aspects of the topic" (WMP7).

The general perception is that media, even when they claim to be independent, have demonstrated political biases as "a power far from being independent" (WMP8). When female politicians' stance does not match with the editorial line, they are excluded as potential interviewees and participants in talk shows, or their commentaries are no longer published. In other words, Albanian media are showing the ideological and political bias identified in the existing literature (Hallin and Mancini 2004; Patterson and Donsbach 1996; Staab 1990) and confirming the reports of international observers and Albanian media scholars about political allegiances in the media and their lack of independence (e.g. Godole 2013: OSCE/ODIHR 2009). There are also a few cases when respondents explicitly criticize media as "superficial in content and not professional" (WMP3).

It is important to point out that women politicians have a more positive perception of their presence in online social media than more traditional media. They perceive social media as a direct way to communicate with the people without having to go through any political or commercial filters mainstream media might apply. They also appreciate the fact that they receive direct feedback on the policies and decisions made by their political parties, the parliament or the commissions. One of them said:

> I have been more skeptical but today I am convinced that it is an extraordinary form of communication. Politicians can communicate with the public, their constituents directly and without having to go through the filters of the media which have their own power, as well … I like to know people's thoughts about the decisions we make, to be closer to them. (WMP5)

Social media were also considered an effective way to increase visibility and overcome gendered mediation, in particular misrepresentation of women politicians.

Gender bias in the media

All of our respondents have noticed some type of bias when it comes to the way media approach and cover women politicians compared to their male colleagues. The general perception is that media frame politics as a male preserve, and therefore pay more attention to male than female members of parliament. They notice that men are more often invited to talk to the press or in talk shows and receive more media coverage in general than women do, which confirms the media studies results of a predominant coverage of men in politics (e.g. ACER 2010). Some women politicians attribute the larger presence of their male colleagues in the media due to the fact that there are more men in the parliament than women, which makes it "normal to invite more men in the media than women" (WMP4).

However, not only are men more present but they are also more prominent. Their male colleagues are mainly invited to talk about "important current political issues" (WMP1), although some say that men receive more media attention despite the topic: " … men are more covered by the media than women, even for issues of less importance to the public" (WMP7).

Meanwhile there is a tendency to invite women politicians to talk about stereotypically feminine topics, such as fashion, family matters, and other gendered social issues which again confirms the results of media studies (ACER 2010). One of our interviewees observed that: "Women politicians are not invited on the same important political programs as their male colleagues, but mostly when the talk is about soft topics" (WMP3).

Our interviewees said that they try to resist media tendencies to invite women politicians to speak on topics that are considered within the domain of "womanhood." While media exposure is considered politically beneficial, they said that they accept invitations only to talk shows that discuss issues of their professional expertise and relate directly to their current engagement in the parliamentary commissions. In the words of one of them: "I try to talk only about my field of expertise. I protect my profile fanatically. When they invite me to talk about other things, I try not to go" (WMP6).

While struggling to protect their professional profile from misrepresentation, women MPs say that they have to pay more attention to their appearance. Although their look does not seem to them to be the dominant topic of women in Albanian politics, which contradicts the results of media monitoring studies (ACER 2010), women politicians seem to be aware that, in the age of mediated politics, they are constantly on display and thus they feel the pressure to manage their image. As one of them observed: "the need to appear serious in attire and outlook has increased" (WMP1). From their explanations we inferred that they feel scrutinized by the public and the media, so they need to reassure the audiences about their worthiness as representatives of their parties as well as women in politics: "My style is sophisticated so that it can be clearer and distinguishable for the public. To convey objective messages to the political force I represent, in service to the reforms that are made, and of course in order to convey an image … but also as a form of respect for women in politics" (WMP2).

Aware of the power of the image, they consider appearance as directly linked to the way they are perceived as women politicians by the electorate. The overall perception is that if they want to be taken seriously, they should look serious. The use of the adjective "serious" by many of them is suggestive of their concern about the way they are perceived by the media and the general public. Despite their professional achievements and their status as members of parliament, it seems like they are still trying to convince everybody that they deserve to be there, that women belong in the political realm. Thus, looks have become "a conscious strategy designed to encourage the perception of themselves as 'serious' politicians" (Ross and Sreberny 2000, 87).

The situation becomes more complicated when political behavior is discussed. Women politicians report two contradictory media attitudes toward their behavior thus providing evidence of the presence of a double bind. The first attitude is shaped by the perception that Albanian politics is aggressive and, in order to be respected as politicians, women have to show that they are aggressive enough. If they adopt a different behavior, the media show little interest and therefore provide less coverage. One MP explained that in talking to her constituents she had found out they think she does not do much because she is not often on television, which is not true as she regularly speaks in parliamentary sessions. However, she is rarely featured or cited in the news, which makes her invisible to her constituents. She confided that she had been told to speak louder and be more aggressive, if she wants to be noticed. Non-confrontational behavior is not considered newsworthy (Trimble 2007), which puts pressure on women to strategically modify their patterns of behavior. On the other hand, when women politicians do adopt the more typical masculine style and are confrontational, they receive more media coverage, but they are also condemned and penalized for it (Gidengil and Everitt 1999). The Speaker of the Parliament explained:

> I believe my strong personality is mistakenly identified as harshness. To understand the difficulties that the Speaker of Parliament has in her line of work, it would be enough to attend the plenary sessions and you would see what happens there. The most difficult job after that of the Prime Minister is that of the Speaker of Parliament.

Thus, we observe the presence of a double bind where women are either criticized for not being aggressive enough to be able to handle Albanian politics, or are criticized for being too aggressive and masculine in the way they do politics. The only thing these two contradictory observations share is the prejudice about women not belonging in the political realm, which the media in Albania apparently continue to reinforce.

Conclusions

The above analysis indicates that the introduction of the gender quota candidates from civil society was considered newsworthy and increased their media coverage temporarily. Women politicians believe that they generally receive much less media coverage than their male colleagues, which is confirmed by some of the content analysis studies conducted in the country after the introduction of the quota system. Furthermore, we found support for all three determinants of parliamentarians' presence in the media: elite status, active involvement, and media bias (Tresch 2009). Women who hold high-level decision-making positions in parliament or serve as spokespeople for their party tend to receive more media attention than the rest. Their visibility increases when they are involved in a newsworthy event and falls back to invisibility at other times. Some of them also perceive political bias in the way the media choose to cover their stories.

But, while in the age of mediated politics these three determinants can be applicable to all members of parliament, women politicians say that they are also affected by the gender bias of the media. Although there are more women in politics after the introduction of the proportional electoral code with a gender quota, studies on media monitoring and the analysis of women's perceptions both confirm that the amount and kind of coverage are influenced by gender. Albanian women parliamentarians are much less proportionally present in the media compared to their male counterparts. They are also more likely to be invited to speak about stereotypically feminine and trivial things and feel scrutinized for their appearance and behavior. When their actions do not follow the common patterns of aggressiveness and confrontation, they fall prey to the "double bind" and are perceived as weak and incapable. However, when they adopt a more masculine confrontational style, they receive more media coverage, but are also condemned and penalized for their behavior (Gidengil and Everitt 1999). Despite all the pressure, many women politicians do not passively accept gendered mediation. They resist trivialization and try to overcome omission by making use of online social media as a direct way to communicate with the people. We were unable to examine the extent of usage and rate of success in social media communication, which could be an area for future research. Another one could also be to compare the relationships of men and women MPs with the media.

To conclude, the examination of the complex relationship between women politicians and the media in Albania confirms that, despite an increased presence of women in politics, women politicians feel that instances of omission, trivialization, and condemnation in the media continue (Fountaine and McGregor 2002; Gidengil and Everitt 1999; Ross and Sreberny 2000). The results lead to the question of how these gender biases are constructed and operate in the media. While efforts to affect politics through the gender quota seem to show some positive results, media demonstrate a higher resistance to change in attitude. Future studies could focus on why this is the case in order to be able to propose effective interventions for overcoming gender bias in Albanian media.

Note

1 List of interviewed women Members of Parliament

Name	Party affiliation	Year elected to parliament
Aliolli, Ledina	Democratic Party	2009
Bulku, Rajmonda	Democratic Party	2009
Gjermeni, Eglantina	Socialist Party	2009
Gjonaj, Adriana	Democratic Party	2009
Hoti, Paulina	Democratic Party	2009
Hysi, Vasilika	Socialist Party	2009
Kodheli, Mimi	Socialist Party	2009
Topalli, Jozefina	Democratic Party	1997

Part Three

Navigating the Public Space: Class and Beauty

14

Michelle Bachelet, President of Chile: A Moving Portrait

Claudia Bucciferro

Michelle Bachelet, the first female President of Chile, is a fascinating political figure—and one that has attracted worldwide media attention in recent years. The *New York Times* (2010), the *Guardian* (Khaleeli 2011), *Der Spiegel* (2006), and a myriad of international media agencies have run stories on her. They present her not just as the President of a small country in the developing South, but as a portentous politician who is smart, kind, and caring (Associated Press 2013; Dixon 2006). Many know she is a woman who survived political imprisonment, prosecution, and exile, and who returned to her home country to work with grassroots organizations, eventually becoming an emblematic figure who defeated, against the odds, a powerful man in a tied presidential race.

But who is Michelle Bachelet and how does her story intertwine with that of her country? In the last fifty years, Chile has changed rapidly. It has gone from having the most stable democratic tradition of Latin America, to a socialist experiment, a brutal military intervention, a harsh and enduring dictatorship, and a negotiated transition to democracy completed by a popularly elected government that embraced European social-democratic values (Castells 2005; Moulian 2002). By the time Bachelet was elected in 2006, the Chilean economy had been transformed by neoliberalism, and was one of the fastest-growing in the developing world. Meanwhile, the country was wrestling with painful memories of a past that could no longer be ignored, and the social landscape was quickly changing due to globalization (Agosín 2008; Bucciferro 2012).

At the dawn of the new millennium, to journalists and scholars from around the world, Chile as a whole was as puzzling as the woman who came to lead its intensely patriarchal political system (Dixon 2006; Morales 2008; Walder 2005). She became a symbol for many things—hope, equality, resilience, forgiveness, strength—yet she remained firmly grounded in her beliefs and values. She has stayed that way over the years, even with controversies surrounding her persona growing as Chilean media outlets continued their attempt to reconcile the symbol with the woman, and both with the times (Balch 2009).

This chapter focuses on understanding Michelle Bachelet as a woman and a politician, considering her against the historical, cultural, and social backdrop of contemporary Chile. It is not so much a biographical sketch as an attempt to make sense of how the personal and the political interweave—as feminist scholars say (Arendt 1959; Randall 1987)—to enable the rise of a particular leader and a certain kind of society. The theoretical framework for this inquiry is Cultural Studies and Gender Studies, and the goal is to better understand the mediated representation of Bachelet's public persona. The analysis is informed by a variety of articles on Michelle Bachelet and Chile, published in national and international media.

The rise of an emblematic figure

Michelle Bachelet was the first democratically elected female to occupy a presidential seat in South America, and before that, she was the first female appointed Minister of Defense (Khaleeli 2011). Despite her saying that she is "a completely normal woman in Chile" (Spiegel 2006), her personal characteristics indicate otherwise: she is a pediatrician with a master's degree in military science, a former political detainee and exile, a single mother of three, a socialist, and an agnostic. She comes from a military family, but her father—a General in the Chilean Air Force—opposed the coup d'état of 11 September 1973, and subsequently died in a torture center (UN Women 2011). Michelle was a politically engaged college student at the time. In 1975, she and her mother were detained and held at *Villa Grimaldi* and *Cuatro Alamos* before being sent into exile. Michelle has never spoken in detail about those painful years, but she has never tried to hide her status as a former political detainee, either. Since her first presidential campaign, when her past became an object of public scrutiny, she gave glimpses into her story and presented it honestly as part of who she was. This mattered at a time when many Chileans were caught in a tangled web of pain, denial, resentment, indignation, oblivion, and trauma (Bucciferro 2012; Spiegel 2006).

In exile, Michelle and her mother went first to Australia and then East Germany, where she continued attending college. They returned to Chile in

1979, when efforts towards democratization began to gain prominence. She finished medical school, specializing in pediatrics and epidemiology, and went to work for a nonprofit organization aiding children affected by the dictatorship's violence (PIDEE, *Fundación de Protección a la Infancia Dañada por los Estados de Emergencia*). Later on, she worked at the National AIDS Commission. Meanwhile, the Socialist Party she belonged to underwent a "renovation" that aligned it with European social democracy and allowed it to fully participate in Chile's upcoming "neoliberal democracy" (Rindefjäll 2009). Along with other center-left parties, it formed the coalition (named *Concertación*) that opposed the military dictatorship and was instrumental in its defeat (Weeks & Borzutzky 2012). Pinochet's power diminished, a plebiscite took place, and a government charged with the duty of implementing a democratic transition was elected.

In 1997, while Christian Democrat President Eduardo Frei Jr. was in power, Bachelet traveled to Washington D.C. to pursue graduate studies in military science (UN Women 2011). Ironically, this brought her to study military strategy at the heart of the capitalist world, in a country that had been involved in bringing about the coup that changed her life (Kornbluh 2008). It was an experience that heightened her awareness of social issues and influenced her career, because upon her return she went to work for the government, eventually moving into very visible posts.

Ricardo Lagos, the first Socialist President since Allende, was elected in the year 2000, and it was his goal to address past wounds and create new opportunities for growth. Lagos was an old-fashioned statesman—strong, outspoken, and decisive—but he had no intention to lead the country back to the populist type of socialism of the 1970s. He knew that things had changed. During the struggle for democratization, in 1988, he had become known for a daring performance: as a guest on live television, he pointed his index finger at the camera, called on General Pinochet directly, and said that all those years of censorship, torture, and human rights' abuses would not be condoned (Wiñazki 2006). It was a bold move that caught national attention—back then, something like that could result in death, but Lagos was allowed to remain free. It was a sign that things were thawing, memories could be stirred, and speech could be loosened. Afterwards, everyone knew that someday Lagos would become President.

Michelle Bachelet worked for years in government positions, even serving a term as Minister of Health. She was catapulted into the national spotlight in 2002, when Lagos appointed her the first female Minister of Defense, and the news media started publishing articles that portrayed her as a political trailblazer (Lehuedé 2010). Famous pictures of the time left a lasting impression: Bachelet dressed in military garb standing on an open tank, surrounded by marines; or ready to fly and accompanied by three pilots, with a fighter jet in the background; or attending a military parade, with the President's authority endorsing her, while the troops pay their respects (Lehuedé 2010). Those powerful images were also ironic—this was a woman whose father had been betrayed by his military comrades, and who had been prosecuted and exiled during Pinochet's regime. Things had changed, and Michelle Bachelet represented the juncture between past and present, memory and hope. Her image fascinated the public and the media, and her personality captivated people's hearts (Morales 2008).

At the beginning of 2005, Lagos was nearing the end of his term and couldn't run for re-election. A new presidential race was gearing up. The parties of the political right built solid alliances and had a strong candidate to challenge the center-left coalition that had been in power for 15 years: his name was Sebastián Piñera, and he was running for the first time. A Harvard-educated billionaire and the son of a diplomat, he had an excellent chance of winning. Who should be nominated by the *Concertación*?, people wondered. In the streets, Michelle Bachelet's name was on everybody's lips, but a woman would never make it, they said.

Bachelet stepped forward, campaigned, and—against the odds—won. The country erupted in a wave of celebration. The public sphere suddenly filled with voices, the editorial pages of national newspapers swelled with debate, and the international media took notice (Dixon 2006; Spiegel 2006). Women put on the Presidential sash *en masse*. What was happening in Chile? In a way, Michelle's election acted as a catalyst for the reactivation of the public sphere, in a country that had been intently depoliticized after the shock of the coup and the years of military dictatorship (Bucciferro 2009; Moulian 2002; Weeks and Borzutzky 2012).

Governing in times of change

Michelle Bachelet took office in March of 2006, and her inauguration was surrounded by big expectations (Weeks and Borzutzky 2012). The Chilean public was ebullient, and international media representatives were intrigued: in a world dominated by men, she was the eleventh female to be elected to higher office (Dixon 2006). Bachelet's uniqueness influenced the ceremony itself—as an agnostic, she held her hand up and "promised" to uphold the Constitution, symbolizing the separation between Church and State that dates back to the nineteenth century. In a place where most people are formally Catholic, having an agnostic President seemed less controversial than a female one, even as the conflation of both characteristics set Michelle up for bitter criticism from conservative groups (Correa 2005). The general public didn't mind, though, because even agnostics respect the Church for its courageous defense of human rights during the dictatorship (Baldez 2002).

There was a honeymoon phase between Bachelet, the media, and the public after her inauguration, which was partly influenced by the favorable articles published in international news sources (Dixon 2006; Spiegel 2006). Chile is invested in a project of re-formulation of its national identity, which involves moving away from the military regime's legacy and embracing a modern image (Bucciferro 2012; Walder 2005). The international attention that Michelle's ascendance attracted rubbed off on the country itself, and people liked it. Local media flirted with her, running flattering articles.

However, the romance was short-lived, and was soon disrupted by an issue that has been at the forefront of women's movements for decades: reproductive rights. A governmental effort to make the "morning-after" pill widely available resulted in explosive clashes between conservative groups, women's organizations, and the liberal left (Bucciferro 2009). The debate occupied all kinds of venues—the streets, the courts, the editorial pages of major newspapers, and meeting rooms across the nation—and was finally sanctioned by a male-dominated committee that voted against the government. The issue became emblematic for what having "a woman President" meant: it mattered on a symbolic level, but on a practical one, it didn't make a great difference (Bucciferro 2012). Many Chileans actually wanted a female President *without* a feminist agenda.

Bachelet's initiatives were sabotaged on other fronts as well. For example, she couldn't enforce the "gender parity" rule that she originally established for appointed government positions. The measure was briefly in place (Dixon 2006), but the first cabinet re-shuffle rendered it ineffective. Still, during her years in office, the presence of women's organizations within civil society was strengthened, undoing the fragmentation that had previously occurred (Valenzuela 1998). Many women became more outspoken and empowered in everyday life, and more willing to participate in the public sphere (Balch 2009).

Awareness of gender issues increased, and some policies oriented towards equality were implemented. Although the changes were not radical, there was a perceptible sense of transformation (Associated Press 2013; Cedem 2011).

Unexpectedly, former dictator Augusto Pinochet died the same year that Michelle took office, and the news shook the national climate. People poured into the streets, some celebrating the death of the oppressor, others mourning the loss of a historical referent. Violent clashes made clear that, more than 30 years after the coup d'état, the country was still divided by the dictatorship's legacy (Agosín 2008). Many attempts were made to bring Pinochet to justice while he was alive, and he was even fingerprinted and put under house arrest (Kornbluh 2008). But he was never sentenced, and died within the protected environment of a military hospital—it was an end that left things pending, especially in the courts. Bachelet ordered a measured official response: to follow the protocol accorded to the demise of a retired Commander in Chief of the Army, without granting the honors given to former heads of State (BBC Mundo 2006). The Minister of Defense, Vivianne Blanlot, attended the funeral.

Soon after, Bachelet's government faced a different challenge: the rise of a vocal citizenry that would not be controlled. The social effervescence that accompanied her ascendance to power was heightened by Pinochet's death, and did not quiet down as time went by, but led to a ripe environment for open conflict. Michelle said that she wanted to "encourage participation" (Bachelet 2007; Spiegel 2006), but it sometimes turned against her (Weeks and Borzutzky 2012). People voiced their demands by any available means, and often took to the streets to exercise pressure and attract public attention. The media reveled in the coverage of protests staged by all kinds of groups, and the government was commonly portrayed as not strong enough to set things in order (Bucciferro 2009).

Among the prominent issues that captured public attention halfway through Bachelet's term were the failed *Transantiago* and the *Movimiento Pingüino*, both of which led to an open conflict between the citizenry and government representatives. *Transantiago* was the name given to a new bus system designed for the capital city, whose implementation presented numerous faults and caused personal inconveniences, disastrous traffic, and business losses for months. *Movimiento Pingüino* was the nickname of the students' movement, which started with a general strike that spread like wildfire through secondary schools and college campuses across the nation, paralyzing much of higher education for weeks (Bucciferro 2009). In both cases, the protests were directed at specific issues, but they were also an expression of the general "discontent" that had reigned in the country for years (Moulian 2002).

Discursively, both issues were represented by critics as illustrating the need for a government that used "manly" styles of management and matched the businesslike disposition of the political right (Bucciferro 2012). Yet this was hardly the case, because these problems extended beyond Bachelet's term and were not handled any better by her male successor. Later on, the students' movement actually grew stronger, catching international media attention and catapulting a young female leader—Camila Vallejo, a member of the Communist Youth—to global fame (Wilson 2012). Finally, just ten days before the end of Bachelet's term, in February of 2010, a massive earthquake hit the central part of Chile, causing major damage and making headlines around the world (Associated Press 2013). It was a stroke of fate that made her last days in office controversial, because amidst the devastation, the governmental response was slow (Coloane 2010).

At the time, Chileans were critical of a fractured governing coalition, but individually, Bachelet had the highest approval rating of any President since the return of democracy (Weeks and Borzutzky 2012). Chilean law did not permit her immediate re-election, though, and there was nobody in the *Concertación* with a charisma to match hers. The opposition won the elections, and the new President, Sebastián Piñera, turned out to be quite the opposite of Michelle—a businessman with strong ties to the conservative elites, who was listed by *Forbes* (2010) among the 500 wealthiest people in the world. Thus, 20 years after the end of the dictatorship, Bachelet handed over the presidential seat to a powerful, right-wing man, in a way that seemed to close a historical cycle.

Walking the gender tightrope

Michelle Bachelet was elected just a few months before Cristina Fernández de Kirchner, the first female President of Argentina. However, the contrast between these two neighbors is notable. Michelle doesn't have Christina's taste for lace, her ability to flirt with the cameras, or the hint of "girl power" that colors her demeanor. She seems stern and understated by comparison, yet she is also kind and warm. She has more in common with Dilma Rousseff, President of Brazil since 2010; but unlike her, she doesn't come across as an "iron lady," even as she commands authority. Perhaps this has charmed journalists and analysts everywhere—Michelle resists stereotyping, and she is all substance, no pose. Some had compared her to Angela Merkel, the German Chancellor, and some of this connection may be granted: they are both women of science, and they are strong but friendly (Dixon 2006). Yet in political and personal terms, they differ: Bachelet is a socialist from South America; Merkel, a conservative born in East Germany. Michelle is also a mother, while Angela is not.

Bachelet's strength contrasts with her low-key, soft-voiced demeanor. She seems uninterested in vanity, although she always looks professional—her style is polished but unpretentious. She doesn't wear much make up and her hair is simply kept. This shouldn't matter, but it does, because she is a woman in the public eye and the media often treat her differently from her male counterparts (Foxley 2005). Every aspect of her life has been scrutinized. For example, during her inauguration in 2006, Michelle looked a bit thinner than usual, and journalists noticed; speculations regarding whether she had been dieting lasted for weeks. Male politicians have openly commented on her body shape: more than once, men have referred to her as "*la gordis*" (literally, "the fat woman"), and a political opponent once accused her of "being overweight in the physical sense and lightweight in the political" (Balch 2009; Dixon 2006). This speaks volumes of how women are often treated in Chile: as objectified beings that must fit certain beauty standards or face public scorn.

Bachelet's characteristics have shaped her public career and fueled people's curiosity (Morales 2008). The ticket that brought her to office was largely based on identity politics, so the scrutiny that followed was expected, but its extent was striking. Nonetheless, unlike other prominent international figures, Bachelet never surrounded herself with a large security operative. She was always measured, open, and accessible. This helped her connect with different kinds of people, but sometimes created a casual environment where formal protocols were not upheld and her authority was challenged. For instance, in the streets, people often referred to her as "Michelle," while male politicians were called by their last names. During her second presidential campaign, she embraced this, using her first name on her webpage and a red, white, and blue "M" as a logo. The implication was that being on a first-name basis brought her closer to people.

Media attention has dwelled on all aspects of Michelle's life: her family, children, romantic history, everyday habits, etc. The public learned that she likes to cook and relies on her own mother's help with the kids, some of whom were still in school when she was first elected (Foxley 2005). Her children have different fathers: two were born while she was married to an architect, while the youngest one was born from a later union (Dixon 2006). A few decades earlier, this would have scandalized "good" society (Montecino 1996); it being openly acknowledged and accepted was a sign of social change. After her election, Bachelet openly dismissed the possibility of any romantic engagements, and she remains among the few women in politics who have built careers without the aid of influential husbands. Raquel Correa, a well-known journalist, directly asked her once: "Wouldn't you rather have a husband instead of the presidential sash?" "Obviously not," answered Michelle, laughing (Correa 2005).

Bachelet's media coverage has always been different from that of male candidates, focusing more on her personal characteristics and less on her political project, despite her efforts to put that project in the forefront. Media outlets catering to wealthy elites, such as *El Mercurio* newspaper, often portray her as a well-educated, upper-middle class mother—all identity markers that present her as non-threatening and position her within a gendered conceptualization of the public sphere. When she was a candidate, they pointed out that despite her being a socialist, her kids attended expensive private schools and they lived in a nice part of Santiago. Disengaging from the Marxist connections that the word "socialism" evokes, commentators said the new establishment was well acquainted with privilege—they even nicknamed it "the Red Set" of Chilean politics (Paz 2006). The designation mattered in a country where concerns over class position abound, and where most politicians come from a specific segment of the population.

Michelle's portrayal as a benevolent, affluent, strong but caring mother had various effects: it made her relatable for women, setting her apart from "hardcore" feminists who disavow motherhood. It made her less threatening to men. It enabled the disenfranchised to perceive her as a caring person who will see to their wellbeing. It allowed the wealthy to indulge her. Finally, it rooted her in Chilean idiosyncrasy, because motherhood constitutes a fundamental social anchor for women there (Montecino 1996). As Walder (2005) says, from the beginning, Bachelet was seen as "a mother for Chile" and many expected her to enable the birth of a new nation.

The boundaries between the public and the private, the real and the symbolic, blur around Michelle's image, yet local media often tried to dig up stories that would make her seem less apt for high office. In deeply patriarchal countries such as Chile, women are held up to unequal standards within the public sphere. Male politicians may be spared an extensive scrutiny into their private lives—their ability to govern a country is not considered to be dependent on their qualities as a spouse or parent. But this is not so for women, who are considered first and foremost mothers, daughters, and wives. Hence, in local media stories, Michelle is usually portrayed as a mother of three, the daughter of a former general, and the ex-wife of an architect. A change in this pattern was only evident after her second election (see also Chapter 9 in this volume).

Hannah Arendt (1959) argues that, since ancient Greece, the public sphere has been a space of "freedom" where people engage in transcendental debates—where they meet as equals to talk about politics, history, and philosophy. Women have been traditionally excluded from it and associated instead with the private realm, where basic human needs are met and life becomes an endless struggle to tackle everyday chores: cooking, cleaning, tending the house, supervising children, etc. The burden of this responsibility has historically fallen on women, who are considered its "natural" bearers; when women enter the public sphere, they are seen as trespassers in a male-dominated realm, which singles them out and attracts attention. Still, they carry their private selves with them and they can't simply disengage from their traditional roles, or they risk being seen as maladjusted. Thus, women in the public eye might as well capitalize on identity politics, making the private public and taking control of how their stories are told (Phillips 1991).

Columnist Caitlin Moran (2011) says media professionals are often pressured to "humanize" women in the spotlight and portray them as normal people, instead of letting them rise above common mortals the way male heroes do. Journalists are asked to report on female leaders' clothes, make-up, emotional state, romantic lives, and personal plans. In the case of men, these topics are usually irrelevant. Moran argues that media should let powerful women like Margaret Thatcher keep their public face, even if it's deemed cold and distant, because later on, there would be time to humanize their profiles. Yet in the case of Michelle Bachelet, she was presented as a relatable character all along. As a woman told me in Chile while I was doing fieldwork research: "when Bachelet was elected, I didn't think she would have enough *garra* [translated loosely as 'grip' or 'claws'] to govern, but she actually did, and I was happy to see it."

From the presidential palace to the United Nations

Bachelet reached an approval rate of almost 80 percent during her last year in office—a number linked to her individual charisma and the respect she inspired (Balch 2009). This did not involve her political coalition, which at the time was succumbing to internal quarrels and losing credibility. Political fragmentation became rampant towards the end of her presidency: some parties pulled out of the coalition, others turned openly against it, and some politicians became vociferous critics. It was a backlash that called for a "return to order" and positioned strong men as desirable candidates for higher office. Michelle didn't set things straight the way it is usually done in Chile, by dominating others, so unrest carried on. Perhaps the times were changing and it was necessary for "hegemonic articulations"—as Laclau and Mouffe (2001) call them—to be questioned everywhere, which brought uncertainty.

By law, Michelle could not be immediately re-elected, and at the time she didn't provide any indications that she would ever run again (Weeks and Borzutzky 2012). When the elections came, Sebastián Piñera, who was endorsed by the right, ran a campaign that promised "change" (*Únete al Cambio*, "Join the Change," was the slogan) and won. Bachelet handed over the presidential seat, and for a short while, faded into the background. A powerful businessman, Piñera was expected to manage the State efficiently and make necessary adjustments to the political establishment (Bucciferro 2012). To his cabinet he appointed young, sophisticated, good-looking people who took to Twitter and Facebook to share insights on public affairs. Traditional media preyed on their images and comments. Because Chile is interested in gaining status and projecting a "successful" image within the international arena, the high-tech twist promoted a dynamic narrative marketable abroad.

However, all this was out of touch with the realities faced by disenfranchised people who have no access to the benefits of economic development in a country where inequality continues to grow (Cedem 2011). While Bachelet tried to address this, Piñera's government didn't seem to care enough, and as the months went by, social unrest increased, coalescing in a highly politicized students' movement with long historical roots. The students garnered public attention and support, called a national strike, and organized marches that brought over 200,000 people to downtown Santiago (Wilson 2012). They demanded an overhaul of the educational system and a re-thinking of the country's larger goals, posing an angry critique to the brutal effects of neoliberalism. Using technology to their advantage, they captivated global media attention by staging creative protests and posting videos on YouTube: they did a "kiss-a-thon," a "march of the zombies," a "superhero day," etc. The most notable student leader, Camila Vallejo, was named "person of the year" by the *Guardian* (Wilson 2012) and was a lot like a young Michelle Bachelet: a charismatic, articulate, fearless, attractive, unorthodox female with leftist affiliations. She ran for Congress in 2013 and was elected.

Meanwhile, people started to compare Michelle's spontaneity with Piñera's carefully managed image. Newspapers pictured her watching a national soccer game at the stadium, cheering the team, casually dressed and smiling in the sun. By contrast, Piñera was seen greeting soccer stars at the Presidential Palace, stiffly shaking their hands in front of the cameras. Not much later came the news of Bachelet's appointment to the United Nations, so her traveling abroad meant multiple things: she was an excellent choice, with her knowledge of foreign languages and her international experience, yet the position also removed her from domestic contingencies. As an official representative living abroad, she couldn't comment on governmental issues and was harder to reach for Chilean journalists, yet her popularity continued to grow (Infolatam/Efe 2012).

Being at the United Nations put Michelle in closer contact with global powers, and reignited international media interest in her. Her profile was further strengthened when she became the first Under-Secretary-General and Executive Director of UN Women, the *UN Entity for Gender Equality and the Empowerment of Women*, created in 2010 (Khaleeli 2011). From there, she engaged with many of the issues that had been prominent for her government: reproductive rights, violence against women, education for girls, equality, poverty alleviation, and the protection of children (Ford 2013). She turned the position into an influential post, expanding her sphere of action to benefit women around the world (Martinson 2011). Her initiatives cemented her presence within foreign media—journalists from all nationalities praised her, and the stories portrayed her in very positive terms.

In Chile, people noticed and started asking her to come home (Infolatam/Efe 2012). On March 16, 2013, Michelle announced that she was stepping down and moving back to Santiago, where her arrival and the announcement of her running again for President were eagerly awaited.

In conclusion: Looking back, moving forward

Michelle Bachelet has governed Chile during times of profound social and political change. When she began her first term, the dragged-out period of transition to democracy was officially over and people were beginning to challenge the silence that had long been established by force and ingrained by fear (Weeks and Borzutzky 2012). The country was being transformed by the influence of globalization, neoliberalism, and transnational information flows, which made Chile's historical isolation a thing of the past (Castells 2005). The nation was hungry for symbolic associations that could undo the damage inflicted by General Pinochet, and Michelle's unique profile enabled a process of re-enchantment (Morales 2008; Walder 2005).

Her first government closed a 20-year cycle of center-left rule, cementing social-democratic principles and contributing to the development of a self-conscious and empowered citizenry (Bucciferro 2012; Weeks and Borzutzky 2012). Many of the reforms introduced moved the country towards equality, even though deep-rooted disparities prevailed because they relate to structural problems (Cedem 2011). There was a transformation, though, even if it didn't meet everyone's expectations—for some people, the changes were not enough; for others, they were either too much or not the right kind of changes. In any case, the country moved away from a government based on hegemonic "consensus" (Laclau and Mouffe 2001) and opened itself to change. As Bachelet (2013) has said: "having women as leaders changes mindsets."

Michelle was congratulated on her fiscal management and the measures she took to strengthen the Chilean economy. While the rest of the world succumbed to the ravaging effects of the economic crisis of 2008, Chile remained relatively buffered by strategic savings and fiscal spending (Khaleeli 2011). As time passed, the social effervescence that was visible during her term continued through the years of Piñera's government. Downtown Santiago became a common site for public demonstrations linked to various social causes. There was a performative aspect to these protests, a sense of postmodern reinvention that people embraced in ambiguous ways. For example, women protested in front of *La Moneda* dressed as superheroes, or painted their bodies from head to toes and paraded naked to represent the peeling of social layers, garnering plenty of media attention. As women's organizations grew stronger and developed a network throughout the country, one thing became clear: they would not be pushed back to the private sphere (CNN Chile 2013).

At the end of her first term, most women were proud of Michelle Bachelet's work and glad that she had opened important doors and put relevant topics on the table. Many were also aware of the contradictions they found in everyday life—deeper social change is still pending, but progress is being made (Bucciferro 2012). Issues that were ignored a few years before, such as domestic violence or equal political representation, were discussed and addressed by governmental policies while Bachelet was in office. The reforms were limited, but significant: they meant that women's issues were no longer marginal, but could be brought to the main agenda (Araneda Briones 2012; Cedem 2011). This mattered because, historically, the demands posed by women's groups had been barely addressed by mainstream political actors (Valenzuela 1998). Having a "woman president" makes a difference, but it should not be confused with achieving full gender equality.

In this sense, Bachelet's election didn't initially reflect a deeper shift in gender dynamics within Chilean society, and this has been publicly pointed out (CNN Chile 2013; Bucciferro 2012). The number of women elected or appointed to governmental posts is still small: in 2012, they occupied between 4 and 26 percent of leadership positions in different areas, which is below the percentages found in other Latin American countries (Araneda Briones 2012). It is known that women don't just "vote woman" (Valenzuela 1998) and Michelle has garnered widespread support not mainly because of her gender. The opposition has tried to raise the profile of other female contenders all along, with only moderate success. Indeed, this shaped the presidential elections that led to Michelle's second term. In the 2013 race, the contenders were Michelle Bachelet (supported by a new center-left coalition), Evelyn Matthei (supported by the political right), and seven other candidates representing minor political groups. The context was interesting because the two runners-up were women, yet their campaigns were not presented in a gendered way. In other aspects, Evelyn and Michelle were very different, and this was noted the most (Romero 2013).

Ever since Bachelet's second candidacy was announced, everyone predicted that she would win, regardless of her opponents. She was supported by a new alliance called *Nueva Mayoría* ("New Majority") and her campaign capitalized on inclusiveness as a theme: the slogan was *El Chile de Todos*, "Everyone's Chile." Media projections indicated that she would win by a landslide, although this didn't materialize until the second round (Associated Press 2013). She won the majority vote right away, though, rising over 20 points above Evelyn Matthei, which made the runoff election a sure win (Servel 2013). Still, Bachelet and

Matthei combined got more than 70 percent of the votes in the first round, and were the only ones competing in the runoff. Conceptually, this is outstanding: two women facing each other in a presidential race, earning most of the votes, and leaving all the male candidates behind.

In this sense, there might be deeper change taking place in Chile, even though it is difficult to determine what it amounts to. From a gender perspective, a look at attitudes, social practices, and structures reveals uneven and contradictory results. Chilean women are gaining a sense of empowerment, but gender inequality prevails in all areas of life, from salary gaps to social expectations (Balch 2009; Bucciferro 2012; Romero 2013). Michelle Bachelet's new governing agenda features a focus on equality that prominently addresses gender and class issues. Since she obtained over 60 percent of the vote, this strong mandate may lead to deeper reforms (Associated Press 2013).

For many people, Bachelet is the type of leader that current times need—so much so, that others acknowledge their envy (Infolatam/Efe 2013; Martinson 2011). Michelle's life experiences inform her leadership style, and facing adversity has led her to cultivate kindness instead of hatred, and empathy instead of detachment. She has a quiet strength and charisma that help her connect with people, and she is able to travel between cultures and contexts, charming journalists everywhere. Upon her appointment to UN Women, Jane Martinson (2011) jokingly said that maybe Bachelet was "a new superhero," a champion for women's rights. Many consider her an inspiration.

Although Michelle alone did not revolutionize Chile's political and social landscape, the country changed during her years in office, and continues to do so, under her towering figure. There is a "before-and-after President Bachelet" in Chilean history, and it is apparent that her legacy will be profound. Beyond Chile, her influence is also notable: she has been named one of the "top 100" influential people by the *Guardian* (Khaleeli 2011) and *Time* magazine. In her article for *Time*, Hillary Clinton (2008) says that Michelle "speaks and leads from the heart," so people "can draw inspiration from leaders like Bachelet, leaders with grace and courage, leaders who never give up and never give in." Because of her sense of commitment, she went back to lead her country's government once again, but her relevance surpasses national boundaries. Michelle Bachelet (2013) has said that the changes that will move whole societies toward gender equality "will happen one woman at a time." She is a woman who embodies those changes, and she is projecting them all around her, one bit at a time.

15

Virgin Venuses: Beauty and Purity for "Public" Women in Venezuela

Elizabeth Gackstetter Nichols

Black women in Venezuela are not beautiful.

Osmel Sousa, Director of Miss Venezuela, *Beauty Obsession* 2002

In Venezuela there are many blacks. Blacks are not decent people. They don't let her hang out with black people.

Ana Isabel: A Decent Girl, Palacios 2009

We Venezuelan men have an ambiguous relationship with our women: we oppress them and we adore them at the same time. Voilà, perhaps there lies the secret, although perverse, of the perpetually renewed crowning of Venezuelan women in international beauty contests of the world and the universe.

The Cult of Venus in Venezuela, Hernández Montoya 2012

In 1998, after a series of economic crises and mass protests, Venezuela held presidential elections, elections that revealed much about the power relationships and gender positions of all the actors involved. The three main candidates for the Venezuelan presidency were businessman Henrique Salas Romer, leftist military Colonel Hugo Chávez Frías, and mayor and former Miss Universe Irene Sáez Conde. Both Sáez and Salas were seen as establishment candidates, while Chávez was recognized as an outsider, a rebel leader of a failed coup in 1992 who sought to completely change the system. Each candidate had their supporters, and those of Chávez were the most militant and strident. Among the most high profile of the Chávez supporters was fiery activist Lina Ron. The positions of these two women—Sáez and Ron, inside and outside the traditional power structure of Venezuelan politics, can tell us much about the issues of public image, the role of the media and women's political participation in Venezuela.

Image building: Race, class, and decency

The Bolivarian Republic of Venezuela has a complex history of race relations, a history too complex to detail in full in this chapter. What this section will provide, therefore, is a brief historical overview of race (understood as both physical appearance and perceived ancestry) and social class in Venezuela, especially as these concepts have become linked to modern notions of "decency" and worth.

In the colonial era of the seventeenth and eighteenth centuries in Venezuela, Spanish settlers imported slaves of African descent to supplement indigenous workers in the production of cacao. As the slave population grew, so did the opportunities for *mestizaje* and the birth of children of mixed ancestry.[1] Except for a small portion of the landed elite who resorted, in some cases, to incestuous marriage to maintain purity of bloodlines, mixed marriages were the norm in the Venezuelan colony (Cunill Grau 1987). By the beginning of the nineteenth century the percentage of the Venezuelan population identified as mixed race was 47 percent (Ferry 1989).

Slaves in the Venezuelan colony labored on extensive rural plantations while the owners themselves often lived far from that production. This situation resulted in a model for the colony that was comprised of separate rural and urban spheres, with white managers preferring to live in cities and leaving the plantations to the *mestizos*, indigenous or African slaves and freedmen in the agricultural areas. These rural areas were then often associated with barbarism, slavery, and disease (Ferry 1989). In this way, national ideologies that equated moral value to racial heritage were partly a product of the plantation model.

The ideological link between moral value and work was additionally encouraged by the elite, through a standard disdain for "vile labor." Skilled professions such as blacksmithing or carpentry fell into this disparaged category. The prejudice meant that slaves and free people of color were allowed to work in trades reserved for European guild members in other colonies (Ferry 1989). While this situation allowed for some social mobility and advancement for slaves, craftsmen were still considered less morally sound and less valuable than the idle elite.

The division of labor, however, promoted racial mixing. The process that allowed slaves to become free, skilled workers also allowed people of color to marry and have families with people of different ancestry. Of course, racial mixing also continued to occur in less official ways. While elite men did not marry women of color, they did not hesitate to make those women concubines. In each situation a stigma of either "vile labor" or illegitimacy attached to the children of mixed-race unions, a stigma that supported the tradition of assumed moral superiority in the elite classes.

This stigma became entrenched in law. By late in the eighteenth century, both the Catholic church and the Venezuelan state passed decrees to forestall legal "whitening"—the process through which free people of color could use earnings to purchase both material goods and even legal whiteness.[2] As the upper classes solidified their position about the difference between those with racially "pure" bloodlines and the mixed race majority, the distance between the two groups began to grow.

By the 1800s, Venezuela's racial reality was problematic for many authors and intellectuals. While "white" continued to be understood as "better," the reality of a mixed Venezuelan majority was impossible to ignore. To deal with the perceived "problem" of race in the colony, many positivist scholars were championing the ideology of *café con leche* [coffee with milk]—a nation of mixed race people. Positivist thinkers began to publish essays that accepted that the Venezuelan nation was "*café con leche.*" These scholars, however, argued that the long process of mixing had wiped out all traces of unique African and indigenous identity and had discarded any negative impulse of the undesirable races. This theory contended that white blood was so superior that centuries of its influence canceled out the negative, undesirable blood (Wright 1995).

What remained as a part of the official ideology was the issue of class. At the same time that positivists explained the ideologically equal value of all *café con leche* citizens, the deciding line between decent and indecent, good and bad, civilized and uncivilized continued to be drawn between rich and poor. In 1853, Manuel Carreño published what proved to be one of Latin America's most influential books, an etiquette manual that is still in print in the twenty-first century. Here Carreño supported the moral superiority of the elites. Therefore, Carreño held, social inequity was neither good nor bad, but part of the God-created social order that favored the more civilized (Carreño 2010).

This type of thinking was a common thread in the positivist argument about race, which held that Anglo-Saxon (white) societies were more successful because they worked harder and had greater intelligence. It was therefore logical that people of color were poorer because they were naturally lazy and unintelligent (Wright 1995). What this type of thinking did revisit was the acquisition of decency through economic power. As the Venezuelan saying "*el dinero blanquea*" [money whitens] suggests, it was possible for people of color to "prove" their worth and status through wealth. In a *café con leche* nation, many citizens could not be differentiated on sight by their physical appearance. Therefore other criteria such as wealth and power could be used to determine a citizen's "decency."

By the early 1900s authors such as the previously cited Antonia Palacios were describing the instruction of young people into the "decency," civilization, and worth of peoples based on both race and social class (Palacios 2009). In her semi-autobiographical 1929 novel, *Ana Isabel, una niña decente* [Ana Isabel, a decent girl], Palacios shows how young women of the time received instruction on how to become a "decent girl" by rejecting the socially unacceptable poor and darker-skinned in social interaction. In this way, a woman's appearance was a signal of her economic standing and worth.

These linkages between class, race, and moral worth, continue to be relevant into the twenty-first century, especially with regard to women and their physical appearance. As Lauren Gulbas found in her 2008 study, Venezuela's social structure "continues to be defined according to a dichotomy between the 'white' and 'wealthy,' on the one hand and the 'dark' and 'poor' on the other hand." Gulbas also found that markers of physical appearance have counted, and still count, for a great deal in deciding the "value" of a person and their family. In Gulbas' interviews, she encountered a strong trend of contemporary women who linked the concept of "white" with "good" or "good enough" (2008, 138). However, it is important to note that in Gulbas' study wealth and access to beauty products and practices are social markers tied integrally to the question of worth: if a woman is not perceived as "white" she can buy that appearance through surgical intervention, hair straightening and cosmetics. In contemporary Venezuela as well as the historical state, race, class and value are inseparable, and money whitens.

Public women and private decency: *Pudor*, *recato*, and body control

A general knowledge of the social dynamics of race and class throughout Venezuela's history helps us understand how *pudor* [modesty] and *recato* [decency] became intrinsically tied to a woman's worth in the history of Venezuela. These concepts are deeply tied to the ideas of race and class as they relate to purity of bloodlines and maintenance of wealth within elite families. In order to maintain this purity, it has always been necessary to control women and their bodies.

Operating from a Spanish tradition in which "men are for the public, and therefore women are for enclosure" (de Leóñ 2011, 23) the moral imperative for Latin American men has traditionally been to keep women confined to the private sphere. On this subject, Debra Castillo notes that Latin American culture has historically supported "the privatized and inward-looking Hispanic house and … the virtual confinement of married women to the home in order to maintain the chastity and purity of 'women of good family'" (1992, 11). In fact, the old-fashioned but widely used term *mujer pública* [public woman] in Latin America is still a euphemism for a prostitute. Castillo's arguments are particularly true in Venezuela. Through history, those women who were forced to work outside the home were those of the lower economic classes, who were generally darker. Elite women, alternately, were protected and taught to reject those of lesser social or racial standing to maintain the family's claim to decency. In each case, the relationship is clear: a woman who leaves the home and enters the public arena is not a decent woman.

The division between public and private, then, is particularly relevant for women seeking to enter politics or other areas of public discourse such as media or film. As Evangelina García Prince notes in her contemporary study of women's political participation in Venezuela, women in the twenty-first century continue to fight against the deeply ingrained ideologies of Venezuelan society, ideologies that, in part, seek to keep women privatized and inward-looking. These ideologies have given rise, according to García Prince to: "strategies of eminently symbolic character that are designed to create solutions of inclusion for women that appear politically correct but preserve the supremacy, *the values*, criteria and practices of the dominant androcentric order" (2012, 12). The values represented in these strategies privilege not just the submission of women, but more generally control of women and their bodies. If the foundational ideology of purity was to maintain bloodlines, it was of paramount importance to control women's access to the public sphere and unacceptable mates. A decent woman, then, was controlled by keeping her in the home, and furthering the project of racial eugenics by attracting a mate who was as white as possible. In order to attract such a mate, she must then appear as beautiful, as white, and as wealthy as possible. As the early twentieth-century novelist Teresa de la Parra observed that women in Venezuela had an "arduous duty to appear beautiful" (2008, 35).

Beauty, here understood as a perfect appearance achieved through hard work, was and still is taught as a mark of self-control. One of Venezuela's leading contemporary cultural icons is beauty expert and designer Titina Penzini. In media interviews upon the launch of her 2009 book *100% Chic*, Penzini declared that her own personal goal in life, decided upon at an early age, was "to always to be *arreglada* [put together/arranged],[3] to always try and make others happy, at least in what they see of me from the outside" (*El Nacional* 2009, 22). Here Penzini asserts that her physical appearance will make others happy. What she has learned, and continues to teach, is the importance of physical beauty for women as social emollient. Indeed, Penzini communicates in the article her desire for the fashion manual to become "the Carreño manual for the twenty-first century" (*El Nacional* 2009, 22), a book that helps each woman earn and communicate their place in the class structure through appearance. Penzini's text continues to instruct that, for women, it is necessary to manage their appearance as a way of demonstrating the socially privileged values of beauty, purity, and hard work.

The effect of this continuing ideology is the root of García Prince's point about the subordinate inclusion of Venezuelan women in politics. If legitimacy is only attached to those women who show careful "arrangement" of their bodies, the playing field is slanted against those women who refuse to participate in traditional beauty practices, including the call for *pudor* and *recato*. Because of this, García Prince argues that the inclusion of women in public life only under restrictive ideologies such as that of beauty practices and body control does not truly represent political inclusion (2012, 16). If a central value of the political and democratic system is the requirement for physical beauty through control, the system can indeed be described as only fictitiously or partially inclusive of women.

Manufacturing the national image: The Miss Venezuela academy

There is little doubt that physical beauty, understood as perfection in European features, is of great importance to Venezuelan society. One specific manifestation of this importance is the unparalleled success of the Miss Venezuela training program. In the 60 years between its founding in 1952 and 2012, Venezuela has won more Miss Universe titles than any other nation, including the only back-to-back winners from the same nation (in 2008 and 2009) and the 2013 Miss Universe, Gabriela Isler, the daughter of a Swiss father and Venezuelan mother. Overall, Venezuela has an unmatched record of success in the training and creation of beauty queens, with over 60 international pageant winners (Koffman 2009).

Venezuela's success in the area of international beauty pageants is directly related to the nation's unique system of training. In Venezuela, the national pageant organization scouts and recruits more than 4,000 young women every year to compete for the title of "Miss Venezuela" (Nichols and Morse 2010, 329). The Miss Venezuela organization, run by Osmel Sousa for more than 25 years, then molds these women into beauty queens with industrial efficiency. At the Miss Venezuela academy, the group of 4,000 is trimmed to 80 young women who expect to participate in a rigorous training program and submit themselves to multiple plastic surgeries.

At the academy, women undergo intensive work in diction, movement, posture, and of course, physical appearance. Not limiting this work on the last to the arrangement of hair and make-up, Sousa is open about the Miss Venezuela program's use of plastic surgery. In a recent year, Dr. Petr Romer, the academy's official plastic surgeon, admitted to performing aesthetic surgery on more than half the contestants in the Miss Venezuela pageant (Koffman 2009). A woman entering the pageant must work hard in training, but must also be willing to suffer to show her willingness to control her body. As Sousa seeks to "change women for the better," he employs all tools at his command (Omestad 2001, 31).

While this award-winning image of physical beauty is often lauded by pageant contestants as a product of Venezuela's *café con leche* heritage, it is worth noting that Sousa is on the record as saying, "black women in Venezuela are not beautiful" (*Beauty Obsession* 2002) and the image manufactured by the pageant is one of traditionally European-descended features and concepts of beauty—thin, straight noses, slim lips, ultra-slim bodies, and voluminous, silky and wavy hair. Even Venezuela's much-ballyhooed first "black" Miss Venezuela (chosen in 1998) had all of these features,[4] and shortly after her victory at Miss Universe in 2013, photos began circulating on the internet of Gabriela Isler before and after plastic surgery. The photos displayed two common "corrections" to mixed heritage—a thinning of the nose and also a thinning of the lips (Despierta 2013).

The training is not all about purely physical appearance, however. The Miss Venezuela academy also stresses the importance of presenting a beautiful personality in public. Knowing how to talk to reporters and answer questions in an appealing way is an integral part of the training process, led by former college professors and psychologists in the academy. In this last stage, women learn the fine art of making "others happy, at least in what they see … from the outside," as Titina Penzini suggests. (*El Nacional* 2009, 22)

Graduates of the Miss Venezuela academy can expect to achieve international and professional success, even if they do not win the pageant. The vast majority of women working in media in Venezuela, as actresses, models, television presenters, and journalists are products of the Miss Venezuela academy (Nichols and Morse 2010, 330). Indeed, in Venezuela, beauty and pageant participation are widely understood as an avenue for entry into public life. This trajectory is understandable as Venezuelan and Latin American pageants continue to be understood and displayed as a method of choosing a woman who represents the values of the nation.

The process of choosing this representative, perfect woman is displayed for the citizenry through a wide variety of highly consumed print and broadcast media. Indeed, in 2013, a new reality television show followed the preparation, training and even surgeries of the contestants (Fernandez 2013). This preparation culminated in the pageant itself, which in 2013, was watched by 65.7 percent of the television audience in Venezuela (*Noticias* 2013).

The pageant remains popular as many Venezuelans continue to accept the idea of one woman representing elements of national identity. As Ingrid Bolívar finds in her study of the national Miss Colombia pageant, the contest creates a sense of a national "we" by selecting one woman who represents the ideals of the nation. This image is then produced and reproduced through various forms of media for consumption by national and international audiences. Nations in Latin America choose one elite woman who can demonstrate "honor, respectability, antiquity" of high morals and the racial and physical ideal of the nation (Bolívar 2007, 80). These women, then, are exhibited publically as a way to "prove the moral value of the whole" (Ibid.).

As in Colombia and Argentina, Venezuelan beauty pageants groom young women to embody the above-mentioned physical and moral values of the nation, a training that is widely accepted and considered worthwhile. In Venezuela, pageants are part of daily life in every public venue from universities to prisons, and parents send their children to beauty training academies often starting as early as age four, because they know "that if they can succeed as beauty queens, their future as celebrities and public figures is assured" (Grainger 2012). This was certainly the case of Miss Universe 1981—Irene Lailin Sáez Conde.

Irene Sáez: Miss Mayor

The fact that barriers of modesty and body control through expectations of beauty have been placed before women in Venezuela does not mean that women have been prohibited from participation in public life. Particularly in the case of those women who are willing to follow the dictates of society's expectations, opportunities for political participation can present themselves. One example is the "Venezuelan Barbie" (Manvel 2012) Irene Sáez, mayor of the Caracas borough of Chacao 1993–8, Governor of the state of Nueva Esparta 1999–2000 and 1998 candidate for the presidency of Venezuela.

Sáez, the daughter of Carlos Sáez, a prominent businessman of an affluent family, entered the Miss Venezuela training program as a 19-year-old engineering student attending the Universidad Central de Venezuela. At 19, Sáez had not only the family pedigree, but also the tall, thin physique, European features, and voluminous hair that fit a traditional Venezuelan vision of beauty (and provoked the creation of an "Irene" doll). When she won not only the Miss Venezuela crown, but also the Miss Universe title, Sáez embarked on the traditional world tour of reigning queens. On this tour, she met leaders like Margaret Thatcher, who impressed her with her strength and agency through her work in public (Arias 1998).

After her reign, Sáez returned to the university, but this time as a student of political science. Earning her degree in 1989, Sáez remarked that "I realized that you change a country through politics first, not engineering" (Arias 1998). The decision to enter politics had specific political consequences, however, as Sáez felt the need to abandon her engagement to a Caracas attorney, explaining: "he wanted me to stay home and not work. I wanted a career" (Arias 1998). This explanation goes to the heart of the public/private dichotomy. Sáez was forced to choose between the *pudor* and *recato* of a private, controlled life, and the potential moral "risk" of a public life. To manage this tension, Sáez worked to maintain an image of the "Virgin Venus," an image that serves as a model of the particular, narrow space in which political women can function. Beautiful, perfect in the physical features that communicated the "honor, respectability, antiquity" of her family, Sáez's appearance went part of the way toward building a successful public image. Some observers, however, have also noted that it is Sáez's control of her body and herself, which is directly responsible for her political successes and failures.

In his essay, "The Cult of Venus in Venezuela," Roberto Hernandez Montoya notes that women such as Sáez manage public lives through the control of their sexuality—by remaining perceptually celibate. Successful public women in Venezuela must be beautiful:

> But it is not an erotic beauty. The most beautiful, Irene Sáez, is after 1962, when she was born, an untouchable figure, a stubborn maiden who has never allowed to be taken as a sex symbol. The queens rest on their asexual pedestal. If they ever marry, they lose their kingdom (or is it a "queendom"?), becoming by that, trivial everyday women, that is, plebeians. Sexual desire voids the charm of being there, immobile, like statues, vestals consecrated to angelic admiration. They are virgin Venuses, that is, a condensation of Venus with the Saint Virgin. (2012)

Here, Hernandez argues that women achieve space for action in public venues through the maintenance of complete body control. If women are not going to stay at home, as Sáez's fiancé insisted, then they must show control of their bodies and their sexuality in other ways.

Indeed, it is interesting to note that some commentators attribute Sáez's lack of success in the presidential election specifically to a perceived loss of control on her part. In an essay on the serenity of Sáez, well-known Venezuelan psychiatrist, author and intellectual Roberto De Vries writes that "Irene Sáez lost the Venezuelan presidency when she lost the power that she had always communicated through her serenity" (2012). She demonstrated this loss of control, according to De Vries (2012), when "she showed herself to be irritated, she pointed her finger, she made faces; in sum, she stopped seeming serene." What is particularly notable about this characterization of Sáez is how serenity is defined by De Vries in nearly exclusively corporeal terms. For De Vries (2012), the fundamentals of an appearance of serenity include muscle tone and tight control of the muscles of a body, a fixed and warm smile, and the control of wide gestures or movements which might "show a loss of control in the effort to attract attention." Indeed, De Vries lists five elements of serenity, of which four are control of the physical body.

After the presidential elections of 1998, Sáez ran for and won the governorship of Nueva Esparta State in Venezuela. In that same year, 1999, Sáez also married. By 2000, Sáez was pregnant and had resigned the governorship, citing a high-risk pregnancy. In this way, Sáez closed the loop between public and private life for a Venezuelan woman.

While single, she left the enclosure of the home to enter into public life, and was able to function in that sphere by careful management of her physical image. When her focus, and her image as a pregnant, married woman indicated a return to the home, however, she left public life, saying, "I've had different roles in my life. It's a constant rebirth. At this time all of my energy is focused on my baby and my family … " (Queen Sáez 2000, 26).

Lina Ron—uncontrollable woman

While the "Venezuelan Barbie," Irene Sáez, represents one type of female public figure in Venezuela, the activist and revolutionary Lina Ninette Ron Pereira represents another. Lina Ron became famous in the early years of the twenty-first century as one of President Hugo Chávez's most ardent and radical supporters. During her career in politics, from 2001 until her death in 2009, Ron led protests outside the US Embassy, organized a violent attack of the offices of a television station and founded a leftist political party, the Venezuelan Popular Union.

Ron, the daughter of a political activist and a school teacher, was not born with the "honor, respectability, antiquity" that Sáez could claim through family connections. Ron, like Sáez, attended the Universidad Central de Venezuela, but her departure from the university differs from that of Sáez, who left to pursue the pageant circuit. Ron attended the UCV for eight semesters as a student of medicine, all the while working in a shopping mall. After her eighth semester, however, she was forced to leave the university for lack of funds (Lina Ron 2011). This difference highlights the social status of both women, pointing to the familial wealth and position that underlie a woman's claim to moral value, and, therefore, control. The fact that Ron differs from Sáez in other ways—in physical appearance, in her forms of public discourse and in her actions, further reinforces the dissimilarity between the two public women. While Sáez forged a successful career in elected office, Ron was marginalized while being perceived as "uncontrollable."

If Irene Sáez was an incarnation of the physical ideal of a Barbie doll, Ron was viewed as a poor child's rag doll. Whereas Sáez displayed a high-class image of female beauty—both superficially and in her controlled behavior—Ron cultivated an unkempt, non-feminine, and out of control image. Indeed, the highly popular Venezuelan comic Benjamín Rausseo, who delivers material through his alter ego "*Er Conde del Guacháro*" famously joked that Ron was a "Barbie doll made by INCE" (Labarca Prieto 2012).

This joke is particularly revealing in its characterization of Ron through a complex associative web of beauty, social class and value. "INCE" in Venezuela refers to the "National Venezuelan Institute for Socialist Education and Worker Training." This institute, a long-standing institution in Venezuela, took on some new connotations under the direction of Socialist President Hugo Chávez. The institute was founded to provide job training to poor Venezuelans, providing the state with skilled workers in key economic areas and continues this mission. INCE, however, has recently become widely ridiculed in Venezuela as ineffective, producing only badly trained workers who in turn, produce poor-quality products. This criticism is linked to the belief that quality job training at the Institute in the last decade has been abandoned in favor of political indoctrination (Capriles 2012). By characterizing Ron as a "Barbie doll made by INCE," Rausseo highlights several elements of Ron's perception in the media. The first of these is her physical appearance. In the joke, it is understood that the poor quality is analogous to Ron's lack of traditional beauty. The joke also aligns Ron with the less affluent classes of Venezuelan society—she is, in this joke, a "poor-man's Barbie doll." Finally, the joke reveals an underlying assumption that the poor cannot afford beauty, and indeed that beauty is inaccessible to them.

Ron, at times also referred to as "the black anti-Barbie," (Duque 2011), was known for a full head of wild platinum blonde hair that most suspected was not natural. Ron's hair was defiant, as was her political stance. Ron was the most incendiary of President Hugo Chávez's supporters, giving fiery speeches, and leading a group of armed militiamen, often repeating her slogan: "*Con Chávez todo; sin Chávez, plomo*" [With Chávez, everything; without Chávez, lead (bullets)]. During her career as an activist, Ron led protests against the United States government as well as other organizations that she considered to be supportive of Chávez's opposition. In 2008, Ron and her supporters staged a violent invasion of the Catholic Archbishop's palace in Caracas and called to the Venezuelan people to reject the church hierarchy which opposed the president. It was the attack by Ron and her supporters on the offices of the television station Globovisión, however, that earned her the disapproval of President Chávez, who on that occasion called her "uncontrollable." It is this combination of wild hair, incendiary rhetoric and violent actions that marginalized Ron from the political and media mainstream. As President Chávez himself noted, "she is a good woman, but she tends toward anarchy" (Rosa 2011).

It is the perceived lack of control, of modesty, and decency that led to the rejection of Ron, even by the president she supported. Ron was, however, a major and recognizable figure. An example of this complex view of Ron's image is found in the 2004 *telenovela* [soap opera] called "*Cosita Rica*." In the *telenovela*, a figure known as "La Chata" stands in as a *doppelgäanger* for the activist. In her essay on the program, Carolina Acosta-Alzuru discusses the generally negative impression that viewers have of both Lina Ron and her representation as "La Chata." "La Chata," as described by Acosta-Alzuru, is portrayed as "vehemence, personified in a woman of quick movements and aggressive speech." In this she is evocative of the real-life figure of Ron as antagonistic political organizer. Together the two women, says Acosta-Alzuru, "distill radicalism and aggressiveness," operating within the show "without any type of *pudor*" (2011, 245).

In "*Cosita Rica*," "La Chata" is both a mother and a presumptive mayoral candidate. Indeed, the first storyline written for the character followed her political campaign. Acosta-Alzuru finds in her study, however, that this type of outspoken and ambitious female figure is perceived as belligerent, confrontational, and without any modesty—a purely negative image. In interviews with a cross-section of Venezuelan citizens (though mostly women), Acosta-Alzuru finds consensus in the rejection of this type of female participation.

Perception of the character of "La Chata," however, changed when the plot and script began to focus more on the character's family and love life, and less on her political goals. Those interviewed expressed a specific preference for the more "passive" Chata over the more "aggressive" version evocative of the "loud" Lina Ron. In Acosta-Alzuru's study, the storylines dealing with "La Chata's" romance scored much higher than those dealing with her run for political office (2011, 260). For many, both La Chata's and Lina Ron's versions of political discourse are inappropriate.

It is hard to overstate the impact of Venezuelan *telenovelas*. Indeed, in her article on the social importance of the Venezuelan *telenovela*, Ana López notes that the programs "create a televisual 'national' in which the imagined community rallies around specific images of itself" (1995, 262). This statement works from the ideas of Benedict Anderson of the "imagined community." For

Anderson, and others that have come after, media help form a community through the creation of fictional images of the nation that juxtapose people, places, and key ideas that can be consumed and understood by members of the community simultaneously (Anderson 1991, 39). In the case of the Venezuelan *telenovela,* recognized by some researchers as Venezuela's common language, the images presented, and accepted or rejected by viewers reflect both assumptions and preferences of the Venezuelan community about women's participation in the public sphere (Stanco 2011, 121).

We see, then, the underlying difficulties for women as they seek to enter politics. In contemporary Venezuela, it is not simply a matter of physically leaving their homes, but ideologically rejecting the *pudor* and *recato* that have traditionally limited their voice. With a national community that has built an ideology of worth and value through body control and physical appearance, this can be an upward struggle for public women in Venezuela.

Conclusions

In September of 2013, 26 Venezuelan women vied to become the new Miss Venezuela for 2014. In a deeply divided country that can agree on very little politically, two-thirds of Venezuela's television viewing audience watched the pageant (Rueda 2013). The Miss Venezuela pageant unifies the Venezuelan people behind an ideal of beauty that goes beyond physical appearance. All Venezuelans can believe in, and support the perfectly controlled, managed and produced image of femininity that parades across their television screens.

The winner of the pageant, who will represent Venezuela in 2014, was Migbelis Castellanos, an 18-year-old student, the youngest of all the contestants. Castellanos, in her first interview for the media conglomerate Venevisión, highlighted how hard it was to reach her position, how much she worked, and how much she controlled her body by losing "a ton of weight" (La nueva Miss 2013). In a two-minute, unscripted monologue, Castellanos mentions her hard work five separate times and the weight loss twice. The new Miss also makes sure to mention how she was just a small-town girl who didn't know anything before coming to the big city (La nueva Miss 2013).

Castellanos' beauty, as well as her youth and inexperience follow closely along with the insistence on innocence, control and hard work as key elements in the image of the "Virgin Venus," the acceptable public image of the *arreglada* woman in Venezuela. The victory of the previous Miss Venezuela, the Swiss-Venezuelan Gabriela Isler, in the Miss Universe pageant, then reinforces the preference for European heritage—the "honor, respectability and antiquity" of her family. The pageants' display to a wide majority of the Venezuelan public—through television, the internet, newspapers, and magazines—sells this particular vision to the Venezuelan people. This aspirational image, traceable back to the beginnings of the Venezuelan state, helps us understand the public, political images of women such as Irene Sáez and Lina Ron.

Sáez and Ron represent two ends of a spectrum of the controlled and modest woman. Miss Venezuela, Irene Sáez was not only the traditionally beautiful blonde who fit perfectly the social expectations of the elite classes, but also maintained careful control of her image and actions. While mayor of Chacao, Sáez became famous for the laws that she passed to ban excessive public displays of affection between men and women—effectively controlling public evidence of erotic or sensual feeling. Sáez projected a perfect, serene, *arreglada* image, and was rewarded by election to multiple elected offices

Lina Ron, on the other hand, was marginalized from the seats of institutional power. In her role as activist, she worked from the periphery, outside the established power structure of the elite. After her death, the Venezuelan daily *El Universal* remembered Ron as:

> ... the queen of the motorcycle taxis, the sovereign of those who collect cans, the General of *La Piedrita* [the Venezuelan Citizen's Army] the ferocious Commander of groups of irregular armed men, who with a cigar between her lips, firing shots and throwing Molotov cocktails, invaded the offices of Globovisión only to later declare retreat without having taken the hill. (Giusti 2011)

Here, Ron is remembered as tightly connected to poverty, violence, and lack of traditional femininity. She is also remembered for failure—her retreat after failing to occupy the station. She was a fervent supporter of the Chávez administration, but never invited to participate formally in politics. As the obituary states, she was never a congresswoman, government minister, nor any other type of elected or appointed official.

A consideration of the gap in experience and official success for these two high-profile Venezuelan women allows us to return to the concepts of beauty, race, class, honor, and decency suggested in the introduction. Physical "beauty" in the Venezuelan social context is a historically traceable concept tightly linked to the idea of purity of race and acquisition of wealth. Both of these (maintenance of bloodline and hard work to earn economic advancement) are then further understood to be markers of self-control, a hard-work ethic, and high moral fiber. Public success, in business as well as politics, then, requires the entry fee of hard work, sacrifice, acceptance of the elite, and a traditional image of beauty. The large difference, then, in media representation and the public perception of Irene Sáez and Lina Ron, describes a fundamental set of social expectations for women in Venezuela seeking to enter public life. Women certainly participate in Venezuelan politics. What remains is to look more closely at the ways in which they are limited—the rules of subordinate inclusion and the ways in which women work within and from outside the system to gain more real inclusion.

Notes

1 The author is aware of the problematic nature of most terms used to describe the processes of intermarriage and mixing in a variety of contexts. The noun, *mestizaje*, in Spanish can be directly and literally translated to "miscegenation," a word with significant pejorative connotations. *Mestizaje*, however, has been used in a variety of contexts to glorify the shared heritage of the peoples of Latin American nations such as Mexico and Venezuela (while arguably covering over entrenched inequities). In this context, and for lack of a better term, *mestizaje*, along with the adjective *mestizo*, will be used.

2 This legal whiteness came in the form of a legal document called a *cédula de gracias al sacar*, which would allow the person access to education to become clergy or to serve in public office.

3 The word here in Spanish, *arreglada,* may be understood to mean arranged, made up, fixed up, packaged, etc. The implied idea is the effort put into the appearance, which results in a beautiful outcome.

4 Lauren Gulbas found in her study of plastic surgery and beauty work in Venezuela that features such as wide noses, wide hips or tightly curly hair were still associated in Venezuela with the idea of dirtiness, ugliness, low social status and deformity, while European physical features continue to be associated with high status and beauty. For more on this phenomenon, please see: Gulbas, Lauren (2008) "Cosmetic Surgery and the Politics of Race, Class, and Gender in Caracas, Venezuela". Ph.D. dissertation. Southern Methodist University.

16

Ultra-Feminine Women of Power: Beauty and the State in Argentina

Elizabeth Gackstetter Nichols

> *My mother had photos of Eva stuck on the door, photos that she still has ... it was that Eva that she remembers, it was the fairy Eva, the Eva with her Dior dresses, with her jewels, she was the image of the benefactor, who granted wishes.*
>
> Bellotta 2012, 30

> *When it comes to Cristina Kirchner, one realizes her emphasis on her femininity ... We see her as a smiling woman, very in tune with her appearance, with her image ... always dressed and made up elegantly. She is an ultra-feminine woman of power.*
>
> Donot 2013

In 1946, Eva Duarte de Perón, more commonly known as "Evita," attempted to give her first public address as part of her husband's presidential campaign. On that occasion Evita stood before twenty-five thousand women, including elite women of the moneyed classes. After lengthy interruptions, catcalls and demands for her husband, Evita abandoned the speech before she had begun. Almost fifty years later, in 1989, the wife of another leading Argentine politician, Cristina Fernández de Kirchner (commonly called "Cristina"), accepted a nomination to run for the national congress. Unlike Evita, Cristina was highly popular with men and women of her political party, and was asked to lead the legislative delegation from the provinces.

The difference in reception for both Argentine women is, of course, partially a product of time. The world was a different place for women in 1946 than in 1989. However, there are other important differences between these two high profile women and their political careers—their family background, their social class, and their level of education. The experience of each woman in her access to public service are partially a product of these differences.

Despite the dissimilarities, the similarities between these two famous female politicians in Argentina are striking. Through their marital connections, beauty, and attention to public image, both left behind the private life of a traditional Latin American woman to achieve public and political success. Indeed, the continuity between the careers of the two women can be understood not only as a reflection of women's appearance and public careers in Argentina, but as "an interpretation of what happens when one generation [of women] takes the baton from the other, trying to understand the essence of its spirit, despite differences of historical context and the advances that result from it" (Bellotta 2012, 13). An examination of the role that corporeal and relational image plays in the life of Argentine women will illuminate the complex process of identity creation and the role of female figures both in the private and the public sectors of Argentina. The way that both women manage and control their appearance and image in the media will further demonstrate the continuity of women's political experience in Argentina.

Nation-building through eugenics: Anglo-Saxon purity and efficiency

The history of Latin America's struggle to integrate diverse populations of indigenous, Afro-descended and European-descended citizens is well documented, as is the persistence of entrenched notions of racial hierarchy established in the colonial era. Even nations such as Venezuela or Mexico that officially celebrate a heritage of mixed blood, of *mestizaje*, continue to demonstrate socially-constructed hierarchies related to race which privilege "white," European heritage and appearance over Afro-descended or indigenous identity.[1] A study of the history of identity creation through the ideology of eugenics in Argentina will help us understand how a national program designed to encourage desirable breeding created a situation in which beauty, industry, and moral worth became intrinsically mixed for women in the nation over time.[2]

What the scholarship on the subject of eugenics in Latin America reveals is that, as they entered the twentieth century, most nations in the region shared an officially held belief that the future of the region lay in a harmonious mixture of the main groups of peoples that made up the citizenry of each nation: European immigrants, former African slaves, and indigenous peoples. This mixture, in the popular and official parlance of the Venezuelan state, for example, was known (and is still known) as *café con leche*—coffee with milk, a mix of the dark and the light. What is important to understand, however, is that the ideal mixture always privileged more milk (for an expanded discussion, see chapter 15).

Latin American intellectuals frequently advocated the value of European milk to lighten the racial coffee in the late nineteenth and early twentieth centuries. As Julie Skurski notes of the Mexican scholar José Vasconcelos (author of the famous treatise on *La raza cosmica* [The Cosmic Race]), "the idea of mixing, or synthesis, [was] part of an evolutionary movement towards 'white,' understood as modern, culture" (Skurski 1994, 642). This is additionally echoed in the Andes region, where indigenous cultures are traditionally imagined and represented as needing "modernization" and "development," suggesting that extant indigenous culture is backwards, uncivilized, and underdeveloped, at best, or at worst, a product of genetic degeneration (Barrig 2001, 113).

At the beginning of the twentieth century, the Bolivian intellectual Alcides Arguedas characterized indigenous Andeans as "sick" in his 1909 work *Pueblo Enfermo* (Arguedas 1996). This text represents a part of a Latin American scientific discourse dedicated to describing "racial degeneration" in the region (Paz-Soldán 1999, 64). Arguedas used the argument of the racial inferiority of non-white genetic heritage to explain the lack of progress toward modernity in nations such as Argentina and Bolivia. Upon the publication of the work in Buenos Aires, it was roundly applauded as an important guide that taught a valuable ideology of breeding that would be of great national benefit to the young nations of the southern cone (Stepan 1991, 61).

The conceptualization of non-white persons as less "civilized" included a generalized perception of people of color as more sexually free and less controlled. In general, as Argentine historian Felipe Pigna notes, the historical record in Latin America generally shows a tendency to characterize non-Europeans "zoologically"—more as animals than as humans. As Pigna notes, one of the earliest examples of literature written in Argentina after European settlement was the myth of Lucía de Miranda, a tale often used as a moral fable to instill sexual control and abstinence. In the 1532 tale, Lucía provokes the lust of an indigenous chief, is kidnapped by him and forbidden to see her white husband. Unable to control themselves, however, Lucía and her husband meet secretly and intimately. Denounced, they were discovered and both were killed (Pigna 2011, 79).

For many years, political and religious leaders in Argentina used this legend "as a moral fable about fidelity, self-control and about the dangers that 'savage' society presented" (Pigna 2011, 79). Related narrations then taught that indigenous women were sexually promiscuous, gave themselves willingly to their captors, and betrayed their own people (Pigna 2011, 79–80). The danger that "less civilized" society taught in these tales is the need for physical beauty to be managed and controlled. For the political and religious elites of the nation, while the bodies of women remained unregulated, the specter of uncontrolled *mestizaje* remained present.

Because of the preference for adding more white blood to the national genetic pool, many nations encouraged as much immigration from Europe as possible, while discouraging or outlawing immigration from Africa or those areas with populations considered to be "too black." Indeed, many positivist thinkers in Latin America attributed the economic success of nations such as the United States to the prevalence of white immigrants, and sought to increase the numbers of those same immigrants to their nations (Nichols and Morse 2010, 165). Argentina, one of the nations with the smallest populations of African-descended citizens, was also one of the most successful nations in the recruitment of European immigrants. For some Argentine intellectuals, it was essential to remember that "those who invoke democracy to the exclusion of good birth, misunderstand both. No matter how many turns society may take, it will never alter the fundamental laws of nature" (Sommer 1991, 96). This sentiment understood those laws of nature to privilege Anglo-Saxon blood over that of Afro-descended or indigenous citizens, who could not truly be expected to participate in the democratic process.

Seeking a "civilized" image: Work, image, and social class

The notion that race and social class were tightly linked follows from the assumption of the superiority of the Anglo-Saxon work ethic and the laziness and barbarism of non-white peoples. Beauty and virtue, understood as adherence to the moral, social, and physical standards represented by Anglo-Saxon immigrants, followed from this assumption. That physical and moral beauty were values intrinsically linked to European features and actions (especially for women) is an ideology represented clearly in the colonial period. In the foundational Argentine novel *Amalia* (1855), the struggle to create a national identity "assumes a social chaos in the absence of legitimate power, and therefore sets about to construct a legitimate nation/family from the elements in flux … " (Sommer 1991, 92). Set during a revolutionary period in which the "uncivilized" rural areas were pitted against the "civilization" and intellectual elite of the capital, the novel seeks to pacify the savage rural elements through marriage. The symbolic method of this construction, as Doris Sommer finds, is the union of two characters: Amalia and Belgrano.

That these two figures represent aspirational images of whiteness and European descent is not surprising (Sommer 1991, 96–7). That Amalia represents a beautiful, wealthy, white woman of the uncivilized "frontier" to Belgrano's civilizing big-city influence also follows well-established ideological patterns. The marriage of the two unites the frontier of Argentina's rural past with the civilization and modernity of the city, while leaving Afro-descended and indigenous citizens on the margins.

What is interesting about Amalia, however, is the author's insistence on her strength and work ethic. Amalia is an active volunteer in the civil war, a woman who declares herself "independent" and courageous (Sommer 1991, 95). The aspirational image of women in the national novel of Argentina is one of beautiful Euro-Americans, yes, but also of women who "know how to defend a dignity which the men have forgotten," and show "a moral valor, a firmness and dignity of character" (Sommer 1991, 95). Here, it is clear that a woman of "good birth" would demonstrate not only beauty and high moral fiber, but also strength and integrity. In the pursuit of whiteness, bodily control, and wealth, women in Argentina have been enculturated to aspire to this model of beauty, self-control and work that reflects the historical precedents of race and class. This model then, demands that women perpetuate the values of work and image by educating future generations.

As Claudia Patricia Uhart notes of the contemporary Argentine state, women's responsibility has been to guard and promote the central value of progress—advancement of family and nation through industry and consumption. In this, women have played a significant role in the creation of national identity through a focus on economic agency and appearance. This association of success through the work of women for their family, according to Uhart, is constructed in Argentina "from the stereotype of a woman who belongs to an elevated, urban, socioeconomic class, in a highly industrialized western nation" (2004, 134). Argentine women, in Uhart's view, demonstrate the moral and economic valor of their families by the acquisition (through fashion, beauty products, etc.) of a wealthy, urban, Euro-descended lifestyle and appearance. In this way, "identity is defined by the appearance that one creates through consumption" (2004, 137).

As in other Latin American nations, this responsibility for Argentine women is closely tied to body image. Returning to the understood supremacy of industrious Anglo-Saxon heritage, Argentine women, according to Uhart, learn to seek the "acquisition of wellbeing, beauty, elegance and comfort" of women who have achieved high economic social positions (2004, 134). Success for women comes in the form of bodily management through cosmetics, hair care, surgeries, and clothing choices that create a wealthy, Euro-descended aspect. This image is then not only demonstrated to society at large to verify the value of the family, but is also then used in the instruction of the family's children into the importance of wealth, industry, and appearance, solidifying a woman's role in maintaining traditional values.

Beauty, virtue, and hard work in Argentina

The combination of physical beauty and the intrinsic, understood value of Anglo-Saxon hard work and industry are clearly represented in the tradition of "Queens of Work" or "Prettiest Little Worker" pageants in Argentina through the 1970s. As demonstrated in recent studies of the pageants, the winners of these competitions represented an ideal "of identification and of new values that were disseminated by means of communication (newspapers, magazines, radio, film, television)"; these images then showed that "a specific corporal appearance exuded a certain moral condition" (Lobato 2005, 177)—a condition that demonstrated hard work, commitment to the traditional family, and self-control.

A review of Argentina's political and media history reveals a well-established tradition of pageants to reward beauty and industry, from regional competitions that chose the prettiest vineyard worker, to those that chose the most beautiful farmworker in a Festival of Wheat. These regional pageants were then linked to the election of a national "Queen of Work" on the international worker's holiday on 1 May—a "Creole beauty"[3] who was either an agricultural worker or a union member (Lobato 2005, 95). This image of a beautiful daughter of immigrants then was combined seamlessly with the conception of a superior work ethic. As Belej et al. contend, "beauty represented and was the vehicle for some of the new elements of a brand-new tradition: immigration and disciplined work united for progress" (2005, 46). Lobato similarly finds that photographic images of these beautiful and industrious women in national media created "a type of ideal beauty, an Argentine beauty" the key to which was "the identity of a feminine 'worker' converted into a queen" (2005, 82).

The creation of regional and national pageants of this type show the importance of the feminine body in the construction of a national Argentine identity. Women, in their physical appearance, functioned as symbols of strength, unity, and modernity, in a way that privileged the beauty of Euro-descended women in the process of creating a "local and national identity on the base of progress and civilization" (Lobato 2005, 179). What is also important to note, however, is the way in which this identity as workers in the public sphere was not contradicted by the image of women as dedicated wives and mothers. Indeed, the two sets of values were understood to be linked. As Lobato (2005) finds:

> The figure of the queen of work represented the perfect combination of worker and beautiful woman, which for decades had been considered incompatible. And so with the incorporation of women in extra-domestic work, the idea that a female worker was first and foremost a mother was supported. (83)

Women, the pageants demonstrated, could be beautiful, could be industrious and aid the modernization of the nation, and were still then symbols of family value and morality.

Until her death in 1952, the national "Queen of Work" in Argentina (and many regional queens) was crowned by first lady Eva Perón. Herself an example of how family relationships and values could be combined with hard work and public image, Eva Perón, her struggles, successes, and attention to physical appearance, represents a key example of the ideology of beauty, power, and virtue in Argentina.

Saint Evita

In the Buenos Aires museum dedicated to the life and work of Eva Duarte de Perón, one of the first things that the visitor encounters is a display detailing the "white myth" and the "black myth" surrounding the first lady. On the left-hand side of the wall, painted black, are shadow boxes with images and text portraying Evita as a prostitute and a corrupt threat to the Argentine people. On the right-hand side of the wall, painted white, are images and texts that portray the organizer and fiery public speaker as a Catholic saint. From the time of her ascendancy to the halls of Argentine power to the present day, both of these images continue to have resonance. Whether scholars and citizens view Evita as a positive or negative figure, there is no difference of opinion on her importance or the power of her beautiful image in Argentine history. The subject of countless plays, films, and texts, the acknowledged inspiration to the first elected female president of Argentina, Evita, as saint or sinner, is an important, if controversial, figure.

Versions of Eva Perón's life differ in the details of her childhood and adolescence.[4] However, most accounts agree that Evita was born illegitimately in 1919 to the mistress of a middle-class rancher, Juan Duarte. After Duarte's death, Evita's family suffered after the rancher's legal family withdrew financial support. In order to survive, Evita's mother took in sewing and boarders while Eva and her siblings worked. Showing an early talent, Evita made the decision to leave her rural home and move to Buenos Aires to pursue an acting career. She received her first part in a vaudeville production in 1935, and then moved on to film.

It was as an actress, participating in a 1944 charity fund-raiser, that Evita met then Colonel Juan Perón. After a scandalous period of living together, in 1945 the couple were joined in a civil ceremony. At the time of their first meeting, Colonel Perón held the position of Secretary of Labor, a position in which he enacted a series of liberal reforms that endeared him to the working classes. However, Perón's political career was only just beginning. After serving as Vice President from 1944–5, Perón was chosen as the 1946 Labor Party Candidate for the presidency of Argentina, a post that he won in that same year.

From the beginnings of Perón's administration, Evita showed astute management of her image both as wife and as an extension of the political platform of her husband. In one of her autobiographical works, Eva noted that: "Perón had a double personality and I would need to have one also: I am Eva Perón, the wife of the President, whose work is simple and agreeable … and I am also Evita, the wife of the leader of a people who have deposited in him all their faith, hope and love" (Eva Perón Foundation 2013). This perception of Evita's dual role is reinforced by a new set of murals by Daniel Santoro and Alejandro Marmo in Buenos Aires. These iron artworks, commissioned by the current president Cristina Kirchner, appear on the main thoroughfare of the Avenida 9 de Julio. Adorning two facing sides of a government building are two images of Evita. One represents the smiling, beautiful fairy godmother of the poor, the other shows the militant Evita giving a fiery speech, fist lifted in the air.

Evita's presentation of herself as both a wife and a political figure fits neatly with the dual roles of work and family promoted to women of the time period; the combination of worker, beautiful woman and mother. While Eva and Juan Perón never had children due to biological difficulties, Evita seamlessly transformed her position as wife of the President into that of mother of the nation. As Gwendolyn Días notes, "Though Evita had a brilliant political mind (some believe more so than Perón) and was a strong woman, she understood that in the society of her time and place a woman would only be allowed to gain power through her connection to a man" (Dias 2003, 184). In this case, Evita used her image and the media to communicate how her role as wife had made her the idealized figure who had achieved an elevated, urban, socioeconomic class and who would use this position for the betterment of her family—the poor and working classes. Through consumption of beauty products and clothing, Evita represented the possibility of advancement for the less privileged segment of the Argentine populace. As such, Evita represented an aspirational ideal for those members of lower socio-economic classes who looked at magazine and film images of Evita and consumed her Cinderella image; that of the fairy Evita.

Evita worked hard to create this position as fairy princess, a "figure that wore clothes like no other" (Moreira and Shaw 1992, 184). She sat for innumerable photo shoots in which she cultivated a fashionable and beautiful appearance, wearing the latest styles, and dying her hair blonde to better approximate a Euro-descended image. Indeed, Evita is perhaps as well known for her careful attention to style as she is for her social work. The Buenos Aires museum created in her honor contains in equal parts information on her social work and dresses, shoes, accessories, and glamorous photos of the first lady. For Evita, this careful attention to image was part and parcel of her desire to prove her worth through the acquisition of the wellbeing, beauty, elegance, and the comfort of the wealthy, as Uhart suggests. For Evita, fashion was a "tool for political expression" (Uhart 2004, 187), a symbolic marker of her hard work and virtue.

And Evita was indeed more than just a fashion icon. She also worked very hard, both politically and socially:

> By the middle of 1949, the roles that Evita played in the Peronist government were clearly defined: she was the delegate and interpreter for Perón to the *descamisados* [shirtless ones], the plenipotentiary of the poor to the leader, the banner carrier of women and the poor through her social work and the president of the Feminine Peronist Party. (Bellotta 2012, 80)

Evita's work with the poor endeared her greatly to them. This association with the morally suspect lower classes, however, did little to impress those in seats of power. In 1951, Evita was encouraged to run as the vice-presidential candidate on her husband's platform. The continuing opposition from the traditional elites, however, scuttled that plan.

Evita would nevertheless become her husband's biggest political advocate, and organized and managed many initiatives before her death in 1952. These projects included homes for unwed mothers, social assistance programs, housing for the poor, and educational programs for lower income children. Perhaps her greatest achievement, however, was her successful advocacy for women's suffrage, which women achieved in Argentina in 1947. In each, Evita revealed her desire to fulfill the role of mother of the disenfranchised—both through her image and through her work.

Beauty, virtue, class, and work: Double standards of social class

As part of the underlying ideologies of work and beauty at play in Argentina, Evita faced significant challenges in the area of her perceived virtue as a member of the lower economic classes. As described earlier, the issue of a woman's beauty and physical appearance was only a part of her whole image, which was tightly linked to issues of wealth, social class, family morals, and individual virtue. Evita could do nothing to change her past as a poor, illegitimate child, but she could manage her image in how she presented herself both as beautiful, and as hard-working.

This work won her the love and admiration of the poor and disenfranchised. Those members of marginalized groups saw a specific image of Evita on billboards, in newspapers, and on screen: the incarnation of Cinderella, a woman who had worked to achieve beauty through industry and moral integrity. For some members of the traditional elite, however, her "low birth" and morally suspect past were difficult to overcome. Indeed, many of her opponents went to great lengths to attack her character through her family, suggesting, for example, that her mother had run not a boarding house, but a brothel.

Evita was well aware of this barrier. Her initial efforts to engage in social work, for example, were stymied by the traditional holders of virtue and industry: the venerable "sociedad de Beneficencia" [Beneficent Society] of wealthy women.

The society was a quasi-governmental organization that received government funds and had worked with the government in charitable works since 1823. In this capacity, the members of the society over time positioned themselves as guardians of feminine virtue. It was traditional for the Argentine first lady to participate in the work of the society. Evita, however, was snubbed thoroughly by the women of the society, who refused her entry. In this way, the society symbolically excluded Evita from the circle of elite women who understood themselves to be carriers of feminine virtue, despite Eva's work to create a wealthy and beautiful image.

The exclusion forced Evita to create her own foundation, an institution that appropriated all the government funds previously given to the Society. Evita was practical in her assessment of her ability to do good works in the face of elite disdain. In her autobiographical text, Evita wrote:

> I could have been a President's wife in the same way that others were. It is a simple and agreeable role: appear on holidays, receive honors, "dress up" and follow protocol which is almost what I did before, and I believe more or less well, in the theater and the cinema. As far as the hostility of the oligarchs goes, I can't help but smile ... Power and money are never bad advantages for a genuine oligarch. (Bellotta 2012, 75)

Here, Evita shows an awareness of both the imperatives to present a well-groomed image, and the need to be "useful" and industrious. The management of a charitable organization allowed her the opportunity to do both, but neither was as useful as the media.

Evita and her husband also made shrewd use of the press to build her image. News-reels and radio programs controlled by the government regularly featured Eva's beauty or good works, and Evita herself bought her own newspaper, *Democracia*, which became her mouthpiece and that of the Peronist administration (Foss 2000). As Clive Foss finds, this newspaper "became the clearest voice of the regime, constantly featuring the President's wife in an array of stories and photos together with national and international news from a Peronist perspective" (2000, 8). The newspaper acquisition was then accompanied by the foundation of a chain of television and radio stations designed to further reinforce the Peronist position and Eva's image as both beautiful and benevolent, a saint (Repoll 2010, 39).

The Perons used Evita's image as a fairy godmother as propaganda, to give glamour and power to their position. The need to control the media to do so was the result of Evita's contested image within the nation. The Perón administration's willingness to manage print and visual media in order to create and protect this image is a tactic that succeeding presidencies would use. Indeed, analysis of the administration of President Cristina Fernández de Kirchner demonstrates the same drive to control the media in order to promote the image of the female leader, her physical appearance, her virtue, and hard work.

Queen Cristina

The trajectory of the political career of Cristina Fernández de Kirchner, Argentina's first elected female president, is similar in many respects to that of Evita Perón. The wife of the president, beautiful in image and work ethic, Cristina has labored to encourage the link between herself and the 1930s' icon. Indeed, in addition to the commission of the previously mentioned mural, Cristina often places herself in front of a portrait of Evita during press conferences, and in 2012 worked intensively to achieve a revision of the Argentine one hundred peso bill. The new bill includes a portrait of the departed first lady and was presented to the nation on the sixtieth anniversary of Evita's death.

Cristina Fernández was born and raised in La Plata, a university town 60 miles to the south of Buenos Aires. The daughter of a politically active family that supported the Peronist party, Cristina excelled at the National University of La Plata. Cristina as a student is remembered by acquaintances not only for the beauty she possessed, but also the intelligence and ambition (Bellotta 2012, 37). Indeed, in terms of care for her appearance, and beauty work, Cristina has always been known for an ultra-feminine and closely managed appearance. In the words of one biographer, Cristina has always presented an "impeccable" image to society (Bellotta 2012, 45). One that "was spectacular, physically perfect. In addition to how great she looked, intellectually … she defended her ideas passionately" (Bellotta 2012, 49). For her contemporaries, the care and discipline with which a youthful Cristina managed her body was reflected in her thinking.

After graduation from the university, Cristina began law school, where she met a politically active Peronist named Néstor Kirchner. Six months after their first meeting, the two were married in 1975. Cristina postponed her graduation to support her husband and care for the couple's children. What she did not give up was her work ethic, activism, or interest in politics. During the early years of the marriage, the couple worked in the management of a law firm founded by Kirchner in the town of Río Gallegos. Despite the demands of marriage and motherhood, Cristina worked as an office assistant in the firm while her husband sought clients. By 1986 Néstor was running for public office as Intendant of Río Gallegos. For that campaign, Cristina managed the publicity and served as the legal and technical secretary (Bellotta 2012, 103). In the same way that Evita had managed dual roles as wife of the president and political ambassador from her husband to the people, Cristina built an image of dedicated, loyal, and hard-working wife and mother, the "perfect combination of worker and beautiful woman" referred to earlier in the context of the prettiest worker pageants.

Cristina's image as hard-working, intelligent and as a beautiful wife and mother gained her support in her husband's party. In 1989, she was nominated to run for a seat in the provincial congress, and won the position, a position she continued to hold as her husband won the governorship of the Province of Santa Cruz and then the presidency of the nation in 2003. In 2005, Cristina ran for and won a seat in the national congress, solidifying her political position.

The Kirchners made a formidable power couple, with Cristina the only member of congress to have an office in the presidential palace. Indeed, some observers took to calling Cristina the "co-president" of the nation (Bellotta 2012, 125). It was therefore not surprising to observers when Cristina announced a run for the presidency for herself after her husband's first term. Indeed, the close support and collaboration between Cristina and Néstor caused some to speculate that the two would continue to trade off presidential campaigns, and presidencies, for the indefinite future.[5]

Cristina ran for president in 2007, both in her position as congresswoman and first lady. Her campaign from that year reveals the careful construction of her image as hard-working and elegant wife and mother, heir to Evita, elegant, fashionable, and friend to the disenfranchised. This image is one continued through her husband's death and her second term as president, as she continues to project a wealthy, benevolent, and beautiful image. Indeed, "she is famously passionate about her clothes and appearance and has deployed her glamour and looks as part of her political armoury—as Evita once did" (Mount and Sherwell 2012). This image for Cristina, however, is also closely and fiercely tied to her work ethic, intelligence, and experience.

Morgan Donot, in her analysis of one the political ads supporting Cristina's first presidential campaign, notes that "Cristina is an elegant 'queen' with carefully arranged hair, ample lips and a top model walk. What's more, this spot highlights the credibility that supports the candidate through her history, her political trajectory" (2011). As Donot observes, the "image transmitted by this spot is of a woman politician with every right to assume her femininity and combativeness" (2011). The research in Donot's study highlights the fundamental elements of a positive female image in Argentina—beauty, self-control, education in image, and a hard work ethic. Cristina's campaign worked to portray her as not only beautiful, but independent, firm, and dignified, just like the title character in *Amalia* one hundred and fifty years earlier.

Cristina's use of the media, and her administration's desire to control it, is not only linked to the use of advertisements. Like Evita in her day, Cristina is also widely criticized for her use of state power to censor and dominate the national press. In 2012, her administration implemented a media law nominally designed to break media monopolies and foment freedom of speech. The law, written in 2009, was seen by many as a bid to silence Cristina's largest media critic, the Clarín media group, which in 2012 owned Argentina's best-selling newspaper, and controlled 59 percent of the television market and 42 percent of the radio markets (Gilbert 2012). The media controlled by Clarín had enormous reach and influence, and the ability to either protect or damage Cristina's image. In 2009, the year of the law, the latter was arguably occurring as 64 percent of the 124 headlines that appeared in the daily newspaper were critical of Cristina's image and policies (Repoll 2010, 49). If indeed the law were passed to silence or reduce Clarín and its power, this can clearly be understood as a desire to repress the media to protect Cristina's image.

Both Eva and Cristina are understood as social reformers. Evita worked for women's rights and social justice for the poor. As a Peronist, Cristina continues this tradition, championing such leftist policies as the nationalization of industry and human rights advances for women, children, and homosexuals. That each leader used their position and arguably their glamour to put forward the perspective of the marginalized or weak in society is another manifestation of their role as "mothers" of the nation.

Conclusion: The power and imperative of humble beauty

Both Evita and Cristina walked a fine line in the creation and the maintenance of their images. While viewed as controlled, managed, and physically beautiful, both were accused publically and in the media of "frivolity" by paying too much attention to their appearance and image (Bellotta 2012, 125). This charge created consternation and anger in both women, who were both proud of their work and their efforts on behalf of the disenfranchised. This criticism also then led the administrations of each figure to seek more control of the means of communication and information dissemination. To manage their images, both Evita and Cristina sought control of newspapers, radio, and television.

What the charge of "frivolity" highlights, however, is the foundational ethic in Argentina for women to be beautiful, hard-working, family women who carry the moral value of humility with them in their lives. While the social expectation for a successful woman was to promote an image of beauty, wellbeing, and comfort, it continues to be equally important for women to aspire to an image of the perfect combination of beauty and work, self-sacrifice, and family loyalty.

In addition to their actions in regard to the media, both Evita and Cristina respond similarly to the criticism of frivolity (instead of work and self-sacrifice). Just as Evita "did not renounce riches like the saints, but renounced pride in front of the poor, who create riches" (Bellotta 2012, 133) as a way to celebrate the work of the poor, Cristina continues to defend her appearance as a part of a necessary image. In 2004, Cristina told a news magazine that her carefully crafted image was necessary "because I represent the Argentine Republic. And one who represents a nation should look appropriate for the task" (Bellotta 2012, 137). For both women, beauty and control are tasks intrinsically aligned with their work and their positions, used as political tools for the advancement of their causes. Female political actors in Argentina draw on a long history of assumed moral high ground that they can occupy through image in order to achieve political goals. Loyalty to family, hard work, and self-sacrifice are combined with bodily control to mark a socially successful woman.

As the nation continues into the twenty-first century, more investigation could be accomplished on the connection between image and power in Argentina. While progress and civilization has traditionally been linked to bodily control, the new millennium may reveal other attitudes. More work could be done on the role that beauty practices and appearance plays for both men and women in positions of power. In the meantime, while the media continue to spill "rivers of ink in the clothing, hair care, shoes, purses and jewels" (Bellotta 2012, 140) of Evita and Cristina, beauty, as a marker of wealth and agency, will still continue to be relevant in Argentina. And ultra-feminine, maternal, and hard-working women will still be those in power.

Notes

1 The author is aware of the problematic nature of most terms used to describe the processes of intermarriage and mixing in a variety of contexts. See note 1 in previous chapter.

2 In this work, we will understand the term "eugenics" to describe any ideology which promotes the improvement of the human race as a whole, or of a specific population of humans, through selective breeding. This may include limiting the reproductive opportunities for those with traits considered undesirable, or promoting the reproduction of persons with traits considered desirable. For more on this topic in relation to Latin America, please see: Stepan, Nancy Leys. *The Hour of Eugenics: Race, Gender and Nation in Latin America*. Ithaca, NY: Cornell University Press 1991.

3 The word, "*criollo*" [creole] in Spanish, here once again refers to the woman's European lineage. *Criollo* was a commonly used term for a person of pure European ancestry born in the Americas.

4 Many biographies have been written about Evita. For examples of further information and detail, please see: Zanatta, Loris. *Eva Perón, una biografía política.* Buenos Aires: Sudamericana 2011; or, in English, Fraser, Nicholas and Marysa Navarro. *Evita: The Real Life of Eva Perón.* New York: W. W. Norton 1996. The Evita Perón foundation's website also has biographies in English and Spanish: http://www.evitaperon.org/evita_peron_biography.htm

5 Argentina's constitution prohibits presidents from serving more than two *consecutive* terms. There is no prohibition to a third or fourth term if alternated with another president. Please see: Carroll, Rory. "Argentina's president to step aside—for wife." The *Guardian*. July 2, 2007.

17

Yulia Tymoshenko's Two Bodies

Tatiana Zhurzhenko

The political phenomenon of Yulia Tymoshenko, her meteoric business career, her triumphant ascent to power, and the consequent drama of her criminal prosecution and imprisonment are unique, even for turbulent, postcommunist Eastern Europe. Having started with a video rental shop at the end of the 1980s, she built a business empire using her husband's family connections. Ten years later, in a move typical of Ukrainian tycoons seeking to protect their business interests, she entered politics. However, upon her election to the Ukrainian parliament, she joined the opposition to president Leonid Kuchma. Dismissed from her post of deputy prime minister in charge of energy policy in 2001, she faced a criminal case and spent 42 days in prison—a fact she later made use of in presenting herself as a victim of the Kuchma regime. In the 2004 presidential elections, Tymoshenko supported Viktor Yushchenko and became the female icon of the Orange Revolution. Her visual appearance from that period evoked a broad variety of cultural connotations: from the Marianne of the Ukrainian revolution and a woman-warrior fighting the dark forces of evil to the traditional Mother of the Nation, the embodiment of chastity, tenderness, and love. Tymoshenko's golden plait, reminiscent of a nimbus or a crown, has become the most successful brand in Ukrainian politics since she appeared on the covers of glossy magazines and on TV screens. Styled as a political celebrity, she did not so much persuade as seduce both the Ukrainian and the international public.

Tymoshenko was appointed prime minister by Viktor Yushchenko, but dismissed seven months later as her political honeymoon with the president ended in the dramatic split of the Orange coalition. In 2007 she returned to the prime minister's office and retained her position despite severely strained relations with the president. The conflict between them, which led to lasting deadlock in Ukrainian politics, threw democratic reforms into disarray. Competing with Viktor Yanukovych in the 2010 presidential elections, Tymoshenko lost by a very narrow margin. One year later she faced criminal charges for "abuse of office" linked to a natural gas imports contract signed with Russia in 2009 and, after two months of hearings, was arrested in the courtroom for "ridiculing court proceedings." Finally, in October 2011, she was found guilty and sentenced to seven years in jail. In December 2011, Tymoshenko was re-arrested (while in prison) as part of a new investigation into alleged tax evasion and theft of public funds by the United Energy Systems of Ukraine, the company she chaired from 1995 to 1997. In January 2013, Tymoshenko was officially notified that she was suspected of ordering the murder of the Donetsk businessman Yevhen Shcherban and his wife in 1996.

Since her imprisonment, Tymoshenko's case has polarized Ukrainian society and been closely followed in the West as an example of selective justice and political repression. While in prison, Tymoshenko went on hunger strike several times and refused to attend court proceedings citing her deteriorating health. Expressing concern for her life, she demanded examination by Western medical experts. While Tymoshenko's supporters posted photos of her bruises on the internet as a prove of her physical abuse, the authorities organized leaks of internal surveillance videotapes showing the jailed opposition leader moving nimbly around her cell. In turn, she appealed to the West, pointing to permanent video surveillance as a violation of privacy and a form of political persecution.

Thus, one can say that Tymoshenko's body made a second appearance in Ukrainian politics, this time as a convict. Her physical condition and health problems, her changing symptoms and controversial diagnoses were constantly discussed by Ukrainian and Western medical experts, lawyers, politicians, and journalists. Tymoshenko's body has become a political battlefield: immobilized, closely watched, and physically tortured, it embodies not only the state of the political opposition, but the general state of Ukrainian society: the whole Ukrainian nation captured by the "criminal regime" of President Yanukovych.

This essay is an intervention in post-Soviet politics and Ukraine's dilemmas concerning democratization and European integration—from the perspective of the role of Yulia Tymoshenko's body in Ukrainian politics. The metaphor of Tymoshenko's two bodies can be understood in more than one sense: on the one hand, I differentiate between her physical and political (symbolic) body. On the other hand, I juxtapose "Tymoshenko-1"—the populist prime minister and political celebrity whose physical appearance was compatible with both the traditional values and the market-driven desires of Ukrainians—and

"Tymoshenko-2"—the imprisoned leader of the political opposition whose immobilized and tortured body became a stage set for the drama of repressed Ukrainian democracy, performed first and foremost for Western eyes.

The gendered body in the postmodern political spectacle

The title of this essay alludes to Ernst Kantorowicz's famous book *The King's Two Bodies*. A medievalist, Kantorowicz argued that the king's natural body had physical attributes, suffering and dying as any human being, while his other, spiritual body symbolized the monarchic power that transcended the earthly. This bodily dimension of power is no longer present in democratic politics, but reappears in authoritarian and totalitarian regimes. For example, the US anthropologist Alexei Yurchak (2013) argues in his account of the Soviet cult of Vladimir Lenin that the public display of Lenin's preserved body in the mausoleum in Red Square played an important role in legitimizing the Soviet polity.

New studies on populism and political celebrities, however, point to the return of the body (male as well as female) and its symbolic dimension to modern politics. A collection of essays edited by Helena Goscilo demonstrates that the physical appearance of president Putin and careful staging contributed to his popularity, turning him into a cultural icon of the new Russian masculinity:

> One of Putin's innovations […] is associated with issues of male sexuality, which were never promoted in relation to the Father of the Nation in Russia before Putin assumed office […] Putin has emerged as an example of fitness and health that both women and men find appealing. In some photos made readily available to the public gaze, Putin happily poses bare-chested, showcasing his well-developed musculature as a visual manifestation of virility. (Mikhailova 2012, 66)

If in the case of Putin these new tendencies can be attributed to an authoritarian cult of personality linked to the legacy of Russia's Stalinist past, the same phenomenon in Western democracies is usually explained with reference to the merging of politics and pop culture, which produces a new style of political communication:

> The advertisement (and the conventions of advertising) come to define political communication. Politicians become stars, politics becomes a series of spectacles and the citizens become spectators. (Street 2004, 441)

Feminist political scientists point to the fact that the female body plays an ambivalent role in representations of women politicians. For example, Elza Ibroscheva and Maria Raicheva-Stover (2009) observe in their study of the 2005 parliamentary elections in Bulgaria that "press coverage of female politicians was refracted through the prism of gender stereotypes, which, in turn, exemplified the current trend of the postcommunist masculinization of democracy" (111). According to their analysis, "politics is treated by the media as a male-oriented realm, where female politicians are either treated as novelty or framed within typical stereotypes of femininity." However, this feminist critique focusing on misrepresentation of women and gender stereotypes fails to explain the high popularity that some female politicians enjoy, despite a rather masculine, and even sexist, political culture. In fact, certain female politicians can profit from contemporary celebrity politics, as argued in one of the studies on Yulia Tymoshenko:

> The female body can be used as a lucrative mode of conveying political representation, as its visual characteristics, such as clothes, looks and postures are generally characterized by a greater variety than those of men and therefore create more possibilities for political communication. (Shulga 2009, 80)

Tymoshenko-1: The glamorous body, political celebrity, and populism in post-Soviet politics

As one of the leaders of the Orange Revolution and later as prime minister, Yulia Tymoshenko, with her capacity for self-fashioning and self-enactment, fascinated gender scholars as a political icon. Marian Rubchak (2005) was probably the first to observe that Tymoshenko, with her traditional plait, modeled herself according to Ukrainian nationalist cultural codes: she evoked the image of Berehynia, a pagan Slavic goddess, a hearth-mother today associated with the guardianship not only of the family, but also the nation. Rubchak argued that Tymoshenko successfully utilized the Ukrainian myth of matriarchal power deeply rooted in Ukrainian culture. However, use of ethnographic elements alone would never have made her a political celebrity in a post-Soviet country longing for global standards of consumption. Tymoshenko's success lay in her particular blend of traditionalism and modernity, merging national archetypes with cosmopolitan clichés of the global fashion industry—high heels and a coat by Louis Vuitton combined with a traditional Ukrainian shawl and embroidery. Brian James Baer calls this feature of post-Soviet self-fashioning bricolage—"a reflection of the post-revolutionary foment and semiotic chaos of post-Soviet society." (Baer 2012, 170)

According to Lviv feminist scholar Oksana Kis, Yulia Tymoshenko's political success is based on her skillful combination of two predominant models of normative femininity in Ukraine—Berehynia and the Barbie doll, which correlate respectively to national and cosmopolitan varieties of femininity:

> A woman interested in a political career in Ukraine is expected to fulfill at least two roles: as Berehynia she has to become a virtuous mother of her nation; as Barbie she must be a national sex symbol. (Kis 2007, 35)

Figure 17.1 Yulia Tymoshenko as prime minister (2009). Source: Tymoshenko's official website: http://www.tymoshenko.ua/en/. Licensed under the Creative Commons Attribution-Share Alike 3.0 Unported License. © Tymoshenko.ua

If Berehynia relates to the formerly forbidden ideology of Ukrainian nationalism, Barbie is a manifestation of Western consumerism, the embodiment of market-driven desires for beauty and fashion. From a feminist perspective, however, both rigid role models place limitations on the political performance of a female politician, who has "to serve—either a man or a patriarchal nation-state" (Kis 2007, 35).

Indeed, in contrast to Western female politicians such as Angela Merkel or Hillary Clinton, Yulia Tymoshenko's image has been aggressively feminine. Natalia Matamoros makes a direct comparison between the highly conformist business style of Hillary Clinton and Tymoshenko's approach:

> The number of elements decorating her clothes is amazing, as well as the selection of exquisite fabric and colors. Tymoshenko's style is "conspicuously not masculine," her "difference to men is strongly signaled" by numerous hyper-feminine details of her clothing. Even her strict military looking jacket […] will always be coupled with a skirt and never trousers. (Matamoros 2010, 342)

However, this "conspicuous femininity" does not necessary signal subjugation to the male political world. Instead, Tymoshenko's visual appearance corresponds to her style of political communication, which appeals to feelings and emotions rather than rational arguments. Its aim is seduction rather than persuasion. Not by chance, the abbreviation of her political force, Block of Yulia Tymoshenko (BYUT), hints strongly at the word "beauty," a word used in one of her electoral slogans, in which she borrowed Fyodor Dostoyevsky's often misunderstood phrase, "Beauty will save the world!"

"Beauty" is of course a social and cultural construct. In the Russian classical tradition (which was maintained to some extent in Soviet literature too), female beauty is usually an expression of a rich inner world and spiritual qualities, a result of internal evolution—in which suffering has often played a role. Tymoshenko, who referred to her martyrdom at the hands of Kuchma's regime in 2001, was fully aware of this cultural pattern. Her transformation from "an ill, pale and exhausted woman—a sacred martyr, a victim of injustice […] into a powerful, determined, beautiful cosmopolitan woman" (Shulga 2009, 50) corresponded to it. Her beauty came to be seen as proof of her inner moral qualities, of her chastity and spiritual purity, signifying her opposition to the corrupt regime and to the dirty world of male politics.

At the same time, "beauty" in post-Soviet Ukraine speaks the language of glamour. Glamour in Russia (and in the post-Soviet space) is about more than just conspicuous consumption among the "new rich."

> The by-product of consumption culture, glamour in Russia is a new utopia, having replaced both the late Soviet project of building a radiant future and the early-1990's vision of a democratic state. Not just an ephemeral vagary of the economic scene, glamour is an ideal of a social structure promulgated and promoted by Putin's regime. Like Soviet projects, the glamour utopia nurtures the aim of constructing a new being—*homo glamuricus*, to replace *homo sovieticus*—of building a new middle class, with its standard bourgeois ideology and taste. (Goscilo and Strukov 2011, 4)

Tymoshenko's glamorous body is certainly bound up with the none-too-deep roots of the Ukrainian political class, which emerged overnight on the ruins of the Soviet economy and secured its high social status with its dubiously accumulated wealth. In post-Soviet Ukraine, glamour has become a form of social distinction (Bourdieu 1987) that provides the new social hierarchy with its stamp of legitimacy. Moreover, the omnipresence of a culture of glamour and conspicuous consumption among the Ukrainian political class signals its organic ties to the oligarchy. To put it more bluntly, glamour is the pseudo-ideology of the "captured state" sometimes referred as "Ukraine Ltd." It attests to the absence of politics in the Weberian sense—as an autonomous sphere of professional political activity.

But glamour, as noted above by Goscilo and Strukov (2011), is not just a culture of the wealthy—it is a popular utopia, and as a new utopia it is linked to post-Soviet populism, the only incarnation of democracy available to Ukrainians after the collapse of the Soviet Union. Populism is a dirty word in the West signifying the decadence of representative democracy. From a post-Soviet perspective, however, populism can be seen as a first step towards democracy, as Francisco Panizza reminds us:

> Populism is not just about the crisis of representation in which people are weaned off their old identities and embrace a new "popular" one. It is also about the beginning of representation, allowing those who have never been represented because of their class, religion, ethnicity or geographic location, to be acknowledged as political actors. (Panizza 2005, 11)

The Orange Revolution in Ukraine was a popular movement that gave many people the feeling of empowerment but failed to achieve its goals in the absence of stable democratic institutions and instruments of public control over politics.

Political competition and media freedom were not enough to defeat corruption and, without fully functional democratic institutions, political reforms lost out to populism.

Yulia Tymoshenko was often called "the queen of Ukrainian populism" (Shulga 2009, 72). Her brand of populism—that of a glamorous princess—differed, however, from its classical versions where "identification is strengthened by the leader's adoption of cultural elements that are considered markers of inferiority by the dominant culture" (Panizza 2005, 26). Promising social justice, love and care to everybody, embracing the elderly and the poor, Tymoshenko appeared as a beautiful stylish lady who did not even try to hide the value of her designer clothes. In fact, her glamorous political body took center stage in the populist spectacle of the Orange Revolution. How can a populist politician wear Louis Vuitton in a country where the average wage is less than a hundred dollars per month? This was a question that Western journalists frequently asked. The answer is simple: glamour as the "opium of the people" has become integral to post-Soviet populist politics.

Tymoshenko-2: The tortured body, immobilized opposition, and Ukraine's defective democracy

In May 2011, one year after losing the presidential elections to Viktor Yanukovych, Tymoshenko was charged with "abuse of office" and, in August the same year, arrested in the courtroom. Criminal cases were also brought against a dozen former officials from the Tymoshenko government, a campaign presented by President Yanukovych as a "battle against corruption" but seen by the Ukrainian opposition as "political persecution." Soon after her arrest, Tymoshenko complained of multiple hematomas and demanded her personal doctor perform blood tests; some BYUT deputies raised concerns that she might have been poisoned, like Viktor Yushchenko in 2004. Some weeks later, Tymoshenko started to suffer from severe back pain; medical tests in a private Kyiv clinic revealed spinal disc herniation. Claiming to be immobilized by pain, Tymoshenko refused to attend court proceedings and complained of physical abuse. Faced with Tymoshenko's boycott on medical grounds, the authorities made tactical mistakes that dealt a serious blow to the president's image. For example, on December 8, 2011, court hearings took place in her cell, where Tymoshenko lay in bed unable to move and heavily anaesthetized;

this was seen by the many Ukrainian and international observers as a severe abuse of human rights.

Tymoshenko's physical and moral suffering in prison (without doubt not faked) was presented by the Ukrainian opposition as torture carried out at the behest of president Yanukovych, who was motivated by personal revenge. While the president publically promised that Tymoshenko would receive medical treatment that "met with European standards," her attorney Serhii Vlasenko expressed deep concern about her security, arguing that "Yanukovych does not need her alive." That Tymoshenko's martyrdom was the center of media attention had a tremendous mobilizing effect during the first months of her imprisonment—thousands of demonstrators regularly gathered on the streets of Kyiv to support the imprisoned opposition leader. On November 27, Tymoshenko's birthday, prayers for her health were held in the Greek Catholic and Orthodox churches of the Kyiv Patriarchy all over the country. In December 2011, BYUT deputies blockaded the Ukrainian parliament under the banner "Yanukovych, don't kill Yulia!" demanding their leader's release.

On December, 30 2011, Tymoshenko was transferred to Kachanivs'ka penal colony in Kharkiv, an east Ukrainian city at the border with Russia. One of the motives of the Ukrainian authorities was to move her away from Kyiv, where she was not only the center of media attention but had significant popular support and could be visited by foreign diplomats. As a means of recapturing fading attention, Tymoshenko responded to this move by focusing even more on her dramatic health condition and physical abuse. She declined the medical assistance that the Ukrainian penitentiary service offered and demanded an independent medical examination. In February 2012, three Canadian and two German doctors, who were permitted to examine Tymoshenko, stated that she was "ill, in constant pain and requires toxicology and other laboratory testing." As a new process focusing on the alleged misappropriation of government funds by United Energy Systems of Ukraine commenced in April 2012 in Kharkiv, she refused to attend on the grounds of poor health. Using her health as a pretext for boycotting court proceedings at the same time as systematically declining medical treatment, Tymoshenko turned her body into a political weapon and effectively sabotaged the plans of her political enemies.

On April 19, 2012, Tymoshenko was moved against her will from Kachanivs'ka prison to a Kharkiv hospital, where she embarked on a hunger strike in protest at the violence and physical abuse she had suffered. A couple of days later, the Ukrainian ombudsman, Nina Karpachova, visited Tymoshenko in hospital and documented hematomas on her stomach and arms that had resulted from physical abuse. Photos of Tymoshenko's bruises appeared in the media and caused huge international outrage; in Ukraine, critical journalists perceived the "beating of Yulia Tymoshenko" as crossing the red line and a sign of the ruling regime's by now obvious moral degradation. In May 2012 new photos of the suffering and immobilized Tymoshenko, skinny and pale after her hunger strike, appeared on the internet, taken during the visit of Lithuanian president Dalia Grybauskaitė to the Kharkiv hospital.

The Yanukovych regime has responded to Tymoshenko turning her body into a political weapon with rather predictable tactics. The Ukrainian penitentiary system and the pro-presidential media denied the existence of her health problems and the facts of her physical abuse; moreover, they tried to compromise Tymoshenko by presenting her stay in the penal colony and later in hospital as luxurious holidays that most Ukrainians could never afford. The

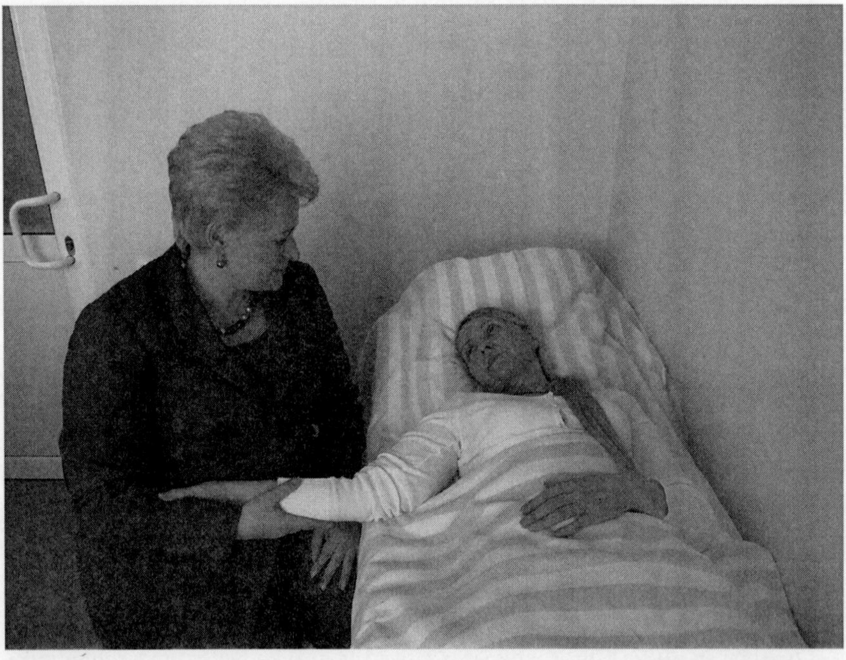

Figure 17.2 Yulia Tymoshenko on hunger strike visited by Lithuanian President Dalia Grybauskaitė on 11 May 2012. Photo: Dzoja Gunda Barysaite. Source: Available for download at the official website of the President of the Republic of Lithuania (http://president.lt/en/press_center/photographs/11-05-2012.html).

special status of Tymoshenko as a glamorous convict, a celebrity who enjoys public attention, receives visitors every day, and can continue her luxurious lifestyle even in prison was thematized in a cartoon, where she appears enjoying a sauna, a fitness session, and even taking drugs while other female inmates are hard at work.

Turning Tymoshenko's celebrity image and her "glamorous body" against her, her political enemies peddled a politics of envy and *schadenfreude*. Tired of Tymoshenko's case and irritated by the permanent discussion of her complaints in the media, a significant section of the Ukrainian public lost sympathy with her. In April 2012, an interview with Tymoshenko's former room-mate appeared in the Ukrainian media, which revealed the details of their everyday routine in the penal colony. According to Yulia Abaplova, Tymoshenko was continually provided with medical care, she was able to sit at the table and work for several hours per day, and did some fitness exercises too. They both enjoyed all kinds of delicious food that Tymoshenko received from her relatives and supporters. This interview was denounced by both Tymoshenko and her lawyer; according to Tymoshenko, her room-mate was blackmailed, put under psychological pressure, and forced to give false information. Tymoshenko's attorney Serhii Vlasenko published a letter allegedly written by Abaplova in March 2012 where she had admitted pressure from the penal colony administration and raised concerns about Tymoshenko's security. Abaplova responded by saying that her letter was dictated by Tymoshenko.

Another PR operation undertaken by the Ukrainian authorities in April 2012 involved leaking a surveillance video containing scenes of Yulia Tymoshenko in Kyiv prison in December 2011. The video shows Yulia moving around her cell wearing high heels despite having claimed to be in severe pain; at the end of the tape, Tymoshenko gives her attorney Serhii Vlasenko a long romantic hug. The video tape was dismissed by both Tymoshenko and Vlasenko as a fake. Another leaked video showing Tymoshenko moving around her hospital room and during fitness exercises appeared on the internet in October 2012 and again was dismissed as a fake and a provocation.

The problem of video surveillance became the subject of the next battle to animate Ukrainian political life for many months. Tymoshenko complained about her room being lit round the clock by electric light and the extensive use of video cameras, which she and her supporters described as "torture." Tymoshenko argued that video cameras, especially those in the shower cabin and in the toilet, violated her privacy and intruded on her intimate sphere.

The representatives of the state penitentiary service first denied the existence of video cameras, but later claimed that cameras were installed "to protect Tymoshenko's health and life."

Clearly, video surveillance was one of the few means of psychological pressure left to the Yanukovych regime with regard to Tymoshenko, not only because every woman would feel humiliated and abused by the voyeuristic gaze of a (male) overseer, but also because videotaping provided authorities with the rich material for their PR operation intended to discredit the opposition leader. Yet, with criminal prosecution, imprisonment, and exclusion from official politics, Tymoshenko's body has gained even more symbolic weight: immobilized, closely watched, tortured, it represents the state of the political opposition in today's Ukraine. Under permanent video surveillance, she is an object of panoptical control, which itself has obviously been used as a means of punishment. But if according to Foucault the panoptical model came to replace the spectacle of public corporal punishment, then in postmodern populist politics, panoptical surveillance itself has become part of the political spectacle. As a particularly perverted case of a "mediated voyeurism" (Calvert 2004), the Ukrainian public was invited to peep at the former prime minister and the leader of the opposition, watch her in her private sphere and make judgments about her health and physical condition that supported the view that her illness was faked.

In January 2013, Tymoshenko once again went on hunger strike and refused to enter her room until the video surveillance equipment was removed. She warned that from now on she refused to cooperate with the state penitentiary system and would attend court only if physically forced. In an open letter, Tymoshenko creatively turned her being an object of male voyeurism to her moral advantage, implying that watching his defeated and imprisoned political enemy gave President Yanukovych some sort of perverse satisfaction:

> From this moment on, I am not going to subdue to your bulling and humiliation. I will not allow anymore searching of me or my belongings. I will defend myself with all the physical force I have, as far as I can. I am not going to enter my room before you, Viktor Fedorovych, remove your video cameras, which you use to pry into my bed, my shower cabin, my toilet, to watch how I undress, eat, sleep, speak to my doctors and lawyers. I wonder if your sons, Oleksandr and Viktor, share this male hobby with you, Viktor Fedorovych. (Tymoshenko 2013a)

A few days prior to the EU-Ukraine summit in March 2013, during his "Dialogue with Ukraine" television campaign, Viktor Yanukovych "recommended" that the state penitentiary service remove the video cameras in Yulia Tymoshenko's hospital room. The same day, the penitentiary service announced that the cameras had been dismantled.

While Tymoshenko's strategy of politicizing her convict body and turning it into a site of personal resistance allowed her to retain the public's attention (with help from the media) for more than two years, this partial success has taken its toll. The trivialization of her body carries with it the serious danger of her "desacralization" as a political leader, as the following Facebook comment illustrates:

> What is Tymoshenko's real tragedy? The problem is her team are dolts! With this permanent show about Tymoshenko's suffering in prison they turned her from a national leader into an alternative heroine of "Dom-2."[1] A national leader must have a political goal and be able to lead to it. Instead, every day we are fed with all these embarrassing details about syringes, pads, soap and so on. This, and not the authorities, ruins her as a leader. […] These dolts do not understand that politics is all about mystery and authority. If a politician appears as an ordinary person, if she behaves as an ordinary person, what should people feel about such a politician?[2]

Under Western eyes

The political spectacle of Yulia Tymoshenko's imprisonment, as well as that of the Orange Revolution some years before, cannot be understood without taking their global dimensions into account. Ukraine, whose geopolitical future remains unclear, is torn between East and West, between post-Soviet Russia and the enlarged European Union. The Orange Revolution raised hopes of democratic reforms and integrating Ukraine into Europe. Though these hopes remain unfulfilled, the EU is still interested in closer cooperation with its Eastern neighbor. The EU Association Agreement with Ukraine was the subject of extended negotiations over a period of several years and was supposed to be signed at end of November 2013 during the Eastern Partnership Summit in Vilnius. Intended to usher in the Deep and Comprehensive Free Trade Area between Ukraine and the EU, closing the Agreement would have brought President Yanukovych significant political dividends and improved his image abroad. But the political prosecution of the Ukrainian opposition remained the main stumbling block in the process. European leaders have denounced the Ukrainian leadership's "selective justice" and made the signing of the agreement conditional on Tymoshenko's release. In summer 2012, after the international scandal surrounding the "beating of Tymoshenko," some European politicians including Angela Merkel called for a boycott of the European football championship in Ukraine.

On April 29, 2013, the European Court of Human Rights in Strasbourg ruled that Tymoshenko's arrest during the 2011 trial was illegal and politically motivated, providing her and her supporters with some long awaited good news. But the court rejected Tymoshenko's claim that conditions in prison were inhumane and degrading: lack of daylight, poor water quality, and lack of heating might have been problematic for her, but they weren't serious. The court also rejected her complaint about 24-hour video surveillance because she had not exhausted the Ukrainian legal system before turning to Strasbourg. The court was not able to determine for sure whether she had been physically abused when she was transferred to a hospital in April 2012, because Tymoshenko had refused medical examination at the time.

All the Ukrainian actors in this drama are of course aware of playing their roles "under Western eyes." Yulia Tymoshenko, as a popular Ukrainian politician with a strong pro-European and pro-democratic image, has repeatedly called on the West for moral and political support in her desperate fight with Yanukovych. Identifying her imprisoned and tortured body with the Ukrainian nation captured and humiliated by a "criminal regime," she has appealed to "Europe" as a moral arbiter and legal authority while painting Yanukovych and his politics as non- and even anti-European. "Because of you, Ukraine has almost lost its chance to become a European state," wrote Tymoshenko (2013a) in the first lines of her open letter to the president. Tymoshenko's victim status in the West, and the political and moral support she has received from Western leaders, constitute a crucial symbolic capital and, in fact, the only advantage she has over her mighty enemy.

The irony of president Yanukovych's politics of surveillance, which he used to "discipline and punish" his political enemy, is that he himself is closely watched by the Western media and political leaders. Under Western pressure, he was facing a difficult dilemma: to comply with Western demands to release a dangerous political opponent who might defeat him in the coming 2015 presidential elections; or to sacrifice the Association Agreement and run the risk of international isolation and even incurring political sanctions.

The stakes were also high for the EU as signing the Agreement with Ukraine was supposed to crown the successful accomplishment of the Eastern Partnership program. In June 2012 the Cox-Kwasniewski mission was launched on the initiative of the European Parliament with the purpose to resolve the Tymoshenko issue. A possible deal, releasing the former prime minister for medical treatment in Germany, required amendments to Ukrainian legislation. Several drafts were submitted by the opposition, but all bills were defeated by the pro-presidential majority as Yanukovych did not get guarantees of Tymoshenko's non-participation in the 2015 presidential elections. On November 21, a few days before the Vilnius Summit, the Ukrainian government officially announced that it had suspended its plans to sign the EU Association Agreement. President Yanukovych indicated that economic pressure from Moscow was the main reason for this decision, but according to many observers the main reason for the pro-Russian turn in Ukrainian politics was the uncompromised stand of the EU in the "Tymoshenko issue."

While the Ukrainian authorities did everything to have Tymoshenko disappear from Ukrainian politics and be forgotten by the larger public, she still remains a key political figure in the country and de facto the leader of the opposition. Moreover, in the tense atmosphere of the last weeks before the Vilnius summit she managed to keep the attention of the Ukrainian and international public, not as a passive hostage waiting to be freed by the West but as a politician still able to think beyond her personal fate. Led by genuine pro-Western convictions, rational calculation, and ingenious political intuition, she appealed to the European leaders to sign the agreement with Ukraine regardless of the question of her release. In this way, Tymoshenko once again presented herself as a true national leader who wants her country to succeed on the way to the EU, and thus in strong contrast to her political opponent, President Yanukovych, who seems to care only about his re-election in 2015. In her open letter from November 22, Tymoshenko warned the president about the danger of international isolation and growing dependency on Russia and called him to put national interests over his personal fears (Tymoshenko 2013d). On November 25, Tymoshenko went on a hunger strike demanding that the Ukrainian government sign the agreement with the EU.

Instead of a conclusion: The Euromaidan and the future of Yulia Tymoshenko

The wave of mass protests in November–December 2013 labeled "Euromaidan" was the most powerful since the Orange Revolution. Provoked by the government's decision to suspend signing the Association Agreement with the EU, protests got a new breath after the brutal beating of students by a riot police unit in the night of November 30. The protesters demanded not only the signing of the Association Agreement, but also the punishment of the officials responsible for the brutal use of force, the resignation of the government, and early elections. The anger of the people focused on the person of President Yanukovych and his highly corrupted close circle. For Yulia Tymoshenko, who had been fighting her mighty enemy alone from a prison cell for more than two years, it was a long awaited great moment when she was finally backed by a powerful demonstration of the general will.

And Tymoshenko proved that she did not lose her political intuition and fighting spirit. In the weeks of protests she appealed to the Ukrainians every second day calling them to rise and not give up until the corrupted authoritarian regime had fallen. She interrupted her hunger strike after 11 days on request of the protesters, in order to stay fit for the fight against the regime. On December 8, Tymoshenko wrote a letter to the protesters suggesting a plan of action, which in her eyes would make the peaceful Ukrainian revolution successful (Tymoshenko 2013b). She claimed that the political regime of Yanukovych had lost its legitimacy and should be replaced by direct rule of the people. She called oppositional parties and civil society to create alternative bodies of power, which should start preparing for early elections. Negotiations with the army and police should be started to bring them to the protesters' side and pro-European Ukrainian diplomats should launch consultations with the Western governments on sanctions against Yanukovych and members of his government.

It is remarkable that in these turbulent days Tymoshenko found the time and strength to write a rather personal letter contemplating on Nelson Mandela's death. She draws some parallels between her own and Mandela's political destinies and sees him as an example to follow. She particularly admires his strength, moral dignity and his belief in the eventual victory of democracy and justice:

> Here, in this place, it is not Mandela the statesman who touches my soul and fires my imagination. "My" Mandela is the prisoner, the Mandela of Robben Island, who endured 27 years behind bars (18 of them on a rock in the South Atlantic) and yet emerged with his spirit intact, brimming with a vision of a tolerant South Africa, a country liberated even for apartheid's architects and beneficiaries. (Tymoshenko 2013c)

Figure 17.3 Poster with Yulia Tymoshenko's portrait in Kyiv during the Euromaidan protests. (Photo by Dmytro Vortman, reproduced with permission)

Tymoshenko's letter was published in Western media, connecting the current drama of the Ukrainian peaceful revolution with the meanwhile emblematic story of the heroic fight against the apartheid regime in South Africa. Drawing parallels between Mandela's and her own imprisonment, Tymoshenko symbolically joined the Western leaders who had gathered in Johannesburg for Mandela's funeral and gently reminded them that some political prisoners are still fighting for their freedom.

Tymoshenko's uncompromised stand on the illegitimacy of President Yanukovych and her flaming appeal to the Ukrainians to stay on the streets until victory is easy to understand—if her powerful enemy survives this political crisis, she might stay in jail for years. Will Western political leaders continue to fight for her freedom? Will oppositional politicians in Ukraine be interested in her comeback to politics or rather afraid of her as a competitor? And probably most important, will Ukrainian society still need Yulia Tymoshenko as a political leader?

The protesters expressed solidarity with Yulia who was listed among the leaders of new popular movement "Maidan." But the current protests differ from the Orange Revolution in one important point—they are not in support of some political leaders as was the case in 2004, and the oppositional parties have only limited influence on the masses. For Ukrainian society the last decade was a period of deep frustration with politicians and political parties and there is a strong demand not just for new faces, but for new rules of the game. A significant part of Ukrainian society perceives Tymoshenko not as a solution, but a part of the problem of corruption. She is a polarizing symbol—the conflict which emerged as a huge portrait of her was put on the Kyiv Christmas tree (which meanwhile has become a symbol of the Ukrainian revolution) is very telling.

Yulia Tymoshenko's prominent but exceptional case does not allow us to generalize about the role of women in post-Soviet politics. As we could see, her case contradicts common wisdom of feminist scholarship which argues that women have only limited options in contemporary celebrity politics as they have to mask their femininity and imitate men (e.g. van Zoonen 2006). Prime Minister Tymoshenko as a glamorous superstar was a perfect illustration (and a product) of post-Soviet populist culture, which obscures the lack of democracy and of real political choice by offering freedom of consumption or at least the promise of it. Exposing her femininity in an assertive way, Tymoshenko for millions of Ukrainian voters represented what "emancipated" Soviet female citizens had not been allowed and could not afford to be—a beautifully styled and fashionably dressed woman. This conspicuous femininity, however, was perfectly compatible with her strong personality, exceptional political talent, and rational thinking. Having lost not only the presidential elections but also her freedom, Tymoshenko remained a political celebrity even behind the bars. As an imprisoned leader of the democratic opposition she managed to keep public attention in Ukraine and in the West alive by turning her body into a site of resistance. As this chapter is written, her fight for personal freedom and for democratic changes in Ukraine is far from being finished. It remains to be seen if female politicians of Tymoshenko's type still have a future in Ukraine given the mass frustration with politics, the radicalization of protests, and the profound political crisis in the country. But even if the Tymoshenko phenomenon is exceptional, it shows that femininity in post-Soviet politics is not confined to the models developed by Western democracies.

This is the updated version of an article written for *Wespennest* and first published in English in *Eurozine*.

Notes

1 Dom-2 (or "House-2") is a Russian reality TV show created by TNT channel and hosted by Russian celebrity Kseniya Sobchak.

2 Yuri Romanenko, note from Facebook, cited in Vozniak 2013.

Concluding Remarks

When we first embarked on this project, our goal was to organize a selection of essays that span the wide gamut of feminist theoretical perspectives and, in doing so, to contribute a new body of knowledge to the growing literature of women, politics, and media. With that said, we contend that the present collection of essays is not to be seen as a comprehensive overview of the topic of women, politics, and media, but rather as a supplement to the notable accomplishments of feminist communication and political science scholars in this area.

Since we, as scholars, advocate for a feminist critique of media and politics, and yet come from Eastern Europe (see Chapter 4) where many of the attributes of this critical perspective do not necessarily apply, the main question that occupied our thoughts was this: What are the interaction dynamics between political women and media in countries that are outside of the group of established, Western democracies?

Our initial expectation was geared towards research focusing on the meditated nature of political representation, with a prevailing emphasis on how media frame female politicians as gendered subjects. Yet, we soon realized that the global outlook we invited in this volume called for a much broader attempt to theorize the extremely dynamic and fluid relationships between women, politics, and media. While gender remains as a variable in the political dynamic, a more nuanced and complex picture emerges when we examine how media play a part in it. The emerging common thread among all contributions to this volume confirms the observation that media frames and media institutions could only be understood if examined in relation to the broader context, in which gender hierarchies are constructed and perpetuated (Norris 1997).

This volume should also be seen as our attempt to address the increasing calls to de-Westernize communication studies and bring to the fore original examinations of the global status of women in positions of power. In spanning the geography of female political success across the globe, one question seems to unify most research inquiries: Is gender becoming less prevalent as a framing device (on the part of media and politicians)? A comparative examination seems to suggest that this is happening in some parts of the world. Yet the results from the 2010 Global Media Monitoring Project still identify disparities, both in terms of representations and effective distribution of power, leading us to believe that gender will not completely disappear as a referent in media coverage.

It is important to recognize that despite our attempt to present an encompassing view of the nexus between gender, politics, and media, we need to be careful about extending generalizations since the majority of essays in this collection are case studies, rather than systematic cross-national examinations of trends. In addition, more replications of the analytical approaches applied in the current volume in different political and cultural settings are needed in order to ascertain their validity.

Finally, we hope that future studies of media representations of women politicians will take globalized media structures into account and will offer an expanded focus on gender and sexuality to capture the evolving definitions and articulations of these terms across cultures. As technology is increasingly becoming a platform for leveling the political playfield, more research on the role of new media across different cultures is needed. Similarly, more work is to be done studying how publics respond to and interpret political messages and how this can have an effect on attitudes and voting behavior affecting women's political advancement. Finally, we also advocate for a more explicitly cross-national comparative perspective through more diverse methodologies and theoretical approaches.

Regardless of these limitations, we hope to have succeeded in compiling a volume that offers a context-sensitive and multi-perspective approach to the study of women, politics, and media. Although we came from different research backgrounds, we managed to find a common language and impetus to describe and analyze the interactions between women politicians and media from more than a dozen nations, spanning all parts of the world.

References

Chapter 1: Introduction

Aalberg, T., and J. Strömbäck. 2011. "Media-driven men and media-critical women? An empirical study of gender and MPs' relationships with the media in Norway and Sweden." *International Political Science Review*, 32(2): 167–87.

Banwart, M. 2006. Webstyles in 2004: The gendering of candidates on campaign web sites? In *Internet Election: Perspectives on the Web in 2004*, eds. A. P. Williams and J. C. Tedesco. Lanham, MD: Rowman and Littlefield, 37–55.

—2010. "Gender and candidate communication: effects of stereotypes in the 2008 election." *American Behavioral Scientist*, 54(3): 265–83.

Blake, A. 2014. "Time Magazine's provocative Hillary Clinton cover." *Washington Post*, January 16, 2014. http://www.washingtonpost.com/blogs/post-politics/wp/2014/01/16/time-magazines-provocative-hillary-clinton-cover/

Bligh, M., M. Schlehofer, B. Casad, and A. Gaffney. 2012. "Competent enough, but would you vote for her? gender stereotypes and media influences on perceptions of women politicians." *Journal of Applied Social Psychology*, 42(3): 560–95.

Braden, M. 1996. *Women Politicians and the Media.* Lexington: University Press of Kentucky.

Byerly, C., and K. Ross. 2006. *Women and Media. A Critical Introduction*. Malden, MA: Blackwell.

Bystrom, Dianne G., T. A. Robertson, and Mary C. Banwart. 2001. "Framing the fight: An analysis of media coverage of female and male candidates in primary races for Governor and U.S. Senate in 2000." *American Behavioral Scientist*, 44(12), 1999–2013.

Bystrom, D., M. Banwart, L. Kaid, and T. Robertson. 2004. *Gender and Political Candidate Communication: VideoStyle, WebStyle, and NewsStyle*. New York: Routledge.

Carilli, T., and J. Campbell. 2005. *Women and the Media: Diverse Perspectives.* Maryland, MD: University Press of America.

Carroll, S., and R. Fox. 2006. *Gender and Elections.* Cambridge: Cambridge University Press.

Carter, C., L. Steiner, and L. McLaughlin. 2014. *Routledge Companion to Media and Gender.* Oxford: Routledge.

Chozick, A. 2014. "Planet Hillary." *New York Times Magazine*, January 24, 2014. http://www.nytimes.com/2014/01/26/magazine/hillary-clinton.html?_r=0

CQ Researcher. 2008. "Women in politics: does gender bias hurt female candidates?" *CQ Researcher*, 18(2): 265–88.

Dahlgren, P., and C. Alvares. 2013. "Political participation in an age of mediatization: Towards a new research agenda." *Javnost-the Public*, 20(2): 47–66.

Devitt, D. 2002. "Framing gender on the campaign trail: female gubernatorial candidates and the press." *Journalism & Mass Communication Quarterly*, 79 (2): 445–63.

Dolan, K. 1998. "Voting for women in the 'Year of the Woman.'" *American Journal of Political Science*, 42: 272–93.

—2005. "Do women candidates play to gender stereotypes? do men candidates play to women? Candidate sex and issues priorities on campaign websites." *Political Research Quarterly*, 58(1): 31–44.

Economist Intelligence Unit. "Democracy Index 2012: Democracy is at a Standstill," http://www.eiu.com/public/topical_report.aspx?campaignid=DemocracyIndex12

Forbes. "World's Most Powerful People." http://www.forbes.com/powerful-people/list/

Fulton, S. 2012. "Running backwards in high heels: the gendered quality gap and incumbent electoral success." *Political Research Quarterly*, 65(2): 303–14.

Gallagher, M. 2001. *Gender Setting: New Agendas for Media Monitoring and Advocacy.* London: Zed Books.

Gidengil, E., and J. Everitt. 1999. "Metaphors and misrepresentation: gendered Mediation in News Coverage of the 1993 Canadian Leaders' Debates." *Harvard International Journal of Press/Politics*, 4(1): 48–65.

Guide to Women Leaders. n.d. "Worldwide Guide to Women in Leadership," http://www.guide2womenleaders.com/index.html

Hanitzsch, T., F. Hanusch, C. Mellado, M. Anikina, R. Berganza, I. Cangoz, M. Coman, B. Hamada, M. E. Hernandez, C. D. Karadjov, S. V. Moreira, P. G. Mwesige, P. L. Plaisance, Z. Reich, J. Seethaler, E. A. Skewes, D. Vardiansyah Noor, D., and K. W. Yuen. 2011. "Mapping Journalism Cultures across Nations: a Comparative Study of 18 Countries." *Journalism Studies*, 12: 273–93.

Inglehart, R., and P. Norris. 2003. *Rising Tide: Gender Equality and Cultural Change Around the World.* Cambridge: Cambridge University Press.

Jalalzai, F. 2006. "Women Candidates and the Media: 1992–2000 Elections." *Politics & Policy*, 34(3): 606–33.

—2013. *Shattered, Cracked, or Firmly Intact?: Women and the Executive Glass Ceiling Worldwide.* New York: Oxford University Press.

Kahn, K. F. 1991. "Women candidates in the news: an examination of gender differences in U.S. Senate campaign coverage." *Public Opinion Quarterly*, 55(2), 180–200.

—1992. "Does being male help? an investigation of the effects of candidate gender and campaign coverage on evaluations of U.S. Senate candidates." *The Journal of Politics*, 54(2): 497–517.

—1994. "The distorted mirror: press coverage of women candidates for statewide office." *The Journal of Politics*, 56(1): 154–73.

—1996. *The Political Consequences of being a Woman.* New York: Columbia University Press.

Kahn, K. F., and E. Goldenberg. 1991. "The media: obstacle or ally of feminists?" *Annals of the American Academy of Political and Social Science*, 55: 104–13.

Kahn, K., and A. Gordon. 1997. "How Women Campaign for the U.S. Senate: Substance and Strategy." In *Women, Media and Politics*, ed. P. Norris. New York: Oxford University Press, 59–75.

Lawless, Jennifer L., and Richard L. Fox. 2010. *It Still Takes a Candidate: Why Women Don't Run for Office.* New York: Cambridge University Press.

Lawrence, R., and M. Rose. 2010. *Hillary Clinton's Race for the White House.* Boulder, CO: Lynne Rienner.

Lünenborg, M. n.d. "Of 'That's That!' Chancellors and Queens of Might: The Media Portrayal of Gender in Politics." *Goethe Institut.* http://www.goethe.de/ges/mol/gen/gef/en4250025.htm

Meeks, L. 2012. "Is she 'Man Enough'? women candidates, executive political offices, and news coverage." *Journal of Communication*, 62: 175–93.

—2013. "All the gender that's fit to print: how the New York Times covered Hillary Clinton and Sarah Palin in 2008." *Journalism & Mass Communication Quarterly*, 90(3): 520–39.

Niven, D. and J. Zilber. 2001. "Do women and men in congress cultivate different images? evidence from congressional web sites." *Political Communication*, 18: 395–405.

Norris, P., ed. 1997. *Women, Media, and Politics.* New York: Oxford University Press.

Norris, P. and R. Inglehart. 2008. "Cracking the marble ceiling: cultural barriers facing women leaders." *Harvard University Report.* Cambridge, MA. http://www.hks.harvard.edu/fs/pnorris/Acrobat/Marble%20ceiling%20professional%20format.pdf

Plan of Action n.d., *Inter-Parliamentary Union.* http://www.ipu.org/wmn-e/Planactn.htm#3

Rakow, L. F., and Kranich, K. 1991. "Women as sign in television news." *Journal of Communication*, 41: 8–23.

Robinson, G., and A. Saint-Jean. 1991. "Women Politicians and their Media Coverage: A Generational Analysis." In *Women in Canadian politics*, ed. K. Megyery. Toronto: Dundurn Press, 127–69.

Ross, K. 2002. *Women, Politics, Media: Uneasy Relations in Comparative Perspective.* Cresskill, NJ: Hampton Press.

—2004. "Women Framed: The Gendered turn in Mediated Politics." In *Women and Media: International perspectives*, eds. Karen Ross and C. Byerly. Malden, MA: Blackwell Publishing, 60–76.

—2010a. "Danse macabre: Politicians, journalists, and the complicated rumba of relationships." The *International Journal of Press/Politics*, 15(3): 272–94.

—2010b. *Gendered Media: Women, Men, and Identity Politics.* Maryland, MD: Rowman and Littlefield.

Ross, K., ed. 2012. *The Handbook of Gender, Sex and Media.* Malden, MA: Wiley-Blackwell.

Ross, K., and A. Sreberny. 2000. "Women in the House: Media Representation of British Politicians." In *Gender, Politics and Communication*, eds. A. Sreberny and L. van Zoonen. Creskill, NJ: Hampton Press, 79–99.

Sreberny A., and L. van Zoonen, eds. 2000. *Gender, Politics and Communication.* Cresskill, NJ: Hampton Press.

Sreberny-Mohammadi, A., and K. Ross. 1996. "Women MPs and Media: representing the body politic." *Parliamentary Affairs*, 49(1): 103–15.

Stromback, J., and P. Van Aelst. 2013. "Why political parties adapt to the media: exploring the fourth dimension of mediatization." *International Communication Gazette*, 75(4): 341–58.

Trimble, L., A. Wagner, S. Sampert, D. Raphael, and B. Gerrits. 2013. "Is it personal? gendered mediation in newspaper coverage of Canadian National Party leadership contents, 1975–2012." The *International Journal of Press/Politics*, 18(4): 462–81.

Tuchman, G. 1979. "Women's depiction by the mass media." *Signs*, 4(3): 528–42.

UN Women. n.d. "Facts and Figures: Leadership and Political Participation." http://www.unwomen.org/en/what-we-do/leadership-and-political-participation/facts-and-figures#notes

Walshe, S. 2013. "Hillary Clinton Calls Women's Rights 'Unfinished Business'." *ABC News*, http://abcnews.go.com/Politics/hillary-clinton-calls-womens-rights-unfinished-business/story?id=18889684

World Bank. "Old concept of 'Third World' outdated, Zoellick says." http://web.worldbank.org/WBSITE/EXTERNAL/NEWS/0,,contentMDK:22541103~pagePK:64257043~piPK:437376~theSitePK:4607,00.html

Zoonen, L. van 2005. *Entertaining the Citizen: When Politics and Popular Culture Converge.* Oxford: Rowman and Littleton.

—2006. "The personal, the political and the popular: a woman's guide to celebrity politics." *European Journal of Cultural Studies*, 9(3): 287–301.

Chapter 2: The Portrayal of Women Politicians in Israeli Popular Women's Magazines

Adcock, C. 2010. "The politician, the wife, the citizen, and her newspaper: rethinking women, democracy, and media(ted) representation." *Feminist Media Studies*, 10(2): 135–59.

Almog, O. 2004. *Farewell to "Srulik": Changing Values among the Israeli Elite.* Haifa: University of Haifa Press and Zmora Bitan. [Hebrew]

At. 5 August 2011. Issue no. 731: 1, 30–3.

Benhabib, S. 1992. "Models of Public Space: Hanna Arendt, the Liberal Tradition, and Jürgen Habermas." In *Habermas and the Public Sphere*, ed. C. Calhoun. Cambridge, MA: MIT Press, pp. 78–98.

Byerly, C. M. and K. Ross. 2006. *Women and Media: A Critical Introduction*. Malden, MA: Blackwell.

Cheker Institute, 2009. http://www.hamil.co.il/upload/ladyglobes.pdf [Hebrew].

Fogiel-Bijaoui, S. 2010. *Democracy and Feminism: Citizenship, Gender and Civil-rights*, Open University: Raanana. [Hebrew]

Fraser, N. 1990. "Rethinking the public sphere: a contribution to the critique of actually existing democracy." *Social Text*, 25/26: 56–80.

Gallagher, M. 2005. *Who Makes the News? Global Media Monitoring Project*. London: WACC.

Garcia-Blanco, I. and K. Wahl-Jorgensen. 2012. "The discursive construction of women politicians in the European press." *Feminist Media Studies*, 12 (3): 422–41.

Gedalya, E., H. Herzog and M. Shamir. 2011. "Tzip(p)ing through the Elections: Gender in the 2009 Elections." In *The Elections in Israel – 2009*, eds. A. Arian and M. Shamir. New Brunswick: Transaction Publications, pp. 165–93.

Gill, R. 2007. *Gender and the Media*. Malden, MA: Polity Press.

Global Media Monitoring Project, 2010. "Who Makes the News." http://whomakesthe news.org/

Gough-Yates, A. 2003. *Understanding Women's Magazines: Publishing, Markets and Readerships*. London: Routledge.

Gramsci, A. 1971. *The Prison Notebooks*, Trans. and ed. by Q. Hoare and G. Nowell Smith. New York: International Publishers.

Habermas, J. 1962/1989. *The Structural Transformation of the Public Sphere*. Cambridge: Cambridge University Press.

Halevi, S. 2012. "Damned if you do, damned if you don't? Tzipi Livni and the debate on a 'feminine' leadership style in the Israeli press". *Feminist Media Studies*, 12 (2): 195–213.

Herzog, H. 2000. "Women's magazines: a mirroring space or a challenging space?" *Kesher*, 28: 43–52. [Hebrew]

Herzog, H. 2006. "Between the lawn and the gravel path: women, politics, and civil society." *Democratic Culture*, 10: 191–214.

Herzog, H. 2013. "The generational and gender perspective on the tent protest." *Theory and Criticism*, 41: 60–72. [Hebrew]

Hollows, J. and R. Moseley. 2006. "Popularity Contests: The Meaning of Popular Feminism." In *Feminism in Popular Culture*, eds. J. Hollows and R. Moseley. Oxford: Berg, pp. 1–22.

Ibroscheva, E. and Raicheva-Stover, M. 2009. "Engendering transition: portrayals of female politicians in the Bulgarian press." *The Howard Journal of Communications*, 20: 111–28.

Ishai, I. 1999. "Old Politics Against New Politics in Elections 1996." In *The Elections in Israel - 1996*, eds. A. Arian and M. Shamir. Jerusalem: The Israel Democracy Institute, 171–201.

Lachover, E. 2009. "Women in the Six Day War through the eye of the media." *The Journal of Israeli History*, 28(2): 117–35.

—2012. "It's not enough just to be a woman: Israeli television news of Israeli women in local elections." *Feminist Media Studies*, 12(3): 442–58.

—2013. "Influential women: Feminist discourse in women's magazines – the case of Israel." *Communication, Culture and Critique*, 6(1): 121–41.

Lady Globes. 2007, September. Issue no. 108: 56.

—2009, December. Issue no. 135: 48–55.

—2011, September. Issue no. 156: 1, 43–54, 72–4.

—2012, August. Issue no. 167: 20–1.

—2012, September. Issue no. 168: 70–2, 194.

La'Isha. 26 September 2008. Issue no. 3207: 48–53.

—2 February 2009. Issue no. 3225: 26–31.

—14 September 2009. Issue no. 3257: 26.

—5 September 2011. Issue no. 3363: 38–9.

—5 March 2012. Issue no. 3386: 30–4.

Lemish, D., and C. E. Tidhar. 1991. "The silenced majority: women in Israel's 1988 television election campaign." *Women and Language*, 14(14): 13–21.

—1999. "Still marginal: women in Israel's 1996 television election campaign." *Sex Roles*, 41(51–6): 389–412.

McCracken, E. 1993. *Decoding Women's Magazines: From Mademoiselle to Ms.* New York: St. Martin's Press.

Norris, P. 1997. *Women, Media and Politics*. New York: Oxford University Press.

Ross, K. 2002. *Women, Politics, Media: Uneasy Relations in Comparative Perspective*. Cresskill, NJ: Hampton Press.

—2010. *Gendered Media: Women, Men, and Identity Politics*. Maryland, MD: Rowman and Littlefield.

Ross, K. and M. Comrie. 2012. "The rules of the (leadership) game: Gender, politics and news." *Journalism*, 13(8): 969–84.

Saarenmaa, L. 2011. "Politicians as Cover girls: Finnish Women's Magazines and the Parliamentary Election 2011 in Finland." Paper presented at *Mapping the Magazine Conference*. Cardiff, Cardiff University, July 7–8, 2011.

Streberny, A. and L. va en Zoonen. 2000. "Gender, Politics And Communication: An Introduction." In *Gender, Politics and Communication*, eds. A. Streberny and L. van Zoonen. Cresskill, NJ: Hampton Press, 1–19.

Winship, J. 1987. *Inside Women's Magazines*. London and New York: Pandora.

Ytre-Arne, B. 2011. "Women's magazines and the public sphere." *European Journal of Communication*, 26(3): 247–61.

Chapter 3: Ambiga Sreenevasan and Malaysian Counter-Publics

Anderson, B. 1991. *Imagined Communities: Reflections on the Origin and Spread of Nationalism*. London: Verso.

Anuar, M.K. 2000. "Malaysian media and democracy." *Media Asia*, 27 (4): 183–90.

—2005. "Journalism, national development and social justice in Malaysia." *Asia Pacific Media Educator*, 16: 63–70.

Asen, R. 2000. "Seeking the 'counter' in counterpublics." *Communication Theory* 10: 424–46.

Bernama.com. 2007. "*Bersih* not given permission to hold rally." November 7, 2007. http://www.bernama.com/bernama/v3/printable.php?id=294788

Bersih. 2006. *Launching of Bersih*. http://www.bersih.org

Boo, Su-Lyn. 2011. "'*Bersih*. rally goes on' says Ambiga," PAS. *Themalaysianinsider.com*. June 11, 2011. http://www.themalaysianinsider.com/malaysia/article/*Bersih*-rally-goes-on-says-ambiga-pas/.htm

Chooi, C. 2013. "In final leg before polls Bersih to train Malaysians to spot GE13 fraud." *Themalaysianinsider.com*, 1 January 2013. http://www.themalaysianinsider.com/malaysia/article/in-final-leg-before-polls-bersih-to-train-malaysians-to-spot-ge13-fraud

Gooch, L. 2011. "A Reluctant Symbol for Electoral Reform in Malaysia." *New York Times*, August 8, 2011. http://www.nytimes.com/2011/08/09/world/asia/09iht-malaysia09.html?pagewanted=all&_r=0

Griffiths, M. 2014. "Notions of Guardianship." In *The Way we are Governed: Investigations in Communication, Media and Democracy*, eds. Philip Dearman and Cathy Greenfield. Cambridge: Cambridge Scholarly Press, 31–52.

Habermas, J. 1991. *The Structural Transformation of the Public Sphere*. Trans. Thomas Burger. Massachusetts: MIT Press.

Hazlan, Z. 2013. "Dr. M: Amend constitution to strip Ambiga's citizenship." *Malaysiakini.com*.February 9, 2013. http://www.Malaysiakini.com/news/221114.htm

Islamic Renaissance Front. 2012. "Muslim group condemns Perkasa's racist threats." April 8, 2012. http://irfront.net/post/news/muslim-group-condemns-perkasas-racist-threats/

Ismail, M. 2011. "Perarakan Haram, Baik Cegah Sebelum Merebak." *Berita Harian*, June 27, 2011.

Kamal, S. M. 2012. "Utusan tried hard to portray *Bersih* as 'evil'," Suhakam inquiry told. *The Malaysian Insider*. April 13, 2012. http://www.themalaysianinsider.com/malaysia/article/utusan-tried-hard-to-portray-Bersih-as-evil-suhakam-inquiry-told/

Lakoff, G. 1995. "Metaphor, morality and politics." *Graduate Faculty of the New School for Social Research: Social Research*, 62(2): 1–23.

Loone, S. 2012. "*Bersih*'s Ambiga connects with the People for Free and Fair Elections."

DinMerican: The Malaysian DJ Blogger. October 23, 2012. http://dinmerican.wordpress.com/2012/10/23/Bersihs-ambiga-connects-with-the-people/

Malaysiakini.com. 2012a. "Top 10 News and 2012 Newsmaker – You Decide." December 21, 2012. http://beta.malaysiakini.com/news/217209

—2012b. "Army veterans do 'Butt Exercises' at Ambiga's house." May 15, 2012. http://beta.malaysiakini.com/news/197928

Malaysian Bar. 2011. "President's roll." 2012. http://www.malaysianbar.org.my/past_presidents.html

Martin, D. 2012. "Ambiga and the fate of women leaders in Malaysia." *TheMalaysianinsider.com.* May 30, 2012. http://www.themalaysianinsider.com/sideviews/article/ambiga-and-the-fate-of-women-leaders-in-malaysia-dahlia-martin/

Patrick Teoh interviews Ambiga. 2012. http://anilnetto.com/democracy/civil-society/patrick-teoh-interviews-ambiga/

Peaceful Assembly Act 2012. *E-Federal Gazette.* "Government of Malaysia." http://www.federalgazette.agc.gov.my/

Rajaratnam, U.D. 2009. "Role of traditional and online media in the 12th General Election, Malaysia." *The Journal of South East Asia Research Centre for Communication and Humanities,* 1(1): 1, 33–58.

Samad, R.A. 2001. "The Double-edged Sword: A Brief Comparison of IT and Internet Development in Malaysia and Some Few Neighboring Countries in the Context of Digital Divide." *67th IFLA Council and General Conference.* August 16–25, 2001, 1–9.

"Sassy MP." Personal blog. Teresa Kok, Seputah MP. http://teresakok.com/

Social Watch. 2012. "Malaysia's gender equality is in the bottom of East Asia, says watchdog organization." March 15, 2012. http://www.socialwatch.org/node/14577

Sreenevasan, A. 2011. "Electoral reform and the quest for democracy in Malaysia." A public address at the Melbourne University Law School, Melbourne, Australia. October 25, 2011. https://www.youtube.com/watch?v=ItL38UqG__g

—2012. "My fellow Malaysians – Ambiga Sreenevasan." *Themalaysianinsider.com.* April, 28, 2012. (This article is restricted access.)

Tang Hang Wu. 2005. "Let a Hundred Flowers Bloom: A Malaysian Case Study on Blogging Towards a Democratic Culture." *20th BILETA Conference: Over-Commoditised; Over Centralised; Over Observed: the New Digital Legal World?* 1–21.

Thestar.com. 2009. "US Honour [*sic*] for Ambiga." March 13. http://www.thestar.com.my/story.aspx/?file=%2f2009%2f3%2f13%2fnation%2f3472311&sec=nation

Thestar.com. 2012. "PSC members given free rein to consider views." April 4, 2012. http://www.thestar.com.my/News/Nation/2012/04/04/PSC-members-given-free-rein-to-consider-views/

United Nations Committee on the Elimination of Discrimination against Women (CEDAW). 2006. "Responses to the list of issues and questions for consideration of the combined initial and second periodic report Malaysia." www.unhchr.ch/tbs/doc.nsf/0/.../$FILE/N0629207.doc

United Nations Development Programme (UNDP). 2007. “Measuring and monitoring gender equality – Malaysia’s gender gap index.” http://www.undp.org.my/measuring-and-monitoring-gender-equality-malaysias-gender-gap-index

—2011. “Human development report.” http://hdr.undp.org/en/media/HDR_2011_EN_Complete.pdf

Utusan Malaysia n.d. AdQrate. http://adqrate.com/newspaper/details?id=64&type=1

—2011a. “Perhimpunan Bersih rugikan Negara,” June 12, 2011. http://www.utusan.com.my/utusan/info.asp?y=2011&dt=0612&pub=Utusan_Malaysia&sec=Terkini&pg=bt_17.htm

—2011b. “NGO berkaitan gerakan Kristian penyumbang dana Bersih?” June 27, 2011. http://www.utusan.com.my/utusan/info.asp?y=2011&dt=0627&pub=utusan_malaysia&sec=Muka_Hadapan&pg=mh_03.htm&arc=hive

—2011c. “Polis berjaya kekang Bersih,” 10 July 2011, http://www.utusan.com.my/utusan/info.asp?y=2011&dt=0710&pub=Utusan_Malaysia&sec=Muka_Hadapan&pg=mh_01.htm

Warner, M. 2002. “Publics and counterpublics.” *Public Culture*, 14(1): 49–90. http://muse.jhu.edu/journals/public_culture/v014/14.1warner.html

World Economic Forum. 2010. “Global Gender Gap Report.” Available at http://www.weforum.org/reports/global-gender-gap-report-2010

Chapter 4: The Girls of Parliament: A Historical Analysis of the Press Coverage of Female Politicians in Bulgaria

Apostolova, I. 2009. “My ambition? Discipline and good laws.” *Trud*, July 16, 2009. http://www.trud.bg/Article.asp?ArticleId=179451

Apostolova, Y., K. Krusteva, and M. Avramova. “Female MPs strut in a vanity fair.” *Trud*, July 21, 2005, 16–17.

Bilefsky, D. 2010. “Women’s influence grows in Bulgarian public life.” *New York Times*. February 7, 2010. http://www.nytimes.com/2010/02/08/world/europe/08iht-bulgwomen.html

Borisov with a club of 700 women. *Trud*, July 14, 2008, 5.

Danova, M. 2006. “Women in Politics in Bulgarian Newspapers: Post-feminism in a Post-totalitarian Society.” In *Stereotyping: Representation of women in print media in Southeast Europe*. A report issued by Mediacentar, 111–32. http://kilden.forskningsradet.no/c16877/publikasjon/vis.html?tid=43074

Daskalova, K. 2000. “Women’s Problem, Women’s Discourses in Bulgaria.” In *Reproducing Gender: Politics, Publics and Everyday Life after Socialism*, eds. S. Gal and G. Kligman. Princeton, NJ: Princeton University Press, 337–369.

Dimitrova, M. 2007. “Four ladies at full speed in the Europarliament.” *Trud*, July 3, 2007, 13.

Herzog, H. 1998. "More than a looking glass: women in Israeli local politics and the media." *Press/Politics*, 3(1): 26–47.

Hristova, L. 2007. "Working girl again in power." *Trud*, July 16, 2007, 8.

Jamieson, K.H. 1995. *Beyond the Double Bind: Women and Leadership*. New York: Oxford University Press.

Kahn, K.F. 1994. "The distorted mirror: press coverage of women candidates for statewide office." *The Journal of Politics*, 56(1): 154–74.

—1996. *The Political Consequences of Being a Woman*. New York: Columbia University Press.

Kostadinova, T. 2003. "Women's Legislative Representation in Post-communist Bulgaria." In *Women's Access to Political Power in Post-communist Europe*, eds. R. Matland and K. Montgomery. Oxford: Oxford Press, 304–320.

Kostova, D. (1998). "Similar or Different? Women in Post-communist Bulgaria." In *Women in the Politics of Post-communist Eastern Europe*, ed. M. Rueschemeyer. Armonk, NJ: M. E. Sharpe, 249–66.

Kotzeva, T. 1999. "Reimagining Bulgaria Women: The Marxist Legacy and Women's Self-identity." In *Gender and Identity in Central and Eastern Europe*, ed. C. Corrin. London: Frank Cass Publishers, 83–99.

Lukic, J. 2000. "Media Representations of Men and Women in Times of War and Crisis: The Case of Serbia." In *Reproducing Gender: Politics, Publics and Everyday Life after Socialism*, eds. S. Gal and G. Kligman. Princeton, NJ: Princeton University Press, 370–93.

Marody, M., and A. Giza-Poleszczuk. 2000. "Changing Images of Identity in Poland: From the Self-sacrificing to the Self-investing Woman?" In *Reproducing gender: Politics, Publics and Everyday Life after Socialism*, eds. S. Gal and G. Kligman. Princeton, NJ: Princeton University Press, 151–76.

Mead, J. 1997. *Bodyjamming: Sexual Harassment, Feminism, and Public life*. Milson Point: Vintage.

Mihaylova, V. 2009. "General's worker bee." *Trud*, July 14, 2009. http://www.trud.bg/Article.asp?ArticleId=178046

Nikolova, I. 2009. "A truthful blonde in charge of parliament." *Trud*, July 13, 2009. http://www.trud.bg/Article.asp?ArticleId=176927

Nikolova, M. 1995. "Even in the minority, women can save the country." *Trud*, April 14, 1995, 10.

Petkova, V., and R. Bratovanova, 2001. "Forward with the ladies." *Trud*, May 18, 2001, 10, 11, 12.

Popova, V. 2004. "Bulgaria." In *Media Ownership and its Impact on Media Independence and Pluralism*, 94–116. http://www.mirovni-institut.si/media_ownership/bulgaria.htm

Profile: Dr. Anka Angelova. (June 14, 1976). *Rabotnichesko Delo*, 2.

Profile: Hristina Petrova. (July 8, 2001). *Trud*, 7.

Profile: Ivanka Vasileva. (April 14, 1976). *Rabotnichesko Delo*, 2.

Profile: Margarita Eftimova. (April 15, 1971). *Rabotnichesko Delo*, 2.

Profile: Muesin Durgurova (June 11, 1971). *Rabotnichesko Delo*, 4.

Profile: Yana Ivanova. (April 19, 1971). *Rabotnichesko Delo*, 2.

Radeva, M. 1991. "Dialogues in the government offices: the unemployment will make us work." *Trud*, 8 January 1911, 1–2.

Rakow, L. F., and K. Kranich, 1991. "Women as sign in television news." *Journal of Communication*, 41: 8–23.

Roman, D. 2001. "Gendering Eastern Europe: pre-feminism, prejudice, and East–West dialogues in post-communist Romania." *Women's Studies International Forum*, 24(1): 55–66.

Ross, K. 2002. *Women, Politics and Media: Uneasy Relations in Comparative Perspective*. Cresskill, NJ: Hampton Press.

Ross, K., and A. Sreberny. 2000. "Women in the House: Media Representation of British politicians." In *Gender, Politics and Communication*, eds. A. Sreberny and L. van Zoonen. Creskill: Hampton Press, 79–99.

Sarnavka, S., K. Mihalec, and N. Sudar. 2002. "Croatian feminists stave off onslaught of sexist media." *Off Our Back*, March.

Spirova, M. 2007. "Political Parties and Women's Representation in the 2005 Bulgarian Parliament." Paper presented at the 2007 SPSA Conference, New Orleans, January 2007.

Todorova, R. 2005. "Miss Parliament." *Trud*, July 15, 2005, 12.

Tokeian, T. 2001. "Siluet." *Trud*, May 4, 2001, 11.

van Zoonen, L. 1994. *Feminist Media Studies*. Thousand Oaks, CA: Sage.

Veleva, V. 1997. "No danger in being bribed." *Trud*, April 26, 1997, 9.

—2005. "Even in walking against the wind, I always succeed." Interview with Eleonora Nikolova. *Trud*, July 23, 2005, 15.

Chapter 5: Zambian Women MPs: An Examination of Coverage by the *Post* and *Zambia Daily Mail*

Carroll, S., and R. Schreiber. 1997. "Media Coverage of Women in the 103rd Congress." In *Women, Media, and Politics*, ed. Pippa Norris. New York: Oxford University Press, 131–48.

Devitt, D. 2002. "Framing gender on the campaign trail: female gubernatorial candidates and the press." *Journalism & Mass Communication Quarterly*, 79(2): 445–63.

Fountaine, Susan, and McGregor, Judy. 2002. "Reconstructing Gender for the 21st Century: News media framing of political women in New Zealand." Australian & New Zealand Communication Association 23rd Annual Conference, July 10–12, 2002, Gold Coast, Queensland. http://webenrol.massey.ac.nz/massey/fms/Colleges/College%20of%20Business/NZCWL/pdfs/JMcGregorSFountainePaper.pdf

Gender Links. 2003. "Gender and Media Baseline Study." http://www.genderlinks.org.za/page/media-gender-and-media-baseline-study

Goffman, E. 1974. *Frame Analysis: An Essay on the Organization of Experience.* Cambridge: Harvard University Press.

Kahn, K. F. 1994. "The distorted mirror: press coverage of women candidates for state office." *The Journal of Politics*, 56(1): 154–73.

Katembo, T. K. 2005. "The Representation of South African women politicians in the *Sunday Times* during the 2004 Presidential and General Elections." (unplublished master's thesis, Rhodes University).

Morna, C., and T. Mtintso. 2005. "Elections, Democracy and Governance." In *Gender in Media Training: A Southern African Toolkit*, ed. Colleen L. Morna, pp. 211–33. Gender Links. http://www.genderlinks.org.za/article/gender-in-media-training---a-southern-african-toolkit-2005-07-01

Sampa, M. K. 2010. "The Election of Women to the Zambian Parliament: An analysis of the under-representation of women in the 2001–2006 Parliamentary Elections." (unpublished master's thesis, UNZA).

Sreberny-Mohammadi, A., and K. Ross. 1996. "Women MPs and media: representing the body politic." *Parliamentary Affairs*, 49(1): 103–15.

Sreberny-Mohammadi, A., and L. van Zoonen, eds. 2000. *Gender, Politics and Communication*. Cresskill, NJ: Hampton Press.

Tankard, J. 1997. "The Empirical Approach to the Study of Media Framing." In *Framing Public Life: Perspectives on Media and Understanding of the Social World*, eds. Stephen D. Reese, Oscar H. Gandy, Jr., and August E. Grant. Mahwah, NJ: Lawrence Erlbaum Associates, 95–106.

Tuchman, G. 1978. "Introduction: The symbolic Annihilation of Women by the Mass Media." In *Hearth and Home: Images of Women in the Mass Media*, eds. Gaye Tuchman, Arlene, K. Daniels, and James Benet. New York: Oxford University Press, 3–38.

Worthington, N. 2011. "Gender discourse and Ubuntu media philosophy." *Journalism Studies*, 12: 608–23.

Yeboah, A. 2011. "Reporting women: do female journalists have a gender agenda?" *African Communication Research*, 4(3): 469–84.

Chapter 6: Media Visibility of Tunisian Women Politicians in Traditional and New Media: Obstacles to Visibility and Media Coverage Strategies

Bourdieu, P. 1981. "La représentation politique." In *Actes de la recherche en sciences sociales*, February/March, 36–7: 3–24.

Derville, G. 1997. *Le pouvoir des médias. Mythes et réalités*, Grenoble: PUG.

El Bour, H. 2009. *Médiatisation de la participation politique de la femme en Algérie, au Maroc et en Tunisie. Rapport de synthèse de l'exercice média.* Tunis: UN-INSTRAW & CAWTAR, 77.

El Bour, H. and A. Mejbri. 2010. "Tunisie: Projet mondial de monitorage des médias (GMMP)." http://cdn.agilitycms.com/who-makes-the-news/Imported/reports_2010/national/Tunisie.pdf

Guard Dogs (Chiennes de garde). 2000. "Qu'est-ce qu'une injure sexiste." http://www.chiennesdegarde.com/article.php3?id_article=9

Hoebeke, S. 2008. *Sexe et stéréotypes dans les médias*, Paris: L'Harmattan.

Honneth, A. 2005. "Invisibility: on the epistemology of recognition." *Networks*, (129–30): 39–57.

Jenkins, H. 2006. *Convergence Culture: Where Old and New Media Collide.* Cambridge, MA: MIT Press.

Macé, E. 2006. "Entre visibilité médiatique et reconnaissance politique." *Mediamorphoses*, 17.

Oger, C. 2006. "Dialectique de la parole et du silence. émergence et fonction de l'politique." *Communication*, 25(1): 11–45.

Sourd, C. 2005. "Femmes ou politiques? la représentation des candidates aux élections françaises de 2002 dans la presse hebdomadaire," *Mots. Les langages du politique* (online), 78 | 2005, posted online on January 31, 2008. http://mots.revues.org/378

Voirol, O. 2005. "Les luttes pour la visibilité: esquisse d'une problématique." *Networks*, (129–30): 89–121.

Women and gender relations over the Tunisian press in transition period. 2011. "Preliminary Report No. 1," Association Tunisienne des Femmes Démocrates (ATFD), August 1–25.

Chapter 7: Understanding the Gender Dynamics of Current Affairs Talk Shows in the Pakistani Television Industry

Alvi, A. 2013. "Concealment and revealment: The Muslim veil in context," *Current Anthropology*, 54 (2): 177–99.

Anderson, N. 1993. "Benazir Bhutto and Dynastic Politics. Her Father's Daughter, her People's Sister." In *Women as National Leaders*, ed. Michael A. Genovese. London and New Delhi: Sage Publications, 41–67.

Anwar, F. 2013. "The feudal culture." The *Nation*, May 19, 2013. http://www.nation.com.pk/pakistan-news-newspaper-daily-english-online/letters/19-May-2013/the-feudal-culture

Crilly, R. 2013. "Hina Rabbani Khar Pakistan's glamorous minister, to step down." *The Telegraph*. 8 April 2013. http://www.telegraph.co.uk/news/worldnews/asia/

pakistan/9978598/Hina-Rabbani-Khar-Pakistans-glamorous-foreign-minister-to-step-down.html

Dolan, K. 2005. "Do women candidates play to gender stereotypes? do men candidates play to women? candidate sex and issues priorities on campaign websites." *Political Research Quarterly*, 58(1): 31–44.

Dow, B., and M. Tonn. 1993. "'Feminine style' and political judgment in the rhetoric of Ann Richards." *Quarterly Journal of Speech*, 79(3): 286–302.

Female Pakistani minister shot dead for refusing to wear veil, *Fox News.com*. February 21, 2007. http://www.foxnews.com/story/2007/02/21/female-pakistani-minister-shot-dead-for-refusing-to-wear-veil/

Gurevitch, M., and A. Kavoori. 1992. "Television spectacles as politics." *Communication Monographs*, 59: 415–20.

Hartley, J. 2003. "Textual Analysis." In *Television Studies*, ed. Toby Miller. London: BFI Publishing.

Hayden, S. 1999. "Negotiating femininity and power in the early twentieth century: domestic ideology and feminine style in the Jeanette Rankin's suffrage rhetoric." *Communication Studies*, 50(2): 83–102.

Imtiaz, H. 2011. "In Pakistani politics, it's still a man's world." *Foreign Policy Journal*, July 19, 2011. http://afpak.foreignpolicy.com/posts/2011/07/19/in_pakistani_politics_its_still_a_mans_world_0

Insight Report. "The Global Gender Gap Report 2012." World Economic Forum. 2012. http://www3.weforum.org/docs/WEF_GenderGap_Report_2012.pdf

Inter Parliamentary Union. "Women in National Parliaments." http://www.ipu.org/wmn-e/classif.htm

Jamieson, K. 1995. *Beyond the Double Bind: Women and Leadership.* New York and Oxford: Oxford University Press.

Kahn, K. F. 1994. "The distorted mirror: press coverage of women candidates for statewide office." *The Journal of Politics*. 56(1): 154–73.

Lee, F. 2004. "Constructing perfect women: the portrayal of female officials in Hong Kong newspapers." *Media, Culture and Society*, 24(2): 207–25.

Lenneberg, C. 1994. "Women and political leadership in India: able politicians or token presences?" *Asian Studies Review*, 17(3): 6–14.

Lovenduski, J. 1993. Introduction: The Dynamics of Gender and Party." In *Gender and Party Politics*, eds. J. Lovenduski and P. Norris. London and Thousand Oaks: Sage Publications, 1–15.

—1996. "Sex, gender and British politics." *Parliamentary Affairs* 49(1): 1–16.

National Assembly of Pakistan. http://www.na.gov.pk/en/bills.php?status=pass

Palmieri, S. 2011. "Gender Sensitive Parliaments: A Global Review of Good Practice." Report and Document No: 64 – 2011, http://www.ipu.org/pdf/publications/gsp11-e.pdf

Pintak, L., and S. J. Nazir. 2013. "Pakistani journalism: at the crossroads of Muslim identity, national priorities and journalistic culture." *Media, Culture & Society*, 35(5): 640–65.

Richter, L. 1990–1. "Exploring theories of female leadership in South and Southeast Asia." *Pacific Affairs*, 63(4): 524–40.

Robson, D. 2000. "Stereotypes and the female politician: a case study of Senator Barbara Mikulski." *Communication Quarterly*, 48(3): 205–22.

Ross, K. 2002. *Women, Politics, Media: Uneasy Relations in Comparative Perspective.* Cresskill, NJ: Hampton Press.

Sreberny-Mohammadi, A, and K. Ross. 1996. "Women MPs and the Media: Representing the Body Politic." In *Women in Politics*, eds. J. Lovenduski and P. Norris. New York, Oxford: Oxford University Press, 105–17.

Syed Ali, N. 2013. "Women in the House." Dawn.com March 3, http://dawn.com/news/789931/women-in-the-house

Walford, G. 2007. "Classification and framing of interviews in ethnographic interviewing." *Ethnography and Education*, 2(2): 147–57.

Willnat, L. and A. Aw. 2008. "Political Communication in Asia: Challenges and Opportunities." In *Handbook of Political Communication Research*, ed. L. Kaid. New Jersey: Lawrence Erlbaum Associates, 479–503.

Yusuf, Z. 2013. "HRCP Concern over Rising Violence Against Women." Human Rights Commission of Pakistan, September 18, 2013. http://hrcp-web.org/hrcpweb/hrcps-concern-over-rising-violence-against-women/

Chapter 8: Between Two Democratic Ideals: Gendering in the Russian Culture of Political Journalism

Azhgikhina, N. 2006. "Kogda Rossiey budet upravlyat' Margaret Thatcher?" *Gendernye issledovanija*, 16. Available online at: http://www.gender.univer.kharkov.ua/gurnal/16/kcgs.org.ua_GS_16.pdf

—2008. *Propuschennyj syuzhet. Istorija novogo nezavisimogo zhenskogo dvizhenija Rossii s nachala 1990-h do nashih dnej v zerkale SMI.* Moscow: Tsentr obschestvennoj informacii.

Braden, M. 1996. *Women Politicians and the Media.* Lexington: University Press of Kentucky.

Byerly, C., and K. Ross. 2006. *Women and Media: A Critical Introduction.* Oxford: Wiley-Blackwell.

Cockburn, C. 1991. "Democracy without women is no democracy: Soviet women hold their first autonomous national conference." *Feminist Review*, 39: 141–8.

Devere, H. and S. G. Davies. 2006. "The Don and Helen New Zealand Election 2005: a media a-gender?" *Pacific Journalism Review*, 12(1): 65–85.

Falk, E. 2008. *Women for President: Media Bias in Eight Campaigns*. Urbana: University of Illinois Press.

Gamble, M., and T. Gamble. 2002. *The Gender Communication Connection*. Boston and London: Houghton Mifflin.

Gidengil, E., and J. Everitt. 1999. "Metaphors and misrepresentation: gendered Mediation in News Coverage of the 1993 Canadian Leaders' Debates." *Harvard International Journal of Press/Politics*, 4(1): 48–65.

Gill, R. 2007. *Gender and the Media*. Cambridge: Polity Press.

Global Media Monitoring Project. 2010. "World Association for Christian Communication (WACC)." http://whomakesthenews.org/images/stories/restricted/global/global_en.pdf

Global Report on the Status of Women in the News Media. 2011. International Women's Media Foundation (IWMF). http://www.iwmf.org/wp-content/uploads/2013/09/IWMF-Global-Report.pdf

Gorshkov, M. K., and N. E. Tikhonova, eds. 2002. *Zhenschina novoj Rossii: Kakaya ona? Kak zhivet? K chemu stremitsya?* Moscow: Rossijskaya politicheskaya entsiklopedıya.

Graber, Doris A. 2005. *Mass Media and American Politics*, 7th edn. Washington, DC: Congressional Quarterly Books.

Hanitzsch, T. 2007. "Deconstructing journalism culture: towards a universal theory." *Communication Theory*, 17: 367–85.

Hausmann, R., L. D. Tyson, Y. Bekhouche, and S. Zahidi, eds. 2013. "The Global Gender Gap Report 2013." World Economic Forum. http://www3.weforum.org/docs/WEF_GenderGap_Report_2013.pdf

Inter-Parliamentary Union. "Women in National Parliaments." http://www.ipu.org/wmn-e/classif.htm

Kahn, K. F. 1996. *The Political Consequences of Being a Woman: How Stereotypes Influence the Conduct and Consequences of Political Campaigns*. New York: Columbia University Press.

Kochkina, E. V. 2004. "Politicheskaya sistema preimuschestv dlya grazhdan muzhskogo pola v Rossii (1917–2002)." In *Gendernaya rekonstruktsiya politicheskikh sistem*, eds. Nataliya M. Stepanova, and Elena V. Kochkina. Saint Petersburg: ALETEYA, 477–523.

Kroon Lundell, Å. and M. Ekström. 2008. "The complex visual gendering of political women in the press." *Journalism Studies*, 9(6): 891–910.

Media Atlas. 2013. http://www.media-atlas.ru/editions/?a=srch&reset=1

Norris, P., ed. 1997. *Women, Media, and Politics*. New York: Oxford University Press.

Nygren, G., ed. 2012. *Journalism in Russia, Poland, and Sweden – Traditions, Cultures, and Research*. Stockholm: Journalistik, Södertörns högskola.

Resnyanskaya, L. 2007. *SMI i politika*. Moscow: Aspect Press.

Ross, K. 2002. *Women, Politics, Media: Uneasy Relations in Comparative Perspective*. Cresskill, NJ: Hampton Press.

—2010. "Danse macabre: politicians, journalists, and the complicated rumba of relationships." *The International Journal of Press/Politics*, 15(3): 272–94.

Ross, K., and C. Byerly, eds. 2004. *Women and Media: International Perspectives*. Malden, MA: Blackwell.

Russian Federal Government. Senior Russian Government Officials. 2013. http://www.government.ru/en/gov/

Russian Federal Subjects. 2013. http://www.gov.ru/main/regions/regioni-44.html

Smirnova, O. 2010. "Zhurnalistika, svobodnaya ot gendernykh stereotipov, nachinaetsya s podgotovki zhurnalistov, svobodnykh ot gendernykh stereotipov." *MediaTrendy*, 3(8): 4.

Sreberny-Mohammadi, A., and K. Ross. 1996. "Women MPs and Media: representing the body politic." *Parliamentary Affairs*, 49(1): 103–15.

Sreberny-Mohammadi, A., and L. van Zoonen, eds. 2000. *Gender, Politics and Communication*. Cresskill, NJ: Hampton Press.

van Zoonen, L. 1994. *Feminist Media Studies*, London: Sage.

—2003. "'After Dallas and Dynasty we have … Democracy': Articulating Soap, Politics and Gender." In *Media and the Restyling of Politics: Consumerism, Celebrity and Cynicism*, eds. John Corner and Dick Pels. London: Sage, 99–116.

Vartanova, E. 2009. *Mass Media Theory: Current Issues*. Moscow: MediaMir.

—2013. *Postsovetskie transformatsii rossijskikh SMI i zhurnalistiki*. Moscow: MediaMir.

Vartanova, E. O. Smirnova, and T. Frolova. 2012. "Gendernoe izmerenie politiki v povestke SMI." In *Gender i SMI. Ezhegodnik 2011*, ed. O. Smirnova. Moscow: Faculty of Journalism, MSU, 67–95.

Voronina, O. 1998. "Gendernaya ekspertiza zakonodatelstva RF o sredstvah massovoi informacii." Moscow: Eslan. http://www.gender.ru/russian/public/voronina/soderj.shtml

Voronova, L. 2011. Media Representation of Women Politicians: Myths and Anti-myths." In *World of Media. Yearbook of Russian Media and Journalism Studies*, ed. E. Vartanova. Moscow: Faculty of Journalism, MSU, 114–27.

Zdravomyslova, O. 2003. *Sem'ya i obschestvo: gendernoe izmerenie rossijskoj transformatsii*. Moscow: Editorial URSS.

Chapter 9: Becoming Less Gendered: A Comparison of (Inter)national Press Coverage of First Female Government Heads Who Win Again at the Polls

Audit Bureau of Circulations of South Africa. 2012. "ABC 2nd Quarter Presentation 2012." www.abc.org.za/Files.aspx/Download/47.

Bachmann, I. and T. Correa. 2013. "Género, medios y participación." In *Intermedios: Medios de Comunicación y Democracia en Chile*, eds. Arturo Arriagada and Patricio Navia. Santiago: Ediciones Universidad Diego Portales, 119–39.

Benson, R. and A. Saguy. 2005. "Constructing social problems in an age of globalization: a French–American comparison." *American Sociological Review*, 70: 233–59.

Blumler, J. and M. Gurevitch. 1995. *The Crisis of Public Communication*. London: Routledge.

Bucy, E. and M. E. Grabe. 2006. "Taking Television Seriously: a Sound and Image Bite Analysis of Presidential Campaign Coverage." *Journal of Communication*, 57: 652–75.

Byerly, C. and K. Ross. 2006. *Women and Media. A Critical Introduction*, Malden, MA: Blackwell Publishing.

Cantrell, T. and I. Bachmann. 2008. "Who is the lady in the window? a comparison of international and national press coverage of first female government heads." *Journalism Studies*, 9: 429–46.

Carlin, D. and K. L. Winfrey. 2009. "Have you come a long way, baby? Hillary Clinton, Sarah Palin, and sexism in 2008 campaign coverage." *Communication Studies*, 60: 326–43.

Carragee, K. and W. Roefs. 2004. "The neglect of power in recent framing research." *Journal of Communication*, 54: 214–33.

Clarke, J. and M. Everest. 2006. "Cancer in the mass print media: fear, uncertainty and the medical model." *Social Science & Medicine*, 62: 2591–600.

Connolly-Ahern, C. and C. Broadway. 2008. "To booze or not to booze? newspaper coverage of fetal alcohol spectrum disorders." *Science Communication*, 29: 362–85.

D'Angelo, P. and J. A. Kuypers, eds. 2010. *Doing News Framing Analysis: Empirical and Theoretical Perspectives*. New York: Routledge.

Devere, H. and S. G. Davies. 2006. "The Don and Helen New Zealand Election 2005: a media a-gender?" *Pacific Journalism Review*, 12(1): 65–85.

Devitt, D. 2002. "Framing gender on the campaign trail: female gubernatorial candidates and the press." *Journalism & Mass Communication Quarterly*, 79(2): 445–63.

Egan, M. E. 2009. "The World's 100 Most Powerful Women." *Forbes*. http://www.forbes.com/2009/08/18/worlds-most-powerful-women-forbes-woman-power-women-09-angela-merkel_land.html

Esser, F. and P. D'Angelo. 2006. "Framing the press and publicity process in U.S., British, and German general election campaigns: a comparative study of metacoverage." *The Harvard International Journal of Press/Politics*, 11: 44–66.

Falk, E. 2008. *Women for President: Media Bias in Eight Campaigns*. Urbana: University of Illinois Press.

Festinger, L. 1957. *A Theory of Cognitive Dissonance.* Stanford, CA: Stanford University Press.

Gamson, W. 1989. "News as framing: comments on Graber." *American Behavioral Scientist,* 33: 157–61.

Gidengil, E., and J. Everitt. 2003. "Talking tough: gender and reported speech in campaign news coverage." *Political Communication*, 20: 209–32.

Han, G. K., T. M. Chock, and P. Shoemaker. 2009. "Issue familiarity and framing effects of online campaign coverage: event perception, issue attitudes, and the 2004 presidential election in Taiwan." *Journalism & Mass Communication Quarterly*, 86: 739–55.

Harp, D., J. Loke, and I. Bachmann. 2010. "First impressions of Sarah Palin: pit bulls, politics, gender performance and a discursive media (re)contextualization." *Communication, Culture & Critique*, 3: 291–309.

Heldman, C., S. J. Carroll, and S. Olson. 2005. "She brought only a skirt: print media coverage of Elizabeth Dole's bid for the Republican presidential nomination." *Political Communication*, 22(3): 315–35.

Hoogensen, G. and B. Solheim. 2006. *Women in Power. World leaders Since 1960.* Westport, CT: Praeger.

Htun, M. 2005. "Women, Political Parties and Electoral Systems in Latin America." In *Women in Parliament: Beyond Numbers, a Revised Edition*. Stockholm: Internacional IDEA, 112–21.

Inglehart, R. and P. Norris. 2003. *Rising Tide: Gender Equality and Cultural Change Around the World.* Cambridge: Cambridge University Press.

Isenson, N. 2009. "Germany poverty atlas shows huge social divide." *Deutsche Welle.* http://www.dw.de/german-poverty-atlas-shows-huge-social-divide/a-4262772

Jamieson, K. H. 1995. *Beyond the Double Bind: Women and Leadership*. New York: Oxford University Press.

Lecheler, S. and C. de Vreese. 2012. "News framing and public opinion: a mediation analysis of framing effects on political attitudes." *Journalism & Mass Communication Quarterly* 89: 185–204.

Lewis, J. J. 1995. "Germany – Status of Women." http://womenshistory.about.com/library/ency/blwh_germany_women.htm

Loke, J., D. Harp, and I. Bachmann. 2011. "Mothering and governing: how news articulates hegemonic gender roles in the case of governors Jane Swift and Sarah Palin." *Journalism Studies* 12: 205–20.

Maher, M. 2003. "Framing: An Emerging Paradigm or a Phase of Agenda Setting?" In *Framing public life*, eds. S. D. Reese, O. H. Gandy, Jr., and A. E. Grant. Mahwah, NJ: Lawrence Erlbaum, 83–94.

McCullough, J. J. 2013. "Female World Leaders Currently in Power." http://www.filibustercartoons.com/charts_rest_female-leaders.php

Meeks, L. 2012. "Is she 'Man Enough'? women candidates, executive political offices, and news coverage." *Journal of Communication*, 62: 175–93.

Neuendorf, K. 2002. *The Content Analysis Guidebook*. Thousand Oaks, CA: Sage.

Niven, D., and J. Zilber. 2001. "Do women and men in congress cultivate different images? evidence from congressional web sites." *Political Communication*, 18: 395–405.

Norris, P., ed. 1997. *Women, Media, and Politics*. New York: Oxford University Press.

Rausch, Jr., J. David, M. Rozell, and H. Wilson. 1999. "When women lose: a study of media coverage of two gubernatorial campaigns." *Women & Politics*, 20: 1–21.

Reese, S. 2003. "Prologue. Framing Public Life: A Bridging Model for Media Research." In *Framing Public Life*, eds. S. D. Reese, O. H. Gandy, Jr., and A. E. Grant, 7.31. Mahwah, NJ: Lawrence Erlbaum.

Rojecki, A. 2005. "Media discourse on globalization and terror." *Political Communication* 22: 63–81.

Rosas-Moreno, T. 2010. "Media representations of race cue the State of Media Opening in Brazil." *International Journal of Communication*, 4: 261–82.

Rosas-Moreno, T., D. Harp, and I. Bachmann. 2013. "Framing ideology: how *Time* magazine represents nationalism and identities through visual reporting." *Communication&Society/Comunicación y Sociedad*, 26: 1–20.

Rosas-Moreno, T. and I. Bachmann. 2012. "Pakistani and U.S. press content on Benazir Bhutto's assassination frame her dynasty, destiny, death and their secrets." *Observatorio*, 6: 281–310.

Ross, K. 2002. *Women, Politics, Media: Uneasy Relations in Comparative Perspective*. Cresskill, NJ: Hampton Press.

—2004. "Women Framed: The Gendered Turn in Mediated Politics." In *Women and Media: International Perspectives*, ed. K. Ross and C. Byerly. Malden, MA: Blackwell Publishing, 60–76.

—2010. *Gendered Media: Women, Men, and Identity Politics*. Maryland, MD: Rowman and Littlefield.

Sanbonmatsu, K. 2003. "Political knowledge and gender stereotypes." *American Politics Research*, 31: 575–94.

Scheufele, D. 2000. "Agenda-setting, priming, and framing revisited: another look at cognitive effects of political communication." *Mass Communication & Society*, 3: 297–316.

Sreberny-Mohammadi, A., and K. Ross. 1996. "Women MPs and Media: representing the body politic." *Parliamentary Affairs*, 49(1): 103–15.

Tuchman, Gaye. 1978. *Making News*. New York: Free Press.

UNICEF. 2014. "At a glance: Liberia." http://www.unicef.org/infobycountry/liberia_statistics.html

World Bank. 2014. "Chile: World Development Indicators." http://data.worldbank.org/country/chile

Chapter 10: "Cameroon's Female Obama": Deconstructing the Kah Walla Phenomenon in the Context of the 2011 Presidential Elections in Cameroon

Aday, S., and J. Devitt. 2001. "Style over substance: newspaper coverage of Elizabeth Dole's presidential bid." *The Harvard International Journal of Press and Politics*, 6(2): 52–73.

Africa Media Barometer. 2011. *Cameroon: 2011*. Windhoek: Friedrich-Ebert Stiftung.

All Voices of 27 November 2010: Cameroon: Kah Wallamania Syndrome Grips Cameroon.

Arriola, L., and M. Johnson. 2013. "Ethnic politics and women's empowerment in Africa: ministerial appointments to executive cabinets." *American Journal of Political Science*. DOI: 10.1111/ajps.12075.

Atkeson, L., and T. Krebs. 2008. "Press coverage of mayoral candidates: the role of gender in news reporting and campaign issue speech." *Political Research Quarterly*, 61(2): 239–52.

Bauer, G. 2012. "Let there be balance: women in African parliaments." *Political Studies Review*, 10(3): 370–84.

Cameroon Tribune 6 March 2011: Le bal des soupirants à la présidentielle 2011.

—21 September 2011: Kah Walla affiche ses soutiens.

—25 September 2011: Edith Kah Walla.

—17 October 2011: Une coalition de candidats pour lannulation de la présidentielle.

—24 October 2011: Le paysage politique relooké du Cameroun

Dan, V., and A. Iorgoveanu. 2013. "Still on the beaten path: how gender impacted the coverage of male and female Romanian candidates for European office." *The Harvard International Journal of Press and Politics*, 18(2): 208–33.

Eyeball to Eyeball of 14 November 2010: Kah Walla: The Audacity to Dream Change.

Garcia-Blanco, I. and K. Wahl-Jorgensen. 2012. "The discursive construction of women politicians in the European press." *Feminist Media Studies*, 12 (3): 422–41.

Gidengil, E. and J. Everitt. 1999. "Metaphors and misrepresentation: gendered Mediation in News Coverage of the 1993 Canadian Leaders' Debates." *Harvard International Journal of Press/Politics*, 4(1): 48–65.

Heldman, C., S. J. Carroll, and S. Olson. 2005. "She brought only a skirt: print media coverage of Elizabeth Dole's bid for the Republican presidential nomination." *Political Communication*, 22(3): 315–35.

Ibroscheva, E. 2012. "Peeking through the looking glass: a comparative analysis of women, politics and media in Lebanon and Bulgaria." *Middle East Media Educator* 1(2): 19–29.

Johnston, A., and A. White. 1994. "Communication styles and female candidates:

a study of the political advertising during the 1986 Senate elections." *Journalism Quarterly*, 71(2): 321–9.
Kahn, K. F., and E. Goldenberg. 1991. "The media: obstacle or ally of feminists?" *Annals of the American Academy of Political and Social Science*, 55: 104–13.
Kahn, K., and A. Gordon. 1997. "How Women Campaign for the U.S. Senate: Substance and Strategy." In *Women, Media and Politics*, ed. P. Norris. New York: Oxford University Press, 59–75.
LAction of 27 September 2011: Paul Biya scores in the media.
La Nouvelle Expression 19 May 2011: Les femmes se solidarisent avec Kah Walla.
—5 September 2011: Sursaut: Ces femmes qui rêvent d'Etoudi.
Larson, S. 2001. "Running as Women? a comparison of female and male Pennsylvania Assembly candidates' campaign brochures." *Women & Politics*, 22(2): 107–24.
Le Jour 6 October 2010: Social democratic front: Kah Walla traduite devant le conseil de discipline.
—22 July 2011: Présidentielle 2011. Ces femmes qui veulent défier Paul Biya.
—13 September 2011:Présidentielle 2011. Les recalés séquestrent les responsablesdElecam.
—8 October 2011: Que largent détourné revienne au pays.
Le Messager of 22 September 2011: Kah Walla: la femme dont la pugnacité fait rêver.
—26 September 2011: Kah Walla: Au moins 13 des 23 candidats ne sont pas de l'opposition.
—11 October 2011: Participation: Le pouvoir pris dans le piège de labstention.
Mbaku, J. 2002. "Cameroon's stalled transition to democratic governance: lessons for Africa's new democrats." *African and Asian Studies*, 1(3): 125–63.
Meeks, L. 2013. "All the gender that's fit to print: how the New York Times covered Hillary Clinton and Sarah Palin in 2008." *Journalism & Mass Communication Quarterly*, 90(3): 520–39.
Mutations 13 September 2010: Kah Walla: Une candidature autre que celle de Fru Ndi est possible au SDF.
—4 February 2011: Kah Walla: Le Cameroun est sans management.
—17 May 2011: Présidentielle 2011: Esther Dang défie Paul Biya.
—23 July 2011: La stratégie 'grassroot' de Kah Walla.
—7 October 2011: Lenjeu du scrutin du 9 octobre.
—17 October 2011: Evaluation: Ombres et lumières dans la nuit noire.
National Statistics Institute. 2012. *Autonomiser Les Femmes Rurales Pour Eradiquer la Faim et la Pauvrete: Que Revelent les Indicateurs?* INS. Yaounde.
The Sun 27 February 2011: I Do Not Regret Leaving SDF – Kah Walla.
Thomas, G. and M. Adams. 2010. "Breaking the final glass ceiling: the influence of gender in the elections of Elle Johnson-Sirleaf and Michelle Bachelet." *Journal of Women, Politics and Policy*, 31(2): 105–31.
Valenzuela, S. and T. Correa. 2009. "Press coverage and public opinion on women

candidates: the case of Chile's Michelle Bachelet." *The International Communication Gazette*, 71(3): 203–23.

Vos, D. 2013. "The vertical glass ceiling: explaining female politicians' under-representation in television news." *Communications – The European Journal of Communication Research*, 38(4): 389–410.

Xinhua 9 September 2011: Présidentielle camerounaise: l`honneur en jeu de Fru Ndi, chef d`une opposition liquéfiée

Chapter 11: The Mother of Brazil: Gender Roles, Campaign Strategy, and the Election of Brazil's First Female President

Abramo, C. W. 2013. "Às Claras." http://www.asclaras.org.br/@index.php?ano=2002

Aleman, E., and G. Tsebelis. 2005. "The origins of presidential conditional agenda-setting power in Latin America." *Latin American Research Review*, 40(2): 3–26.

Alencar, K. 2009. "Lula de Saia." *Folha de Sao Paulo*. http://www1.folha.uol.com.br/folha/pensata/kennedyalencar/ult511u609735.shtml

Alvares, R. 2010. "Eu Vou Ser a Mãe Do Povo Brasileiro, Afirma Dilma Rousseff Em Natal." *Politics*. http://blogs.estadao.com.br/radar-politico/2010/07/28/eu-vou-ser-a-mae-do-povo-brasileiro-afirma-dilma-rousseff-em-natal

Alves, J. E. D. 2012. "Diferenças Sociais e de Gênero Nas Intenções de Voto Para Presidente Em 2010." In *Mulheres nas eleições 2010*, eds. Celi Regina Jardim Pinto, José Eustáquio Diniz Alves, and Fatima Jordao. Sao Paulo: ABCP/SPM, 21–46.

Amaral, R. 2011. *A Vida Quer e Coragem – A Trajetoria de Dilma Rousseff, a Primeira Presidenta Do Brasil*. Rio de Janeiro: Sextame.

Araújo, C. 2010. Rotas de Ingresso, "Trajetórias e Acesso Das Mulheres Ao Legislativo: Um Estudo Comparado Entre Brasil e Argentina." *Revista Estudos Feministas*, 18(2): 567–84.

Azevedo, F. 2006. "Mídia e Democracia No Brasil: Relações Entre o Sistema de Mídia e o Sistema Político." *Opinião Pública*, 12(1): 88–113.

Backes, A. and L. Claudio Pires dos Santos. 2012. Gastos Em Campanhas Eleitorais No Brasil. *Caderno Aslegis*, 46: 47–59.

Baldwin, J. and E. DeSouza. 2001. "Modelo de María and Machismo: the social construction of gender in Brazil." *Revista Interamericana de Psicología*, 35(1): 9–29.

Bencke, C. 2010. PT "Lança Dilma Reforçando Imagem de Mãe, Mulher e Escolhida de Lula." *Folha de Sao Paulo*. http://eleicoes.uol.com.br/2010/ultimas-noticias/2010/06/13/pt-lanca-dilma-reforcando-imagem-de-mae-mulher-e-escolhida-de-lula.jhtm

Bertazzo, J. 2012. "An initial survey of the Dilma Rousseff administration in Brazil." *Critical Sociology*, 38(6), 889–92.

Biroli, F. 2010. "Gender and politics in Brazilian news magazines: absences and stereotypes." *Cadernos Pagu*, (34): 269–99.

Bonin, R. 2009. "Marina Silva Anuncia Saída Do PT e Deve Se Filiar Ao PV." *G1 Politica*. http://g1.globo.com/Noticias/Politica/0,,MUL1272525-5601,00-MARINA+SILVA+ANUNCIA+SAIDA+DO+PT+E+DEVE+SE+FILIAR+AO+PV.html

"Brasil mantendrá su política económica". 2003. *BBC*. http://news.bbc.co.uk/hi/spanish/business/newsid_2623000/2623635.stm

Carlin, D. and K. L. Winfrey. 2009. "Have you come a long way, baby? Hillary Clinton, Sarah Palin, and sexism in 2008 campaign coverage." *Communication Studies*, 60: 326–43.

Carvalho, L. 2005. "Dilma Diz Ter Orgulho de Ideais Da Guerrilha." *Folha de Sao Paulo*. http://www1.folha.uol.com.br/fsp/brasil/fc2106200508.htm

Cox, G. and S. Morgenstern. 2001. "Latin America's reactive assemblies and proactive presidents." *Comparative Politics*, 33(2): 171–89.

Downie, A. 2010. "Brazil's new President: Can Dilma be another Lula?" *Time*. http://www.time.com/time/world/article/0,8599,2028581,00.html

Fernandes, C. 2012. "As representações midiáticas de Dilma Rousseff no cenário político brasileiro." *Aurora. Revista de Arte, Mídia e Política ISSN 1982-6672* 5(14): 69–85.

Flor, A., and F. Victor. 2010. "A Hollywood de Dilma." *Folha de Sao Paulo*. http://www1.folha.uol.com.br/fsp/poder/po2609201027.htm

Goertzel, T. 2011. *Lula: The Most Popular Politician on Earth*. Boca Raton, FL: Brown Walker Press.

Gomes, M. 2011. "Corpo, Política e Tecnologização: Um Estudo Da Representação De Dilma Rousseff No Contexto Da Mídia." *Cadernos de Linguagem e Sociedade* 12(1): 11–29.

Gonzalez, C. 2010. "Campanha de Dilma Traça Estratégia Para Conquistar Voto Feminino." *Portal Vermelho*. http://www.vermelho.org.br/noticia.php?id_noticia=133288&id_secao=1

Guedes, J. 2010. "Nasce Neto de Dilma Rousseff." *O Globo*. http://oglobo.globo.com/eleicoes-2010/nasce-neto-de-dilma-rousseff-4989036

Heldman, C., S. J. Carroll, and S. Olson. 2005. "She brought only a skirt: print media coverage of Elizabeth Dole's bid for the Republican presidential nomination." *Political Communication* 22(3): 315–35.

Hunter, W., and T. Power. 2007. "Rewarding Lula: executive power, social policy, and the Brazilian Elections of 2006." *Latin American Politics and Society*, 49(1): 1–30.

Inter-Parliamentary Union (IPU). n.d. "Women In National Parliaments." http://www.ipu.org/wmn-e/classif.htm

Jalalzai, F. 2008. "Women rule: shattering the executive glass ceiling." *Politics & Gender*, 4(02): 205–31.

—2012. "Firme y Honesta: Costa Rica's First Female President, Laura Chinchilla."

Paper presented at the annual meeting of the Northeastern Political Science Association, Omni Parker House, Boston, MA.

—2013. *Shattered, Cracked, or Firmly Intact?: Women and the Executive Glass Ceiling Worldwide*. New York: Oxford University Press.

Jamieson, K. H. 1995. *Beyond the Double Bind: Women and Leadership*. New York: Oxford University Press.

Kinzo, Maria D'Alva, and J. Dunkerley, eds. 2003. *Brazil Since 1985: Economy, Polity, and Society*. London: Institute of Latin American Studies.

Lago, R. 2009. "Sem Peruca, Dilma Aparece de Cabelos Curtos." *Congresso em Foco*. http://congressoemfoco.uol.com.br/noticias/sem-peruca-dilma-aparece-de-cabelos-curtos

Martins, J. M. 2013. Dilma Rousseff: Vestígios Da Construção de Uma Candidata. Quinto Congresso da Associação Brasileira de Pesquisadores em Comunicação Politica (5th Congress of the Brazilian Association of Political Communication Researchers). May 8–10. Curitiba, PR-Brazil.

Miguel, L. 2006. "From equality to opportunity: transformations in the discourse of the Workers' Party in the 2002 elections." *Latin American Perspectives*, 33(4): 122–43.

—2008. "Political representation and gender in Brazil: quotas for women and their impact." *Bulletin of Latin American Research*, 27(2): 197–214.

Murray, R. 2010. "Linear trajectories or vicious circles? the causes and consequences of gendered career paths in the National Assembly." *Modern & Contemporary France*, 18(4): 445–59.

Oms, C. 2010. "Dilma Ganha Voto Feminino Após Dizer Que é Mãe, Diz Pesquisa." *Terra – Política*. http://terramagazine.terra.com.br/interna/0,,OI4619887-EI6578,00-Dilma+ganha+voto+feminino+apos+dizer+que+e+mae+diz+pesquisa.html

Panke, L. 2011. "Análise Comparativa entre as Campanhas Eleitorais dos Brasileiros Dilma Rousseff e Luiz Inácio Lula da Ailva." *ComHumanitas*, 3(3): 39–47.

Pires, T. M. de Carvalho Cruz. 2011. "A Construção Da Imagem Política De Dilma Rousseff Como Mãe Do Povo Brasileiro." *Revista Debates*, 5(1): 139–62.

Preite Sobrinho, W. 2010. "Lula Diz Que Dilma é Dura 'como Uma Mãe'." *R-7 Noticias*. http://noticias.r7.com/brasil/noticias/lula-diz-que-dilma-e-dura-como-uma-mae-20100410.html

Queiroz, A. and F. R. Martins Jr. 2011. "Presidente Dilma, com que roupa eu vou?" *Compolítica*, 1(1): 133–48. http://compolitica.org/revista/index.php/revista/article/view/9

Ribeiro, T. 2009. "Ministra Dilma Diz Que Faz Quimioterapia Contra Linfoma." *Estadão*. http://www.estadao.com.br/noticias/nacional,ministra-dilma-diz-que-faz-quimioterapia-contra-linfoma,360409,0.htm

Rohter, L. 2007. "Argentina's president steps aside to support wife as his successor." *New York Times*. http://www.nytimes.com/2007/07/03/world/americas/03argentina.html

Romero, S. 2012. "Brazil's Ex-President Da Silva back on political front lines." *New York*

Times. http://www.nytimes.com/2012/08/26/world/americas/brazils-ex-president-lula-back-on-political-front-lines.html

dos Santos, P. G. 2007. "Punishing corruption: the impact of corruption allegations in the 2006 Brazilian Congressional Elections". University of Kansas, M.A. Thesis.

Schmitt, Rogério. 1999. Estratégias de Campanha No Horário Gratuito de Propaganda Eleitoral Em Eleições Proporcionais. *Dados*, 42(2).

Scolese, E. and A. Flor. 2005. "Lula Demite Olívio, Mas Adia Anúncio Por Pressão Do PT." *Folha de Sao Paulo*. http://www1.folha.uol.com.br/fsp/brasil/fc2007200526.htm

da Silva, J. M. 2011. "Intelectuais E Mídia Na Eleição De Dilma Rousseff." *Santa Cruz do Sul*, 36(1): 41–50.

da Silveira, B. S. and J. M. P. de Mello. 2011. "Campaign advertising and election outcomes: quasi-natural experiment evidence from gubernatorial elections in Brazil." *Review of Economic Studies*, 78(2): 590–612.

de Souza, Amaury 2011. "The politics of personality in Brazil." *Journal of Democracy*, 22(2): 75–88.

Thomas, G., and M. Adams. 2010. "Breaking the final glass ceiling: the influence of gender in the elections of Elle Johnson-Sirleaf and Michelle Bachelet." *Journal of Women, Politics and Policy*, 31(2): 105–31.

Villaméa, Luiza. 2005. "Companheiras de Armas." *Istoé* (1864).

Weir, S. 1993. "Peronisma: Isabel Peron and the Politics of Argentina." In *Women as National Leaders*. London: Sage.

Chapter 12: The Visual Framing of Romanian Women Politicians in Personal Campaign Blogs during the 2012 Romanian Parliamentary Elections

Banwart, M. 2010. "Gender and candidate communication: effects of stereotypes in the 2008 election." *American Behavioral Scientist*, 54(3): 265–83.

Bichard, S. 2006. "Building blogs: a multi-dimensional analysis of distribution of frames in the 2004 Presidential candidate websites." *Journalism and Mass Communication Quarterly*, 83(2): 329–45.

Biroul Electoral Central (Central Electoral Bureau). 2012. "Statistici nivel colegiu." www.becparlamentare2012.ro/ADOCUMENTE/Statistici/StatisticiNivelColegiu.xls.

Blood, R. 2005. "At the Interface: New Intimacies, New Cultures." In *Living in the Information Age: A New Media Reader*, ed. E. P. Bucy. Belmont. CA: Wadsworth, 129–33.

Bourdieu, P. 1990. *Photography. A Middle-brow Art*. Cambridge: Polity Press.

Burgin, Vi. 1982. *Thinking Photography*. London: Macmillan.

Bystrom, D. 2004. "Women as Political Communication Sources and Audiences." In

Handbook of Political Communication Research, ed. Lynda Lee Kaid. Mahwah. NJ and London: Lawrence Erlbaum Associates, 435–62.

Bystrom, D., M. Banwart, L. Kaid, and T. Robertson. 2004. *Gender and Political Candidate Communication: VideoStyle, WebStyle, and NewsStyle*. New York: Routledge.

Cismaru, D. 2012. *Social media şi managementul reputaţiei*. Bucureşti: Tritonic.

Dan, V., and A. Iorgoveanu. 2013. "Still on the beaten path: how gender impacted the coverage of male and female Romanian candidates for European office." *The International Journal of Press/Politics* 18(2): 208–33.

Dolan, K. 2005. "Do women candidates play to gender stereotypes? do men candidates play to women? Candidate sex and issues priorities on campaign websites." *Political Research Quarterly*, 58(1): 31–44.

Goffman, E. 1974. *Frame Analysis: An Essay on the Organization of Experience*. Cambridge, MA: Harvard University Press.

Goodnow, T. 2013. "Facing off: a comparative analysis of Obama and Romney Facebook timeline photographs." *American Behavioral Scientist*, 57(11): 1584–95.

Hacker, K. 1995. *Candidate Images in Presidential Elections*. Westport, CT: Praeger.

Hertog, J. and D. McLeod. 2001. "A Multiperspectival Approach to Framing Analysis: A Field Guide." In *Framing Public Life: Perspective on Media and our Understanding of the Social World*, eds. S. Reese, O. Gandy, Jr., and A. Grant. Mahwah, NJ: Lawrence Erlbaum Associates, 139–62.

INSCOP. 2013. "The Barometer of Public Opinion – the Truth about Romania." http://www.inscop.ro/septembrie-2013-increderea-in-institutii/

Internetworldstats.com.2013. http://www.internetworldstats.com/stats4.htm

Jamieson, K. H. 1995. *Beyond the Double Bind: Women and Leadership*. New York: Oxford University Press.

Jewitt, C. and R. Oyama. 2001. "Visual Meaning: A Social Semiotic Approach." In *Handbook of Visual Analysis*, eds. Theo van Leeuwen and Carey Jewitt. Los Angeles, London, New Delhi and Singapore: Sage, 134–56.

Kaplan, A. and M. Haenlein. 2010. "Users of the world, unite! the challenge and opportunities of social media." *Business Horizons*, 53 (1): 59–68.

Kress, G. and T. van Leeuwen. 2006. *Reading Images: The Grammar of Visual Design*, 2nd edn. London, New York: Routledge.

Lawson-Borders, G. and R. Kirk. 2005. "Blogs in campaign communication." *American Behavioral Scientist*, 49(4): 548–59.

van Leeuwen, T. 2005. *Introducing Social Semiotics*. London, New York: Routledge.

Marcu, D. and L. Nedelcu. 2013. "Evoluţia reprezentării femeilor în Parlamentul României." *Expert Electoral* (*Electoral Expert*), 1: 19–21.

Markstedt, H. 2007. "Political Handbags. The representation of women politicians. A case study of the websites and newspaper coverage of the women candidates in the Labour Party Deputy Leadership Election." Ph.D. diss., Media@lse. http://www.

lse.ac.uk/media@lse/research/mediaWorkingPapers/MScDissertationSeries/Past/Markstedt_final.pdf
Messaris, P. and L. Abraham. 2001. "The Role of Images in Framing News Stories." In *Framing Public Life: Perspective on media and our understanding of the social world*, eds. S. Reese, O. Gandy, Jr., and A. Grant. Mahwah, NJ: Lawrence Erlbaum Associates, 215–26.
Miroiu, M. 2004. *Drumul către autonomie. Teorii politice feministe*. Iaşi: Polirom.
Nineo'clock.ro. 2013. "INSCOP Survey: Citizens Trust Town Hall and the Government Most." http://www.nineoclock.ro/inscop-survey-citizens-trust-town-hall-and-the-government-most/
Niven, D. and J. Zilber. 2001. "Do women and men in congress cultivate different images? evidence from congressional web sites." *Political Communication*, 18: 395–405.
Paul Vass, A. 2012. "Consultare publică cu privire la îmbunătăţirea reprezentării politice de gen în România." http://www.femeileinpolitica.ro/
PDL.ro 2013. "Viziunea PDL despre România." http://www.pdl.org.ro/viziunea-pdl-pentru-romania
—2013. "În ce credem." http://www.psd.ro/despre/in-ce-credem/
Report on the Romanian Blogosphere. 2011. http://www.dailybusiness.ro/stiri-new-media/cat-bani-face-blogosfera-din-romania-76154/
Semetko, H. and H. Boomgaarden. 2007. "Reporting Germany's 2005 Bundestag election campaign: was gender an issue?" *The Harvard International Journal of Press/Politics*, 12 (4): 154–71.
Ţăruş, A. 2008. "Condiţia femeii în politica din România – învingerea *malestreamului*." *Revista română de comunicare şi relaţii publice* 12: 61–77.
Vannini, P. 2007. "Social semiotics and fieldwork: method and analytics." *Qualitative Inquiry*, 13(1): 113–40.
Verschueren, P. 2012. *Picturing Afghanistan: The Photography of Foreign Conflict*. New York: Hampton Press.

Chapter 13: Gender, Politics, and the Albanian Media: A Women Parliamentarians' Account

Aalberg, T., and J. Strömbäck. 2011. "Media-driven men and media-critical women? an empirical study of gender and MPs' relationships with the media in Norway and Sweden." *International Political Science Review*, 32(2): 167–87.
ACER. 2010. *A Baseline Analysis: The Situation of Women Leaders at the Local Level in Albania*. Tirana: UNIFEM Albania.
ACER and ASET. 2009. *Parliamentary Election in Albania: Monitoring the Implementation of Gender and Women Participation*. Tirana: UNIFEM.

Albanian Assembly. 2003. *Women in Parliament*. Tirana.

Antić, M., and S. Lokar. 2006. "The Balkans: From Total Rejection to Gradual Acceptance of Gender Quotas." In *Women, Quotas and Politics*, ed. D. Dahlerup. London/New York: Routledge, 138–67.

Bell, A. 1991. *The Language of News Media*. Oxford: Blackwell.

Dragoti, E., I. Tahsini, E. Dhëmbo, and J. Ajdini. 2011. *Monitoring Albania's Steps Towards Gender Equality: The Case of Gender Quotas in Politics*. Tirana: University of Tirana, Social Sciences Department.

Ekonomi, M., L. Sokoli, S. Danaj, and B. Picari. 2006. *Representation and the Quality of Democracy in Albania: A Gender Perspective*. Tirana: Gender Alliance for Development.

Equality in Decision-Making Women's Network. 2010. *A e solli kuota gruan në vendimmarrje?* Pogradec: D.I.J.A.

Fountaine, S. and J. McGregor. 2002. "Reconstructing Gender for the 21st Century: News media framing of political women in New Zealand." Australian & New Zealand Communication Association 23rd Annual Conference, July 10–12, 2002, Gold Coast, Queensland. http://webenrol.massey.ac.nz/massey/fms/Colleges/College%20of%20Business/NZCWLI pdfs/JMcGregorSFountainePaper.pdf

Gender Alliance for Development. 2009. *Addressing Social Issues in the Media: A Gender Perspective*. Tirana: Gender Alliance for Development.

Gidengil, E. and J. Everitt. 1999. "Metaphors and misrepresentation: gendered Mediation in News Coverage of the 1993 Canadian Leaders' Debates." *Harvard International Journal of Press/Politics*, 4(1): 48–65.

Godole, J. 2013. "Journalism culture in Albania after 1990." (unpublished doctoral dissertation, University of Tirana).

Hallin, D., and P. Mancini. 2004. *Comparing Media Systems: Three Models of Media and Politics*. New York: Cambridge University Press.

IDRA and FML. 2009. *Promoting Financial Transparency and Accountability of Political Parties Participating in Parliamentary Elections in Albania*. Tirana.

Iyengar, S. and D. Kinder. 1987. *News that Matters: Television and American Opinion*. Chicago: University of Chicago Press.

Kahn, K. F. 1994. "The distorted mirror: press coverage of women candidates for statewide office." The *Journal of Politics*, 56(1): 154–73.

Kahn, Kim F. and E. Goldenberg. 1991. "Women candidates in the news: an examination of gender differences in U.S. Senate campaign coverage." *Public Opinion Quarterly*, 55: 180–99.

Lundell, Å. and M. Ekström. 2008. "The complex visual gendering of political women in the press." *Journalism Studies*, 9(6): 891–910.

Mazzoleni, G. and W. Schulz. 1999. "Mediatization of politics: a challenge for democracy?" *Political Communication*. 16(3): 247–61.

McQuail, D. 1992. *Media Performance: Mass Communication and the Public Interest*. London: Sage.

OSCE/ODIHR. 2009. *OSCE/ODIHR Election Observation Mission Final Report*. Warsaw: OSCE/ODIHR.

—2011. *OSCE/ODIHR Election Observation Mission Final Report*. Warsaw: OSCE/ODIHR.

OSFA (Open Society Foundation in Albania). 2012. *Political discourse analysis. Report No. 3. The Main Political Actors and Media's Discourse on Women, Religious and Ethnic Minorities Issues*. Tirana. htpp://www.soros.al/2010/article.php?id=420

Patterson, T. and W. Donsbach. 1996. "News decisions: journalists as partisan actors." *Political Communication*, 13(4): 455–68.

Ross, K. 2010. "Danse macabre: politicians, journalists, and the complicated rumba of relationships." *The International Journal of Press/Politics*, 15(3): 272–94.

Ross, K. and A. Sreberny. 2000. "Women in the House: Media Representation of British Politicians." In *Gender, Politics and Communication*, eds. A. Sreberny and L. van Zoonen. Creskill: Hampton Press, 79–99.

Staab, J. 1990. "The role of news factors in news selection: a theoretical reconsideration." *European Journal of Communication*, 5(4): 423–43.

Tresch, A. 2009. "Politicians in the media: determinants of legislators' presence and prominence in Swiss newspapers." *The International Journal of Press/Politics*. 14: 67–90.

Trimble, L. 2007. "Gender, political leadership and media visibility: *Globe and Mail* coverage of conservative party of Canada leadership contests." *Canadian Journal of Political Science*, 40(4): 969–93.

Tuchman, G. 1978. *Making News: A Study in the Construction of Reality*. New York: Free Press.

UNDP. 2013. *National Statistics Reveal Increased Level of Domestic Violence in Albania – Men and Boys Unite to end it*. Tirana, December 6, 2013. http://www.al.undp.org/content/albania/en/home/presscenter/pressreleases/2013/12/06/national-statistics-reveal-increased-level-of-domestic-violence-in-albania-men-and-boys-unite-to-end-it/

Wolfsfeld, G. 1997. *Media and Political Conflict: News from the Middle East*. New York: Cambridge University Press.

Chapter 14: Michelle Bachelet, President of Chile: A Moving Portrait

Agosín, M. 2008. *Tapestries of Hope, Threads of Love: The Arpillera movement in Chile*. Lanham: Rowman & Littlefield.

Araneda Briones, S. 2012. "Participación Política de las Mujeres en Chile 2011." *Revista*

Derecho Electoral, 13, January–June 2012. http://www.tse.go.cr/revista/art/13/sonia_arenada.pdf

Arendt, H. 1959. *The Human Condition*. New York: Doubleday Anchor Books.

Associated Press, 2013. "Chile's once and future President, Michelle Bachelet, wins runoff election." *Guardian*, December 15, 2013. http://www.theguardian.com/world/2013/dec/15/chile-president-michelle-bachelet-wins-election

Bachelet, Michelle. 2013. "Lean In: Former Chilean president Michelle Bachelet on how gender equality has to become the norm." *Daily Beast: Women in the World*, April 5, 2013. http://www.thedailybeast.com/witw/articles/2013/04/05/lean-in-former-chilean-president-michelle-bachelet-on-how-gender-equality-has-to-become-the-norm.html

—2007. "Los Sueños que Inspiran mi Mandato." *El Mercurio*, April 22, 2007. http://www.pschile.cl/ps-prensa-detalle.php?id=10

Balch, O. 2009. "The Bachelet factor: The cultural legacy of Chile's first female president." *Guardian*, December 13, 2009. http://www.guardian.co.uk/world/2009/dec/13/michelle-bachelet-chile-president-legacy

Baldez, L. 2002. *Why Women Protest: Women's Movements in Chile*. Cambridge: Cambridge University Press.

BBC Mundo. 2006. "Velan a Pinochet en Escuela Militar." *BBC Mundo*, December 11, 2006. http://news.bbc.co.uk/hi/spanish/latin_america/newsid_6167000/6167565.stm

Bucciferro, C. 2012. *FOR-GET: Identity, Media, and Democracy in Chile*. Lanham and New York: University Press of America.

—2009. "President Michelle Bachelet and the Chilean media: a complicated affair." *Journal of Global Communication*, 2(1): 289–312.

Castells, M. 2005. *Globalización, Desarrollo y Democracia: Chile en el Contexto Mundial*. México: Fondo de Cultura Económica.

Cedem. 2011. "The gender equality 'Social Watch': following Bachelet's government." *Centro de Estudios para el Desarrollo de la Mujer*, evaluation report. http://www.un.org/democracyfund/sites/dr7.un.org.democracyfund/files/UDF-RLC-07-198_Evaluation%20Report.pdf

Clinton, H. 2008. "The 2008 Time 100, leaders and revolutionaries: Michelle Bachelet." *Time Magazine*, May 12, 2008. http://www.time.com/time/specials/2007/article/0,28804,1733748_1733757_1735593,00.html

Coloane, J. 2010. "La Última Semana de Michelle Bachelet." *Blogs La Tercera*, March 4, 2010. http://blog.latercera.com/blog/jfcoloane/entry/la_%C3%BAltima_semana_de_michelle

Correa, R. 2005. Entrevista a Michelle Bachelet: "Me la puedo para ser Presidenta de Chile." *El Mercurio*, December 25, 2005, reprinted in *Archivo Chile*. http://www.archivochile.com/Chile_actual/Elecciones_2005/Bachelet/16_bachellet.pdf

CNN Chile. 2013. "Campaña 'Más Mujeres al Poder' Busca Aumentar la Participación Femenina en Política." *CNN Chile*, July 23, 2013. http://www.cnnchile.com/noticia/

2013/07/23/campana-mas-mujeres-al-poder-busca-aumentar-la-participacion-femenina-en-politica-

Dixon, D. 2006. "Michelle: Top woman in a macho world." *Observer*, April 1, 2006. http://www.theguardian.com/world/2006/apr/02/gender.chile

Forbes. 2010. "The World's Billionaires: #437 Sebastián Piñera." *Forbes Magazine*, March 10, 2010. http://www.forbes.com/lists/2010/10/billionaires-2010_Sebastian-Pinera_YLRC.html

Ford, L. 2013. "Bachelet ready to tone down language on UN Women proposals." *Guardian*, March 5, 2013. http://www.guardian.co.uk/global-development/2013/mar/05/michelle-bachelet-language-un-women

Foxley, V. 2005. "Sebastián Dávalos: 'Mi Madre Representa al Chile de Hoy'." *Revista Cosas*, 2005. http://www.cosas.cl/reportajes/92-revista-n-766/994-862

Infolatam/Efe. 2012. "Chile: Piñera Admite que Envidia la Popularidad de Michelle Bachelet." *Infolatam: Información y Análisis de América Latina*, March 13, 2013. http://www.infolatam.com/2012/11/12/chile-pinera-admite-que-envidia-la-popularidad-de-michelle-bachelet/

Khaleeli, H. 2011. "Top 100 Women in Politics: Michelle Bachelet." *Guardian*, March 7, 2011. http://www.guardian.co.uk/world/2011/mar/08/michelle-bachelet-100-women

Kornbluh, P. 2008. *Introduction* to *Tapestries of Hope, Threads of Love: The Arpillera Movement in Chile*, Marjorie Agosín, 1–12. Lanham: Rowman & Littlefield.

Laclau, E. and C. Mouffe. 2001. *Hegemony and Socialist Strategy*, 2nd edn. London: Verso.

Lehuedé, S. 2010. "Michelle Bachelet: La Revolucionaria de Defensa y las FF.AA." *Política Rock*, February 6, 2010. http://politicarock.cl/michelle-bachelet-revolucionaria-defensa/

Martinson, J. 2011. "UN Women's head Michelle Bachelet: A new superhero?" *Guardian*, April 21, 2011. http://www.guardian.co.uk/lifeandstyle/2011/apr/22/michelle-bachelet-un-women

Montecino, S. 1996. *Madres y Huachos: Alegorías del Mestizaje Chileno*. Santiago: Sudamericana.

Morales, M. 2008. "La Primera Mujer Presidenta de Chile: ¿Qué Explicó el Triunfo de Michelle Bachelet en las Elecciones de 2005–2006?" *Latin American Research Review*, 43(1): 7–32.

Moran, C. 2011. *How to be a Woman*. New York: Harper Perennial.

Moulian, T. 2002. *Chile Actual: Anatomía de un Mito*. Santiago: LOM Ediciones.

New York Times. 2010. "Times Topics: Michelle Bachelet." *New York Times*, March 11, 2010. http://topics.nytimes.com/top/reference/timestopics/people/b/michelle_bachelet/index.html

Paz, M. 2006. "La Joya del Red Set." *La Nación*, January 29, 2006. http://prontus2.lanacion.cl/la-joya-del-red-set/noticias/2006-01-28/224348.html

Phillips, A. 1991. *Engendering Gemocracy*. University Park: Pennsylvania State University Press.

Randall, V. 1987. *Women and Politics: An International Perspective,* 2nd edn. Chicago: University of Chicago Press.

Rindefjäll, T. 2009. "Continuity and Change in Chile's Neoliberal Democracy." In *Governance after neoliberalism in Latin America*, eds. Jean Grugel and Pía Riggirozzi. New York: Palgrave Macmillan, 175–194.

Romero, S. 2013. "On Election day, Latin America Willingly Trades Machismo for Female Clout." *New York Times*, December 14, 2013. http://www.nytimes.com/2013/12/15/world/americas/on-election-day-latin-america-willingly-trades-machismo-for-female-clout.html?ref=michellebachelet&_r=1&

Servel. 2013. "Presidenciales: Información País." *Servicio Electoral.* http://www.eleccionservel.cl/ELECCIONES2013/vistaPaisPresidente

Spiegel, Der. 2006. SPIEGEL's Interview with Chile's Michelle Bachelet: "Only Cleaned Wounds can Heal." *Der Spiegel*, March 9, 2006. http://www.spiegel.de/international/spiegel/spiegel-interview-with-chile-s-michelle-bachelet-only-cleaned-wounds-can-heal-a-404859.html

UN Women. 2011. "Biographical Sketch: Michelle Bachelet." http://www.unwomen.org/about-us/directorate/executive-director/biographical-sketch-michelle-bachelet/

Valenzuela, M. 1998. "Women and the Democratization Process in Chile." In *Women and democracy: Latin America and Central and Eastern Europe*, eds. J. Jaquette and S. Wolchik. Baltimore and London: John Hopkins University Press, 47–74.

Walder, P. 2005. "Michelle: Una Madre para Chile?" *Red Voltaire*. December 21, 2005. http://www.voltairenet.org/article135456.html

Weeks, G. and S. Borzutzky. 2012. "Michelle Bachelet's government: the paradoxes of a Chilean president." *Journal of Politics in Latin America*, 4(3): 97–121.

Wilson, W. 2012. "Just don't call her Che." *New York Times*, January 28, 2012. http://www.nytimes.com/2012/01/29/opinion/sunday/student-protests-rile-chile.html?ref=magazine&pagewanted=print

Wiñazki, M. 2006. "El dedo de Lagos." *Blogs El Clarín*, September 20, 2006. http://weblogs.clarin.com/aparienc

Chapter 15: Virgin Venuses: Beauty and Purity for "Public" Women in Venezuela

Acosta-Alzuru, C. 2011. "Venezuela's Telenovela." In *Venezuela's Bolivarian Democracy: Participation, Politics, and Culture under Chávez*, eds. D. Smilde and D. Hellinger. Durham: Duke University Press, 244–70.

Anderson, B. 1991. *Imagined Communities: Reflections on the Origin and Spread of Nationalism.* London: Verso.

Arias, R. 1998. "Not Just Another Pretty Face." *People.* (50)8.

Beauty Obsession. 2002. ABC Australia, Journeyman Pictures, Film.

Bolivar Ramírez, I. 2007. "Reinados de belleza y nacionalización de las sociedades latinoamericanas." *Iconos: Revista de Ciencias Sociales*, May 28, 2007, 80.

Capriles promete un millón de empleos a los jóvenes de Venezuela. 2012. http://www.lacelosia.com/capriles-promete-un-millon-de-empleos-a-los-jovenes-de-venezuela/.

Carreño, M. 2010. *Manuel de urbanidad y buenas maneras*. Whitefish, MO: Kessinger.

Castillo, D. 1992. *Talking Back: Toward a Latin American Feminist Literary Criticism*. Ithaca, NY: Cornell University Press.

Cunill Grau, Pedro. 1987. *Geografía del poblamiento venezolano en el siglo xix*. Caracas: Ediciones de la Presidencia de la República.

De Vries, R. 2012. "El Poder de la Serenidad." http://www.robertodevries.com/index.php?accion=ver_articulo&arti_id=1179&articulo=el-poder-de-la-serenidad.--irene-s%C3%A1ez-conde.

Despierta America. 2013. "La Miss Universo antes y después." http://entretenimiento.univision.com/despierta-america/el-revoltillo/video/2013-11-12/la-miss-universo-antes-y-despues

Duque, J. 2011. "La anti-Barbie." http://discursodeloeste.blogspot.com/2011/03/la-anti-barbie.html

El Nacional. 2009. "Titina Penzini: ¡Qué viva lo alurdo!" October 4, 2009, 22.

Fernández, N. 2013. "New reality show to focus on Miss Venezuela contest." *Fox News Latino*. http://latino.foxnews.com/latino/lifestyle/2013/07/14/new-reality-show-to-focus-on-miss-venezuela-contest/

Ferry, Robert J. 1989. *The Colonial Elite of Early Caracas: Formation and Crisis, 1567–1767*. Berkeley: University of California Press.

García Prince, E. 2012. "Seminario: La participación política de las mujeres en Venezuela: Desafíos y propuestas." Seminar, Caracas, Venezuela, March 21, 2012.

Giusti, R. 2011. "La otra muerte de Lina Ron." *El Universal*. March 8, 2011.

Grainger, S. 2012. "Inside a Venezuelan school for child beauty queens." *BBC News Magazine*. September 2, 2012. http://www.bbc.co.uk/news/magazine-19373488

Gulbas, L. 2008. "Cosmetic surgery and the politics of race, class, and gender in Caracas, Venezuela." Unpublished doctoral dissertation, Southern Methodist University.

Hernández Montoya, R. 2012. The cult of Venus in Venezuela." http://www.analitica.com/bitblioteca/roberto/venus-i.asp

Koffman, J. 2009. "In Venezuela, beauty is born … and made." *ABC News*, October 8, 2009. http://abcnews.go.com/Nightline/miss-venezuela-beauty-pageant/story?id=8780813

La nueva Miss Venezuela da sus impresiones luego de ser coronada. 2013. http://www.missvenezuela.com/Videos/?idMedia=635171111312&idSeccion=2013&idCategoria=130&la-nueva-miss-venezuela-da-sus-impresiones-luego-de-ser-coronada-

Labarca Prieto, D. 2012. "Lina Ron funda un partido." http://www.analitica.com/va/politica/opinion/3206845.asp

de León, Fray Luís. 2011. "La perfecta casada [the perfect wife]" Cited in Pignia, Felipe. *Mujeres tenían que ser.* Planeta: Buenos Aires. 23.

Lina Ron: Biografía de una revolucionaria venezolana 1959–2011. 2011. *Patria Grande.* March 5, 2011. http://www.patriagrande.com.ve/temas/politica/lina-ron-biografia-una-revolucionaria-venezolana-1959-2011

López, A. 1995. "Our Welcomed Guests: Telenovelas in Latin America." In *To be Continued: Soap Operas Around the World,* ed. R. C. Allen. London: Routledge, 256–75.

Manvel, N. 2012. "Tal día como hoy nació Irene Saez, la 'Barbie' que se convirtió en figura política." *Noticias 24.* December 13, 2012.

Nichols, E. G., and K. Morse. 2010. *Venezuela: In focus.* Santa Barbara, CA: ABC-Clio.

Noticias 24. 2013. "El Miss Venezuela Mundo 2013 se adueñó del rating." http://www.noticias24.com/gente/noticia/104910/el-miss-venezuela-mundo-2013-se-adueno-del-rating/

Omestad, T. 2001. "In the Land of Mirror, Mirror on the Wall." *US News and World Report,* July 2001.

Palacios, A. 2009. *Ana Isabel: Una niña decente.* Caracas: Otero Ediciones. 78.

Parra, Teresa de la. 2008. *Memorias de mama blanca.* Caracas, Monte Avila.

Queen Saez Change. 2000. *Latin Trade* (English). September 8, 2000, 26.

Rosa, Alicia de la. 2011. "Falleció la dirigente de UPV Lina Ron." *El Universal,* March 5, 2011.

Rueda, J. 2013. "Miss Venezuela pageant bridges political divide." *Latinovoices,* November 10, 2013. http://www.huffingtonpost.com/2013/10/12/miss-venezuela-pageant-political-divide_n_4089018.html

Stanco, E. 2011. "Caracas en nuestra (tele)novela de todas las noches: Mujeres de un solo zarcillo y la novela telenovelizada." *Hispanic Review.* 79: 1.

Wright, W. 1995. *Café con leche: Race, Class and National Image in Venezuela.* Austin: Texas University Press.

Chapter 16: Ultra-Feminine Women of Power: Beauty and the State in Argentina

Arguedas, A. 1996. *Pueblo enfermo.* La Paz, Bolivia: Libreria Editorial Juventud.

Barrig, M. 2001. *El mundo al revés: Imágenes de la mujer indígena.* Buenos Aires: CLASCO.

Belej, C., A. L. Martin and A. Silveira. 2005. "La más bella de los viñedos." In *Cuando las mujeres reinaban: Belleza, virtud y poder en la Argentina del siglo XX (20th century),* ed. M. Z. Lobato. Buenos Aires: Biblos, 45–72.

Bellotta, A. 2012. *Eva y Cristina: La razón de sus vidas*. Vergara: Buenos Aires.

Carozzi, M. J., M. B. Maya and G. E. Magrassi. 1980. *Conceptos de antropología social.* Centro Editor de América Latina; Buenos Aires.

Carroll, R. 2007. "Argentina's president to step aside – for wife." *Guardian*. July 2, 2007. http://www.guardian.co.uk/world/2007/jul/03/argentina.rorycarroll/print

Díaz, G. 2003. "Making the myth of Evita Perón: Saint, martyr, prostitute." *Studies In Latin American Popular Culture*, 22, 181–92.

Donot, M. 2011. "Cristina Fernández de Kirchner, de 'una reina' a la encarnación del pueblo de la Argentina." *Ensemble: Revista electrónica de la Casa Argentina en Paris*.5: No. 6. http://ensemble.educ.ar/?p=2078&numero=24 (accessed January 15, 2013).

Eva Perón Foundation. 2013. "To Be Evita." http://www.evitaperon.org/part2.htm

Foss, C. 2000. "Propaganda and the Perons." *History Today*, 50(3): 8.

Fraser, N., and M. Navarro. 1996. *Evita: The real life of Eva Perón*. New York: W. W. Norton.

Gilbert, J. 2012. "Showdown looms between Argentina's Kirchner and her biggest media critic." *Christian Science Monitor*, December 5, 2012, 1.

Lobato, M., ed. 2005. *Cuando las mujeres reinaban: Belleza, virtud y poder en la Argentina del siglo XX (20th century)*. Buenos Aires: Biblos.

Moreira, E. and E. Shaw. 1992. "High fashion: the search for a style." *The Journal of Decorative and Propaganda Arts*, 18: 170–87.

Mount, I., and P. Sherwell. 2012. "The Argentine President and her Empire to the South." *Telegraph*. February 12, 2012. http://www.telegraph.co.uk/news/worldnews/southamerica/argentina/9076133/The-Argentine-president-and-her-empire-in-the-south.html

Nichols, E. G. and K. Morse. 2010. *Venezuela: In focus*. Santa Barbara, CA: ABC-Clio.

Paz-Soldán, E.1999. "Nación enferma y narración: El Discurso de la degeneración en *Pueblo Enf*ermo de Alcides Arguedas." *Revista Hispana Moderna*, 52(1): 60–76.

Pigna, F. 2011. *Mujeres tenían que ser*. Buenos Aires: Planeta.

Repoll, J. 2010. "Política y medios de comunicación en Argentina: Kirchner Clarín y la ley." *Andaminos*, 7(14): 35–67.

Skurski, J. 1994. "The ambiguities of authenticity in Latin America." *Poetics Today*, 15(4): 605–42.

Sommer, D. 1991. *Foundational Fictions: The National Romances of Latin America.* Berkeley: University of California Press.

Stepan, N. 1991. *The Hour of Eugenics: Race, Gender and Nation in Latin America.* Ithaca, New York: Cornell University Press.

Uhart, C. 2004. "La mujer en los Noventa: Procesos Ideológicos, Consumo Eidentidad." In *Cartógrafías de la Argentina de los '90: Cultura mediática, política y sociedad*, ed. M. A. Antonelli. Buenos Aires: Ferreyra.

Zanatta, L. 2011. *Eva Perón, una biografía política*. Buenos Aires: Sudamericana.

Chapter 17: Yulia Tymoshenko's Two Bodies

Baer, B. J. 2012. "Post-Soviet Self-Fashioning and the Politics of Representation." In *Putin as celebrity and cultural Icon*, ed. H. Goscilo. London: Routledge, 160–79.

Bourdieu, P. 1987. *Distinction: A Social Critique of the Judgement of Taste*. Harvard: Harvard University Press.

Calvert, C. 2004. *Voyeur Nation: Media, Privacy and Peering in Modern Culture*. Boulder: Westview Press.

Goscilo, H., and V. Strukov. 2011. "Introduction." In *Celebrity and Glamour in Contemporary Russia: Shocking Chick*, eds. H. Goscilo and V. Strukov. London: Routledge, 1–26.

Ibroscheva, E., and M. Raicheva-Stover. 2009. "Engendering transition: portrayals of female politicians in the Bulgarian press." *The Howard Journal of Communications*, 20(2): 111–28.

Kantorowicz, E. 1957/1998. *The King's Two Bodies*. Princeton: Princeton University Press.

Kis, O. 2007. "Beauty will save the world!: feminine strategies in Ukrainian politics and the case of Yulia Tymoshenko." *Spaces of Identity* 7(2), pi.library.yorku.ca/ojs/index.php/soi/article/view/7970.

Matamoros, N. 2010. "Visual representation of women in politics: an intercultural perspective (Based on Hillary Rodham Clinton, USA, and Yulia Tymoshenko, Ukraine)." *Observatorio (OBS*)* 4(4): 325–44.

Mikhailova, T. 2012. "Putin as the Father of the Nation: his family and Other Animals." In *Putin as Celebrity and Cultural Icon*, ed. H. Goscilo. London: Routledge, 65–81.

Panizza, F. 2005. Introduction. In *Populism and the Mirror of Democracy*, ed. F. Panizza. London and New York: Verso, 1–31.

Rubchak, M. J. 2005. "Goddess of the Orange Revolution." In *Transitions Online*. http://www.tol.org/client/article/13378-goddess-of-the-orange-revolution

Shulga, Y. 2009. *Gender and Ukrainian Politics: The Making of Yulia Tymoshenko*. Saarbrücken: VDM Verlag.

Street, J. 2004. "Celebrity politicians: popular culture and political representation." *British Journal of Politics and International Relations*, 6.

Tymoshenko, Yu. 2013a. "Ia oholoshuiu aktsiiu hromadians'koi nepokory," *Ukrainska Pravda*, January 8, 2013. www.pravda.com.ua/columns/2013/01/8/6981072/

—2013b. "The authoritarian regime must be removed from power." http://www.tymoshenko.ua/en/article/yulia_tymoshenko_08_12_2013_01

—2013c. "A Prisoner's Reflections on Nelson Mandela," *Project Syndicate*. http://www.project-syndicate.org/commentary/yuliya-tymoshenko-reflects-on-imprisonment-and-nelson-mandela#V70j3zC7K6IjPar5.99

—2013d. "Tymoshenko to Yanukovych: 'Your fear is so evident.'" *Kyiv Post*. http://

www.kyivpost.com/opinion/op-ed/tymoshenko-to-yanukovych-your-fear-is-so-evident-332338.html
van Zoonen, L. 2006. "The personal, the political and the popular. a women's guide to celebrity politics." *European Journal of Cultural Studies*, 9(3): 287–301.
Vozniak, T. 2013. "Trahediia Tymoshenko chy nash z vamy diahnoz?" *Ukrainska Pravda*. www.blogs.pravda.com.ua/authors/voznyak/50ffd2acc17ac/
Yurchak, A. 2013. "Netlennost' formy: Leninizm i material'nost' mavzoleinogo tela." *Neprikosnovennyi Zapas*, 3 (89).

Concluding Remarks

Global Media Monitoring Project, 2010. "Who makes the news," http://whomakesthenews.org/
Norris,. P., ed. 1997. *Women, Media and Politics*. New York: Oxford University Press.

Index